Aligning Perspectives on Health, Safety and Well-Being

Series Editors

Stavroula Leka, University College Cork, Cork, Ireland

Aditya Jain, Nottingham University Business School and Centre for Organizational Health and Development, University of Nottingham, Nottingham, UK

Gerard Zwetsloot, University of Nottingham, Centre for Organizational Health and Development, Nottingham, United Kingdom, TNO InGerard Zwetsloot Research & Consultancy, Amsterdam, The Netherlands

Raising awareness of the interdisciplinary and complementary relationship of different research perspectives on health, safety and well-being is the main aim of the book series Aligning Perspectives on Health, Safety and Well-being. Combined research approaches on health, safety and well-being are becoming more and more popular in several research disciplines across and between the social, behavioural and medical sciences. Therefore, Aligning Perspectives on Health, Safety and Well-being stimulates the publication of interdisciplinary approaches to the promotion of health, safety and well-being. Recognizing a need within societies and workplaces for more integrated approaches to problem solving, the series caters to the notion that most innovation stems from combining knowledge and research results from related but so far separated areas. Volumes will be edited by expert authors and editors and will contain contributions from different disciplines. All authors, and especially volume editors are encouraged to engage in developing more robust theoretical models that can be applied in actual practice and lead to policy development.

Lara Christina Roll • Hans De Witte
Sebastiaan Rothmann
Editors

Global Perspectives on Job Insecurity in Higher Education

Precarity in the Ivory Tower

Springer

Editors
Lara Christina Roll
Research Group Work
Organizational and Personnel Psychology
(O2L-WOPP), FPPW, KU Leuven
Leuven, Belgium

Optentia Research Unit
North-West University
Vanderbijlpark, South Africa

Hans De Witte
Research Group Work
Organizational and Personnel Psychology
(O2L-WOPP), FPPW, KU Leuven
Leuven, Belgium

Optentia Research Unit
North-West University
Vanderbijlpark, South Africa

Sebastiaan Rothmann
Optentia Research Unit
North-West University
Vanderbijlpark, South Africa

ISSN 2213-0497 ISSN 2213-0470 (electronic)
Aligning Perspectives on Health, Safety and Well-Being
ISBN 978-3-031-85771-3 ISBN 978-3-031-85772-0 (eBook)
https://doi.org/10.1007/978-3-031-85772-0

This Springer imprint is published by the registered company Springer Nature Switzerland AG
The registered company address is: Gewerbestrasse 11, 6330 Cham, Switzerland

Acknowledgments

We extend our sincere gratitude to the National Research Foundation (NRF) of South Africa for their generous support through the Knowledge Interchange and Collaboration grant (Reference No. KIC170419227844), which made this collaboration possible.

Contents

List of Abbreviations

BAT	Burnout Assessment Tool
BIC	Bayesian Information Criterion
CFA	Confirmatory Factor Analysis
CWB	Counterproductive Work Behavior
GHQ	General Health Questionnaire
IWB	Innovative Work Behavior
JI	Job Insecurity
JDR	Job Demands-Resources (Model)
MBI	Maslach Burnout Inventory
PE	Preventive Effect
SD	Standard Deviation
UWES	Utrecht Work Engagement Scale

Chapter 1
Introduction: The Growing Crisis of Job Insecurity in Academia

Lara Christina Roll, Hans De Witte, and Sebastiaan Rothmann

Job insecurity in academia is a burgeoning crisis that profoundly impacts the well-being of individuals, the stability of academic institutions, and the future of education and research. Over recent years, we have witnessed a troubling decline in tenure-track positions,[1] paralleled by a rise in non-tenure track roles such as part-time lecturers, postdoctoral fellows, and contract faculty (American Association of University Professors, 2023). This shift has rendered many academics vulnerable to unemployment or underemployment, fostering a highly competitive and unstable work environment. Moreover, the rapid rise of automation and technological advancements has further intensified job insecurity, with traditional academic roles increasingly being replaced or supplemented by automated systems and online education platforms (Broughman & Haar, 2018).

The impact on individuals is profound. Many academics grapple with financial insecurity, struggling to make ends meet on meager salaries and limited benefits (Dill, 2018). This precarious financial situation often leads to stress, anxiety, and depression, as individuals fret over their future prospects and their ability to support themselves and their families (American Psychological Association, 2020).

[1] Throughout this book, we refer to "tenure-track positions" as they are defined in the U.S., denoting academic roles intended to lead to permanent employment, contingent upon the individual meeting specified standards.

L. C. Roll (✉) · H. De Witte
Research Group Work, Organizational and Personnel Psychology (O2L-WOPP), FPPW, KU Leuven, Leuven, Belgium

Optentia Research Unit, North-West University, Vanderbijlpark, South Africa
e-mail: hans.dewitte@kuleuven.be

S. Rothmann
Optentia Research Unit, North-West University, Vanderbijlpark, South Africa
e-mail: ian@ianrothmann.com

L. C. Roll et al. (eds.), *Global Perspectives on Job Insecurity in Higher Education*, Aligning Perspectives on Health, Safety and Well-Being,
https://doi.org/10.1007/978-3-031-85772-0_1

Research indicates that non-tenure track faculty experience higher levels of stress and burnout compared to their tenure-track counterparts (Toutkoushian, 2015). The constant threat of job loss fosters a pervasive sense of uncertainty, frustration, and disappointment, severely affecting mental health and well-being (Menéndez-Espina et al., 2019).

The repercussions of job insecurity extend beyond individuals, threatening the very fabric of academic institutions. The incessant turnover of non-tenure track faculty erodes institutional knowledge and disrupts continuity in programs and courses (Flaherty, 2020). This instability compromises the ability of institutions to sustain high standards of education and research, ultimately diminishing the quality of education students receive (Inside Higher Ed, 2023). A 2023 report by the American Association of University Professors (AAUP) underscores the detrimental impact of job insecurity on academic institutions and the quality of education they offer.

Despite these significant challenges, job insecurity in academia remains a largely undiscussed and unaddressed issue. Many academics feel powerless to effect change and fear that voicing their concerns could jeopardize their career prospects (Redden, 2019). A 2012 study by the Coalition on the Academic Workforce (CAW) revealed that adjunct and non-tenure track faculty face substantial barriers to speaking out about their working conditions, including fear of retaliation and lack of job security (CAW, 2012). This underscores the urgent need to raise awareness about these challenges and seek viable solutions.

In this book, we aim to provide a comprehensive overview of job insecurity in higher education and elucidate its impact on individuals and institutions. We will offer evidence-based recommendations for enhancing job security in academia, drawing on the latest research and best practices. By raising awareness and proposing solutions, we hope this book will significantly contribute to supporting the well-being of individuals and the stability of academic institutions.

1.1 The Basis of This Book

The basis of this book is a collaborative effort between a core project team and ten country teams, each consisting of multiple researchers. The aim of this project was to thoroughly examine the issue of job insecurity in higher education. The core project team coordinated the efforts of the country teams, ensuring that the research was conducted in a consistent and comprehensive manner. Each country team conducted extensive research within their own country to gain a local perspective on the issue of job insecurity. The ten countries involved cover a wide and heterogeneous variety of countries from no less than four different continents of the globe: different parts of Europe (e.g. Belgium, UK, Croatia, Greece), Asia (China), North America (the USA) and Africa (South Africa). The results of these efforts provide the basis for this book, which offers a comprehensive examination of the impact of job insecurity in higher education. The members of the project were as follows:

Core Project Team (also covering Belgium and South Africa)
Dr. Lara C. Roll (KU Leuven, Belgium and Optentia Research Unit, North-West University, South Africa),
Prof. Hans De Witte (KU Leuven, Belgium and Optentia Research Unit, North-West University, South Africa), and
Prof. S. Rothmann (Optentia Research Unit, North-West University, South Africa)
China
Prof. Haijiang Wang (Huazhong University of Science and Technology)
Croatia
Prof. Darja Maslic Sersic (University of Zagreb)
Dr. Jasmina Tomas (University of Zagreb)
Greece
Prof. Despoina Xanthopoulou (Aristotle University of Thessaloniki)
Dr. Andreas Tsounis (Aristotle University of Thessaloniki)
Lithuania
Prof. Jurgita Lazauskaite-Zabielske (Vilnius University)
Prof. Ieva Urbanaviciute (Vilnius University)
Romania
Prof. Dragos Iliescu (Bucharest University)
Prof. Coralia Sulea (West University of Timisoara)
Switzerland
Prof. Ieva Urbanaviciute (Vilnius University, Lithuania)
United Kingdom (UK)
Prof. Eva Selenko (Loughborough University)
United States of America (USA)
Prof. Tahira M. Probst (Washington State University Vancouver)
Prof. Lixin Jiang (University of Auckland, New Zealand)

1.2 Higher Education Institutions

In this book, we refer to higher education institutions as the umbrella term for all educational establishments that provide tertiary education, i.e., education beyond secondary school level. Those are typically universities, colleges, and polytechnics that offer degrees, diplomas, and certificates. Universities offer a range of undergraduate and postgraduate programs in arts, humanities, sciences, and professional fields, while colleges and polytechnics tend to focus on practical and vocational training. Universities of technology, on the other hand, offer a combination of technical and academic education and specialize in science, engineering, and technology-related disciplines. Other forms of higher education institutions include teacher training colleges, medical schools, and specialized institutions that offer courses in specific areas of study such as fine arts, business, or law. All those higher education institutions were eligible to be included in this research.

The target groups are referred to using different terms across various chapters: job title (Chap. 2), position (Chaps. 5 & 8), and professional category/categories (Chaps. 4 & 9). They are also collectively grouped under the term staff category. Professors are described as holding an academic role or academic contract (Chap. 4), and are also referred to as faculty teaching staff (Chap. 10) and professors (Chaps. 4

& 9). PhD students and post-doctoral researchers are identified as junior (research) staff (Chaps. 4 & 7). Administrative personnel are labelled as administrative staff or (administrative) support staff, depending on the context.

1.3 Target Groups in Academia

In this project, three distinct sample groups were considered. The first group consisted of *academics*, which included professors, lecturers, and other academic personnel. The second group was *university support staff*, including administrative assistants, IT experts, security personnel, and similar roles. Finally, the third sample group was made up of *PhD students and postdoctoral researchers*, who are typically engaged in research activities after completing their PhDs. These three groups were selected to provide a comprehensive representation of the university population and to examine potential differences in their experiences and perspectives.

1.4 The Job Insecurity Concept: Quantitative and Qualitative Job Insecurity

About 30 years ago, the publication of "Job Insecurity: Toward Conceptual Clarity" by Greenhalgh and Rosenblatt (1984) sparked scientific interest in job insecurity. This started an extensive research tradition, especially after the year 2000. Nowadays, job insecurity is considered one of the major psychosocial risks in the workplace, along with factors such as workload, lack of control, role stressors, and poor work relationships, leading to psychological and physical harm (Leka & Jain, 2010).

Job insecurity is characterized by the fear of job loss (Mohr, 2000) and can be defined as a general concern about the future existence of one's job (van Vuuren, 1990). Scholars agree that it is a subjective experience resulting from an individual's interpretation of the work environment. The same objective situation can lead to different levels of uncertainty for different employees (Klandermans & van Vuuren, 1999; Sverke et al., 2002). Perceived job insecurity generally reflects the objective labour market position of the worker (De Witte, 2005). It involves uncertainty about the future and hinders preparation because employees do not know if they will keep their job (Sverke & Hellgren, 2002).

The definition of job insecurity distinguishes between its qualitative and quantitative dimensions (Hellgren et al., 1999). *Qualitative* insecurity involves the fear of losing valuable aspects of the job, while *quantitative* insecurity involves the potential loss of the entire job (Greenhalgh & Rosenblatt, 1984; Hellgren et al., 1999). The concept of quantitative job insecurity covers a wider scope, meaning it can encompass qualitative job insecurity. However, research has shown that the occurrence of qualitative job insecurity is more prevalent and distinct from quantitative job insecurity, with higher mean levels of qualitative job insecurity being observed when both are measured together (Chirumbolo et al., 2017; Nawrocka et al., 2021; Tu et al., 2019). In this book, both types of job insecurity in the higher education context will be explored (see Chap. 2 for further elaboration on the quantitative and qualitative job insecurity concepts and related theories).

1.5 Reasons for Job Insecurity in Higher Education

Job insecurity in higher education is a growing concern worldwide, driven by several common themes across different countries. These include economic pressures, changes in employment practices, advancements in technology, and political influences.

1.5.1 Economic Pressures

Budget cuts and financial constraints are prevalent in higher education institutions globally. These financial pressures are often exacerbated by economic crises, leading to reduced funding for universities. This, in turn, forces institutions to implement cost-saving measures such as hiring freezes, job cuts, and increased reliance on temporary contracts (Tight, 2020; Woodhouse, 2015).

1.5.2 Changes in Employment Practices

There has been a notable shift towards more flexible employment practices, including the increased use of fixed-term and part-time contracts. These contracts often lack the job security and benefits associated with permanent positions, contributing to a precarious work environment for many academic staff. This trend towards casualisation is a significant factor in job insecurity across various countries (Kezar & Maxey, 2014; Courtois & O'Keefe, 2015).

1.5.3 Advancements in Technology and Online Education

The rise of online education and advancements in technology have disrupted traditional higher education practices. Universities are increasingly adopting online platforms and automated systems, which can lead to fears of job loss among faculty and staff who may feel their roles are becoming obsolete or undervalued (McMurtrie, 2020; Czerniewicz, 2018).

1.5.4 Political Influences and Reforms

Political decisions and reforms in higher education policy can create uncertainty and instability. Governmental austerity measures, changes in funding policies, and political scrutiny of educational institutions often contribute to an unstable environment, exacerbating job insecurity for academic staff (Marginson, 2013; Sabri, 2011).

1.5.5 Impact of the COVID-19 Pandemic

The COVID-19 pandemic has had a profound impact on higher education worldwide. The pandemic led to significant disruptions in traditional teaching methods, reduced student enrollment, and financial uncertainties. These challenges forced many universities to implement additional cost-cutting measures, increasing job insecurity among academic staff (Johnson et al., 2020; Marinoni et al., 2020).

1.6 Specific Reasons for Job Insecurity in Higher Education

Apart from the general reasons for job insecurity in higher education outlined above, there are also specific factors unique to each country discussed in this book. These factors are elaborated upon in the following.

1.6.1 Belgium and Switzerland

The higher education sectors in Western societies like Belgium and Switzerland have long valued the implicit understanding between employees and employers, known as the psychological contract (Griep et al., 2021). This unwritten agreement encompasses mutual expectations and obligations beyond the formal employment contract, influencing workplace culture and employee behaviour. Historically, higher education employees have expected stability, fair treatment, and opportunities for career advancement in exchange for their loyalty, dedication, and performance. However, economic shifts, technological advancements, and evolving business models have increasingly challenged these expectations. This shift towards more precarious employment conditions, such as fixed-term and part-time contracts in higher education, and various budget cuts by governments over time have heightened job insecurity, fundamentally altering these psychological contracts. The resulting perceived breaches have significantly impacted employee morale, trust, and overall job satisfaction in the Belgian and Swiss higher education sectors (Chan et al., 2020; OECD, 2023a).

1.6.2 China

Job insecurity in Chinese higher education has been a pressing issue for several years due to a variety of ongoing reforms and changes in universities. China's ambition to elevate the status of its higher education sector to match its economic power has driven a series of policy shifts aimed at enhancing teaching and research quality. This effort has led to significant changes in human resource policies at universities.

1.6.2.1 Reforms and Changes

Recruitment of International Talent: Chinese universities are increasingly focusing on recruiting talent from overseas. This strategy is intended to bring in diverse perspectives and enhance the global standing of Chinese higher education. However, this also creates competition and uncertainty among existing faculty members, who may feel their positions are at risk with the influx of international academics (Ministry of Education of the People's Republic of China, 2023).

1.6.2.2 Performance Evaluation System

There is a shift towards a more rigorous performance evaluation system. Faculty members are now required to meet higher standards in their teaching and research outputs. For instance, the requirement to publish a certain number of high-quality papers annually has become a norm, even for full professors. This continuous pressure to perform can lead to significant job insecurity, as failing to meet these standards can jeopardize one's position (Wang, 2022).

1.6.2.3 Tenure-Track Appointments

The adoption of tenure-track appointments is another major change. Unlike the traditional system, where job security was relatively high once a faculty member was hired, the tenure-track system introduces periodic evaluations that faculty must pass to retain their positions. This system aims to ensure ongoing productivity and quality but also introduces a significant level of uncertainty and insecurity among faculty members (Chen, 2021).

1.6.2.4 Impact on Faculty

The cumulative effect of these reforms is a heightened sense of job insecurity among academic staff. Faculty members now face the dual pressures of meeting high performance standards and competing with international talent. This environment requires constant output and improvement, which can be stressful and destabilizing. The data collected from two STEM-focused universities in China, which were slowly implementing these changes, suggest that faculty in these institutions are likely experiencing various levels of job insecurity, influenced by factors such as job nature and organizational tenure (Zhang, 2022; Li, 2021).

Overall, the drive to improve the quality and global standing of higher education in China has led to significant changes in human resource policies at universities. These reforms, while aimed at enhancing teaching and research, have also increased job insecurity among faculty members. The continuous need to produce high-quality research and the introduction of tenure-track systems contribute to an unstable job environment, reflecting broader trends in Chinese higher education reform.

1.6.3 Croatia

Job insecurity in higher education in Croatia is influenced by both quantitative and qualitative factors, affecting different categories of academic and supporting staff in various ways.

1.6.3.1 Quantitative Job Insecurity

For tenure-tracked academics at public universities in Croatia, quantitative job insecurity, characterized by concerns about the likelihood of job loss, is relatively low. Assistant professors, associate professors, and full professors generally enjoy high job security as they are employed on permanent contracts. These positions require evaluations and re-elections every 5 years, but actual layoffs are extremely rare. Supporting staff with permanent contracts in the public sector also share this high level of job security, making it almost impossible for them to lose their jobs (Hebrang Grgić & Žilić, 2018).

However, this high level of job security has slightly changed, especially among academics employed at smaller and newer universities. While these tenure-tracked positions still offer a significant degree of stability, there is a noted increase in job insecurity due to the evolving dynamics of the higher education sector in these institutions (Šćukanec Schmidt, 2020). Research assistants and early-career academics, particularly those on temporary contracts, face higher levels of general job insecurity. The lack of permanent positions and the instability associated with temporary contracts contribute to a pervasive sense of job insecurity among these staff members (Vrbanec, 2019).

1.6.3.2 Qualitative Job Insecurity

Even those in more secure, tenure-tracked positions experience qualitative job insecurity, reflecting worries about their professional growth, workplace conditions, and overall job satisfaction.

Many academics are concerned about the limited opportunities for professional development and career advancement. The hierarchical and often rigid structure of Croatian universities can impede career progression, leaving many academics feeling stagnant in their roles. This can be particularly disheartening for younger faculty who aspire to advance their careers but find few pathways to do so within the current system (Farnell, 2020).

Workplace conditions also contribute significantly to qualitative job insecurity. Academics frequently report heavy workloads, inadequate administrative support, and insufficient resources for research. These conditions can lead to burnout and job dissatisfaction. The pressure to publish and secure funding, often with limited institutional support, exacerbates this stress, further impacting the overall well-being of academic staff (Doolan, 2021).

Job satisfaction among Croatian academics is also affected by factors such as bureaucratic inefficiencies and a lack of recognition for their work. Many feel that the administrative burden detracts from their primary roles of teaching and research. Additionally, the lack of transparent evaluation criteria for promotions and a perceived bias in decision-making processes can undermine morale and job satisfaction (Matković, 2017).

1.6.3.3 Emigration and Demographic Challenges

Croatia faces high emigration rates among young professionals and academics. This brain drain, coupled with low birthrates, heightens job insecurity in higher education by depleting the pool of skilled talent (Vidović, 2021; Bačić Karković, 2019).

In conclusion, job insecurity in Croatian higher education is multifaceted, influenced by both quantitative and qualitative factors. While tenure-tracked positions offer some stability, evolving sector dynamics and demographic challenges exacerbate insecurities, particularly for early-career academics and those on temporary contracts.

1.6.4 Greece

Job insecurity in Greek higher education is influenced by several interconnected factors, including economic crises, mismatches between education and labor market needs, and extensive educational reforms.

1.6.4.1 Economic Crisis and Financial Pressures

Greece's prolonged economic crisis, which began in the late 2000s, has had a significant impact on higher education. The crisis led to austerity measures and severe budget cuts across the public sector, including universities. This resulted in reduced funding for higher education institutions, which in turn affected job security for academic staff. Many universities faced financial difficulties, leading to hiring freezes and increased reliance on temporary contracts for new staff members (Kottaridi & Tsakloglou, 2020; Ladi, 2014).

1.6.4.2 Mismatch Between Education and Labour Market

There is a significant mismatch between the skills provided by Greek universities and the needs of the labor market. Many university courses are seen as too theoretical and not aligned with the practical skills required by employers. This mismatch has led to high unemployment rates among graduates, further exacerbating job insecurity for those in academia. The difficulty in finding suitable employment after graduation has been a persistent issue, reflecting broader problems in the Greek labor market (Patrinos, 2017; OECD, 2020).

1.6.4.3 Europeanization and Educational Reforms

Greece's efforts to align its higher education system with European standards have also contributed to job insecurity. The process of Europeanization, which includes implementing policies related to evaluation, accountability, and efficiency, has pressured Greek universities to restructure and adapt. These reforms, while aimed at improving the quality of education, have often led to job cuts and increased workloads for remaining staff, adding to job insecurity (Featherstone, 2016; Papadimitriou, 2015).

In summary, job insecurity in Greek higher education has been driven by a combination of economic crises, shifting employment practices, systemic mismatches between education and labor market needs, and the impacts of Europeanization and reforms.

1.6.5 *Lithuania*

Job insecurity in higher education in Lithuania has been shaped by several socio-economic and political factors, reflecting broader trends experienced by many new EU member states.

1.6.5.1 Economic and Social Changes

Lithuania has undergone significant social, political, and economic changes, particularly since joining the EU in 2004. As a developing economy, it remains sensitive to external shocks, such as the global financial crisis of 2008, which had lasting impacts on employment and economic stability. These economic fluctuations have contributed to job insecurity across various sectors, including higher education (Stankevičiūtė et al., 2021).

1.6.5.2 Higher Education Reforms

The Lithuanian higher education sector is undergoing significant reforms, including planned university mergers and the closure of some regional branches. These changes are aimed at improving the quality of education and research but have also led to heightened job insecurity among academic staff due to the anticipated restructuring and potential job losses (Stankevičiūtė et al., 2021).

1.6.5.3 Emigration and Demographic Challenges

Lithuania, like Croatia, faces high rates of emigration, which exacerbates job insecurity. Many young professionals, including academics, leave the country seeking better opportunities abroad. This emigration, coupled with low birthrates and rising income inequality, creates additional pressures on the higher education sector, further contributing to job insecurity (OECD, 2021).

Overall, the combination of economic pressures, demographic challenges, and extensive reforms has significantly contributes to the growing sense of job insecurity among higher education professionals in Lithuania.

1.6.6 *Romania*

In recent years, although contracts in Romania's higher education sector are generally secure, job insecurity has been influenced by a combination of socio-economic changes, political dynamics, and systemic issues.

1.6.6.1 Higher Education Reforms

The Romanian higher education sector is undergoing significant reforms aimed at improving the quality of education and research. These reforms include measures to enhance governance, funding, and inclusivity within the higher education system, as outlined in the new Higher Education Law 199/2023 (European Commission, 2023; Eurydice, 2023). The "Educated Romania" initiative supports these reforms with European funding, aiming to address the challenges identified in the national education system (European Commission, 2024; OECD, 2023b).

However, some aspects of these reforms, such as the removal of rectors' term limits and the effective amnesty on doctoral plagiarism, have faced criticism for potentially undermining academic integrity (Times Higher Education, 2022). These contentious changes highlight ongoing debates within the academic community regarding the overall impact of the reforms on the sector.

1.6.6.2 Emigration and Demographic Challenges

Similar to Croatia and Lithuania, Romania faces significant emigration rates, which intensify job insecurity. A considerable number of young professionals, including academics, are emigrating in search of better opportunities abroad. This brain drain, combined with declining birthrates and growing income inequality, adds further strain to the higher education sector, exacerbating job insecurity (OECD, 2023b).

1.6.6.3 Trust in the Evolution of Economic Conditions

The general trust in the positive evolution of the economic situation is indeed lower in Romania compared to other EU countries. According to the European Commission's Spring 2024 Economic Forecast, Romania faces significant economic challenges including high inflation and a persistent government deficit projected to reach about 7% of GDP in 2024 and 2025. This economic strain contributes to lower confidence among the population regarding the country's economic prospects (European Commission, 2024).

Additionally, a report from the OECD highlights that while Romania has shown some resilience and growth in specific sectors, it still lags behind many EU countries in terms of economic stability and innovation. The slow pace of economic reforms and external economic dependencies further dampen public trust in economic improvements (OECD, 2023b; McKinsey & Company, 2024).

These factors collectively result in a lower level of general trust in the economic future of Romania compared to other EU member states.

1.6.7 South Africa

In South Africa, job insecurity within higher education has become increasingly pronounced over the past decade. This issue has been shaped by a multitude of socio-economic and political factors, leading to significant changes in the landscape of academic employment.

1.6.7.1 Historical Context and Student Protests

One of the most notable events in recent South African higher education history is the #FeesMustFall movement, which began in 2015. This student-led protest called for the elimination of tuition fees, decolonisation of the curriculum, and better funding for universities. The protests highlighted the financial strains and systemic inequalities within the higher education system, and although they led to some concessions, they also resulted in significant disruptions and heightened job insecurity for academic staff due to the financial instability faced by many institutions (Svongoro, 2023).

1.6.7.2 Labour Market Inequalities

Labour market inequalities also play a significant role in job insecurity. Issues such as gender, race, and socioeconomic status continue to affect employment opportunities and conditions within the higher education sector. Efforts to address these inequalities have been ongoing, but progress has been slow, and many academics still face significant challenges in securing stable and fair employment (Solomon & Du Plessis, 2024).

1.6.7.3 Political Climate and Funding Issues

The political climate in South Africa has also influenced job insecurity in higher education. Government funding for universities has been inconsistent, and political decisions often impact the financial stability of higher education institutions. The pressures from both the government and public to reduce tuition fees while maintaining high-quality education standards have created a challenging environment for universities to navigate (Svongoro, 2023).

In summary, the landscape of higher education in South Africa has been significantly affected by historical student protests, systemic labour market inequalities, and political funding issues. These factors have collectively contributed to an increasing sense of job insecurity among academic professionals in the country over the past 10 years.

1.6.8 The United Kingdom

In the United Kingdom, job insecurity in higher education has evolved significantly over the past decade, influenced by various socio-economic and political factors.

1.6.8.1 Historical Context and Strikes

Since 2018, UK higher education has experienced a series of strikes primarily driven by disputes over pay, pensions, and working conditions. The University and College Union (UCU) has been at the forefront of these actions. The strikes have highlighted deep-rooted issues within the sector, such as the shift towards fixed-term and part-time contracts, which has increased job insecurity. Notably, the strikes from 2018 to 2023 were some of the largest in UK higher education history, involving over 70,000 staff and impacting more than a million students. These strikes were initially triggered by proposed changes to the Universities Superannuation Scheme (USS), which would have significantly reduced pension benefits (Times Higher Education, 2023a, 2023b; UCU, 2022).

1.6.8.2 Brexit and Its Implications

The Brexit referendum in 2016 added a layer of uncertainty, impacting funding and collaboration opportunities with European institutions. The exit from the European Union has strained financial resources and collaboration opportunities, leading to a more uncertain and competitive environment for securing research grants and other funding sources (Times Higher Education, 2023a, 2023b).

1.6.8.3 Cost-of-Living Crisis

The cost-of-living crisis has significantly impacted the higher education sector. Rising living costs have left many academics struggling to make ends meet, exacerbating financial insecurity. Universities have attempted various measures to support their staff, but these have often been insufficient to alleviate the financial pressures faced by many (Hunterlodge, 2023).

In summary, the combination of historical labour disputes, the impact of Brexit, and the ongoing cost-of-living crisis have significantly contributed to the growing sense of job insecurity among higher education professionals in the UK over the past decade.

1.6.9 The United States

In the USA, job insecurity in higher education is influenced by a multitude of different factors, including the so-called "enrolment cliff", migration trends, changes in faculty positions, the political climate and rising skepticism towards college education.

1.6.9.1 The Enrollment Cliff

One significant issue is the "enrollment cliff," a term that describes the anticipated decline in college-aged students due to the lower birth rates following the 2008 financial crisis. As the number of high school graduates drops, universities face smaller pools of potential students, leading to decreased enrollment numbers. This reduction can result in less funding and potential job cuts (Hechinger Report, 2022).

1.6.9.2 Migration Trends

Additionally, a significant migration trend has emerged, with more students and their families relocating to the southern United States. This demographic shift is influenced by factors such as a lower cost of living, warmer climates, and better job opportunities, which are attracting people from the northern states (North American Van Lines, 2023; USAFacts, 2023). This migration can create disparities in enrolment numbers across different regions, further contributing to job insecurity in northern institutions while potentially increasing stability in southern ones.

1.6.9.3 Changes in Faculty Positions

Moreover, there is an increasing dependence on temporary faculty positions in the USA. There has been a shift from tenured and tenure-track positions, which provide permanent job security, to non-tenure-track, instructor, and adjunct roles. These positions typically offer less job security and are more precarious, making the academic profession less stable overall (American Psychological Association, 2024; NASFAA, 2023).

1.6.9.4 Political Climate

In addition to these trends, the political climate has also had an impact. Science and academia have faced increasing skepticism and scrutiny (Carroll, 2023), which has been demoralizing for faculty members dedicated to scientific research and empirically-driven recommendations. This skepticism, coupled with budget cuts and political pressures, further exacerbates job insecurity for those in higher education.

1.6.9.5 Rising Skepticism Towards College Education

A growing number of Americans are opting to skip college, questioning its value and cost. This trend is fueled by rising student loan debts and a belief that trade jobs offer more immediate and practical financial benefits. Polls indicate increasing skepticism about the return on investment for a college degree, with many families favoring direct entry into the workforce or vocational training over traditional four-year college pathways (AP News, 2024; CNN, 2024). This decline in college attendance rates further threatens the financial stability of higher education institutions, leading to additional job insecurity for academic staff.

Overall, the combination of demographic shifts, economic pressures, changes in employment practices, the political climate, and the rising skepticism towards college education contribute to the growing sense of job insecurity among higher education professionals in the United States.

1.7 The Analytic Framework for the Study

In our examination of job insecurity within higher education, we selected variables inspired by the model proposed by Shoss (2017). This model offers a comprehensive framework that elucidates the multifaceted nature of job insecurity, making it particularly pertinent to our study. We identified specific variables that are especially relevant to the higher education context, addressing gaps in existing literature and incorporating insights from our scholarly expertise. By doing so, we aim to provide a nuanced understanding of job insecurity among higher education professionals, shedding light on the unique challenges and dynamics within this sector. The model depicted in Fig. 1.1 was used as a generic heuristic model that could be used by our participants to develop specific research questions. All variables were operationalized in a standardized questionnaire, based on internationally validated scales. All countries collected the same data, but in analyzing their specific research questions, they focused on testing a selection of variables and their relationships.

1.7.1 Measures

For the following description of measures, all answer options ranged from "1 = strongly disagree" to "5 = strongly agree", unless noted otherwise. Specific scales can be obtained upon request from the first Editor of this book (contact: lara.roll@kuleuven.be).

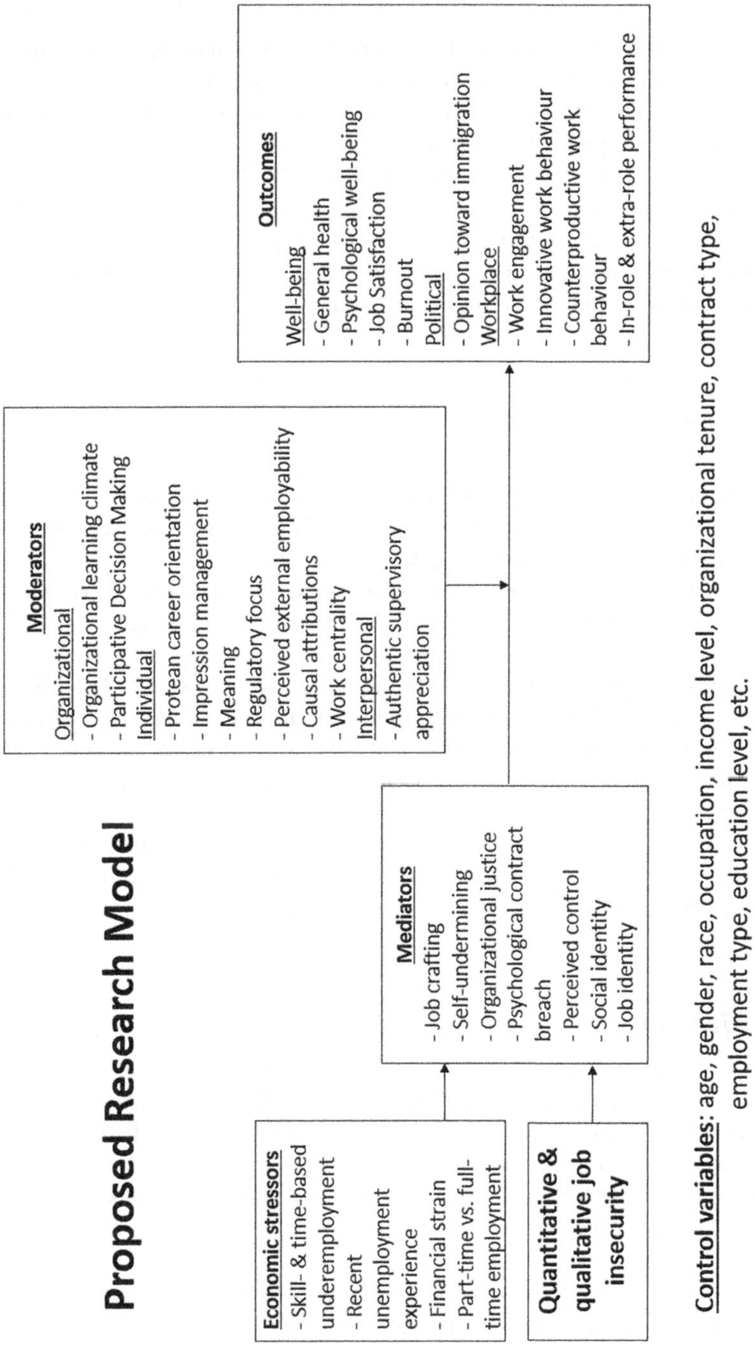

Fig. 1.1 Theoretical model

1.7.2 Job Insecurity

Quantitative job insecurity (Vander Elst et al., 2014) was assessed with four items: "Chances are, I will soon lose my job (item 1)," "I am sure I can keep my job" (reverse coded; item 2), "I feel insecure about the future of my job (item 3)," and "I think I might lose my job in the near future (item 4)."

Qualitative job insecurity (Fischmann et al., 2022) was measured with the following four items: "I think my job will change for the worse (item 5)," "Chances are, my job will change in a negative way (item 6)," "I feel insecure about the characteristics and conditions of my job in the future (item 7)," "I am worried about how my job will look like in the future (item 8)."

1.7.3 Economic Stressors

Skill-based underemployment was measured with one item ("My current position is a match for my level of occupational skills and training."), rated on a scale from "1 = strongly disagree" to "7 = strongly agree".

Recent involuntary unemployment was measured with the item, "Have you been involuntarily unemployed in the past 2 years?" Answer options were "1 = Yes" and "2 = No".

Employment type was measured with one item "Do you work…?" with answer options "1 = full-time", 2 = part-time (followed up by the questions, "How many hours do you work at this university?" and "Would you prefer to work: __fewer ___the same ___more hours each week at this university?" to identify time-based underemployment), "3 = other, please specify."

Financial strain was assessed with the item "I am stressed by my financial situation" (Pettita et al., 2020), with answer options ranging from "1 = totally disagree" to "5 = totally agree".

1.7.4 Mediators

Job crafting was assessed using four items created by Vanbelle et al. (n.d., accepted, online). An example item is: "I make changes to my job to perform better." Response options ranged from "1 = never" to "7 = daily".

Self-undermining was evaluated with six items developed by Bakker and Wang (2016). An example statement is: "I create a backlog in my tasks." Responses were rated from "1 = never" to "5 = very often".

Organizational justice was measured with three items crafted by Ambrose and Schminke (2009). An example item is: "In general, I can count on this organization to be fair."

Psychological contract breach was gauged with four items from Robinson and Morrison (2000). An example item is: "My employer has broken many of its promises to me even though I've upheld my side of the deal."

Perceived control was assessed using three items developed by Ashford et al. (1989). An example item is: "I have enough power in this organization to control events that might affect my job." For this study, we considered perceived control as a mediator, despite ongoing debate in the job insecurity literature about whether it is a mediator or a moderator (Vander Elst et al., 2011).

Social identity was measured with four items created by Doosje et al. (1995). An example item is: "I see myself as a part of the <country's name> workforce."

Job identity was evaluated using three items also developed by Doosje et al. (1995). An example statement is: "My job is a central part of my identity." These items were adapted from the social identity scale (Doosje et al., 1995) and rephrased by the authors of this research.

1.7.5 Moderators

1.7.5.1 Organizational

Organizational learning climate was assessed using three items from the facilitation dimension of the learning climate scale created by Nikolova et al. (2014). An example item is: "My organization provides sufficient resources to develop competences." One item was modified to suit the university context: "My organization provides me with further educational opportunities." Responses were rated on a scale from "1 = not applicable at all" to "5 = fully applicable".

Participative decision making was measured with six items developed by Probst (2005). An example statement is: "Supervisors encourage workers to set their own work-related goals."

1.7.5.2 Individual

Protean career orientation was measured using five items developed by Briscoe (2006). An example item is: "I am in charge of my own career." Responses ranged from "1 = totally disagree" to "5 = totally agree."

Impression management was evaluated using four items originally developed by Wayne et al. (1990) and later adapted by Bolino & Turnley (1999). The final items for this study were published by De Cuyper and De Witte (2010). An example item is: "I arrive at work early in order to look good in front of my supervisor." Responses ranged from "1 = never" to "7 = always."

Meaning, based on the PERMA model by Seligman (2011), was measured using three items developed by Khaw and Kern (2014). An example item is: "To what extent do you lead a purposeful and meaningful life?" Responses were rated from "1 = not at all" to "5 = completely."

Regulatory focus was assessed using three items to measure prevention focus and three items to measure promotion focus, all part of the Work Regulatory Focus Scale (WRF) developed by Neubert et al. (2008). An example item for prevention focus is: "Job security is an important factor for me in any job search." A sample item for promotion focus is: "A chance to grow is an important factor for me when looking for a job."

Perceived external employability was evaluated using four items developed by De Witte (1992), as used in the Psycones-project (Guest et al., 2010). An example item is: "I will easily find another job if I lose this job."

Causal attributions were assessed using seven items based on van Vuuren (1990) and adapted for this study. Participants were asked: "In your country of residence, job insecurity is increased because of:" They then rated seven potential causes, such as poor employee performance. Responses ranged from "1 = totally disagree" to "5 = totally agree."

Work centrality was measured using three items developed by Lodahl and Kejner (1965). An example item is: "The major satisfaction in my life comes from my job." Responses ranged from "1 = strongly disagree" to "7 = strongly agree."

1.7.5.3 Interpersonal

Authentic supervisory appreciation was assessed using one item created by White (2016). An example item is: "My supervisor knows how to show appreciation in ways that are meaningful to me."

1.7.6 Outcomes

1.7.6.1 Well-Being

General health and psychological well-being were evaluated using one item each, created by Ai et al. (2017). The item for physical health was: "How would you rate your overall physical health?" and the item for psychological well-being was: "How would you rate your overall mental health?" Response options ranged from "0 = very poor" to "4 = very good."

Job satisfaction was assessed with a single item from Quinn and Shepard (1974): "Taking everything into consideration, how satisfied are you with your current job?" Responses ranged from "1 = highly dissatisfied" to "7 = highly satisfied."

Burnout was measured with four items derived from the Burnout Assessment Tool (BAT) by Schaufeli et al. (2020), similar to those in Hadžibajramović et al. (2024). Response options ranged from "0 = never" to "6 = every day." An example item is: "At work, I feel mentally exhausted."

1.7.6.2 Political

Opinion toward immigration was measured using a single item from Park and Kang (2013): "Do you think the number of immigrants to your country of residence nowadays should be ...?" with response options ranging from "1 = increased a lot" to "5 = reduced a lot," and "6 = I don't know."

1.7.6.3 Workplace

Work engagement was evaluated using the three items from the Utrecht Work Engagement Scale—3 (UWES-3) by Schaufeli et al. (2017). The item for vigor was: "At my work, I feel bursting with energy." The item for dedication was: "I am enthusiastic about my job." The item for absorption was: "I am immersed in my work." Response options ranged from "0 = never" to "6 = every day."

Innovative work behaviour was measured using four items from De Jong and Den Hartog (2010). Participants were asked: "In your job, how often do you..." with options like "...wonder how things can be improved?" Responses ranged from "1 = never" to "5 = daily."

Counterproductive work behaviour was evaluated with four items from Bennett and Robinson (2000). Participants were asked: "To what extent have you engaged in each of the following behaviours in the last year:" with options like "...come in late to work without permission?" Responses ranged from "1 = never" to "7 = daily."

In-role and extra-role performance were assessed using four items each. The in-role performance items were developed by Williams and Anderson (1991), with an example being: "I fulfil the responsibilities specified in my job description." The extra-role performance items were created by Podsakoff et al. (1990) and modified by Morrison (1994). Participants were asked: "During the last six months, how often have you enacted the following in the workplace?" with an example being: "Helping others who have heavy workloads." Responses for extra-role performance ranged from "1 = never" to "5 = daily."

1.7.7 The Control Variables

As control variables, we measured age, gender (1 = male; 2 = female; 3 = transgender; 4 = other), education level (based on ISCED classification), whether participants are presently pursuing further education (1 = yes; 2 = no), nationality, citizenship, organizational tenure (in years and months), job level (based on International Standard Classification of Occupation ISCO-08, e.g. elementary occupation or senior official), position (1 = Academic faculty, e.g. professors, lecturers,...; 2 = University support staff, e.g. administrative staff, secretaries,...; 3 = Graduate student/PhD; 4 = Post-doc), contract type at the present university of employment (1 = Permanent, e.g., tenured/tenure-track faculty, permanent staff; 2 = Temporary/ Fixed term, e.g., non-tenure-track faculty, temp staff; graduate student/post-doc; 3 = Other, please indicate…). Whether participants had a paid second job was measured with the item, "Do you currently have a paid second job outside of your position at the university" (1 = Yes, 2 = No).

1.8 Data Collection Strategy

1.8.1 Procedure

Research teams from ten different countries collaborated in this international study examining the evolving nature of work in higher education, with a particular emphasis on job insecurity. Data were gathered over a two-week period in early 2018 through anonymous online surveys conducted primarily at traditional universities, unless specified otherwise. The survey was translated into the appropriate language for each country's data collection. In cases where no pre-existing scale was available in the target language, the research team employed a rigorous translation-back translation method and/or a committee approach to ensure accurate translation of the questionnaire (Brislin, 1970). Due to variations in data collection procedures across countries, specific methods used in each country are detailed below.

1.8.1.1 Belgium

The project received approval from the SMEC council (File # G-2017 121,039). A total of 596 participants, recruited from two universities, were entered into a raffle for one of ten vouchers worth 50 euros (approximately $57 USD) as an incentive. Participants could complete the survey in either English or Dutch, using a back-translation approach. Survey invitations were distributed via the Websurvey service of KU Leuven or through their HR departments.

1.8.1.2 China

Approval for the project and data collection was granted by the research committee of the School of Management at Huazhong University of Science and Technology. A total of 160 participants from two technological universities were offered $20 USD as an incentive to complete the survey. Invitations were sent through WeChat, a versatile Chinese app that includes messaging, social media, and mobile payment functions.

1.8.1.3 Croatia

The project was approved by the Research Ethics Committee of the Department of Psychology, Faculty of Humanities and Social Sciences, University of Zagreb. In collaboration with the Agency for Science and Higher Education in Croatia, 722 participants from 24 universities were recruited and invited via email to participate in the survey, which was conducted in Croatian using a back-translation approach.

1.8.1.4 Greece

The project received approval from the Research Ethics Committee of the School of Psychology at Aristotle University of Thessaloniki (# 020/03-01-2018). A total of 403 participants were recruited via email to complete the survey in Greek using a committee approach. Email addresses were obtained from 14 university intranet portals or public websites, and no incentives were provided for participation.

1.8.1.5 Lithuania

Ethical board approval was not required. A total of 530 participants from one university were recruited via email to complete the survey in Lithuanian, using a combined back-translation and committee approach. Ten participants were randomly selected to receive a souvenir as an incentive for participation.

1.8.1.6 Romania

Ethical board approval was not required. Data collection was conducted in partnership with D&D Research, a Romanian market research company. Invitations were sent via email and posted in a closed group used by university employees (e.g., Facebook, WhatsApp). A total of 476 participants from five universities were recruited, and no incentives were offered for participation.

1.8.1.7 South Africa

The project was approved by the governing ethics board (# NWU-HS-2016-0207). Participants from three traditional universities and three universities of technology were recruited via email provided by their university. A total of 1096 participants were entered into a lottery to win one of six grocery vouchers worth ZAR100 (about $7 USD) as an incentive.

1.8.1.8 Switzerland

Ethical board approval was not required. A total of 318 participants from one university were recruited via email to complete the survey in their preferred language (English or French) using a combined back-translation and committee approach. No incentives were provided.

1.8.1.9 The United Kingdom

The project was approved by the governing ethics board (# C17-76). Seventy participants from one university were recruited via email to complete the survey. Participants could enter a raffle to win one Amazon voucher worth £50 (about $63 USD) or choose to donate £1 to a homeless and housing charity as an incentive.

1.8.1.10 The United States

The project was classified as exempt by the Washington State University IRB (#16619). A total of 372 participants were recruited, with 333 from 30 four-year universities (selected based on the ten institution categories outlined by the Carnegie Classification of Institutions website). Email addresses were obtained from university public websites, and no incentives were offered. An additional sample of 8 participants was recruited via Amazon Mechanical Turk (MTurk) to improve representation from graduate students, with each MTurk participant offered $2.50 USD as an incentive. Evidence supports the viability of MTurk for recruiting reliable samples (Mortensen & Hughes, 2018).

1.8.2 Overall Sample Characteristics

The total sample was comprised of 4741 participants. Participants had an average age of 41.2 years ($SD = 11.3$). Women constituted a majority of 61.3%. Of the total population, 36.5% held a permanent contract. In terms of job positions, 47.4% were faculty members, 34.1% were support staff, and 18.5% were graduate students (i.e., PhDs and postdocs).

1.8.2.1 Belgian Sample

In total, 596 participants provided usable data for this study. The majority of participants were female (72.2%), whereas the remaining 27.8% self-identified as male. The mean age of the sample was 39.24 years ($SD = 11.26$). Most participants were highly educated (15.9% held a bachelor's degree, 54.3% held a master's degree and 27.8% held a doctoral degree or other equivalent). Permanent academic staff and junior research staff were approximately equally represented in the sample (39.2% and 37.7%, respectively), while the remaining 23.1% of the sample was composed of support and administrative staff. Approximately half of the employees (51.1%) were permanently employed, and a majority (71.2%) worked full-time.

1.8.2.2 Chinese Sample

Usable data were obtained from 160 participants (response rate of 58.8%). Half of the participants self-identified as female and half as male. The mean age was 36.50 years ($SD = 7.49$). With regards to education level, the majority of employees had obtained some level of higher education (20.0% held a bachelor's degree, 65.0% held a master's degree and 11.9% held a doctoral degree or other equivalent). A majority of the sample were permanent academic staff (61.3%), with an additional 26.3% made up of administrative staff and 12.5% of junior research staff. Participants were to a large extent permanently employed (80%), and nearly all of them (96.3%) worked full-time.

1.8.2.3 Croatian Sample

In total, 722 employees participated in the study (precise response rate is unknown due to an unprecise number of active e-mail addresses), and 430 provided usable data for this study. The mean age was 40.47 years ($SD = 9.98$), and the majority of participants were female (67.3%). Similarly, the majority were highly educated (2.1% held a bachelor's degree, 34.4% held a master's degree and 59.1% held a doctoral degree or other equivalent), permanently employed (67.7%) and worked full-time (98.1%). With regards to the staff category, just over half of the employees were permanent academic staff (51.4%), whereas support and administrative staff and junior research staff were equally represented in the sample (24.3%).

1.8.2.4 Greek Sample

A total of 403 participants contributed usable data to this study. A precise response rate cannot be obtained, as there are no reliable data on the number of active accounts and the number of participants who were on leave during data collection. The sample was composed of 54.6% female, 44.2% male and 0.7% transgender participants, with an additional 0.5% indicating the response "Other". The mean age was 46.88 years ($SD = 8.91$). A large proportion of the sample was highly educated, where 5.9% participants held a bachelor's degree, 17.6% a master's degree and 67.8% a doctoral degree or other equivalent. Furthermore, 48.6% of participants were permanent academic staff, 39.7% were support and administrative staff and

11.7% were junior research staff. Approximately half of the employees (55.4%) had a permanent contract with their university, and the vast majority (91.4%) were employed full-time.

1.8.2.5 Lithuanian Sample

Altogether, 530 participants provided data suitable for analysis (response rate unknown). Slightly more than half of the participants were female (54.6%), while all others self-identified as males. The mean age was 40.66 years ($SD = 11.13$). Most of them were highly educated (10.4% held a bachelor's degree, 40.4% held a master's degree and 46.4% held a doctoral degree or other equivalent). The sample was composed of 56.3% permanent academic staff, 36.3% support and administrative staff and 7.4% junior research staff. Most employees worked full-time (70.3%). Data on the type of work contract were not collected.

The *Romanian sample* was composed of 476 employees. The average age was 42.95 years ($SD = 9.16$), and the majority were female (76.1%). Slightly more than half of the participants were academic staff (58.6%), 17.9% were administrative staff, and 23.5% were supportive staff. The vast majority of participants worked full-time (95.6%).

1.8.2.6 South African Sample

The final sample comprised 1096 participants with usable data. The response rate cannot be calculated due to an unknown number of employees who received an invitation to participate in the study. Slightly more than half of the participants were male (54.1%), 45% were female and 0.9% indicated the response "Other". The mean age was 38.93 years ($SD = 12.26$). The majority of the participants had obtained some level of higher education (41.1% held a bachelor's degree, 22.3% held a master's degree and 15.4% held a doctoral degree or other equivalent). With regards to the staff category, 34.7% of the participants were permanent academic staff, 46.8% were support and administrative staff and 18.5% were junior research staff. More than half of the participants were permanent employees (65.6%) and employed full-time (79.4%).

1.8.2.7 Swiss Sample

Data from 318 participants met the criteria for inclusion in the study (response rate could not be precisely computed). The mean age was 41.48 years ($SD = 10.42$). The majority were female (i.e., 62.3%, whereas 37.7% participants self-identified as male). Most employees indicated high levels of education (10.1% held a bachelor's degree, 20.8% held a master's degree and 52.3% held a doctoral degree or other equivalent). Approximately equal proportions of the sample were support and administrative staff (41.6%) and junior research staff (36.5%), while the remaining 21.9% were permanent academic staff. The majority of the sample was composed of participants who worked full-time (62.9%). Approximately half of the sample was employed on a permanent contract (50.8%).

The *UK sample* consisted of 68 academic employees. The average age was 42.37 years ($SD = 11.41$), and 66.2% of the sample was female. The majority of the sample was highly educated (17.6% had obtained a bachelor's degree, 16.2% had a master's degree, and 63.2% had a doctoral degree or another equivalent). A total of 58.2% worked full time. The sample was predominantly composed of academic staff (64.7%), whereas 29.4% were supportive and 5.9% were administrative staff.

1.8.2.8 US Sample

Hypotheses were tested among 372 employees who provided usable data for this study (response rate: 7.3%). Slightly more than half of the participants were female (54.2%), 45.2% were male, 0.3% were transgender, and 0.3% indicated the response "Other". The mean age was 47.31 years ($SD = 13.17$). The majority of the sample was highly educated (6.5% held obtained a bachelor's degree, 29.7% held a master's degree and 59.5% held a doctoral degree or other equivalent). In addition, the majority were permanently employed (75.14%) and worked full-time (89.5%). The sample was predominantly composed of permanent academic staff (65%), whereas 33% were support and administrative staff and 2% were junior research staff.

The composition of the sample in each chapter may vary depending on the variables included in the respective studies. Therefore, a brief description of the sample is provided in each chapter concerning the specific variables utilized.

1.9 The Structure of the Book

Following this introductory chapter, Chaps. 2 and 3 address the equivalence of scales used in the following chapters of this book. Establishing measurement equivalence is crucial to ensure that accurate and meaningful comparisons can be made across countries. Moreover, achieving equivalence in measurement can lend credibility and confidence to future researchers who may wish to apply this scale in different cultural and national contexts.

Chapter 2 provides support for metric invariance of both quantitative and qualitative job insecurity scales across ten countries. Although evidence of scalar invariance, which would allow for cross-country comparisons of job insecurity, was not found, additional alignment analyses were conducted to facilitate specific cross-country comparisons. Furthermore, the chapter uncovers global trends related to job insecurity.

Chapter 3 analyses the measurement equivalence of nine predictors, moderators, and outcomes of job insecurity used in subsequent chapters. By demonstrating equivalence, it shows the suitability of comparing results from multiple countries using the same measures. Item- and scale-level invariances were tested using maximum likelihood alignment. While strict alignment could not be demonstrated for those measures, the findings suggest a level of confidence for comparing results across countries.

Chapter 4 investigates the well-being of academics, exploring the coexistence of burnout and work engagement, often seen as contradictory. Using latent class analysis on the comprehensive international dataset, it identifies three distinct types of well-being in academia: the 'exhausted', the 'moderate' and the 'engaged'. These types are only weakly associated with background variables, like gender, age, professional position, and country, suggesting some universality across contexts and categories. The associations with both kinds of job insecurity are stronger and in line with the expectation that job demands are related with burnout. The results indicate that the various professional categories in academia are much more engaged than burned out.

Chapter 5 examines self-undermining as a mediator between job insecurity, in-role performance, and counterproductive work behavior across ten countries. The findings show that qualitative job insecurity increases self-undermining, leading to poorer performance and more counterproductive behaviors. Quantitative job insecurity showed mixed results, highlighting the complexity of these relationships in different contexts.

Chapter 6 argues that academics would have a stronger identification with their job than other people working at university, due to the lengthy socialization process, exclusive status, and strong group culture. Both qualitative and quantitative job insecurity would hence pose an identity threat, which would lead to subsequent problems for mental health. Results of the study confirmed the core assumptions: Academics indeed reported a higher job identification than non-academics in 9 out of 10 countries. Qualitative job insecurity was found to reduce identification with the job and working population (quantitative insecurity only reduced identification with the working population). The latter was also found to be related to burnout. The results vary by country, indicating a different interpretation of job insecurity in each country. Academic identity is not just a matter of personal choice, but is informed by the contextual job circumstances.

Chapter 7 investigated the relationship between qualitative job insecurity and work performance in the higher education sector. The key finding is that qualitative job insecurity relates to higher levels of burnout, which in turn negatively relates to in-role performance. The study also found a consistent trend across multiple countries in its results.

In Chap. 8 the relationship between job insecurity and organizational justice is examined, with a focus on the often-overlooked aspect of overall organizational fairness. The authors present new insights on how perceptions of fairness can impact job insecurity and its effects in a more nuanced manner than previously believed.

Chapter 9 examines the relationship between three indicators of insecurity (subjective quantitative and qualitative job insecurity and the temporary employment contract) with various performance indicators among the three professional categories in academia (professors, PhD-students and administrative staff). Contrasting hypotheses are tested: is insecurity related to more or to less job performance? Does the employment contract moderate these relationships, and if so, does it buffer or boost the association between subjective job insecurity and job performance? Using the data from 10 countries, the results show that—when statistically significant—job insecurity is associated with a decrease in productive work behaviour and an increase in counterproductive work behaviour. Additionally, when a significant interaction effect is found, working on a temporary contract seems to buffer these relationships. The results suggest that job insecurity in academia is problematic for performance, as it is not conducive to the development and accumulation of scientific knowledge, but rather jeopardises its creation and dissemination.

Chapters 10 and 11 are special case studies within the country contexts of China and Greece. Chapter 10 shows the impact of qualitative job insecurity on faculty teaching staff in higher education institutions in China. The results revealed that qualitative job insecurity was linked to decreased work motivation, work adjustment, and life satisfaction among this population. Additionally, staff who had a stronger focus on promotions were more negatively affected by qualitative job insecurity, as shown by a further decline in work adjustment and life wellbeing.

Chapter 11 explores the role of workplace social capital (measured by trust, reciprocity and social network) as a buffer against the negative effects of job insecurity on work engagement and in-role performance in Greece. Contrary to expectations, results showed that job insecurity related negatively to work engagement only in conditions of higher workplace social capital, while insecurity related positively to in-role performance in conditions of lower workplace social capital. These findings that are mainly attributed to the network sub dimension of workplace social capital imply that employees' centrality in organizational networks determines their access to the available resources that forms job insecurity outcomes.

Finally, Chap. 12 consolidates the findings from the preceding chapters, offering a comprehensive overview and integration. It explores potential future directions for the field, highlighting key areas needing further investigation. Additionally, the chapter includes some new results on causal attributions that have not been presented in one of the chapters.

References

Ai, A. L., Aisenberg, E., Weiss, S. I., & Salazar, D. (2017). Measures of general health and psychological well-being. *Journal of Health Psychology, 22*, 156–169.

Ambrose, M. L., & Schminke, M. (2009). The role of overall justice judgments in organizational justice research: A test of mediation. *Journal of Applied Psychology, 94*, 491–500.

American Association of University Professors. (2023). *Data snapshot: Tenure and contingency in US higher education*. AAUP. https://www.aaup.org/sites/default/files/AAUP%20Data%20Snapshot.pdf
American Psychological Association. (2020). *The toll of job loss*. APA. https://www.apa.org/monitor/2020/10/toll-job-loss
American Psychological Association. (2024, March). College enrollment drop: Psychology's response to declining numbers. *APA Monitor*. https://www.apa.org/monitor/2024/03/college-enrollment-drop-psychology
AP News. (2024, July 8). *More Americans skipping college, raising concerns about the value of higher education*. https://apnews.com/article/skipping-college-student-loans-trade-jobs-efc1f6d6067ab770f6e512b3f7719cc0
Ashford, S. J., Lee, C., & Bobko, P. (1989). Content, causes, and consequences of job insecurity: A theory-based measure and substantive test. *Academy of Management Journal, 32*, 803–829.
Bačić Karković, D. (2019). Brain drain in Croatia: The emigration of highly educated professionals. *Migration and Development, 8*, 326–344.
Bakker, A. B., & Wang, Y. (2016). Self-undermining behavior at work: Evidence of construct validity. *International Journal of Stress Management, 23*, 135–158.
Bennett, R. J., & Robinson, S. L. (2000). Development of a measure of workplace deviance. *Journal of Applied Psychology, 85*, 349–360.
Bolino, M. C., & Turnley, W. H. (1999). Measuring impression management in organizations: A scale development based on the Jones and Pittman taxonomy. *Organizational Research Methods, 2*, 187–206.
Briscoe, J. P. (2006). Protean career orientation: Findings and implications for career development. *Journal of Vocational Behavior, 69*, 78–94.
Brislin, R. W. (1970). Back-translation for cross-cultural research. *Journal of cross-cultural psychology, 1*(3), 185–216.
Broughman, S. P., & Haar, C. K. (2018). *Characteristics of public and private elementary and secondary school principals in the United States: Results from the 2015-16 National Teacher and Principal Survey First Look*. National Center for Education Statistics. https://nces.ed.gov/pubs2018/2017070.pdf
Carroll, A. E. (2023, October 3). Science in America: Why do we trust it? *The New York Times*. https://www.nytimes.com/2023/10/03/opinion/science-americans-trust-covid.html
Chan, W. Y., Ho, G. W. K., Chernyshenko, O. S., Ho, R., & Sam, Y. L. (2020). Stress adaptation and resilience of academics in higher education. *Asia Pacific Education Review, 21*(1), 23–33.
Chen, X. (2021). The impact of tenure-track systems on job security in Chinese higher education. *Journal of Higher Education Policy and Management, 43*, 205–221.
Chirumbolo, A., Callea, A., Urbini, F., & Lo Presti, A. (2017). The effect of job insecurity and life uncertainty on everyday consumptions and broader life projects. *Psicologia Sociale, 12*, 297–312.
CNN. (2024, July 8). *Americans increasingly skeptical about the value of a college degree, poll shows*. https://edition.cnn.com/2024/07/08/us/college-value-cost-americans-skeptical-poll/index.html
Coalition on the Academic Workforce (CAW). (2012). *A portrait of part-time faculty members*. CAW. http://www.academicworkforce.org/CAW_portrait_2012.pdf
Courtois, A., & O'Keefe, T. (2015). Precarity in the ivory tower: Gendered impacts of casualisation of academic work in Ireland. *Journal of Higher Education Policy and Management, 37*, 15–27.
Czerniewicz, L. (2018). Inequities in higher education contexts: The politics of digital learning. *British Journal of Educational Technology, 49*, 1283–1293.
De Cuyper, N., & De Witte, H. (2010). Temporary employment and perceived employability: Mediation by impression management. *Journal of Career Development, 37*(3), 635–652.
De Jong, J., & Den Hartog, D. (2010). Measuring innovative work behavior. *Creativity and Innovation Management, 19*, 23–36.

De Witte, H. (1992). *Between optimism and withdrawal. Empirical study of the long-term unemployed in Flanders, Belgium*. Hoger Instituut voor de Arbeid—KU Leuven.
De Witte, H. (2005). Job insecurity: Review of the international literature on definitions, prevalence, antecedents and consequences. *SA Journal of Industrial Psychology, 31*, 1–6.
Dill, E. (2018, November 8). *Adjunct professors battle low pay, lack of job security*. Herald-Tribune. https://www.heraldtribune.com/news/20181108/adjunct-professors-battle-low-pay-lack-of-job-security
Doolan, K. (2021). Workload, burnout, and the value of academic work in Croatian higher education. *Croatian Journal of Education, 23*, 11–27.
Doosje, B., Ellemers, N., & Spears, R. (1995). Social identity and perceived group variability. *Journal of Experimental Social Psychology, 31*, 410–436.
European Commission. (2023). *Higher Education Law 199/2023*.
European Commission. (2024). *Educated Romania initiative*. https://ec.europa.eu/education/educated-romania_en
Eurydice. (2023). *Reforms in Romanian higher education*. https://eacea.ec.europa.eu/national-policies/eurydice/content/national-reforms-higher-education-55_en
Farnell, T. (2020). Professional development in Croatian higher education. *European Journal of Education, 55*, 337–349.
Featherstone, K. (2016). The Greek crisis and the challenge to reform higher education. *Journal of Modern Greek Studies, 34*, 323–345.
Fischmann, G., De Witte, H., Sulea, C., Vander Elst, T., De Cuyper, N., & Iliescu, D. (2022). Validation of a Short and Generic Qualitative Job Insecurity Scale (QUAL-JIS). *European Journal of Career Assessment, 38*(5), 397–411. https://doi.org/10.1027/1015-5759/a000674
Flaherty, C. (2020, May 21). *COVID-19 and the future of faculty work*. Inside Higher Ed. https://www.insidehighered.com/news/2020/05/21/covid-19-and-future-faculty-work
Greenhalgh, L., & Rosenblatt, Z. (1984). Job insecurity: Toward conceptual clarity. *Academy of Management Review, 9*, 438–448.
Griep, Y., Bankins, S., Vander Elst, T., & De Witte, H. (2021). How psychological contract breach affects long-term mental and physical health: The longitudinal role of effort–reward imbalance. *Applied Psychology: Health and Well-Being, 13*(2), 263–281.
Guest, D. E., Isaksson, K., & De Witte, H. (Eds.). (2010). *Employment contracts, psychological contracts & employee Well-Being. An international study*. Oxford University Press.
Hadžibajramović, E., Schaufeli, W. B., & De Witte, H. (2024). The ultra-short version of the Burnout Assessment Tool (BAT4)—development, validation, and measurement invariance across countries, age and gender. *PLoS ONE, 19*(2), e0297843. https://doi.org/10.1371/journal.pone.0297843
Hebrang Grgić, I., & Žilić, A. (2018). Job security and academic performance in Croatian higher education. *Journal of Higher Education Policy and Management, 40*, 365–377.
Hechinger Report. (2022, August 31). College students predicted to fall by more than 15% after the year 2025. The Hechinger Report. https://hechingerreport.org/college-students-predicted-to-fall-by-more-than-15-after-the-year-2025/
Hellgren, J., Sverke, M., & Isaksson, K. (1999). A two-dimensional approach to job insecurity: Consequences for employee attitudes and well-being. *European Journal of Work and Organizational Psychology, 8*, 179–195.
Hunterlodge. (2023). *The trends shaping UK higher education in 2023 and beyond*. https://www.hunterlodge.co.uk
Inside Higher Ed. (2023, May 3). *Tenure and promotion barriers persist for women, faculty of color*. Inside Higher Ed. https://www.insidehighered.com/news/2023/05/03/tenure-and-promotion-barriers-persist-women-faculty-color
Johnson, N., Veletsianos, G., & Seaman, J. (2020). U.S. faculty and administrators' experiences and approaches in the early weeks of the COVID-19 pandemic. *Online Learning, 24*, 6–21.

Kezar, A., & Maxey, D. (2014). The changing academic workforce. *Association of American Colleges and Universities.* https://www.aacu.org/publications-research/periodicals/changing-academic-workforce

Khaw, D., & Kern, M. L. (2014). PERMA profiles and subjective well-being. *Journal of Positive Psychology, 9*, 181–194.

Klandermans, B., & van Vuuren, T. (1999). Job insecurity: Introduction. *European Journal of Work and Organizational Psychology, 8*, 145–153.

Kottaridi, C., & Tsakloglou, P. (2020). The impact of the economic crisis on higher education in Greece. *Higher Education Policy, 33*, 5–24.

Ladi, S. (2014). Austerity politics and administrative reform: The Eurozone crisis and its impact upon Greek public administration. *Comparative European Politics, 12*, 184–208.

Leka, S., & Jain, A. (2010). *Health impact of psychosocial hazards at work: An overview*. World Health Organization. https://www.who.int/publications/i/item/9789241500272

Li, J. (2021). Faculty perceptions of job security and performance expectations in Chinese higher education. *Chinese Education & Society, 54*, 251–266.

Lodahl, T. M., & Kejner, M. (1965). The definition and measurement of job involvement. *Journal of Applied Psychology, 49*, 24–33.

Marginson, S. (2013). The impossibility of capitalist markets in higher education. *Journal of Education Policy, 28*, 353–370.

Marinoni, G., van't Land, H., & Jensen, T. (2020). The impact of COVID-19 on higher education around the world. *International Association of Universities.* https://www.iau-aiu.net/IMG/pdf/iau_covid19_and_he_survey_report_final_may_2020.pdf

Matković, T. (2017). Bureaucratic inefficiencies and academic job satisfaction in Croatia. *Studies in Higher Education, 42*(5), 897–912.

McKinsey & Company. (2024). *Economic challenges in Romania.* Retrieved from https://www.mckinsey.com/ro/economic-challenges-2024

McMurtrie, B. (2020). How the shift to remote learning might affect college staffing. *The Chronicle of Higher Education.* https://www.chronicle.com/article/how-the-shift-to-remote-learning-might-affect-college-staffing

Menéndez-Espina, S., Llosa, J. A., Agulló-Tomás, E., Rodríguez-Suárez, J., Sáiz-Villar, R., & Lahseras-Díez, H. F. (2019). Job insecurity and mental health: The moderating role of coping strategies from a gender perspective. *Frontiers in Psychology, 10*, 286. https://doi.org/10.3389/fpsyg.2019.00286

Ministry of Education of the People's Republic of China. (2023). *China sets direction for world-class universities.* https://internationaleducation.gov.au/News/Latest-News/Pages/China-sets-direction-for-world-class-universities.aspx

Mohr, G. B. (2000). The changing significance of different stressors after the announcement of bankruptcy: A longitudinal investigation with special emphasis on job insecurity. *Journal of Organizational Behavior, 21*, 337–359.

Morrison, E. W. (1994). Role definitions and organizational citizenship behavior: The importance of the employee's perspective. *Academy of Management Journal, 37*, 1543–1567.

National Association of Student Financial Aid Administrators. (2023). *Demographic changes and pandemic fallout could alter higher ed enrollment trends.* NASFAA. https://www.nasfaa.org

Nawrocka, S., De Witte, H., Brondino, M., & Pasini, M. (2021). On the reciprocal relationship between quantitative and qualitative job insecurity and outcomes. Testing a cross-lagged longitudinal mediation model. *International Journal of Environmental Research and Public Health, 18*, 6392. https://doi.org/10.3390/ijerph18126392

Neubert, M. J., Kacmar, K. M., Carlson, D. S., Chonko, L. B., & Roberts, J. A. (2008). Regulatory focus as a mediator of the influence of initiating structure and servant leadership on employee behavior. *Journal of Applied Psychology, 93*, 1220–1233.

Nikolova, I., Van Ruysseveldt, J., De Witte, H., & Van Dam, K. (2014). Learning climate scale: Construction, reliability and initial validity evidence. *Journal of Vocational Behavior, 85*, 258–265. https://doi.org/10.1016/j.jvb.2014.07.007

North American Van Lines. (2023). 2023 U.S. moving migration patterns report. North American Van Lines. https://www.northamerican.com/migration-map

OECD. (2021). *Lithuania: Education at a Glance.* https://www.oecd-ilibrary.org

OECD. (2023a). *Education at a glance 2023: OECD indicators. OECD Publishing.* https://doi.org/10.1787/69096873-en

OECD. (2023b). *Economic outlook and challenges in Romania.* https://www.oecd.org/economy/romania-economic-outlook-2023

Organisation for Economic Co-operation and Development (OECD). (2020). *Education policy outlook: Greece. OECD Publishing.* https://doi.org/10.1787/0b8fdca0-en

Papadimitriou, A. (2015). Higher education reforms in Greece: An international comparative perspective. *European Journal of Higher Education, 5*, 49–65.

Park, H. J., & Kang, S. W. (2013). Attitudes toward immigration and the role of the labor market: Evidence from OECD countries. *International Journal of Social Economics, 40*, 421–434.

Patrinos, H. A. (2017). *Higher education and the labor market in Greece. World Bank.* https://documents.worldbank.org/en/publication/documents-reports/documentdetail/220631490636651210/higher-education-and-the-labor-market-in-greece

Pettita, J., McCune, E., & Loughlin, C. (2020). Financial strain and its impact on employee well-being. *Journal of Occupational Health Psychology, 25*, 118–127.

Podsakoff, P. M., MacKenzie, S. B., & Fetter, R. (1990). Organizational citizenship behavior and objective productivity as determinants of managerial evaluations of employee performance. *Organizational Behavior and Human Decision Processes, 50*, 123–150.

Probst, T. M. (2005). Countering the negative effects of job insecurity through participative decision making: Lessons from the demand-control model. *Journal of Occupational Health Psychology, 10*, 320–329.

Quinn, R. P., & Shepard, L. J. (1974). *The 1972–1973 quality of employment survey*. University of Michigan, Institute for Social Research.

Redden, E. (2019, May 10). *The decline of tenure track positions.* The Guardian. https://www.theguardian.com/education/2019/may/10/the-decline-of-tenure-track-positions

Robinson, S. L., & Morrison, E. W. (2000). The development of psychological contract breach and violation: A longitudinal study. *Journal of Organizational Behavior, 21*, 525–546.

Sabri, D. (2011). What's wrong with 'the student experience'? *Discourse: Studies in the Cultural Politics of Education, 32*, 657–667.

Schaufeli, W. B., Desart, S., & De Witte, H. (2020). Burnout Assessment Tool (BAT)—Development, validity, and reliability. *International Journal of Environmental Research and Public Health, 17*, 9495.

Schaufeli, W. B., Shimazu, A., Hakanen, J., Salanova, M., & De Witte, H. (2017). An ultra-short measure for work engagement: The UWES-3 validation across five countries. *European Journal of Psychological Assessment, 33*, 171–182.

Šćukanec Schmidt, N. (2020). Dynamics of academic employment at new universities in Croatia. *European Education Research Journal, 19*, 445–462.

Seligman, M. E. P. (2011). *Flourish: A visionary new understanding of happiness and well-being*. Free Press.

Shoss, M. K. (2017). Job insecurity: An integrative review and agenda for future research. *Journal of Management, 43*, 1911–1939.

Solomon, S., & Du Plessis, M. (2024). Precarious employment practices in South African universities. *SA Journal of Human Resource Management, 22*, 2490.

Stankevičiūtė, Ž., Staniškienė, E., & Ramanauskaitė, J. (2021). The impact of job insecurity on employee happiness at work: A case of robotised production line operators in the furniture industry in Lithuania. *Sustainability, 13*(3), 1563.

Sverke, M., & Hellgren, J. (2002). The nature of job insecurity: Understanding employment uncertainty on the brink of a new millennium. *Applied Psychology: An International Review, 51*, 23–42.

Sverke, M., Hellgren, J., & Näswall, K. (2002). No security: A meta-analysis and review of job insecurity and its consequences. *Journal of Occupational Health Psychology, 7*, 242–264.

Svongoro, P. (2023). Understanding higher education: Alternative perspectives (2022) by C. Boughey, and S. McKenna. – African Minds, Cape Town. *Journal of Education (University of KwaZulu-Natal), 93*, 212–218.

Tight, M. (2020). Higher education financial management. *Journal of Higher Education Policy and Management, 42*, 229–239.

Times Higher Education. (2022). *Controversial reforms in Romanian higher education*. https://www.timeshighereducation.com/romania-reforms-2022

Times Higher Education. (2023a). *UK university strikes 2023: A guide to what the dispute is about*. https://www.timeshighereducation.com/news/uk-university-strikes-2023-guide-what-dispute-about

Times Higher Education. (2023b). *University strikes: why staff are taking action*. https://www.timeshighereducation.com

Toutkoushian, R. K. (2015). Stress and burnout among non-tenure track faculty. *Research in Higher Education, 56*(6), 571–592. https://link.springer.com/article/10.1007/s11162-015-9367-7

Tu, Y., Long, L., Wang, H., & Jiang, L. (2019). To prevent or to promote: How regulatory focus moderates the differentiated effects of quantitative versus qualitative job insecurity on employee stress and motivation. *Journal of Organizational Behavior, 40*, 825–838.

University and College Union. (2022). *Biggest ever university strike begins in fight over pay, pensions & conditions*. https://www.ucu.org.uk

USAFacts. (2023, April 12). Where are students moving to attend college? USAFacts. https://usafacts.org/articles/where-are-students-moving-to-attend-college/

van Vuuren, T. (1990). *Met ontslag bedreigd: Werknemers in onzekerheid over hun arbeidsplaats bij veranderingen in de organisatie [Threatened with dismissal: Employees in uncertainty about their job position in organizational changes]. PhD dissertation*. VU University Amsterdam.

Vanbelle, E., Griep, Y., Van den Broeck, A., & De Witte, H. (n.d.). (accepted, online). Development and validation of a short broad job crafting scale. *Group & Organization Management*. https://doi.org/10.1177/10596011231208924.

Vander Elst, T., De Cuyper, N., & De Witte, H. (2011). The role of perceived control in the relationship between job insecurity and psychosocial outcomes: moderator or mediator? *Stress and Health, 27*, 215–227.

Vander Elst, T., De Witte, H., & De Cuyper, N. (2014). The job insecurity scale: A psychometric evaluation across five European countries. *European Journal of Work and Organizational Psychology, 23*(3), 364–380. https://doi.org/10.1080/1359432X.2012.745989

Vidović, D. (2021). Emigration and its impact on the Croatian labor market. *South East European Journal of Economics and Business, 16*, 41–53.

Vrbanec, S. (2019). Early-career academics in Croatia: Challenges and opportunities. *International Journal of Educational Development, 68*, 77–85.

Wang, Y. (2022). Performance evaluation and job insecurity in Chinese academia. *Higher Education Research & Development, 41*, 676–690.

Wayne, S. J., Shore, L. M., & Liden, R. C. (1990). Perceived organizational support and leader-member exchange: A social exchange perspective. *Academy of Management Journal, 40*, 82–111.

White, J. K. (2016). Authentic supervisory appreciation and its impact on employee motivation. *Journal of Managerial Psychology, 31*, 128–142.

Williams, L. J., & Anderson, S. E. (1991). Job satisfaction and organizational commitment as predictors of organizational citizenship and in-role behaviors. *Journal of Management, 17*, 601–617.

Woodhouse, K. (2015). The financial pressures facing higher education institutions. *Inside Higher Ed.* https://www.insidehighered.com/news/2015/04/14/financial-pressures-facing-higher-education-institutions

Zhang, L. (2022). Job insecurity among academic staff in China: The impact of ongoing reforms. *Asia Pacific Education Review, 23*, 89–103.

Lara Christina Roll (PhD in Work and Organizational Psychology) is a Senior Associate at PwC Belgium, an External Researcher at KU Leuven (Belgium) and an Extraordinary Professor with the Optentia Research Unit at North-West University (South Africa). Her primary research focuses on workplace insecurity, particularly on how employees perceive the impact of technological advancements on their occupations. From 2022 until 2024 she has served as vice-chair of Algoright e.V., a think tank comprised of young scholars to support research exchange and good digitalisation in Germany (https://algoright.de/). Furthermore, from 2023 to 2024, she served as an expert panel member for the Flemish Minister for Economy, Innovation, Work, Social Economy, and Agriculture, contributing to the development of future scenarios on the role of technology in creating an inclusive job market.

Hans De Witte (PhD in Psychology) was Full Professor in Work Psychology at the Faculty of Psychology and Educational Sciences of the KU Leuven, Belgium (Research Group Work, Organizational and Personnel Psychology). He is academically active since October 2023 as emeritus with assignment. He is also appointed as Extraordinary Professor at the North-West University of South Africa (Optentia Research Unit, Vanderbijlpark Campus). His research includes the study of the psychological consequences of job insecurity, unemployment, temporary employment and downsizing, as well as mobbing and burnout versus work engagement. He (co-)authored about 300 articles in English peer-reviewed journals, published 30 books (14 English and 16 in Dutch, most as co-editor) and is (co-)author of about 80 chapters in English academic books.

Sebastiaan Rothmann Sr. Ph.D. is Professor in industrial/organizational psychology at the North-West University (Vanderbijlpark Campus) and Director of the Optentia Research Unit in South Africa. His research journey started with the topics of stress, burnout, and work engagement and has evolved toward prospering and flourishing of people in work and organizational contexts. People who prosper in work and organizational contexts are satisfied with their jobs; experience positive emotions; are energetic, learning, and dedicated; experience satisfaction.

Chapter 2
Job Insecurity Within Higher Education: An Assessment of Measurement Invariance and Global Trends

Lixin Jiang, Andrea Bazzoli, Melissa R. Jenkins, and Tahira M. Probst

Artificial intelligence and machine learning, automation of jobs and tasks, and the gig economy and contract work have emerged as key themes in the new world of work and led to increasingly precarious working arrangements (Ashford et al., 2018). For example, automation is predicted to replace 40% of jobs within the next 15 years (Reisinger, 2019), readily substituting for human labor in a wide range of routine and non-routine cognitive tasks (Frey & Osborne, 2017). The utilization of online labor platforms (i.e., gig work) is growing at an annual rate of 26% (Kässi & Lehdonvirta, 2016); and 83% of 2718 executives surveyed across 27 countries indicate that they plan to increase use of contingent, intermittent, or consultant employees in the next 3 years (Oxford Economics, 2014). Consequently, job insecurity is called "the disease of the 21st century" (Parramore, 2012) and "the single largest cause of uncertainty in the high-risk society" (Mandel, 1996, p. 160).

Although we do not examine the impact of the coronavirus disease (COVID-19; World Health Organization, 2020) pandemic on job insecurity as our data were collected prior, the pandemic further compounds the threat to the continuity and stability of people's employment. In the United States, the unemployment rate rose from 3.5% in February (pre-pandemic) to 14.7% in April, 13.3% in May, and 11.1% in June 2020 (U.S. Bureau of Labor Statistics, 2020). Almost half of Britain's workforce were worried that their livelihoods stand in immediate danger because

L. Jiang (✉)
School of Psychology, University of Auckland, Auckland, New Zealand
e-mail: l.jiang@auckland.ac.nz

A. Bazzoli
Department of Psychology, Baruch College & CUNY Graduate Center, New York, NY, USA
e-mail: andrea.bazzoli@baruch.cuny.edu

M. R. Jenkins · T. M. Probst
Department of Psychology, Washington State University, Vancouver, WA, USA
e-mail: melissa.jenkins@wsu.edu; probst@wsu.edu

L. C. Roll et al. (eds.), *Global Perspectives on Job Insecurity in Higher Education*,
Aligning Perspectives on Health, Safety and Well-Being,
https://doi.org/10.1007/978-3-031-85772-0_2

of the impact of COVID-19 (The Sunday Times, 2020). The International Labour Organization (2020) revealed that nearly half of the global workforce faced significant declines in working hours and was at risk of becoming jobless due to the prolongation and extension of lockdown measures. Together, social, political, economic, and technological changes have transformed working life, causing job insecurity to be one of the most common stressors in the contemporary workplace.

Higher education around the world is not immune from these fundamental changes to the workplace. For example, a 2011 study from the American Association of University Professors (AAUP Research Office, 2013) estimated that 76% of college professors within the United States are contingent instructional staff, including full-time non-tenure-track faculty, part-time faculty, and graduate student employees. AAUP (2016, p. 13) further indicated that "Over the past forty years, the proportion of the academic labor force holding full-time tenured positions[1] has declined by 26 percent and the share holding full-time tenure-track positions has declined by an astonishing 50 percent. Conversely, there has been a 62 percent increase in full-time non-tenure-track faculty appointments and a 70 percent increase in part-time instructional faculty appointments."

Similarly, the University and College Union (UCU, 2019) revealed that the UK university sector underwent casualization of academic workforce where about 70% of the 49,000 researchers are on fixed-term contracts, 37,000 teaching staff are on fixed-term contracts, and a further 71,000 teachers are employed as "atypical academics" who are paid hourly and on the lowest contract levels. Consequently, 85% of 2646 surveyed participants indicated that they had considered leaving the higher education sector in the past year, with 77% of participants listing a high level of job insecurity being their reason for doing so (UCU, 2019).

Higher education in China also undertook radical changes abolishing the former practice of lifetime employment within the ivory tower; instead, each university is now required to set their own performance evaluations to determine whether their academic staff members are "up or out." Consequently, the academic standards for promotion are constantly changing. Moreover, universities have fixed limits on the number of faculty that can be granted promotion in any given year, leading to a highly competitive climate within higher education (Guoxue, 2020).

When specific crises like COVID-19 appear, the global higher education landscape undergoes significant changes, exacerbating job insecurity among university employees. In response to the pandemic, institutions worldwide have been compelled to switch to online learning and digital tools, cancel internships and study abroad programs, and close campus doors. Travel restrictions and closed borders have led to a substantial drop in international students, causing a significant decline in revenue for the higher education system (QS survey, 2020). As a result, universities have implemented hiring freezes, halted pay and benefit increases, reduced various expenditures, cut services, asked staff to do more with less, and consolidated or eliminated academic programs.

[1]A tenured position in the US is an indefinite appointment that can be terminated only under extraordinary circumstances.

Because of the international prevalence of the job insecurity experience within and outside the higher education system, scholars have investigated job insecurity across the globe. For instance, Debus et al. (2012) have examined job insecurity across 24 countries, while Probst and Jiang (2017) have focused on job insecurity in 19 European countries. Moreover, a meta-analysis (Jiang et al., 2021) has compiled job-insecurity studies from 39 countries, including U.S., China, Belgium, Canada, Finland, Sweden, South Africa, Italy, Germany, Australia, South Korea, Spain, Pakistan, U.K., Turkey, Netherlands, Norway, Romania, Switzerland, Israel, Egypt, Demark, Estonia, Lithuania, Nigeria, Peru, Poland, Portugal, Singapore, Austria, Chile, Croatia, Greece, Lebanon, Malaysia, New Zealand, Oman, United Arab Emirates, and Russia. As inclusive as these studies are, it is unknown whether the job insecurity construct being measured is comparable across these different countries.

To facilitate the comparability of job-insecurity research and make sure that survey respondents from different countries interpret the job insecurity construct in a conceptually equivalent manner, the purpose of this chapter is to cross-nationally validate a Quantitative Job Insecurity scale (Vander Elst et al., 2014) and a Qualitative Job Insecurity scale (Fischmann et al., 2022). As non-equivalence of job insecurity may invalidate cross-country comparisons, there is a strong need to investigate invariance, which, if supported, can facilitate meaningful group comparisons. Moreover, the factor alignment that can reduce statistical biases involved with comparing scores from individuals across diverse observed groups are advantageous when accessing equivalence across a large number of groups. Thus, building on the previous research showing construct validity, reliability, and criterion validity of the Quantitative Job Insecurity scale across five European countries (i.e., Belgium, The Netherlands, Spain, Sweden, the UK; Vander Elst et al., 2014), we examine measurement invariance of the Quantitative and Qualitative Job Insecurity scales across ten countries (i.e., Belgium, China, Croatia, Greece, Lithuania, Romania, South Africa, Switzerland, the UK, and the US).

2.1 Definitions, Theoretical Frameworks, and Outcomes of Job Insecurity

Scholars have defined job insecurity in multiple ways. For example, Greenhalgh and Rosenblatt (1984, p. 438) referred to job insecurity as "powerlessness to maintain desired continuity in a threatened job situation" (also see Ashford et al., 1989, p. 804); Van Vuuren and Klandermans (1990) as "concern about the future permanence of the job"; Jacobson and Hartley (1991, p. 1431) as "a discrepancy between the level of security a person experiences and the level she or he might prefer"; Heaney et al. (1994, p. 1431) as "an employee's perception of a potential threat to continuity in his or her current job"; Davy et al. (1997, p. 323) as "one's expectations about continuity in a job situation"; and Probst (2003, p. 452) as "perceived level of stability and continuance of one's job as one knows it".

Based on the diverse definitions of job insecurity, we summarize three defining features of job insecurity containing subjectivity, uncertainty, and vulnerability. First, job insecurity is "in the eye of the beholders" (Probst et al., 2018). Regardless of any actual objective level of job security, job insecurity is contingent upon individuals' subjective evaluations regarding the future of one's job, which can be impacted by individual, organizational, social, and economic factors (Lee et al., 2018; Shoss, 2017; Sinclair et al., 2010). In other words, some might feel insecure even in the absence of "objective reasons" for such insecurity, while others may feel secure even when their employment is actually at risk (De Witte, 1999). Second, without knowing when and what outcomes will become reality, job insecurity involves an uncertain and unpredictable job situation (De Witte, 1999; Probst, 2003; Shoss, 2017; Sverke et al., 2002). Indeed, Shoss (2017) posits that job insecurity is a future-focused phenomenon reflecting one's anticipation of a loss event that has not yet taken place. Thus, it is unclear what might happen next and what has to be done. Third, insecurity implies vulnerability. With regards to employment relationships, individual employees are at a disadvantage because employment relationships represent an unequal distribution of power and dependence between employees and their employer (Emerson, 1972a, 1972b; Hipp, 2016). Job insecurity, where an employee is unable to maintain the desired continuity of a job situation (Greenhalgh & Rosenblatt, 1984), compounds that disadvantage. This also reflects the involuntary, uncontrollable nature of job insecurity (De Witte, 1999; Lee et al., 2018; Sverke & Hellgren, 2002).

Not surprisingly, job insecurity is considered a work stressor with negative consequences. Several theories provide excellent theoretical frameworks to understand the associations between job insecurity and its adverse outcomes. First, the latent deprivation model of Jahoda (1981) proposes that employment provides one manifest benefit (i.e., income) and five latent benefits (i.e., collective purpose, social contact, status, time structure, and activity). Thus, job insecurity, where employees perceive and fear that they may lose one or more of these benefits associated with their work, may lead to damaging outcomes, including decreased psychological well-being and health and increased strain consequences (e.g., Vander Elst et al., 2016). Moreover, Conservation of Resources theory (Hobfoll, 1989) argues that employees may report psychological strain when experiencing the threat to their valued resources. Because job insecurity represents the threat to employee latent and manifest benefits (Jahoda, 1981; Vander Elst et al., 2016), job-insecure employees tend to report decreased psychological well-being and poor health.

On the other hand, the job demands-resources model (Bakker & Demerouti, 2017) proposes that job demands are those physical, psychosocial, or organizational aspects of the job that require sustained physical and/or mental effort and are related to physiological and/or psychological costs by activating an energy depletion process. Job insecurity is one such job demand (Probst, 2005) that may lead to constant overtaxing and health problems (e.g., fatigue, burnout). According to the transactional theory of stress (Lazarus & Folkman, 1984), employees appraise stressful situations such as job demands in terms of their significance for well-being as either potentially challenging or threatening. Integrating knowledge from the transactional theory of stress (Lazarus & Folkman, 1984), job demands can be appraised by employees as either hindrances or challenges (Bazzoli et al., 2020; Cavanaugh et al., 2000). Job insecurity has been categorized as one of the hindrance stressors (Armstrong-Stassen, 1993; De Witte, 1999; Piccoli et al., 2019) that hamper personal growth, learning, and goal attainment, as well as trigger negative emotions (e.g., fear, anxiety, anger), cognitions (e.g., rumination), and a passive, disengaging style of coping (e.g., withdrawing from the situation; Jiang & Lavaysse, 2018).

Finally, social exchange theories provide another lens to understand the harmful outcomes of job insecurity. Deriving from social exchange theory (Cropanzano & Mitchell, 2005), the norm of reciprocity suggests that one party will feel a sense of obligation to return good deeds from the other party. Applying the perspective of social exchange to the workplace indicates that employees repay a favorable workplace treatment with favorable attitudes and behaviors of their own, as well as adjust their attitudes and behaviors downward in response to unfavorable treatment. Therefore, when employees experience job insecurity, an infraction of the implicit or explicit social exchange agreement (Mauno et al., 2005), they will decrease their job attitudes and job performance in return.

Together, these above theoretical perspectives propose that job insecurity as a work stressor may trigger adverse employee outcomes. Empirically, decades of studies documenting the detrimental outcomes of job insecurity have provided strong support for these theoretical frameworks. A meta-analysis (Jiang & Lavaysse, 2018) based on 535 independent samples confirms the significant associations between job insecurity and 41 of its adverse outcomes. A review of 30 years of longitudinal studies also suggests that job insecurity causally leads to subsequent declines in health and well-being (De Witte et al., 2016).

2.2 Dimensions and Measures of Job Insecurity

In their pioneering work, Greenhalgh and Rosenblatt (1984, p. 440) argued that the potential loss of continuity in a job situation can range from "permanent loss of the job itself" (i.e., job loss insecurity) to "loss of some subjectively important feature of the job" (i.e., job feature insecurity). Accordingly, Ashford et al. (1989) developed a multidimensional measure of job insecurity and calculated job insecurity as a function of (1) the importance of job features that could be at risk (17 items); (2) the subjective probability of losing each feature (17 items); (3) the importance of possible job loss (10 items); (4) the perceived likelihood of job loss (10 items); and (5) one's perceived powerlessness to counter job threats (3 items).

Although theory-driven, Ashford et al.'s scale (1989) faces several criticisms. A common criticism is its length (54 items in total; Kinnunen et al., 1999; Mauno et al., 2005), making it impractical in the applied setting. Moreover, their job insecurity measure includes factors that do not belong to the core experiences of job insecurity, such as the importance of the job and job features as well as powerlessness (Jacobson, 1991; Rosenblatt & Ruvio, 1996; Probst, 2003; Vander Elst et al., 2014). Additionally, it has been criticized for including theorized multiplication (e.g., the perceived likelihood of job loss X the importance of the job to the person; Lee et al., 2006). Indeed, Cheng and Chan's (2008) meta-analysis on job insecurity excludes studies using Ashford et al.'s scale because research has shown that the relationship between multiplicative measures and criterion variables is susceptible to a scaling effect that may generate spurious results in bivariate correlational analyses (Evans, 1991). Finally, although deteriorated working conditions as part of the job insecurity construct are included in Ashford et al.'s measurement, scholars have increasingly acknowledged that job feature insecurity is a unique dimension of job insecurity, independent of job loss insecurity.

Therefore, Hellgren et al. (1999) coined the terms "quantitative job insecurity" (i.e., job loss insecurity) and "qualitative job insecurity" (i.e., job feature insecurity) to reflect the threat to the continuity of the job itself and the threat to the continuity of important job features, respectively. Some examples of qualitative job insecurity may include erosion of working conditions, demotion, lack of career opportunities, and decreases in salary development (Sverke & Hellgren, 2002).

Empirically, principal component analyses have supported a two-factor solution of quantitative job insecurity and qualitative job insecurity, and these two dimensions are only moderated correlated ($r = .28$; Hellgren et al., 1999). Moreover, Reisel and Banai (2002) demonstrated that quantitative job insecurity is a better predictor of employee attitudes (i.e., organizational commitment, organizational trust) and behaviors (i.e., job search behavior) than qualitative job insecurity. On the other hand, Ashford et al. (1989) found that role ambiguity, role conflict, and anticipated organizational change exhibit stronger relationships with qualitative job insecurity than quantitative job insecurity. Similarly, Lee et al. (2006) revealed that organizational change displays a stronger relationship with qualitative job insecurity than quantitative job insecurity. Tu et al. (2019) found that quantitative job insecurity is more strongly associated with employee physical and behavioral stress symptoms than qualitative job insecurity, whereas qualitative job insecurity is more strongly associated with employee work engagement than quantitative job insecurity. Together, these studies demonstrate that quantitative and qualitative job insecurity are two dimensions of job insecurity, each displaying unique relationships with predictors and outcomes.

Practically speaking, as the new world of work is on our doorstep, researchers (e.g., Lee et al., 2018) have expected qualitative job insecurity to become more common. Indeed, technological revolutions are likely to computerize certain tasks but not others and therefore change the nature of work across industries and occupations. For example, diagnostics tasks in health care (Cohn, 2013), pre-trail research in legal services (Markoff, 2011), and condition monitoring for batteries (Saha et al., 2007), aircraft engines (King et al., 2009) and water quality (Osborne et al., 2012) have been computerizing (Frey & Osborne, 2017). On the other hand, tasks requiring creative and social intelligence are non-susceptible to computerization. Thus, studies on qualitative job insecurity, in addition to quantitative job insecurity, could help reveal whether employees may be able to stay in the same organization but have to experience fundamental job feature changes (Lee et al., 2018).

2.3 The Current Study

In as early as 1984, Greenhalgh and Rosenblatt concluded that "loss of valued job features is an important but often overlooked aspect of job insecurity" (p. 441). Unfortunately, the reality has not changed much since their early remark in that the bulk of research attention has been paid to quantitative job insecurity as opposed to qualitative job insecurity (Lee et al., 2018). To respond to Lee et al.'s (2018) call for more research on qualitative job insecurity, on job insecurity measurement, and on job-insecurity experiences across different cultures, the purpose of this chapter is to conduct a multigroup measurement invariance test of the Quantitative Job Insecurity Scale and the Qualitative Job Insecurity Scale across ten countries, representing the most rigorous examination of the job insecurity scales to date.

Notably, we evaluate the Quantitative Job Insecurity scale (De Witte, 2000; Vander Elst et al., 2014) with four items and the Qualitative Job Insecurity scale (Fischmann et al., 2022) with four items for two main reasons. First, the Quantitative Job Insecurity scale (Vander Elst et al., 2014) is the most commonly employed job insecurity measure, which has been used 47 times since 2003; by comparison, the second frequently adopted measure — Hellgren et al.'s (1999) scale — has been used by 15 studies (Lee et al., 2018). Second, although Hellgren et al.'s scale has been popular among scholars who are interested in qualitative job insecurity, their scale with four items — (1) My future career opportunities in [the organization] are favorable; (2) I feel that [the organization] can provide me with a stimulating job content in the near future; (3) I believe that [the organization] will need my competence also in the future; and (4) My pay development in this organization is promising — are too specific to be inclusive, especially in today's ever-changing work environment, while other scales (see, e.g., Brondino et al., 2020) are multidimensional. By contrast, the Qualitative Job Insecurity scale (Fischmann et al., 2022) focusing on insecurity about unfavorable job changes in general does not specify the content of such changes and is unidimensional. Instead, it captures the core experiences of qualitative job insecurity by asking employees to evaluate the extent to which their job may change for the worse in the future. Thus, such a qualitative job insecurity scale can be applied in a wide variety of organizations and settings.

Taking stock of past validation studies on job insecurity, we commend the work of Vander Elst et al. (2014), which provided initial evidence for the generalizability of the Quantitative Job Insecurity scale across five European countries. However, we contend that more focused approaches are needed to comprehensively address questions of cross-cultural equivalence of both quantitative and qualitative job insecurity. We therefore contribute a more detailed understanding of the measurement equivalence (or lack thereof) of the Quantitative Job Insecurity scale (Vander Elst et al., 2014) and the Qualitative Job Insecurity scale (Fischmann et al., 2022).

2.4 Method

2.4.1 Participants and Procedure

Participants were 4629 faculty, staff, and graduate students (e.g., masters' students, doctoral students, research/teaching assistants) from universities across ten countries, namely, Belgium, China, Croatia, Greece, Lithuania, Romania, South Africa, Switzerland, the UK, and the US. Table 2.1 shows the description of the total sample and the subsamples based on different background characteristics. The mean age of the employees in the total sample was 41.21 years ($SD = 11.29$). Most of the total sample identified as women ($n = 2755$, 59.52%), 1725 identified as men (37.27%), and four respondents identified as transgender (0.09%; 11 respondents did not provide gender information). Although 41.64% of participants did not indicate their employment status, of those participants who indicated their employment status, a large portion of the sample worked on permanent contracts ($n = 1729$, 36.45%), 896 (18.89%) participants worked on temporary contracts, and 143 (3.01%) participants reported their employment status as "other." A plurality of the total sample was faculty ($n = 1938$, 47.40%), 1395 were university support staff (34.12%), and 756 respondents were graduate students (18.49%). Most of the sample had received a doctoral degree or the equivalent ($n = 1335$, 38.77%), 31.54% had received a master's degree ($n = 1086$), 19.23% had received a bachelor's degree ($n = 662$), and 10.46% had received post-secondary education or less ($n = 360$). See Chap. 1 for details on the data collection procedure.

2.4.2 Measures

Quantitative job insecurity (Vander Elst et al., 2014) was measured using four items: "Chances are, I will soon lose my job (item 1)," "I am sure I can keep my job" (reverse coded; item 2), "I feel insecure about the future of my job (item 3)," and "I think I might lose my job in the near future (item 4)." *Qualitative job insecurity* (Fischmann et al., 2022) was measured using four items: "I think my job will change for the worse (item 5)," "Chances are, my job will change in a negative way (item 6)," "I feel insecure about the characteristics and conditions of my job in the future (item 7)," "I am worried about how my job will look like in the future (item 8)." Participants responded on a five-point Likert scale from 1 (*strongly disagree*) to 5 (*strongly agree*).

Table 2.1 Sample characteristics

Characteristic	Total sample	Subsamples				
		Belgium	China	Croatia	Greece	Lithuania
N (*N*miss)	4629(114)	594(2)	160(0)	692(30)	402(1)	501(29)
Age in years						
Mean (SD)	41.21(11.29)	39.24(11.26)	36.50(7.49)	40.47(9.98)	46.88(8.91)	40.66(11.13)
Min-Max	17–85	23–64	23–60	22–78	22–67	21–77
Median	40	38	36	40	47	39
Gender						
Female	2755(61.29%)	429(72.22%)	80(50%)	468(67.34%)	220(54.59%)	343(68.46%)
Male	1725(38.38%)	165(27.78%)	80(50%)	227(32.66%)	178(44.17%)	158(31.54%)
Transgender	4(0.09%)	–	–	–	–	–
Other	11(0.24%)	–	–	–	–	–
Contract						
Permanent	1729(36.45%)	303(50.84%)	128(80.00%)	–	160(39.70%)	–
Temporary	896(18.89%)	269(45.13%)	27(16.88%)	–	34(8.44%)	–
Other	143(3.01%)	21(3.52%)	5(3.13%)	–	95(23.57%)	–
Missing	1975(41.65%)	3(0.50%)	–	–	114 (28.3%)	–
Classification						
Faculty	1938(47.40%)	233(39.23%)	98(61.25%)	222(51.27%)	196(48.64%)	205(56.32%)
Staff	1395(34.12%)	137(23.06%)	42(26.25%)	106(24.48%)	160(39.70%)	132(36.26%)
Graduate student	756(18.49%)	224(37.71%)	20(12.50%)	105(24.25%)	47(11.66%)	27(7.42%)
Education level						
Lower secondary	8(0.23%)	–	–	–	–	1(0.27%)
Upper secondary	56(1.63%)	2(0.50%)	1(0.63%)	2(0.46%)	10(3.66%)	7(1.92%)
Pre-university	124(3.60%)	2(0.50%)	–	12(2.76%)	4(1.47%)	1(0.27%)
Post-secondary	172(5.00%)	4(0.99%)	4(2.50%)	5(1.15%)	10(3.66%)	1(0.27%)

(continued)

Table 2.1 (continued)

Characteristic	Total sample	Subsamples				
		Belgium	China	Croatia	Greece	Lithuania
Bachelor's degree	662(19.23%)	64(15.88%)	32(20.00%)	9(2.07%)	16(5.86%)	38(10.44%)
Master's degree	1086(31.54%)	219(54.34%)	104(65.00%)	150(34.56%)	48(17.58%)	147(40.38%)
Doctoral degree or equivalent	1335(38.77%)	112(27.79%)	19(11.88%)	256(58.99%)	185(67.77%)	169(46.43%)
Characteristic	Subsamples					
	Romania	South Africa	Switzerland	UK	US	
N (*N*miss)	476(0)	1076(20)	317(1)	70(0)	341(31)	
Age in years						
Mean (SD)	42.95(9.16)	38.75(12.24)	41.48(10.42)	42.33(11.29)	47.31(13.15)	
Min-Max	23–78	19–78	17–65	23–71	24–85	
Median	43	37	39	42.5	47	
Gender						
Female	362(76.05%)	411(45.02%)	197(62.34%)	46(65.71%)	199(54.22%)	
Male	114(23.95%)	494(54.11%)	119(37.66%)	24(34.29%)	166(45.23%)	
Transgender	–	–	–	–	1(0.27%)	
Other	–	8(0.88%)	–	–	1(0.27%)	
Contract						
Permanent	–	654(59.70%)	160(50.31%)	52(74.29%)	272(73.12%)	
Temporary	–	330(30.10%)	146(45.91%)	15(21.43%)	75(20.16%)	
Other	–	–	9(2.83%)	3(4.29%)	10(2.69%)	
Missing	–	112(10.22%)	3(0.94%)	–	15(4.03%)	
Classification						
Faculty	318(75.18%)	369(35.28%)	69(21.90%)	–	228(64.96%)	
Staff	86(20.33%)	486(46.46%)	131(41.59%)	–	115(32.76%)	
Graduate Student	19(4.49%)	191(18.26%)	115(36.51%)	–	8(2.28%)	

Characteristic	Total sample	Subsamples				
		Belgium	China	Croatia	Greece	Lithuania
Education level						
Lower secondary	–	4(0.37%)	3(0.97%)	–	–	
Upper secondary	–	4(0.37%)	28(9.09%)	1(1.43%)	1(0.28%)	
Pre-university	–	92(8.54%)	6(1.95%)	1(1.43%)	6(1.69%)	
Post-secondary	–	125(11.61%)	15(4.87%)	–	8(2.26%)	
Bachelor's degree	–	437(40.58%)	31(10.06%)	12(17.14%)	23(6.50%)	
Master's degree	–	238(22.10%)	64(20.78%)	11(15.71%)	105(29.66%)	
Doctoral degree or equivalent	–	177(16.43%)	161(52.27%)	45(64.29%)	211(59.60%)	

Note: Valid percentages used. *N*miss = any missing data

2.4.3 Data Analyses

Psychometric theory commonly approaches a factor analysis of multiple groups by considering three degrees of increasingly restrictive tests (see Brown, 2015; Kline, 2015): configural (i.e., equal factorial form across the groups), metric (i.e., weak factorial invariance or equal loadings model), and scalar measurement invariance (i.e., strong factorial invariance or equal intercepts model). Configural invariance places no restrictions across groups, and all parameters are freely estimated. Metric invariance holds the value of factor loadings equal across groups, which allows researchers to make group comparisons of factor variances and structural relationships. Scalar invariance holds both factor loadings and item intercepts equal across groups and allows researchers to compare factor means and intercepts across groups.

Cross-group invariance is established by sequentially imposing more restrictive equality constraints on the equal forms model (i.e., like-items equal loadings and subsequently like-items equal intercepts; Brown, 2015). If the more constrained models do not show a significant decrement in fit, then there is empirical evidence to claim measurement invariance. Change in chi-square (Brown, 2015), change in Comparative Fit Index (i.e., Δ CFI $\leq .010$; Chen, 2007), and change in Root Mean Square Error of Approximation (i.e., Δ RMSEA $\leq .015$; Chen, 2007) can be used to infer measurement invariance. Following Brown's recommendation (2015), we only consider the change in CFI. This is consistent with simulation studies showing that change in CFI can accurately detect measurement (non)invariance (Cheung & Rensvold, 2000). Additionally, we use a more liberal cutoff criterion (Δ CFI $\leq .020$; Rutkovski & Svetina, 2014) for testing metric invariance due to the high number of groups ($n = 10$), whereas we use the traditional cutoff criterion for scalar invariance (i.e., Δ CFI $\leq .010$) because it seems to be appropriate even with a large number of groups (Rutkovski & Svetina, 2014).

For historical reasons, scholars have focused on metric invariance, perhaps because the scalar invariance model rarely fits the data adequately when there are more than two groups in the analysis (Muthén & Asparouhov, 2018). To achieve *partial* measurement invariance, psychometric theory recommends releasing a few parameters until the invariance threshold is met (Sörbom, 1989). Issues may arise when there are several large modification indices due to many violations of invariance, which could lead to a mis-specified model only because the invariance model may be far from the true model. Additionally, many models have to be manually estimated to reach a reasonably well-fitting model. Granted, this approach is not guaranteed to lead to the most parsimonious and easy-to-interpret model. Even with as few as three groups in the analysis, a well-fitting model may not be so obvious.

To address this issue, psychometricians have proposed the alignment method (Asparouhov & Muthén, 2014). Recall that in the equal forms model, unconstrained factor loadings and intercepts are estimated, and the factor means and variances need to be fixed for identification purposes, typically to 0 and 1, respectively. It follows that each factor is on a different scale in each group, and comparisons cannot be made. By using the alignment approach that first estimates the equal forms model and then another model in which factor means and variances are also freely estimated, researchers are able to make meaningful comparisons. Estimating this apparently empirically unidentifiable model requires adding a simplicity function similar to the rotation criterion commonly used in exploratory factor analysis, which aims to minimize non-invariance across groups. The simplicity function is optimized at a few, large, varying parameters and many approximately invariant parameters. Further details and the computational steps associated with this procedure can be found in Asparouhov and Muthén (2014).

Three pieces of information are reported: (i) the item's intercept and loading contribution to the simplicity function (i.e., the fit function contribution, in which a lower contribution is more desirable), (ii) an R^2 statistic that shows how much variation of the model parameter is due to variation in the factor means and variances (i.e., a high R^2 can be interpreted as evidence of a high degree of measurement invariance), and (iii) the variance in the alignment parameters across groups (lower variance indicates parameter invariance). Taken together, these pieces of information give an idea of the empirical plausibility of the invariance assumption.

The results section is organized as follows: we first investigate the factorial structure of the Quantitative Job Insecurity scale and the Qualitative Job Insecurity via separate confirmatory factor analyses (CFAs) for each country. Next, we assess the measurement invariance of the Job Insecurity Scale. Second, we implement an alignment analysis to further investigate non-invariance in each dimension of job insecurity separately. Last, we outline country-level differences that were apparent in the data. All analyses were conducted using M*plus* 8.6 (Muthén & Muthén, 1998–2017) with a maximum likelihood estimator.

2.5 Results

Table 2.2 shows the global fit indices for two-factor models from CFAs, reliability, correlations, and descriptive statistics for each country separately.

2.5.1 Measurement Invariance Analysis across Countries

Before running the analyses, we checked whether the data met the normality assumption. We found that skewness (range: 0.27–0.90) and kurtosis (range: −1.02—0.88) of the quantitative job insecurity items did not approach known cutoff values (Brown, 2015), suggesting univariate normality. Likewise, we confirmed that skewness (range: −0.19—0.28) and kurtosis (range: −1.03—0.02) of the qualitative job insecurity items did not exceed scholarly guidelines (Brown, 2015).

As Table 2.3 shows, we estimated four increasingly restrictive models. The configural model (model 1) did not fit the data well, according to scholarly guidelines (Hu & Bentler, 1999); therefore, we added one covariance between residuals

Table 2.2 Global fit indices for the single sample CFAs (df = 18), correlations, reliability, and descriptive statistics of the Quantitative Job Insecurity scale and the Qualitative Job Insecurity scale in 10 countries

	Global fit indices					Quantitative Job insecurity		Qualitative Job insecurity		Correlation between quantitative and qualitative job insecurity	
Country	⊆	$\vert^2$	CFI	RMSEA	SRMR	alpha	*M (SD)*	alpha	*M (SD)*	Raw	Latent
Belgium	596	264.45	.913	.152	.114	.89	2.33 (1.07)	.85	2.70 (0.90)	.36	.18
China	160	54.22	.903	.112	.060	.65	2.28 (0.57)	.73	2.47 (0.67)	.64	.94
Croatia	719	103.75	.978	.081	.060	.88	2.15 (0.95)	.88	3.04 (0.97)	.48	.47
Greece	403	195.70	.901	.157	.108	.84	2.20 (0.88)	.85	3.16 (0.87)	.51	.44
Lithuania	530	210.02	.932	.142	.079	.87	2.53 (0.87)	.86	3.06 (0.87)	.68	.69
Romania	476	187.12	.893	.140	.075	.74	2.00 (0.69)	.83	2.40 (0.90)	.53	.72
South Africa	1096	267.07	.942	.112	.060	.77	2.54 (0.87)	.85	2.81 (0.92)	.60	.70
Switzerland	318	201.86	.879	.179	.160	.90	2.44 (1.21)	.78	2.74 (0.90)	.59	.41
UK	70	75.93	.860	.214	.141	.89	2.70 (1.14)	.87	3.29 (0.99)	.43	.26
US	372	175.11	.930	.153	.105	.87	2.21 (1.00)	.90	2.99 (1.13)	.65	.49

Note. The means presented in this table were computed using the full scales and therefore are not suitable for cross-country comparisons. Global fit indices and the latent correlation between quantitative job insecurity and qualitative job insecurity are based on two-factor models CFAs with residual covariances of item 7 and item 8

Table 2.3 Measurement invariance analysis across countries

Model	I^2	df	CFI	TLI	RMSEA	SRMR	⊗CFI	Comparison
1. Configural Invariance (Equal forms)	2906.73	190	.878	.817	.174	.082	–	–
1b. Configural Invariance (Revised)	1735.24	180	.929	.890	.135	.091	–	–
2. Metric Invariance (Equal Loadings)	2128.78	234	.914	.897	.131	.111	.015	1b vs 2
3. Scalar Invariance (Equal Intercepts)	2830.19	288	.884	.887	.136	.117	.030	2 vs 3

Note. χ^2 = chi square, CFI = Comparative Fit Index, TLI = Tucker Lewis Index, RMSEA = Root Mean Square Error of Approximation, SRMR = Standardized Root Mean Square Residual, ΔCFI = change in Comparative Fit Index

(items 7 "I feel insecure about the characteristics and conditions of my job in the future" and 8 "I am worried about how my job will look like in the future") to improve the model's fit. The revised configural model (model 1b) fit the data acceptably.[2] Subsequently, we estimated the metric (model 2) and scalar invariance models (model 3). Our data showed that the criterion for metric invariance was met (Δ CFI = .015), but the threshold for scalar invariance was not (Δ CFI = .030). To further explore item-level contributions to this non-invariance, we ran two alignment analyses, presented below.

2.5.2 Measurement Invariance Across Major Demographics

We also tested whether the quantitative and qualitative job insecurity scales were invariant across gender (male vs. female), contract type (temporary vs. permanent), job title (faculty member vs. support staff vs. graduate student), and educational level (Ph.D. or equivalent vs. MA/MS or equivalent vs. BA/BS or equivalent). We used Brown's (2015) criterion to detect measurement noninvariance (i.e., Δ CFI $\leq$ .010). The results of measurement invariance analyses are reported in Table 2.4. As it can be seen, the qualitative and quantitative job insecurity scales were fully invariant (i.e., met the criterion for scalar invariance) across gender,

[2] The RMSEA and SRMR values of Model 1b were above traditional scholarly guidelines (Hu & Bentler, 1999). However, given the complexity of the tested model, a good fitting model may be extremely difficult to obtain, not-so-obvious to identify, and still far from the "true" model (Asparouhov & Muthén, 2014; Marsh et al., 2018). For these reasons, we proceeded with the measurement invariance analyses even though the revised baseline model did not meet all scholarly guidelines.

Table 2.4 Measurement invariance analysis across major demographics

Model	I^2	df	CFI	TLI	RMSEA	SRMR	⊗CFI	Comparison
Gender								
1. Configural Invariance (Equal forms)	1284.53	36	.936	.901	.124	.085	–	–
2. Metric Invariance (Equal Loadings)	1327.33	42	.934	.913	.117	.088	.002	1 vs 2
3. Scalar Invariance (Equal Intercepts)	1394.04	48	.931	.920	.112	.089	.003	2 vs 3
Job title								
1. Configural Invariance (Equal forms)	1220.75	54	.931	.893	.126	.083	–	–
2. Metric Invariance (Equal Loadings)	1358.82	66	.924	.903	.120	.093	.007	1 vs 2
3. Scalar Invariance (Equal Intercepts)	1504.22	78	.916	.910	.116	.098	.008	2 vs 3
Contract type								
1. Configural Invariance (Equal forms)	876.60	36	.919	.873	.133	.088	–	–
2. Metric Invariance (Equal Loadings)	975.78	42	.910	.880	.130	.101	.009	1 vs 2
3. Scalar Invariance (Equal Intercepts)	1162.72	48	.892	.874	.133	.113	.018	2 vs 3
Education								
1. Configural Invariance (Equal forms)	1095.28	54	.931	.893	.130	.091	–	–
2. Metric Invariance (Equal Loadings)	1143.60	66	.929	.909	.119	.096	.002	1 vs 2
3. Scalar Invariance (Equal Intercepts)	1192.00	78	.926	.921	.112	.096	.003	2 vs 3

Note. χ^2 = chi square, CFI = Comparative Fit Index, TLI = Tucker Lewis Index, RMSEA = Root Mean Square Error of Approximation, SRMR = Standardized Root Mean Square Residual, ΔCFI = change in Comparative Fit Index

education attainment, and job title, whereas we were only able to establish equal factor loadings invariance across contract type (i.e., metric invariance).

2.5.3 *Quantitative Job Insecurity Alignment Analysis*

We ran an alignment analysis of the items tapping into quantitative job insecurity. As can be seen in Table 2.5, item 1, 3 and 4 factor loadings were approximately invariant in nine out of ten countries (Belgium excluded), and item 2's factor loading was approximately invariant in seven countries (Switzerland, South Africa, and Belgium excluded). Conversely, item 1 and 2 intercepts were approximately invariant in all countries, while item 4's intercept was invariant in eight countries (Croatia

Table 2.5 Approximate measurement invariance for intercepts and loadings of quantitative job insecurity

Item	Description	Invariant intercepts	Invariant loadings
1	Chances are, I will soon lose my job	US, UK, Switzerland, South Africa, Romania, Lithuania, Greece, Croatia, China, Belgium	US, UK, Switzerland, South Africa, Romania, Lithuania, Greece, Croatia, China
2	I am sure I can keep my job	US, UK, Switzerland, South Africa, Romania, Lithuania, Greece, Croatia, China	US, UK, Romania, Lithuania, Greece, Croatia, China
3	I feel insecure about the future of my job	US, UK, Switzerland, Romania, Lithuania, China, Belgium	US, UK, Switzerland, South Africa, Romania, Lithuania, Greece, Croatia, China
4	I think I might lose my job in the near future	US, UK, Switzerland, South Africa, Romania, Lithuania, Greece, China	US, UK, Switzerland, South Africa, Romania, Lithuania, Greece, Croatia, China

Note. The columns Invariant Intercepts and Invariant Loadings show the countries for which a given item's intercept or factor loading was found to be approximately invariant

Table 2.6 Alignment fit statistics of quantitative job insecurity

	Intercepts			Loadings			Total
Item	Fit function contribution	R^2	Variance	Fit function contribution	R^2	Variance	Fit function contribution
1	−15.29	.92	0.002	−19.24	.83	0.028	−34.53
2	−21.66	.67	0.017	−23.77	.70	0.033	−45.43
3	−19.94	.77	0.018	−18.67	.28	0.015	−38.63
4	−18.32	.75	0.009	−17.13	.79	0.008	−35.45

and Belgium excluded), and item 3 was approximately invariant in seven countries (South Africa, Greece, Croatia, and Belgium excluded). Thus, three out of four items show a significant degree of non-invariance across countries.

Table 2.6 shows each item's contribution to the simplicity function. It seems that item 1 contributes the least to the simplicity function optimization for both loadings and intercepts. Additionally, this item's variation is, for the most part, attributable to variation in groups' factor means and variances (i.e., it shows a high R^2), suggesting some degree of invariance. Last, the variance column in Table 2.6 shows very minimal variation in the alignment parameter across groups. Taken together, evidence suggests that item 1 is the most invariant; however, no item showed invariance across all countries.

2.5.4 *Qualitative Job Insecurity Alignment Analysis*

We also ran an alignment analysis on the four items assessing qualitative job insecurity. Table 2.7 shows that all of the four items' loadings are invariant across

Table 2.7 Approximate measurement invariance for intercepts and loadings of qualitative job insecurity

Item	Description	Invariant intercepts	Invariant loadings
5	I think my job will change for the worse	US, UK, Switzerland, South Africa, Romania, Lithuania, Greece, Croatia, China, Belgium	US, UK, Switzerland, South Africa, Romania, Lithuania, Greece, Croatia, China, Belgium
6	Chances are, my job will change in a negative way	US, Switzerland, Romania, Greece, China, Belgium	US, UK, Switzerland, South Africa, Romania, Lithuania, Greece, Croatia, China, Belgium
7	I feel insecure about the characteristics and conditions of my job in the future	US, UK, Switzerland, South Africa, Romania, Lithuania, Greece, China	US, UK, Switzerland, South Africa, Romania, Lithuania, Greece, Croatia, China, Belgium
8	I am worried about how my job will look like in the future	US, UK, Switzerland, South Africa, Romania, Lithuania, Greece, Croatia, China, Belgium	US, UK, Switzerland, South Africa, Romania, Lithuania, Greece, Croatia, China, Belgium

Note. The columns Invariant Intercepts and Invariant Loadings show the countries for which a given item's intercept or factor loading was found to be approximately invariant

Table 2.8 Alignment fit statistics of qualitative job insecurity

	Intercepts			Loadings			Total
Item	Fit function contribution	R^2	Variance	Fit function contribution	R^2	Variance	Fit function contribution
5	−15.13	.98	0.001	−16.13	.85	0.003	−31.26
6	−19.55	.85	0.015	−15.79	.81	0.003	−35.34
7	−22.24	.84	0.022	−16.91	.71	0.004	−39.15
8	−16.75	.93	0.003	−15.29	.89	0.003	−33.04

countries. Additionally, Table 2.7 shows that item 5 and 8 intercepts are invariant across countries, while there is a substantial degree of non-invariance in item 6 and 7 intercepts, where item 6 intercept is invariant only in six countries, and item 7 intercept is invariant across eight countries.

Table 2.8 shows each item's contribution to the simplicity function. As expected, the items' contribution to the optimized simplicity function for the factor loadings is similar, as they all are invariant across countries (see Table 2.6), and their variability is, in large part, due to variation in the group means and variances (i.e., they show a high R^2). Additionally, there is minimal variance of the alignment parameters across countries, suggesting that the factor loadings are indeed invariant. Coherent with results presented in Table 2.6, the contribution to the optimized simplicity function for the intercepts show that items 5 and 8 contribute less, compared to item 6 and 7. Furthermore, almost all of the variance in item 5 and 8 intercepts is due to variation of the groups means and variances, supporting the assumption that these items' intercepts are invariant across countries. The variance index in Table 2.8 also indicates little to no variation in alignment parameters across groups. Taken together, these results seem to support measurement invariance for items 5 and 8.

2.5.5 Country-level Differences in Job Insecurity

The alignment method produced estimates of latent factor means, which are useful to compare countries on variables of theoretical interest to identify global patterns and trends. It should be noted that because these parameters were estimated using the alignment algorithm, scalar invariance is not a necessary condition to make meaningful comparisons (Asparouhov & Muthén, 2014; Muthén & Asparouhov, 2018). Tables 2.9 and 2.10 show the estimated factor means. For ease of interpretation, these means are ranked from the highest to the lowest, and groups that have a significant difference between their respective means (at the 5% level) are shown.

Table 2.9 Country-level differences in quantitative job insecurity

Ranking	Country	Factor mean	Countries with a significantly smaller factor mean
1	UK	0.306	Belgium, China, US, Croatia, Greece, Romania
2	South Africa	0.248	Belgium, China, US, Croatia, Greece, Romania
3	Lithuania	0.239	Belgium, China, US, Croatia, Greece, Romania
4	Switzerland	0.130	US, Croatia, Greece, Romania
5	Belgium	0.000	Croatia, Greece, Romania
6	China	−0.004	Croatia, Greece, Romania
7	US	−0.100	Romania
8	Croatia	−0.145	Romania
9	Greece	−0.145	Romania
10	Romania	−0.309	

Table 2.10 Country-level differences in qualitative job insecurity

Ranking	Country	Factor mean	Countries with a significantly smaller factor mean
1	UK	0.687	Croatia, US, South Africa, Switzerland, Belgium, China, Romania
2	Greece	0.562	Croatia, US, South Africa, Switzerland, Belgium, China, Romania
3	Lithuania	0.461	South Africa, Switzerland, Belgium, China, Romania
4	Croatia	0.386	South Africa, Switzerland, Belgium, China, Romania
5	US	0.347	South Africa, Switzerland, Belgium, China, Romania
6	South Africa	0.155	Belgium, China, Romania
7	Switzerland	0.038	China, Romania
8	Belgium	0.000	China, Romania
9	China	−0.285	
10	Romania	−0.403	

Notably, academicians working in the UK reported the highest levels of both quantitative and qualitative job insecurity. Similarly, Lithuanian participants reported high levels of both types of job insecurity. Conversely, those working in Romania reported the lowest levels in both types of job insecurity. Greek and Croatian participants, however, reported high levels of qualitative job insecurity and low levels of quantitative job insecurity. On a more general note, participants in the UK, South Africa, Lithuania, and Switzerland reported comparably high levels of quantitative job insecurity, while participants in the UK, Greece, and Lithuania reported comparably high levels of qualitative job insecurity.

2.6 Discussion

To respond to the calls to formally examine job insecurity scales and to facilitate the comparisons of results across studies and countries (Lee et al., 2018), the current chapter was designed to cross-nationally examine the measurement invariance of the Quantitative Job Insecurity scale and the Qualitative Job Insecurity scale. Measurement invariance of a scale across different countries — especially with regard to the general structure (configural invariance) and loadings (metric invariance) — is often considered a vital prerequisite for the comparability of the construct values obtained in these countries. Given this importance, we aim at providing a large-scale test of measurement invariance of both job insecurity scales across ten countries with diverse languages. To the best of our knowledge, this study is the first to test and support the equivalence of the Quantitative Job Insecurity scale and the Qualitative Job Insecurity scale using samples of the higher education systems drawn from ten countries (i.e., Belgium, China, Croatia, Greece, Lithuania, Romania, South Africa, Switzerland, the UK, and the US), eight languages, and four continents.

In conducting the multigroup CFA, we addressed the question: do the job insecurity scales and their underlying latent factors measure the same construct across countries? Are they interpreted in the same way by each sample? Overall, results from the multigroup CFA provide support for metric invariance of both job insecurity scales across ten countries. First, this implies that the factor structure of the job insecurity dimensions is similar across countries, meaning that the same facets load on the same factors and the country-specific models involve the same number of latent variables and the same pattern of indicator-factor relationships. The configural invariance of both job insecurity scales suggests that the construct measured by the instrument is conceptualized in the same way across the subgroups; that is, the respondents from the different subsamples employ the same conceptual frame of reference to make item responses.

Second, it implies that the latent job insecurity factors have the same meaning across countries, given that the factors are described by the same facets in equal measure (i.e., equivalent factor loadings). The metric invariance of the Quantitative Job Insecurity scale and the Qualitative Job Insecurity scale indicates that the measurement units are the same and factor loadings are comparable across these countries, and the observed scores on the job insecurity items are calibrated to the scores on the latent factor of job insecurity in the same way across subgroups (i.e., equality of scaling units across countries). As a result, item scores and differences in item scores may be meaningfully compared across countries.

Although these results confirm that the Quantitative Job Insecurity scale and the Qualitative Job Insecurity scale are equivalent across countries and the instrument measures the same concept and in the same way, analyses do not provide support for scalar invariance or equivalence of like-intercepts across countries. This raises the question of whether observed differences in facet and factor means between countries can actually be attributed to "true" differences in the latent constructs or rather to differences in the measurement of these constructs. Lack of scalar (strong) invariance suggests that the scale is used differently across various subgroups of respondents (Davidov et al., 2014). Lack of scalar invariance can be caused by translations, response styles, or a combination of both (Boer et al., 2018). However, this result is not surprising because participants in different countries responding in different languages may anchor their responses differently (Peng et al., 1997), and it has consistently been demonstrated that it is difficult to show higher levels of metric or scalar equivalence in cross-cultural studies (e.g., Cieciuch et al., 2015).

Although some scholars have argued that "meaningful comparisons of mean scores across cultures…require scalar invariance" (Church et al., 2011, p. 1069; also see Steinmetz, 2013; Van de Schoot et al., 2012), others (e.g., Davidov et al., 2014; McCrae, 2015; Vandenberg & Lance, 2000) have argued that scalar non-invariance does not necessarily prevent meaningful mean-level comparisons. Instead, measurement non-invariance itself might be a phenomenon of substantive interest. For example, Vandenberg and Lance (2000, p. 38) point out that "intercept differences may not reflect biases (undesirable) but response threshold differences that might be predicted based on known group differences (desirable)." Nonetheless, future research is needed to clarify the sources of scalar non-invariance as observed across ten countries.

Because scalar invariance is not achieved, we use the alignment analyses to identify non-invariant parameters and make the latent means comparisons more trustworthy. In particular, we find that item 1 ("Chances are, I will soon lose my job"), measuring quantitative job insecurity, as well as item 5 ("I think my job will change for the worse") and item 8 ("I am worried about how my job will look like in the future") measuring qualitative job insecurity, are predominantly invariant across countries.

Based on the measurement invariance results, we offer a few recommendations regarding which items should be used when conducting cross-country research (see Table 2.11). Specifically, when testing a research question involving the comparison of means, only item 1 assessing quantitative job insecurity and/or items 5 and 8 assessing qualitative job insecurity should be used. On the other hand, when testing hypotheses involving associations using a regression-based approach, the full scales for either job insecurity dimension may be used (although item 1 is still preferred for quantitative job insecurity).

Table 2.11 Recommendations for future cross-country applications of the quantitative job insecurity scale and the qualitative job insecurity scale

Research question	Quantitative job insecurity	Qualitative job insecurity
Comparing means (e.g., t-tests, ANOVA-like analyses, SEM with mean structure)	Item 1	Items 5 and 8
Regression-based (e.g., path analysis, SEM without mean structure)	Item 1 (preferred) or full scale	Full scale

Additionally, measurement invariance tests for the Quantitative Job Insecurity scale and the Qualitative Job Insecurity scale across major demographics reveal scalar invariance (i.e., strong invariance) across gender (male vs. female), job title (faculty member vs. support staff vs. graduate student), and educational level (Ph.D. or equivalent vs. MA/MS or equivalent vs. BA/BS or equivalent) but metric invariance (i.e., weak invariance) across contract type (temporary vs. permanent).

This study is a contribution to the literature because, to date, little attention has been paid to issues of comparability, and invariance is too often assumed but not tested. Establishing measurement invariance has important implications on what can or cannot be compared across countries. Although our study is limited by its reliance on academic staff samples, the aim was only to confirm the reliability and validity of the Quantitative Job Insecurity scale and the Qualitative Job Insecurity scale in different countries. In this case, the homogeneous employee samples in the higher education sector are ideal for cross-country comparisons.

2.6.1 Job Insecurity in Different Countries — Global Trends

Despite the limitations in our ability to achieve strong invariance across countries, we can use the results of the alignment analyses to draw some conclusions regarding the levels of job insecurity across the ten countries examined in this project. Although country-level rankings of job insecurity differed somewhat as a function of the dimension being examined, i.e., quantitative vs. qualitative, some trends are clear. First, among all ten countries, respondents in the UK reported the highest levels of job insecurity on both dimensions, whereas respondents in Romania reported the least job insecurity on both dimensions. An examination of trends within higher education in these countries reveals some explanatory insights.

For example, within the UK, as mentioned before, an analysis (UCU, 2019) found that a large proportion of academicians are on fixed-term contracts. Moreover, many UK institutions utilize so-called “zero-hours contracts”, which make no guarantees regarding the future need for their employment. Additionally, the high levels of both quantitative and qualitative job insecurity in the UK may be in part attributed to Brexit, which was ongoing and salient during the study period. Macroeconomic changes and structural reforms resulting from Brexit could affect perceptions of job insecurity, particularly among the many non-native UK academics

(Edwards et al., 2020). On the other hand, academic faculty within Romania have permanent positions once they achieve the rank of associate professor, and administrative staff are typically on permanent contracts as well. Thus, it is perhaps not surprising that these stark differences between the two countries' approaches to employment within the higher education sector are reflected in the latent mean differences between respondents in those two samples.

Interestingly, whereas most countries had similar rankings with respect to respondent levels of quantitative and qualitative job insecurity, Greek respondents reported some of the lowest levels of quantitative job insecurity in our 10-country sample but simultaneously some of the highest levels of qualitative job insecurity. Similar to the higher education system in Romania, associate professors in Greece have permanent (i.e., quantitatively secure) positions, although assistant professors may be on a permanent or fixed-term contract. Additionally, most of the administrative staff members have permanent positions. Thus, it is perhaps not surprising that Greek respondents are among the lowest in the country-rankings of quantitative job insecurity.

Yet, with respect to qualitative job insecurity, Greece ranks among the highest. Again, this is perhaps not unexpected when one considers the modernization pressures that the Greek higher education system has faced in the years since austerity measures were imposed as a condition of receiving bailout funding from the IMF and the EU (Prokou, 2013). Moreover, with the 2011 passage of the Framework Act for Higher Education, there have been mounting pressures to overhaul the higher education system, rethink entrance standards and curricula, enhance accountability, and implement other major reforms to the system. Such changes stemming from this framework would not necessarily affect the quantitative job security of academicians (most of whom are public sector civil servants) but could certainly affect the qualitative nature of those positions due to wage reductions, newly implemented forced distribution performance assessments, merged units, and job relocations (see Mouza & Souchamvali, 2016 and Mouza, 2017, for studies on the stress-related effects of these policy changes). Figure 2.1 graphically depicts each country's standing with respect to quantitative and qualitative job insecurity.

2.6.2 Limitations and Future Research Directions

This study is not without its limitations. First, the Quantitative Job Insecurity scale and the Qualitative Job Insecurity scale did not reach scalar invariance, indicating that there may be some differences in interpreting some of the items across countries. However, it is impossible to conclusively explain why these items did not perform as well without additional studies. Although we were not able to explore possible mechanisms for non-invariance, future research should consider how external variables might explain non-invariance of job insecurity across countries by using the alignment and/or alignment-within-CFA frameworks (Marsh et al., 2018). Moreover, despite representation from four continents, most of the ten samples came from

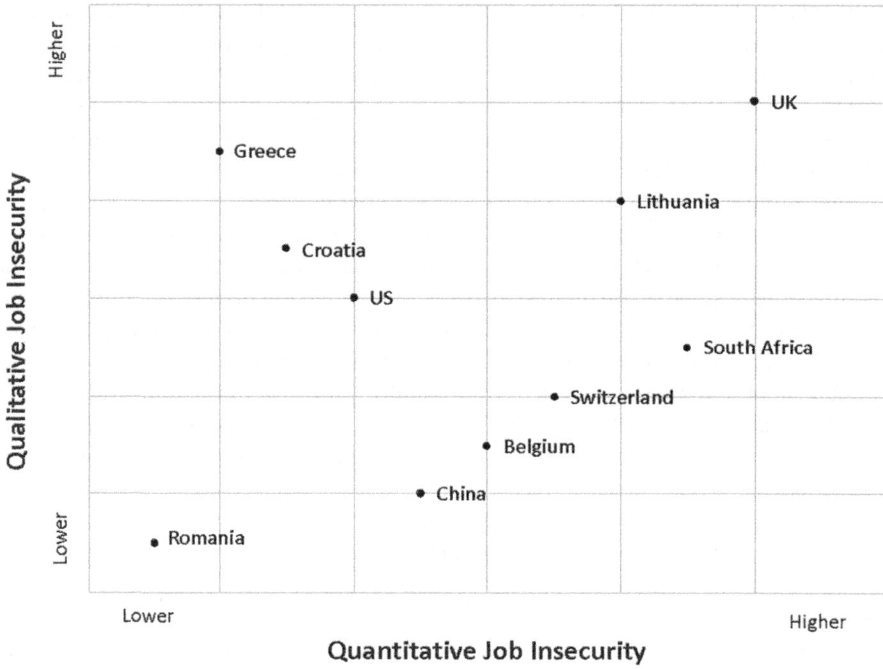

Fig. 2.1 Graphical cross-country comparison

European countries; we were unable to include South or Central American countries. In addition, as in most psychological research, our participants are from highly literate populations, many of them having a doctoral degree. In order to more deeply address the universality and cultural specificity of the construct and the instrument, we would need to also sample countries with lower levels of education, less participation in market economies, lower income, and less urbanization.

2.6.3 Conclusion and Take Home Message

Our large-scale test of measurement invariance of the Quantitative Job Insecurity scale and the Qualitative Job Insecurity scale suggests that this instrument provides largely comparable measurement of the two dimensions of job insecurity (i.e., quantitative job insecurity and qualitative job insecurity) across ten countries. Although facet intercepts show a substantial degree of non-invariance (i.e., a lack of scalar invariance), the factor structure of the job insecurity scale strongly converges across the ten countries under examination (i.e., configural and metric invariance). This study indicates that the Quantitative Job Insecurity scale and the Qualitative Job Insecurity scale could be successfully used by researchers in a wide range of countries, and their results could be to some extent compared and integrated. Given the prevalence of job insecurity experiences, it is possible to examine the nomological network of the scale in cross-cultural data and to integrate the knowledge about sources, correlates, and outcomes of job insecurity from different countries across cultures.

References

American Association of University Professors Research Office. (2013). Retrieved from https://www.aaup.org/sites/default/files/files/AAUP_Report_InstrStaff-75-11_apr2013.pdf

American Association of University Professors Research Office. (2016). Higher Education at a crossroads: The economic value of tenure and the security of the pression. Retrieved from https://www.aaup.org/sites/default/files/2015-16EconomicStatusReport.pdf

Armstrong-Stassen, M. (1993). Production workers' reactions to a plant closing: The role of transfer, stress, and support. *Anxiety, Stress and Coping, 6*(3), 201–214.

Ashford, S. J., Caza, B. B., & Reid, E. M. (2018). From surviving to thriving in the gig economy: A research agenda for individuals in the new world of work. *Research in Organizational Behavior, 38*, 23–41.

Ashford, S. J., Lee, C., & Bobko, P. (1989). Content, cause, and consequences of job insecurity: A theory-based measure and substantive test. *Academy of Management Journal, 32*(4), 803–829.

Asparouhov, T., & Muthén, B. O. (2014). Multiple-group factor analysis alignment. *Structural Equation Modeling, 21*, 495–508. https://doi.org/10.1080/10705511.2014.919210

Bakker, A. B., & Demerouti, E. (2017). Job demands–resources theory: taking stock and looking forward. *Journal of Occupational Health Psychology, 22*(3), 273.

Bazzoli, A., Brondino, M., De Witte, H., & Pasini, M. (2020). Development and psychometric properties of the job insecurity appraisals scale. *European Journal of Psychological Assessment. Advance Online Publication, 37*(4), 313–324. https://doi.org/10.1027/1015-5759/a000611

Boer, D., Hanke, K., & He, J. (2018). On detecting systematic measurement error in cross-cultural research: A review and critical reflection on equivalence and invariance tests. *Journal of Cross-Cultural Psychology, 49*(5), 713–734.

Brondino, M., Bazzoli, A., Vander Elst, T., De Witte, H., & Pasini, M. (2020). Validation and measurement invariance of the multidimensional qualitative job insecurity scale. *Quality & Quantity, 54*(3), 925–942. https://doi.org/10.1007/s11135-020-00966-y

Brown, T. A. (2015). *Confirmatory factor analysis for applied research*. Guilford.

Cavanaugh, M. A., Boswell, W. R., Roehling, M. V., & Boudreau, J. W. (2000). An empirical examination of self-reported work stress among US managers. *Journal of Applied Psychology, 85*(1), 65.

Chen, F. F. (2007). Sensitivity of goodness of fit indices to lack of measurement invariance. *Structural Equation Modeling, 14*, 464–504. https://doi.org/10.1080/10705510701301834

Cheng, G. H.-L., & Chan, D. K.-S. (2008). Who suffers more from job insecurity? A meta-analytic review. *Applied Psychology: An International Review, 57*, 272–303.

Cheung, G. W., & Rensvold, R. B. (2000). Assessing extreme and acquiescence response sets in cross-cultural research using structural equations modeling. *Journal of Cross-Cultural Psychology, 31*(2), 187–212.

Church, A. T., Alvarez, J. M., Mai, N. T., French, B. F., Katigbak, M. S., & Ortiz, F. A. (2011). Are cross-cultural comparisons of personality profiles meaningful? Differential item and facet functioning in the Revised NEO Personality Inventory. *Journal of Personality and Social Psychology, 101*(5), 1068.

Cieciuch, J., Davidov, E., Oberski, D. L., & Algesheimer, R. (2015). Testing for measurement invariance by detecting local misspecification and an illustration across online and paper-and-pencil samples. *European Political Science, 14*, 521–538.

Cohn, J. (2013, February 20). The robot will see you now. *The Atlantic.*

Cropanzano, R., & Mitchell, M. S. (2005). Social exchange theory: An interdisciplinary review. *Journal of Management, 31*(6), 874–900.

Davidov, E., Meuleman, B., Cieciuch, J., Schmidt, P., & Billiet, J. (2014). Measurement equivalence in cross-national research. *Annual Review of Sociology, 40*, 55–75.

Davy, J. A., Kinicki, A. J., & Scheck, C. L. (1997). A test of job security's direct and mediated effects on withdrawal cognitions. *Journal of Organizational Behavior: The International Journal of Industrial, Occupational and Organizational Psychology and Behavior, 18*(4), 323–349.

De Witte, H. (1999). Job insecurity and psychological well-being: Review of the literature and exploration of some unresolved issues. *European Journal of Work and Organizational Psychology, 8*(2), 155–177.

De Witte, H. (2000). Arbeidsethos en jobonzekerheid: Meting en gevolgen voor welzijn, tevredenheid en inzet op het werk [Work ethic and job insecurity: Assessment and consequences for well-being, satisfaction and performance at work]. In R. Bouwen, K. De Witte, H. De Witte, & T. Taillieu (Eds.), *Van groep naar gemeenschap [From group to community]. Liber Amicorum Prof. Dr. Leo Lagrou* (pp. 325–350). Garant.

De Witte, H., Pienaar, J., & De Cuyper, N. (2016). Review of 30 years of longitudinal studies on the association between job insecurity and health and well-being: Is there causal evidence? *Australian Psychologist, 51*(1), 18–31.

Debus, M. E., Probst, T. M., König, C. J., & Kleinmann, M. (2012). Catch me if I fall! Enacted uncertainty avoidance and the social safety net as country-level moderators in the job insecurity–job attitudes link. *Journal of Applied Psychology, 97*(3), 690.

Edwards, M. R., Leite, A. C., Randsley de Moura, G., & Marques, A. G. (2020). Let's talk about Brexit: intra-organizational communication, citizenship status, procedural justice, and job insecurity in a context of potential immigration threat. *The International Journal of Human Resource Management, 33*(5), 1–28. https://doi.org/10.1080/09585192.2020.1754883

Emerson, R. M. (1972a). Exchange theory part I: A psychological basis for social exchange rules and networks. In J. Berger, M. J. Zelditch, & B. Anderson (Eds.), *Sociological theories in progress* (p. 38e57). Houghton-Mifflin.

Emerson, R. M. (1972b). Exchange theory part II: exchange rules and networks. In J. Berger, M. J. Zelditch, & B. Anderson (Eds.), *Sociological theories in progress* (p. 58e87). Houghton-Mifflin.

Evans, M. G. (1991). The problem of analyzing multiplicative composites: Interactions revisited. *American Psychologist, 46*, 6–15.

Fischmann, G., De Witte, H., Sulea, C., Vander Elst, T., De Cuyper, N., & Iliescu, D. (2022). Validation of a Short and Generic Qualitative Job Insecurity Scale (QUAL-JIS). *European Journal of Career Assessment, 38*(5), 397–411. https://doi.org/10.1027/1015-5759/a000674

Frey, C. B., & Osborne, M. A. (2017). The future of employment: How susceptible are jobs to computerisation? *Technological Forecasting and Social Change, 114*, 254–280.

Greenhalgh, L., & Rosenblatt, Z. (1984). Job insecurity: Toward conceptual clarity. *Academy of Management Review, 9*(3), 438–448.

Guoxue. (2020). Fixed limits on the number of faculty that can be granted promotion. Retrieved from http://www.guoxue.com/?p=22330

Heaney, C. A., Israel, B. A., & House, J. S. (1994). Chronic job insecurity among automobile workers: Effects on job satisfaction and health. *Social Science & Medicine, 38*(10), 1431–1437.

Hellgren, J., Sverke, M., & Isaksson, K. (1999). A two-dimensional approach to job insecurity: Consequences for employee attitudes and well-being. *European Journal of Work and Organizational Psychology, 8*(2), 179–195.

Hipp, L. (2016). Insecure times? Workers' perceived job and labor market security in 23 OECD countries. *Social Science Research, 60*(4), 1–14.

Hobfoll, S. E. (1989). Conservation of resources: A new attempt at conceptualizing stress. *American Psychologist, 44*(3), 513–524.

Hu, L., & Bentler, P. M. (1999). Cutoff criteria for fit indices in covariance structure analysis: Conventional criteria versus new alternatives. *Structural Equation Modeling, 6*, 1–55. https://doi.org/10.1080/10705519909540118

International Labour Organization. (2020). ILO: As job losses escalate, nearly half of global workforce at risk of losing livelihoods. Retrieved from https://www.ilo.org/global/about-the-ilo/newsroom/news/WCMS_743036/lang%2D%2Den/index.htm

Jacobson, D. (1991). Toward a theoretical distinction between the stress components of the job insecurity and job loss experiences. In S. B. Bacharach (Ed.), *Research in the sociology of organizations* (Vol. 9, pp. 1–19). JAI Press.

Jacobson, D., & Hartley, J. (1991). Mapping the context. Job insecurity: Coping with jobs at risk, 1–22.

Jahoda, M. (1981). Work, employment, and unemployment: Values, theories, and approaches in social research. *American Psychologist, 36*(2), 184–191.

Jiang, L., & Lavaysse, L. M. (2018). Cognitive and affective job insecurity: A meta-analysis and a primary study. *Journal of Management, 44*(6), 2307–2342.

Jiang, L., Xu, X., & Wang, H-J. (2021). A resources-demands approach to sources of job insecurity: A multilevel, meta-analytic investigation. *Journal of Occupational Health Psychology, 26*, 108–126.

Kässi, O., & Lehdonvirta, V. (2016). Online labour index: Measuring the online gig economy for policy and research. Paper presented at Internet, Politics & Policy, 22–23 September, Oxford. Retrieved from https://mpra.ub.uni-muenchen.de/74943/1/MPRA_paper_74943.pdf

King, S., Bannister, P., Clifton, D., & Tarassenko, L. (2009). Probabilistic approach to the condition monitoring of aerospace engines. *Proceedings of the Institution of Mechanical Engineers, Part G: Journal of Aerospace Engineering, 223*(5), 533–541.

Kinnunen, U., Mauno, S., Nätti, J., & Happonen, M. (1999). Perceived job insecurity: A longitudinal study among Finnish employees. *European Journal of Work and Organizational Psychology, 8*, 243–260.

Kline, R. B. (2015). *Principles and practice of structural equation modeling*. Guilford.

Lazarus, R. S., & Folkman, S. (1984). *Stress, appraisal, and coping*. Springer Publishing Company.

Lee, C., Bobko, P., & Chen, Z. X. (2006). Investigation of the multidimensional model of job insecurity in China and the USA. *Applied Psychology, 55*(4), 512–540.

Lee, C., Huang, G. H., & Ashford, S. J. (2018). Job insecurity and the changing workplace: recent developments and the future trends in job insecurity research. *Annual Review of Organizational Psychology and Organizational Behavior, 5*(10), 335–359.

Mandel, M. J. (1996). *The high-risk society: Peril and promise in the new economy*. Crown Business.

Markoff, J. (2011, March 4). Armies of expensive lawyers replaced by cheaper software. *New York Times*.

Marsh, H. W., Guo, J., Parker, P. D., Nagengast, B., Asparouhov, T., & Muth. n, B., & Dicke, T. (2018). What to do when scalar invariance fails: The extended alignment method for multi-group factor analysis comparison of latent means across many groups. *Psychological Methods, 23*, 524–545.

Mauno, S., Kinnunen, U., Mäkikangas, A., & Natti, J. (2005). Psychological consequences of fixed-term employment and perceived job insecurity among health care staff. *European Journal of Work and Organizational Psychology, 14*, 209–237.

McCrae, R. R. (2015). A more nuanced view of reliability: Specificity in the trait hierarchy. *Personality and Social Psychology Review, 19*(2), 97–112.

Mouza, A. M. (2017). Continuous unplanned changes and stress in Greek public sector due to economic crisis. *International Journal of Humanities and Social Science, 7*, 70–78.

Mouza, A. M., & Souchamvali, D. (2016). Effect of Greece's new reforms and unplanned organizational changes on the stress levels of primary school teachers. *Social Indicators Research, 128*, 981–994.

Muthén, B. O., & Asparouhov, T. (2018). Recent methods for the study of measurement invariance with many groups: Alignment and random effects. *Sociological Methods & Research, 47*, 637–664. https://doi.org/10.1177/0049124117701488
Muthén, L. K., & Muthén, B. O. (1998–2017). *Mplus user's guide* (8th ed.). Muthén & Muthén.
Osborne, M. A., Garnett, R., Swersky, K., & de Freitas, N. (2012). Prediction and fault detection of environmental signals with uncharacterised faults. Twenty-Sixth AAAI Conference on Artificial Intelligence (AAAI-12).
Oxford Economics. (2014). Workforce 2020. Retrieved from https://ler.illinois.edu/wpcontent/uploads/2015/01/LER-Slides-Bringing-the-Future-into-Focus.pdf
Parramore, L. S. (2012). Job insecurity: It's the disease of the 21st century, and it's killing us. https://truthout.org/articles/job-insecurity-its-the-disease-of-the-21st-century-and-its-killing-us/
Peng, K., Nisbett, R. E., & Wong, N. Y. (1997). Validity problems comparing values across cultures and possible solutions. *Psychological Methods, 2*(4), 329–344.
Piccoli, B., Reisel, W. D., & De Witte, H. (2019). Understanding the relationship between job insecurity and performance: Hindrance or challenge effect? *Journal of Career Development, 48*(2), 0894845319833189.
Probst, T. M. (2003). Development and validation of the Job Security Index and the Job Security Satisfaction Scale: A classical test theory and IRT approach. *Journal of Occupational and Organizational Psychology, 76*, 451–467.
Probst, T. M. (2005). Countering the negative effects of job insecurity through participative decision making: Lessons from the demand-control model. *Journal of Occupational Health Psychology, 10*(4), 320.
Probst, T. M., & Jiang, L. (2017). European flexicurity policies: Multilevel effects on employee psychosocial reactions to job insecurity. *Safety Science, 100*, 83–90.
Probst, T. M., Jiang, L., & Benson, W. L. (2018). Job insecurity and anticipated job loss: A primer and exploration of possible interventions. In U. Klehe & E. van Hooft (Eds.), *The Oxford handbook of job loss and job search* (pp. 31–53). Oxford University Press.
Prokou, E. (2013). Equity and efficiency in Greek higher education policies in the past three decades: A shift of emphasis to the issue of efficiency "quality assurance" in the 2000s. *Journal of Critical Education Policy Studies, 11*(3), 29–51.
QS Survey. (2020). The impact of the coronavirus on global higher education. Retrieved from https://info.qs.com/rs/335-VIN-535/images/The-Impact-of-the-Coronavirus-on-Global-Higher-Education.pdf
Reisel, W. D., & Banai, M. (2002). Comparison of a multidimensional and a global measure of job insecurity: Predicting job attitudes and work behaviors. *Psychological Reports, 90*, 913–922.
Reisinger, D. (2019). A.I. Expert says automation could replace 40% of jobs in 15 years. Retrieved from https://fortune.com/2019/01/10/automation-replace-jobs/
Rosenblatt, Z., & Ruvio, A. (1996). A test of a multidimensional model of job insecurity: The case of Israeli teachers. *Journal of Organizational Behavior, 17*, 587–605.
Rutkovski, L., & Svetina, D. (2014). Assessing the hypothesis of measurement invariance in the context of large-scale international surveys. *Education and Psychological Measurement, 74*, 31–57. https://doi.org/10.1177/0013164413498257
Saha, B., Goebel, K., Poll, S., & Christophersen, J. (2007). An integrated approach to battery health monitoring using Bayesian regression and state estimation. In *Autotestcon, 2007 IEEE* (pp. 646–653). IEEE.
Shoss, M. K. (2017). Job insecurity: An integrative review and agenda for future research. *Journal of Management, 43*(6), 1911–1939.
Sinclair, R., Sears, L. E., Probst, T., & Zajack, M. (2010). A multilevel model of economic stress and employee well-being. *Contemporary Occupational Health Psychology: Global Perspectives on Research and Practice, 1*, 1–20.
Sörbom, D. (1989). Model modification. *Psychometrika, 54*, 371–384. https://doi.org/10.1007/BF02294623

Steinmetz, H. (2013). Analyzing observed composite differences across groups. Is partial measurement invariance enough? *Methodology, 9*, 1–12.

Sverke, M., & Hellgren, J. (2002). The nature of job insecurity: Understanding employment uncertainty on the brink of a new millennium. *Applied Psychology, 51*(1), 23–42.

Sverke, M., Hellgren, J., & Näswall, K. (2002). No security: A meta-analysis and review of job insecurity and its consequences. *Journal of Occupational Health Psychology, 7*(3), 242–264.

The Sunday Times. (2020). The Times view on job insecurity: The economy after Covid-19. Retrieved from https://www.thetimes.co.uk/article/the-times-view-on-job-insecurity-the-economy-after-covid-19-t9c052pg3

Tu, Y., Long, L., Wang, H. J., & Jiang, L. (2019). To prevent or to promote: How regulatory focus moderates the differentiated effects of quantitative versus qualitative job insecurity on employee stress and motivation. *International Journal of Stress Management, 27*(2), 135.

U.S. Bureau of Labor Statistics. (2020). Labor force statistics from the current population survey. Retrieved from https://www.bls.gov/web/empsit/cpseea03.htm

University and College Union. (2019, June). Counting the costs of casualization in higher education. Retrieved from https://www.ucu.org.uk/media/10336/Counting-the-costs-of-casualisation-in-higher-education-Jun-19/pdf/ucu_casualisation_in_HE_survey_report_Jun19.pdf

Van de Schoot, R., Lugtig, P., & Hox, J. (2012). A checklist for testing measurement invariance. *European Journal of Developmental Psychology, 9*(4), 486–492.

van Vuuren, C. V., & Klandermans, P. G. (1990). Individual reactions to job insecurity: An integrated model. In P. J. D. Drenth, J. A. Sergeant, & R. J. Takens (Eds.), *European perspectives in psychology, Vol. 3. Work and organizational, social and economic, cross-cultural* (pp. 133–146). John Wiley & Sons.

Vandenberg, R. J., & Lance, C. E. (2000). A review and synthesis of the measurement invariance literature: Suggestions, practices, and recommendations for organizational research. *Organizational Research Methods, 3*(1), 4–7.

Vander Elst, T., De Witte, H., & De Cuyper, N. (2014). The Job Insecurity Scale: A psychometric evaluation across five European countries. *European Journal of Work and Organizational Psychology, 23*, 364–380.

Vander Elst, T., Näswall, K., Bernhard-Oettel, C., De Witte, H., & Sverke, M. (2016). The effect of job insecurity on employee health complaints: A within-person analysis of the explanatory role of threats to the manifest and latent benefits of work. *Journal of Occupational Health Psychology, 21*(1), 65.

World Health Organization. (2020). Coronavirus disease (COVID-19) pandemic. Retrieved from https://www.who.int/emergencies/diseases/novel-coronavirus-2019

Lixin Jiang is an Associate Professor of Industrial and Organizational Psychology and the Director of the Master of Organizational Psychology program at the University of Auckland, New Zealand. Before relocating to New Zealand, she was an Assistant Professor at University of Wisconsin Oshkosh in the U.S.. Her research focuses on occupational health psychology, with a particular emphasis on workplace uncertainty and job insecurity. She currently serves as the Deputy Editor for *Stress and Health* and as an Associate Editor for the *Journal of Occupational Health Psychology*. Additionally, she sits on the Editorial Boards of the *Journal of Organizational Behavior* and *Occupational Health Science*.

Andrea Bazzoli is an Assistant Professor of Industrial-Organizational Psychology at Baruch College and CUNY Graduate Center. His research is focused on three areas: (i) investigating the experiences of job insecure and financially strained workers to improve their outcomes,

(ii) enhancing workplace safety (e.g., by investigating safety climate and accident (under)-reporting), and (iii) examining how advancements in quantitative and qualitative methods can be best utilized to inform empirical work in the organizational sciences. His work has appeared in some of the leading outlets in the field and he serves on the editorial board of *Occupational Health Science*.

Melissa R. Jenkins is a Scholarly Assistant Professor in Psychology at Washington State University Vancouver (USA). In addition to teaching courses in Psychology, Industrial-Organizational Psychology, and Occupational Health Psychology, Dr. Jenkins' areas of expertise include workplace diversity, training and development, and the effects of work-related stressors on employee performance and well-being.

Tahira M. Probst is a Professor of Psychology at Washington State University (USA) where she directs the Coalition for Healthy and Equitable Workplaces lab. Her research focuses on the health, safety and performance-related outcomes of economic stressors (including job insecurity, financial strain, and underemployment), as well as multilevel contextual variables that influence these relationships. She is past Editor of *Stress & Health* and sits on the Editorial Boards of the *Journal of Occupational Health Psychology*, *Occupational Health Science*, *International Journal of Stress Management*, *Military Psychology,* and the *Journal of Business and Psychology*.

Chapter 3
The Cross-Cultural Equivalence of Predictor, Moderator and Outcome Variables Related to Job Insecurity in Academic Settings: A Maximum Likelihood Alignment Approach

Dragoş Iliescu, Andreea Butucescu, Andreea Corbeanu, and Roxana Spinu

Globalization has, over the past decades, led to an increasingly interconnected world in terms of economies, cultures and populations: a steady swell of cross-border trade of goods, services and technology, as well as flows of investment, people and information. Globalization has also led to increased immigration rates, increased cross-border job mobility, a more diverse workforce and, as a result, to a stronger general need to make decisions that encompass individuals from diverse cultures, thus fueling cross-cultural research on individual differences.

In cases where decisions on culturally diverse groups of individuals need to be made, one might be tempted to hand out to both groups scales developed in the dominant culture and then make decisions based on the result (Chen, 2008). This is, however, a perilous path unless we are secure in the knowledge that we measure the exact same construct across the different groups. This situation is known as "equivalence". In the absence of equivalence, such cross-cultural comparisons are meaningless—simple comparisons of scores will yield results that are not only devoid of meaning but may also attract serious consequences, such as systematic bias and altered decision-making processes, a particularly dire consequence in high-stake contexts.

The present chapter studies the degree of equivalence for nine measures in a sample of more than 4000 participants from ten countries. The chapter will not focus on the general research model for the entire study, nor will it focus on in-depth descriptions of the actual variables or of the rationale for selecting them in this study.

D. Iliescu (✉) · A. Butucescu · A. Corbeanu · R. Spinu
Department of Psychology and Cognitive Science, Assessment and Individual Differences Lab, University of Bucharest, Bucharest, Romania
e-mail: dragos.iliescu@fpse.unibuc.ro; andreea.butucescu@unibuc.ro; andreea.corbeanu@drd.unibuc.ro; roxana.spinu@drd.unibuc.ro

L. C. Roll et al. (eds.), *Global Perspectives on Job Insecurity in Higher Education*, Aligning Perspectives on Health, Safety and Well-Being,
https://doi.org/10.1007/978-3-031-85772-0_3

These aspects are handled in a different chapter in the current volume (see the introduction chapter). We will focus, however, on all the variables that were measured, except the focal variable of job insecurity, which was investigated separately in a different chapter in this volume (see Chap. 2) The present chapter will, however, look at the degree of comparability and some of the differences between countries in these nine variables.

3.1 Equivalence and Bias

When comparing data collected in different cultures with the same measure, or possibly with different language forms of that measure, the concepts of "equivalence", "invariance" and (lack of) "bias" are used almost interchangeably. These are central constructs in the testing literature and intimately linked terms. Bias is considered a reflection of nonequivalence and is often associated with error or the presence of nuisance factors, which, in turn, taint the comparability of scores. If the internal structure of a test varies between different-language forms of the test, it is for all practical purposes a different test—we say that the two forms are not equivalent, or in more statistical terms, that the structure is not invariant (because it varies).

If the initial (source) and adapted (target) forms of a measure do not have equivalence (or, in more statistical lingo, invariance), not only is it impossible to directly compare responses gathered with the two forms of the test, but any conclusions drawn from evidence stemming from the original measure cannot be generalized to the adapted one. In other words, when scores are biased, "differences within a culture (within culture differences) do not have the same meaning as cultural differences (between-cultural differences)" (Greiff & Iliescu, 2017, p. 147). For example, scores of a measure of self-esteem that exhibit bias can indeed be valid measures of self-esteem within a single culture, while cross-culturally, responses collected with this measure may be exposed to a number of tainting factors, including item incongruity, differential response styles or translation deficiencies.

As a crucial part of test adaptation, the concept of equivalence reflects a particular type of validity that posits that test scores (and, naturally, the latent attributes they are designed to measure) have the same relationship across groups, conditions, or testing circumstances. As noted, this is of critical importance to any decision based on cross-cultural measurement—but despite comprehensive handbooks on test adaptation (Iliescu, 2017) and cross-cultural research (Matsumoto & Van de Vijver, 2011), a handful of articles (e.g., Chen, 2008; Ion & Iliescu, 2017), and the paramount importance equivalence has within psychological assessment, scientific literature on this topic is still scarce. The topic is present in cross-cultural research (where it has a central role) and psychometrics/assessment but was by and large absent in domains of applied research, such as clinical, educational or work and organizational psychology, where it has been adopted only recently and timidly.

An important tenet of equivalence is that it is always established through comparisons (Iliescu, 2017): a measure is never equivalent on its own but rather in connection to another. Establishing equivalence brings with it two crucial consequences. First, test scores recorded with the one measure can be directly compared to scores derived from the equivalent one. Second, and perhaps more importantly, validity of evidence is transferable, meaning that evidence recorded from one test form will also be valid for its equivalent counterpart (Greiff & Iliescu, 2017). On this note, the importance of establishing construct comparability across distinct cultural or ethnic groups has long been acknowledged in cross-cultural research (Chen, 2008; Poortinga, 1989; Van de Vijver & Leung, 1997). However, carrying out rigorous assessments of measurement invariance only became possible through the recent emergence of easy-to-use advanced statistical tools and the development of tests of measurement invariance (Chen, 2008; Meredith, 1993; Widaman & Reise, 1997).

3.2 Degrees of Equivalence

Despite the length that researchers often go to in order to ensure comparability of scores, equivalence in measures is never utterly perfect and is rather a matter of degree. Tests might seem to be completely equivalent on a certain level (for a review, see Schmitt & Kuljanin, 2008), though this also implies that they are non-invariant (non-equivalent) on another level. For example, when testing for equivalence models with different constraints (and a different degree of severity) are tested for fit and against each other, in a hierarchy of ever more constrained models, one can test (1) if the item variance-covariance matrix is identical for both groups, (2) if the factor structure is the same for both groups, (3) if the factor loadings are equal across groups, (4) if the factor intercepts are equal across groups, (5) if the residuals are equal across groups, (6) if the variances of the latent factors are equal across groups, (7) if the covariance of the latent factors are equal across groups, (8) or if the means of the latent factors are equal across groups. In a hypothetical case where the best accepted model is (3) if the factor loadings are equal across groups, metric invariance is accepted—but all the other, more constrained models are rejected, i.e., the test is equivalent across the two compared groups from a metric point of view, but not from other points of view—it does not exhibit scalar invariance, strict invariance, etc. We also emphasize that while the statistical approach can robustly detect lack of invariance based on *a posteriori* analyses, researchers should always carefully document the sources of bias encountered in their studies—and this cannot be done solely based on an *a posteriori* analysis but instead calls for depth of reasoning, qualitative analysis and additional (oftentimes qualitative) data (Iliescu, 2017).

The important work of van de Vijver and colleagues (e.g., van de Vijver & Poortinga, 2004) has structured the way in which the most common sources of bias are currently understood and analyzed: (a) construct bias (i.e., an incomplete overlap of the measured constructs in the original and adapted versions of the test), (b) method bias (i.e., nuisance factors arising from aspects of the method, e.g., sample, instrument, or administration conditions), and (c) item bias (i.e., anomalies in items such as those stemming from incorrect or poor item translation, differential item familiarity, cultural appropriateness, etc.). These are all possible sources of inequivalence, i.e., they lead to the situation where the compared forms of a measure are not equivalent. However, simply analyzing the two sets of data will not point to one or another of these specific forms of bias but at the best will give a hint—as noted above, their specific detection requires a dedicated qualitative approach. The current study has not been designed to point to a specific form of bias, and in those cases where we detected inequivalence, we could only speculate regarding the reason.

3.3 Consequences of Inequivalence

Lack of equivalence has insidious effects on a measure's reliability and validity (Ion & Iliescu, 2017) and has been linked to non-trivial decreases in observed reliabilities (Schmitt & Kuljanin, 2008), which in turn can assumably lead to systematic biases (van de Vijver & Poortinga, 2004), affecting the entire decision-making process. The consequences of employing non-equivalent measures for comparisons have been explored both empirically (e.g., Schmitt et al., 2011), as well as in simulation studies (e.g., Millsap & Kwok, 2004). For example, in the case of decisions that are based on data provided with such a test, evidence supports that selection accuracy is seriously influenced by even the smallest group differences in factor structure, especially when it comes to sensitivity, which is the accuracy with which a test discerns true positives. To illustrate, in Millsap and Kwok's (2004) simulation of selection bias in school admission settings, sensitivity plunged from 64.2% to 22.1%, once the percentage of non-equivalence increased from 0% (in the control condition) to 75%. Therefore, if any measures used in high-stake contexts prove to be non-invariant, making decisions on the basis of comparing individual test scores can have dire consequences, such as systematic discrimination, admission of false positive candidates and rejection of false negative ones (Nye & Drasgow, 2011).

3.4 The Present Study

As part of the larger international project studying job insecurity across different nations, this chapter focuses on testing the equivalence of nine variables that are used in the project (individual differences and work attitudes) across ten countries. In simpler studies, equivalence is usually tested through multi-group confirmatory factor analysis (CFA), which is the current gold standard for measurement invariance across distinct populations (Millsap & Kwok, 2004; Vandenberg, 2002). Multigroup CFA is, however, uniquely suited to compare two samples (i.e., two countries) and is unsuited to compare a larger number of countries unless several dyads of such comparisons are conducted. To counter these drawbacks, the maximum likelihood alignment method ("the alignment method", AM) was recently introduced by Asparouhov and Muthén (2014) as a better way of performing multi-group CFA in such situations and has rapidly become the new gold standard.

Unlike multi-group CFA, where model parameters are forced to assume moderate strength across all groups, factor alignment analysis is conceptually closer to rotational algorithms in exploratory factor analysis, where factor loadings are either maximized or minimized (Mclarnon & Romero, 2020). This places fewer constraints on the model parameters across groups and essentially automates and greatly simplifies measurement invariance analysis (Asparouhov & Muthén, 2014). The method also provides a detailed account of parameter invariance for every model parameter in every group, which is very suitable for making comparisons across data across countries.

3.5 Method

3.5.1 Participants

Our sample was comprised of a total of 4101 participants from ten countries, namely, Belgium (N = 404; 9.9%), China (N = 161; 3.9%), Croatia (N = 586; 14.3%), Greece (N = 273; 6.7%), Lithuania (N = 383; 9.3%), Romania (N = 476; 11.6%), South Africa (N = 1081; 26.4%), Switzerland (N = 322; 7.9%), the UK (N = 68; 1.7%), and the USA (N = 347; 8.5%). Overall, there were 1590 (38.8%) male participants, 2292 (55.9%) female and 3 (.1%) transgender respondents, while 9 (.3%) people chose not to disclose their gender. Participants ranged between 17 and 85 years old, with an overall average age of 40.71 years old ($SD = 11.34$). Full demographic information on the participant sample is available in Table 3.1.

3.5.2 Measures

3.5.2.1 Burnout

Burnout was measured with an abbreviation of the Burnout Assessment Tool (Schaufeli et al., 2020). The measure contains four items (e.g., "At work, I feel mentally exhausted."), scaled from 0 = "Never" to 6 = "Every day". The median reliability (alpha) in the current study was .77, ranging from .68 (Country 1) to .81 (Country 2).

3.5.2.2 Work Engagement

Work engagement was measured with UWES-3 (Schaufeli et al., 2020). The measure contains three items, one for each dimension—e.g., "At my work, I feel bursting

Table 3.1 Country-level descriptive statistics for the participant sample

		Belgium	China	Croatia	Greece	Lithuania	Romania	South Africa	Switzerland	UK	USA
N		404	158	571	272	364	476	1073	321	52	320
Excluded cases		195	3	268	131	231	0	437	28	20	93
Age	Mean	37.23	36.28	40.65	46.77	39.85	42.95	38.72	41.34	30.77	47.52
	Minimum	23	23	22	27	21	23	19	17	18	24
	Maximum	64	60	78	67	70	78	75	65	55	85
Gender	Male	96	81	189	124	110	114	495	202	23	156
	Female	308	80	385	146	254	362	408	119	45	185
	Transgender	0	0	0	2	0	0	0	0	0	1
	Undisclosed	0	0	0	1	0	0	0	0	0	1
Education Level	Lower Secondary	0	–	0	–	0	–	4	–	–	0
	Upper Secondary	2	–	2	–	0	–	4	–	–	1
	Pre-University	2	–	12	–	1	–	92	–	–	6
	Post-Secondary	4	–	7	–	7	–	124	–	–	7
	Bachelor Degree	59	–	10	–	1	–	433	–	–	23
	Master Degree	192	–	139	–	39	–	236	–	–	98
	Doctoral Degree	102	–	231	–	147	–	174	–	–	181
Occupation	Elementary Occupation (e.g., cleaner)	0	0	4	0	1	0	30	–	4	2
	Office Worker (e.g., secretary; electrician)	92	19	77	45	50	72	243	–	44	44
	Technicians/Associates/Professional/ Students	187	29	65	10	126	40	218	–	11	6
	Professionals (e.g., professor; university lecturer)	106	103	400	203	16	279	434	–	9	174
	Senior Official/Manager (e.g., chancellor, dean, campus rector, director)	19	10	28	15	11	85	124	–	0	16
Type of employment	Full Time	292	155	560	249	256	455	802	203	–	309
	Part Time	88	4	12	19	108	21	212	108	–	31
	Other	24	2	0	0	0	0	0	0	–	4

with energy." for vigor; "I am enthusiastic about my job." for dedication; and "I am immersed in my work." for absorption. The items were scaled from 0 = "Never" to 6 = "Every day". The median reliability (alpha) for this construct was .82, ranging from .75 (Country 1) to .89 (Country 2).

3.5.2.3 Innovative Work Behaviour

Innovative work behaviour was measured with a questionnaire by De Jong and Den Hartog (2010). The measure contains four items (e.g., "In your job, how often do you wonder how things can be improved?"), scaled from 1 = "Never" to 5 = "Daily". The median reliability (alpha) for this construct was .85, ranging from .80 to .89.

3.5.2.4 In-role Performance

In-role performance was measured with a questionnaire by Williams and Anderson (1991). The measure contains four items (e.g., "I fulfil the responsibilities specified in my job description."), scaled from 1 = "Strongly disagree" to 5 = "Strongly agree". The median reliability (alpha) for this construct was .88, ranging from .66 to .92.

3.5.2.5 Job Crafting

Job crafting was measured with a generic questionnaire by Vanbelle (2017, see also Vanbelle et al., 2023, online). The measure contains four items (e.g., "I make changes to my job to feel better."), scaled from 1 = "Never" to 7 = "Daily". The median reliability (alpha) for this construct was .91, ranging from .71 to .95.

3.5.2.6 Overall Organizational Justice

Overall organizational justice was measured with a questionnaire by Ambrose and Schminke (2009). The measure contains three items (e.g., "Overall, I'm treated fairly by my organization."), scaled from 1 = "Strongly disagree" to 5 = "Strongly agree". The median reliability (alpha) for this construct was 93, ranging from .77 to .95.

3.5.2.7 Social Identity

Social identity was measured with a questionnaire by Doosje et al. (1995). The measure contains four items (e.g., "I see myself as a part of the [country's name] workforce."), scaled from 1 = "Strongly disagree" to 5 = "Strongly agree". The median reliability (alpha) for this construct was .85, ranging from .80 to .91.

3.5.2.8 Job Identity

Job identity was measured with three items based on the social identity scale developed by Doosje et al. (1995). The items were reworded to reflect how much individuals identify with their jobs. The three items were: (1). "My job is a central part of my identity.", (2). "My job defines who I am.", and (3). "My personal identity is defined by my job." The scale ranged from 1 = "Strongly disagree" to 5 = "Strongly agree". The median reliability (alpha) for this construct was .86, ranging from .77 to .92.

3.5.2.9 Regulatory Focus

Social identity was measured with the Work Regulatory Focus Scale (Neubert et al., 2008). The measure contains six items and two dimensions, namely, "prevention" (e.g., "Job security is an important factor for me in any job search.") and "promotion" (e.g., "A chance to grow is an important factor for me when looking for a job."). The items were measured on a scale ranging from 1 = "Strongly disagree" to 5 = "Strongly agree". The median reliability (alpha) for this construct was .67, ranging from .52 to .80.

3.6 Results

All analyses were conducted with Mplus 8.5 (Muthen & Muthen, 2020). All analyses were conducted separately for each measure.

3.6.1 Decision on Procedure

We started the approach with a preliminary look at the data structure, trying to detect the extent to which the data can be described as "noisy" (i.e., many small and meaningless intercorrelations of residuals and a large number of cross-loadings). In case of noisy data or of unfitting baseline models, different approaches to the problem of equivalence are recommended, such as approximate invariance or Bayesian alignment. We looked specifically at any major imbalance in the country samples and significant and major differences in the endorsement rates specific for any of the items or in the intercorrelations for any of the scales (see Table 3.2). We also conducted CFAs of the basic structural models for each scale and noted that the data are relatively "clean of noise". Also, we noted that by only having ten country groups, a more sophisticated random effects multilevel CFA model (Byrne & Van de Vijver, 2014a, 2014b) is not warranted. As a result, we concluded that the maximum

Table 3.2 Country-level descriptive statistics for the items measuring the nine variables

		Total sample			C1			C2			C3			C4			C5		
Variable	Item	n	M	SD	n	M	SD	n	M	SD	n	M	SD	n	M	SD	n	M	SD
Burnout		4403	1.91	1.34	598	1.73	1.14	161	0.83	0.79	601	1.69	1.02	273	1.12	1.02	398	1.19	1.12
	i1	–	2.82	1.87	–	2.42	1.59	–	1.34	1.20	–	2.85	1.65	–	2.12	1.59	–	1.83	1.64
	i2	–	1.86	1.75	–	1.46	1.48	–	0.81	1.11	–	1.46	1.45	–	1.00	1.46	–	1.31	1.49
	i3	–	1.19	1.40	–	0.94	1.23	–	0.57	0.89	–	0.94	1.22	–	0.53	1.09	–	0.48	0.92
	i4	–	1.78	1.65	–	2.09	1.65	–	0.60	0.90	–	1.48	1.36	–	0.84	1.23	–	1.15	1.46
Engagement		4408	4.32	1.41	598	4.37	1.21	161	2.20	1.26	601	4.48	1.23	273	3.23	1.29	398	3.24	1.34
	i1	–	3.99	1.65	–	4.18	1.30	–	2.01	1.38	–	4.15	1.45	–	3.04	1.54	–	2.65	1.56
	i2	–	4.30	1.64	–	4.45	1.36	–	2.27	1.40	–	4.25	1.52	–	2.97	1.67	–	3.20	1.64
	i3	–	4.65	1.49	–	4.49	1.39	–	2.31	1.38	–	5.03	1.29	–	3.68	1.37	–	3.88	1.38
Innovative work behaviour		4433	3.55	0.88	598	3.29	0.72	161	3.28	0.91	609	3.79	0.85	273	3.51	0.80	398	3.22	0.90
	i1	–	3.87	1.05	–	3.68	0.92	–	3.43	1.12	–	4.18	0.89	–	3.86	0.99	–	3.35	1.06
	i2	–	3.58	1.05	–	3.26	0.87	–	3.30	1.07	–	3.89	1.01	–	3.59	1.00	–	3.38	1.07
	i3	–	3.41	1.08	–	3.33	0.93	–	3.14	1.02	–	3.48	1.08	–	3.30	1.04	–	3.10	1.05
	i4	–	3.34	1.09	–	2.90	0.86	–	3.25	1.07	–	3.60	1.10	–	3.27	1.01	–	3.05	1.01
In-role performance		4652	4.36	0.61	598	4.30	0.59	161	3.97	0.49	616	4.53	0.52	273	4.45	0.57	442	4.26	0.58
	i1	–	4.33	0.75	–	4.25	0.71	–	4.06	0.58	–	4.53	0.63	–	4.46	0.66	–	4.26	0.67
	i2	–	4.42	0.68	–	4.37	0.63	–	4.20	0.61	–	4.56	0.58	–	4.51	0.58	–	4.37	0.62
	i3	–	4.31	0.73	–	4.23	0.70	–	3.58	0.85	–	4.54	0.58	–	4.36	0.70	–	4.15	0.69
	i4	–	4.39	0.67	–	4.33	0.66	–	4.04	0.72	–	4.49	0.63	–	4.48	0.60	–	4.24	0.66
Job crafting		4377	3.97	1.59	596	3.43	1.37	161	3.58	1.31	601	4.63	1.55	273	3.78	1.61	398	3.98	1.69
	i1	–	3.93	1.75	–	3.52	1.41	–	3.39	1.40	–	4.29	1.69	–	3.64	1.67	–	3.92	1.81
	i2	–	3.70	1.90	–	3.34	1.52	–	3.50	1.40	–	4.68	1.85	–	3.51	1.83	–	3.77	1.83
	i3	–	4.23	1.78	–	3.47	1.45	–	3.73	1.52	–	4.73	1.68	–	4.00	1.67	–	4.27	1.78
	i4	–	4.01	1.86	–	3.40	1.53	–	3.69	1.53	–	4.79	1.78	–	3.95	1.79	–	3.97	1.81

(continued)

Table 3.2 (continued)

Variable	Item	Total sample			C1			C2			C3			C4			C5		
		n	M	SD	n	M	SD	n	M	SD	n	M	SD	n	M	SD	n	M	SD
Job identity		4336	3.48	0.96	596	3.35	0.83	161	3.77	0.70	592	3.24	1.02	273	3.50	0.96	383	3.50	0.98
	i1	–	3.88	0.99	–	4.10	0.83	–	4.00	0.77	–	3.42	1.07	–	4.09	0.98	–	3.52	1.12
	i2	–	3.37	1.14	–	3.09	1.01	–	3.74	0.86	–	3.15	1.10	–	3.33	1.11	–	3.45	1.10
	i3	–	3.18	1.14	–	2.85	1.03	–	3.58	0.91	–	3.14	1.11	–	3.10	1.12	–	3.54	1.03
Overall organizational justice		4704	3.45	0.96	598	3.88	0.78	161	3.30	0.73	630	3.40	0.99	273	3.05	0.98	442	3.15	0.86
	i1	–	3.50	1.03	–	3.89	0.82	–	3.25	0.89	–	3.43	1.01	–	3.19	1.04	–	3.20	0.91
	i2	–	3.33	1.06	–	3.80	0.84	–	3.35	0.88	–	3.28	1.10	–	2.84	1.03	–	3.01	0.93
	i3	–	3.52	1.01	–	3.94	0.81	–	3.29	0.86	–	3.48	1.00	–	3.11	1.07	–	3.24	0.90
Social identity		4335	3.95	0.82	596	4.07	0.72	161	4.00	0.62	592	3.86	0.81	273	3.54	0.91	383	3.81	0.82
	i1	–	4.32	0.84	–	4.60	0.64	–	4.06	0.77	–	4.47	0.79	–	4.01	0.97	–	4.27	0.82
	i2	–	4.11	0.93	–	4.48	0.69	–	4.02	0.79	–	4.04	1.01	–	3.57	1.10	–	4.10	0.92
	i3	–	3.66	1.08	–	3.59	1.11	–	3.98	0.74	–	3.43	1.10	–	3.30	1.17	–	3.39	1.15
	i4	–	3.70	1.05	–	3.61	1.09	–	3.94	0.67	–	3.50	1.09	–	3.30	1.07	–	3.49	1.15
Regulatory focus		4353	3.90	0.59	405	3.82	0.48	161	3.68	0.46	612	3.76	0.53	273	4.07	0.57	442	3.74	0.53
	i1	–	4.08	0.85	–	3.95	0.89	–	3.74	0.78	–	4.00	0.80	–	4.11	0.93	–	3.85	0.86
	i2	–	3.86	0.96	–	4.03	0.88	–	3.37	0.86	–	3.56	1.00	–	4.11	0.74	–	3.91	0.82
	i3	–	3.62	0.98	–	3.32	0.98	–	3.76	0.68	–	3.14	0.98	–	3.92	0.88	–	3.55	0.90
	i4	–	4.18	0.82	–	3.98	0.87	–	3.78	0.72	–	4.25	0.71	–	4.19	0.85	–	4.26	0.69
	i5	–	3.84	0.96	–	4.02	0.78	–	3.81	0.73	–	3.82	0.88	–	3.95	0.86	–	3.21	0.98
	i6	–	3.83	0.92	–	3.61	0.87	–	3.60	0.80	–	3.80	0.89	–	4.12	0.82	–	3.66	0.93

Variable	Item	C6			C7			C8			C9			C10		
		n	M	SD	n	M	SD	n	M	SD	n	M	SD	n	M	SD
Burnout		476	1.52	1.14	1133	2.94	1.27	328	1.39	1.14	70	2.65	1.35	365	2.07	1.27
	i1	–	2.05	1.63	–	4.10	1.70	–	1.87	1.64	–	3.74	1.70	–	3.38	1.77
	i2	–	1.48	1.45	–	3.04	1.80	–	1.27	1.52	–	2.56	1.81	–	2.07	1.74
	i3	–	1.25	1.34	–	2.13	1.41	–	0.79	1.46	–	1.33	1.38	–	0.85	1.23
	i4	–	1.29	1.47	–	2.51	1.64	–	1.64	1.67	–	2.96	1.84	–	1.96	1.75
Engagement		476	4.61	1.06	1138	5.19	1.05	328	3.47	1.29	70	4.27	1.16	365	4.52	1.19
	i1	–	4.66	1.20	–	4.80	1.51	–	3.12	1.46	–	3.61	1.43	–	3.88	1.52
	i2	–	4.34	1.30	–	5.35	1.20	–	3.61	1.54	–	4.46	1.38	–	4.55	1.45
	i3	–	4.84	1.24	–	5.42	1.11	–	3.69	1.42	–	4.74	1.30	–	5.13	1.23
Innovative work behaviour		476	3.42	0.88	1156	3.80	0.90	328	3.30	0.86	70	3.41	0.87	364	3.71	0.82
	i1	–	3.74	1.02	–	4.06	1.12	–	3.71	1.08	–	4.01	0.94	–	4.12	0.97
	i2	–	3.62	0.95	–	3.74	1.14	–	3.35	1.10	–	3.43	0.94	–	3.61	1.00
	i3	–	3.19	1.08	–	3.72	1.14	–	3.16	1.04	–	3.13	1.06	–	3.58	0.97
	i4	–	3.14	1.14	–	3.70	1.12	–	2.98	1.04	–	3.06	1.06	–	3.52	0.98
In-role performance		476	4.20	0.67	1299	4.33	0.61	349	4.21	0.65	70	4.63	0.52	368	4.82	0.34
	i1	–	4.27	0.81	–	4.26	0.73	–	3.93	1.04	–	4.64	0.57	–	4.83	0.45
	i2	–	4.23	0.83	–	4.35	0.71	–	4.29	0.81	–	4.69	0.60	–	4.87	0.35
	i3	–	4.03	0.88	–	4.33	0.69	–	4.28	0.74	–	4.53	0.61	–	4.77	0.49
	i4	–	4.27	0.73	–	4.37	0.68	–	4.33	0.68	–	4.66	0.63	–	4.84	0.38
Job crafting		476	3.84	1.42	1116	4.16	1.68	328	3.90	1.43	70	3.48	1.37	358	3.79	1.59
	i1	–	3.60	1.96	–	4.29	1.85	–	3.87	1.52	–	3.53	1.55	–	3.87	1.80
	i2	–	3.83	2.00	–	3.55	2.08	–	3.65	1.62	–	3.26	1.66	–	3.28	1.84
	i3	–	4.08	1.91	–	4.61	1.90	–	4.09	1.58	–	3.70	1.37	–	4.26	1.72
	i4	–	3.84	1.90	–	4.19	2.02	–	3.98	1.62	–	3.43	1.59	–	3.77	1.89

(continued)

Table 3.2 (continued)

Variable	Item	C6			C7			C8			C9			C10		
		n	M	SD	n	M	SD	n	M	SD	n	M	SD	n	M	SD
Job identity		476	3.89	0.82	1085	3.56	0.99	322	3.31	0.95	70	3.38	0.99	378	3.31	0.97
	i1	–	3.95	0.86	–	4.00	0.95	–	3.98	0.97	–	3.91	1.07	–	3.94	0.98
	i2	–	3.96	0.92	–	3.51	1.21	–	3.10	1.15	–	3.26	1.10	–	3.06	1.16
	i3	–	3.77	1.03	–	3.17	1.21	–	2.85	1.11	–	2.97	1.18	–	2.93	1.14
Overall organizational justice		476	3.52	0.84	1328	3.38	0.93	349	3.59	1.01	69	3.68	1.08	378	3.56	1.18
	i1	–	3.45	1.00	–	3.45	1.03	–	3.67	1.10	–	3.64	1.18	–	3.69	1.21
	i2	–	3.46	0.95	–	3.26	1.06	–	3.47	1.10	–	3.57	1.16	–	3.34	1.27
	i3	–	3.65	0.94	–	3.42	1.01	–	3.64	1.04	–	3.83	1.08	–	3.65	1.22
Social identity		476	3.64	0.74	1085	4.23	0.77	322	3.85	0.85	70	4.13	0.81	377	3.92	0.83
	i1	–	4.10	0.84	–	4.38	0.80	–	4.29	1.03	–	4.36	0.89	–	4.12	0.89
	i2	–	3.70	0.93	–	4.27	0.88	–	4.19	0.85	–	4.21	0.93	–	4.05	0.88
	i3	–	3.37	0.95	–	4.12	0.94	–	3.47	1.11	–	3.94	1.02	–	3.72	1.07
	i4	–	3.40	0.98	–	4.15	0.86	–	3.44	1.12	–	4.01	1.00	–	3.79	0.98
Regulatory focus		476	3.69	0.54	1190	4.24	0.54	349	3.51	0.59	70	3.94	0.64	375	3.92	0.60
	i1	–	3.96	0.81	–	4.28	0.79	–	4.00	0.90	–	4.24	0.91	–	4.31	0.78
	i2	–	3.20	0.93	–	4.19	0.79	–	4.07	0.86	–	4.00	1.12	–	3.66	1.16
	i3	–	3.48	0.92	–	4.10	0.79	–	3.39	1.00	–	3.71	1.07	–	3.36	1.13
	i4	–	4.16	0.81	–	4.40	0.69	–	3.37	1.08	–	4.33	0.83	–	4.35	0.67
	i5	–	3.59	0.99	–	4.30	0.73	–	3.09	1.09	–	3.71	0.98	–	3.93	0.94
	i6	–	3.75	0.85	–	4.16	0.77	–	3.15	1.12	–	3.64	0.99	–	3.94	0.91

likelihood alignment method is probably the best suited to analyze our data: this method will show for what country groups invariance holds and what items are less invariant in terms of loadings and/or intercepts for certain country groups. The method also has the advantage of providing approximate latent means for the country groups (and tests of difference for these latent means), even in those cases when no exact measurement invariance is established, thus making the direct comparison of these country groups possible.

3.6.2 Acceptable Models of Configural Invariance

The alignment procedure is, like every other multigroup CFA procedure, based on the assumption of an acceptable fit for the configural invariance model. We have therefore conducted CFA analyses for all nine scales on the combined sample, in order to establish the best fitting model. The simple models (with no errors correlated) have shown a good to acceptable fit for all variables, with the exception of regulatory focus ($\chi^2[9] = 1900.98$, CFI = .691, TLI = .485, RMSEA = .220). All models were then tweaked by specifying one correlated error (three error correlations for regulatory focus) to obtain the best possible baseline model. All these baseline models have excellent to very good fit, as shown in Table 3.3. For engagement, job identity and overall organizational justice, fit indices could not be computed: these scales are composed of only three items each and therefore provide perfectly defined models.

3.6.3 Alignment Models

We have first conducted a free alignment procedure. For seven of our variables (burnout, innovative work behaviour, job crafting, social identity, engagement, job identity, overall organizational justice), this procedure did not converge, and the output recommended a specific country group (2, 7, 7, 1, 7, 6, 1, respectively) as the reference for the fixed alignment process. For the other two variables (in-role performance, social identity), we nevertheless conducted the fixed alignment procedure, fixing country group 1 (Belgium) as the reference for the fixed alignment process.

3.6.4 Invariance of Item-Level Loadings and Intercepts

Table 3.4 shows the results of the alignment procedure. Specifically, the table reports on the invariance of item-level intercepts and loadings across the ten country groups. A cell that contains a "-" signifies a non-invariant case. For example, in the case of

Table 3.3 Fit indices for the baseline CFA models of the nine variables

		Simple model (no error correlations)						Best baseline model						
	Number of items	X^2	df	CFI	TLI	RMSEA	SRMR	X^2	df	CFI	TLI	RMSEA	SRMR	Number of error correlations
Burnout	4	56.39	2	.991	.972	.079	.016	1.73	1	1.000	.999	.013	.003	1
Engagement	3	0.00	0	1.000	1.000	.000	.000	0.00	0	1.000	1.000	.000	.000	–
Innovative work behaviour	4	397.40	2	.952	.855	.211	.040	4.55	1	1.000	.997	.028	.003	1
In-role performance	4	517.24	2	.948	.843	.235	.034	3.12	1	1.000	.999	.021	.002	1
Job crafting	4	360.96	2	.966	.897	.202	.023	1.04	1	1.000	.999	.003	.002	1
Job identity	3	0.00	0	1.000	1.000	.000	.000	0.00	0	1.000	1.000	.000	.000	–
Overall organizational justice	3	0.00	0	1.000	1.000	.000	.000	0.00	0	1.000	1.000	.000	.000	–
Social identity	4	844.00	2	.905	.715	.312	.064	16.78	1	.998	.989	.060	.006	1
Regulatory focus	6	1900.98	9	.691	.485	.220	.104	46.92	6	.993	.983	.040	.015	3

Table 3.4 Item-level invariance: item invariance index and invariance by country

		Loadings											Intercepts										
		R^2	C1	C2	C3	C4	C5	C6	C7	C8	C9	C10	R^2	C1	C2	C3	C4	C5	C6	C7	C8	C9	C10
Burnout	i1	.37						–					.81	–	–		–	–	–		–		
	i2	.94											.99										
	i3	.17			–		–						.76					–					–
	i4	.75											.81	–							–		
Engagement	i1	.50											.90	–					–				
	i2	.69						–					.98										
	i3	.00	–	–						–			.94										
Innovative work behaviour	i1	.26											.56			–		–					
	i2	.43											.80							–			–
	i3	.65											.73	–		–							
	i4	.29			–								.90										
In-role performance	i1	.80											.81							–	–		
	i2	.86											.97					–					
	i3	.91											.83	–		–				–			
	i4	.57					–						.97										
Job crafting	i1	.73					–						.83	–						–			
	i2	.84											.65				–	–		–	–		–
	i3	.30											.92	–		–							
	i4	.51	–										.94	–						–			
Job identity	i1	.24			–		–	–					.00		–	–		–	–	–			
	i2	.90											.99							–			
	i3	.93											.88			–		–	–				

(continued)

Table 3.4 (continued)

		Loadings											Intercepts										
		R^2	C1	C2	C3	C4	C5	C6	C7	C8	C9	C10	R^2	C1	C2	C3	C4	C5	C6	C7	C8	C9	C10
Overall organizational justice	i1	.88											.92										–
	i2	.86			–								.88				–						–
	i3	.98											.98										
Social identity	i1	.00	–	–					–			–	.04	–		–				–			
	i2	.00	–				–			–			.46	–						–			
	i3	.80											.86		–								
	i4	.47		–									.90										
Regulatory focus	i1	.21											.33										–
	i2	.28								–			.10		–	–			–				–
	i3	.48											.36	–		–							–
	i4	.13											.58			–		–	–			–	–
	i5	.00							–				.52		–			–					
	i6	.00							–				.77										

Note: C1 = Belgium, C2 = China, C3 = Croatia, C4 = Greece, C5 = Lithuania, C6 = Romania, C7 = South Africa, C8 = Switzerland, C9 = UK, C10 = USA. R^2 is the parameter invariance index burnout, item 1 ("At work, I feel mentally exhausted.") has non-invariant loadings for country group 6 (Romania) and non-invariant intercepts for country groups 1 (Belgium), 2 (China), 4 (Greece), 5 (Lithuania), 6 (Romania) and 8 (Switzerland). In contrast, item 2 ("I struggle to find any enthusiasm for my work.") is completely invariant in both loadings and intercepts across all ten country groups.

There is a fundamental difference between loading and intercept invariance (Schmitt & Kuljanin, 2008). Constraining factor loadings to be equal (i.e., testing for the equality of loadings) defines a metric invariance model (or "weak factorial" model). A metric invariance model tests in essence if respondents in the various groups (in our case, in the ten country groups) attribute the same meaning to the focal latent construct (i.e., the latent construct is composed from the same "mix" of item meanings, or each item contributes to the latent construct to a similar degree). Constraining the intercepts (thresholds) to be equal (i.e., testing for the equality of intercepts) tests in essence if respondents in the various groups attribute the same meaning to the levels of the underlying items (i.e., the endorsement for the items is equally strong, or the scaling levels of the items are similar). Constraining both the loadings and intercepts to be equal (i.e., testing for the equality of intercepts) defines a scalar invariance model (or "strong factorial" model). This model tests if both the meaning of the construct and the endorsement levels of the items are equal in the various groups. In such a case, the groups can be directly compared on their mean latent scores.

3.6.5 Latent Means and Their Comparison

Table 3.5 visualizes the estimated latent means of each of the variables for each of the country groups and compares these means. Two issues are important in this regard. First, these latent means for each scale are estimated with the assumption of invariance, i.e., they ignore measurement non-invariance. They should thus only be considered with confidence if the rest of the output supports at least some level of invariance. Second, the comparisons are conducted not by comparing each of the country groups with each other but by rank ordering the country groups in descending order of the latent mean and then comparing each group with those consecutive; the last column shows a list of those consecutive country groups that have latent means that are different from the focal country group (row). In order to simplify this comparison, we recomputed the means so that the largest group is set to zero (Putnick & Bornstein, 2016). For example, for burnout, the largest latent mean was computed for country group 7 (South Africa); this is set to zero. The next latent mean is for country group 9 (UK), −0.488, and is not significantly different—the next, however, for country group 10 (USA), which is −1.296, is significantly different from South Africa. Country group 7 (South Africa) has a latent mean that is significantly different from those of country groups 10, 3, 1, 6, 8, 5, 4, and 2; country group 4 (Greece) has a latent mean that is not significantly different from that of country group 2 (China), and so on.

Table 3.5 Factor means and factor mean comparison by country for the nine variables

		Country	Factor mean	Groups with significantly smaller factor mean
Burnout				
	7	South Africa	0.000	10 3 1 6 8 5 4 2
	9	UK	−0.488	10 3 1 6 8 5 4 2
	10	USA	−1.296	3 1 6 8 5 4 2
	3	Croatia	−1.953	8 5 4 2
	1	Belgium	−2.048	8 5 4 2
	6	Romania	−2.062	8 5 4 2
	8	Switzerland	−2.401	4 2
	5	Lithuania	−2.456	4 2
	4	Greece	−2.828	
	2	China	−3.077	
Engagement				
	7	South Africa	0.000	10 6 3 1 9 8 4 5 2
	10	USA	−0.698	8 4 5 2
	6	Romania	−0.699	8 4 5 2
	3	Croatia	−0.817	8 4 5 2
	1	Belgium	−0.893	8 4 5 2
	9	UK	−0.972	8 4 5 2
	8	Switzerland	−1.906	2
	4	Greece	−2.055	
	5	Lithuania	−2.093	
	2	China	−3.246	
Innovative work behaviour				
	7	South Africa	0.000	10 4 6 9 8 2 5 1
	3	Croatia	−0.038	4 6 9 8 2 5 1
	10	USA	−0.136	4 6 9 8 2 5 1
	4	Greece	−0.394	8 2 5 1
	6	Romania	−0.509	5 1
	9	UK	−0.552	
	8	Switzerland	−0.616	
	2	China	−0.639	
	5	Lithuania	−0.659	
	1	Belgium	−0.689	
In-role performance				
	10	USA	0.000	9 3 4 7 1 8 5 6 2
	9	UK	−0.390	4 7 1 8 5 6 2
	3	Croatia	−0.598	7 1 8 5 6 2
	4	Greece	−0.717	7 1 8 5 6 2
	7	South Africa	−0.967	6 2
	1	Belgium	−1.005	6 2
	8	Switzerland	−1.049	2

(continued)

Table 3.5 (continued)

		Country	Factor mean	Groups with significantly smaller factor mean
	5	Lithuania	−1.079	2
	6	Romania	−1.163	2
	2	China	−1.444	
Job crafting				
	3	Croatia	0.000	7 5 8 6 10 4 2 9 1
	7	South Africa	−0.238	5 8 6 10 4 2 9 1
	5	Lithuania	−0.418	2 9 1
	8	Switzerland	−0.467	2 9 1
	6	Romania	−0.505	2 9 1
	10	USA	−0.509	9 1
	4	Greece	−0.540	1
	2	China	−0.676	
	9	UK	−0.759	
	1	Belgium	−0.781	
Job identity				
	6	Romania	0.000	2 7 5 4 9 3 1 8 10
	2	China	−0.242	7 5 4 9 3 1 8 10
	7	South Africa	−0.549	3 1 8 10
	5	Lithuania	−0.607	3 1 8 10
	4	Greece	−0.725	3 1 8 10
	9	UK	−0.856	
	3	Croatia	−0.955	
	10	USA	−0.997	
	8	Switzerland	−0.982	
			−0.607	
Overall organizational justice				
	1	Belgium	0.000	8 10 6 3 7 2 5 4
	9	UK	−0.256	3 7 2 5 4
	8	Switzerland	−0.377	3 7 2 5 4
	10	USA	−0.393	3 7 2 5 4
	6	Romania	−0.462	3 7 2 5 4
	3	Croatia	−0.633	2 5 4
	7	South Africa	−0.661	2 5 4
	2	China	−0.847	
	5	Lithuania	−0.958	
	4	Greece	−1.036	
Social identity				
	7	South Africa	0.000	10 2 1 3 8 5 6 4
	9	UK	−0.194	1 3 8 5 6 4
	10	USA	−0.458	3 8 5 6 4
	2	China	−0.480	3 5 6 4
	1	Belgium	−0.542	3 8 5 6 4

(continued)

Table 3.5 (continued)

		Country	Factor mean	Groups with significantly smaller factor mean
	3	Croatia	−0.698	6 4
	8	Switzerland	−0.707	6 4
	5	Lithuania	−0.735	4
	6	Romania	−0.876	
	4	Greece	−1.052	
Regulatory focus				
	7	South Africa	0.000	4 10 9 3 1 5 6 2 8
	4	Greece	−0.718	9 3 1 5 6 2 8
	10	USA	−1.080	3 5 6 2 8
	9	UK	−1.421	8
	3	Croatia	−1.423	2 8
	1	Belgium	−1.459	8
	5	Lithuania	−1.597	8
	6	Romania	−1.665	8
	2	China	−1.762	8
	8	Switzerland	−2.589	

3.6.6 *Other Indices*

The alignment method produces a number of other indices, such as R^2 indicators for the degree of invariance of item parameters (loadings and intercepts) across groups, as well as an average R^2, a so-called average invariance index (a global score of both metric and scalar invariance). These are confusing to interpret and can be severely impacted by variations in other parameters that are trivial to the actual issue of equivalence, such as the non-occurrence of a particular category in one or several groups or a small factor mean variability in one or several of the groups. We have nevertheless reported them as global indicators of invariance, that should be interpreted in corroboration with other results.

Table 3.4 contains a column with the R^2 invariance index for each parameter (loadings and intercepts) for each item. This should be interpreted (Muthen & Asparouhov, 2018) as the variation across groups in the respective parameter that is explained by a variation in the corresponding factor-level indicators (e.g., in the case of intercepts, the variation in factor mean and in the case of loadings, the variation in factor variance across groups). Table 3.6 also contains a number of more synthetic indices that give an overview of the level of invariance for each of the 9 variables. Specifically, the table contains for each variable the percentage of loadings and respectively of intercepts that are invariant (number of invariant parameters from the total number of parameters that are also visualized in Table 3.4). Also, Table 3.6 contains a column with the Average Invariance Index

Table 3.6 Summary of invariance statistics for the nine variables

Variable	Number of items	Median reliability alpha over countries [Min-Max]	Median parameter over countries [Min-Max]		Parameter invariance status[a]		Average Invariance Index (R^2)
			Loadings	Intercepts	Loadings	Intercepts	
Burnout	4	.77 [68–.81]	0.643 [0.281–0.871]	0.739 [0.039–2.582]	92.50%	75.00%	0.699
Engagement	3	.82 [75–.89]	0.894 [0.726–1.401]	4.426 [3.503–5.002]	86.67%	93.33%	0.668
Innovative work behaviour	4	.85 [80–.89]	0.843 [0.323–1.092]	3.740 [3.473–4.263]	97.50%	85.00%	0.576
In-role performance	4	.88 [66–.92]	0.537 [0.359–0.693]	4.313 [3.847–4.431]	97.50%	85.00%	0.838
Job crafting	4	.91 [71–.95]	1.514 [0.981–2.008]	3.829 [3.087–4.260]	95.00%	72.50%	0.714
Job identity	3	.86 [77–.92]	0.874 [0.440–0.957]	3.113 [2.849–4.104]	90.00%	70.00%	0.656
Overall organizational justice	3	.93 [77–.95]	0.747 [0.547–0.874]	3.901 [3.513–4.025]	96.67%	90.00%	0.917
Social identity	4	.85 [80–.91]	0.726 [0.229–1.001]	4.319 [4.060–4.725]	80.00%	85.00%	0.441
Regulatory focus	6	.67 [52–.80]	0.284 [0.018–0.982]	3.832 [3.132–4.311]	95.00%	75.00%	0.313

[a] Percentage of invariant parameters based on the alignment method, i.e., total number of approximate measurement invariance groups across indicators divided by total number of groups across indicators

(R^2), which is a global score of invariance (both metric and scalar), ranging from 0 (complete non-invariance) to 1 (full scalar invariance).

3.7 Discussion

3.7.1 Interpretation of Results

The results should be approached with finesse and from several perspectives. First, we draw attention to the fact that strict alignment is not present for any of the investigated variables/measures. Table 3.5 offers a look at the countries that are more often not aligned on each of the variables. For example, some of the country groups have consistently higher (SA, USA) or lower (China, Lithuania) scores than the others. This could have pointed to a specific pattern of wellbeing typical for these countries, but some of these patterns are contradictory; for example, South Africa has the highest score, and China has the lowest score both on Burnout and on Engagement, which is perhaps difficult or impossible to reconcile. These consistent patterns point more likely to cultural response sets, which have been considered threats to validity by some (Cronbach, 1946; Messick, 1962) and as *bona fide* cross-cultural differences by other authors (Benet-Martinez, 2007). According to these latter authors, cultural responses are thus "tendencies for members of a given culture to use certain parts of a scale when responding" (Benet-Martinez, 2007, p. 179) and are not an expression of bias but reflect actual "true" differences (albeit not related to the target variable) between the two cultures, such as cultural norms about appropriate self-expression (He & van de Vijver, 2013), in general or related to the measured construct. The actual status and mechanisms of these cultural response sets are impossible to ascertain from statistical data alone but require qualitative investigations related to the cognitive processes and cultural expressions typical for the compared cultures. This investigation therefore exceeds the objectives of the current analysis but is pointed out as a possible follow-up study into the registered differences.

Interesting conclusions also result from the investigation of those countries that occasionally score very high or low on some scales, such as Romania in job identity. This very specific high average score could point to a real cultural difference in how participants from Romania shape their self-identity based on their specific identity as an "academic", deriving social status and respect and suggesting that an academic job may in this case be more than "just another job".

Based on Table 3.6, we consider it important to look at the actual evidence in terms of the summary of invariance. It is obvious that we do not have absolutely full invariance in any of these investigated measures. Invariance is present for some measures to a higher (job crafting, in-role performance) or lesser (regulatory focus especially, maybe also social identity) degree. At the same time, the volume of misalignment is actually small to spurious: the invariance status of loadings and intercepts shows that the overwhelming majority of these parameters are usually aligned. It is also visible that loadings fare better than intercepts, suggesting that the measurement model is more robust than the score offsets.

This information should be corroborated with Table 3.4, investigating the actual items that have better alignment. No item is absolutely perfectly aligned across all countries except item 2 of the Burnout measure ("I struggle to find any enthusiasm for my work"), that has non-significant deviations of both loadings and intercepts across the ten country groups. Anchor items that behave excellently, almost perfectly, across all countries can then be used to compare specific behaviors with very good to complete confidence. Examples of such items would be item 2 of the Engagement measure ("I am enthusiastic about my job"), item 3 of the Innovative work behavior measure ("In your job, how often do you generate original solutions for problems"), item 2 of the In-role performance measure ("I perform the tasks that are expected as part of the job"), item 1 of the Job crafting measure ("I make changes to my job to feel better"), item 2 of the Job identity measure ("My job defines who I am"), item 3 of the Overall organizational justice measure ("In general, the treatment I receive around here is fair"), item 3 of the Social identity measure ("I feel strong ties with the [country's name] workforce"), and item 3 of the Regulatory focus measure ("I am very careful to avoid exposing myself to potential losses at work").

In conclusion, and in light of previous results in cross-cultural comparisons of the kind conducted in our analysis and of the vague recommendations extant in the field, we consider that scores on regulatory focus and social identity should be compared with prudence and that scores for the other variables can be compared with a reasonable degree of confidence, being mindful of the limitation suggested by the results in Table 3.6.

3.8 Conclusions

Scalar invariance is the minimal condition for the meaningful comparison of latent mean scores across groups. However, "scalar invariance is an unachievable ideal that in practice can only be approximated" (Marsh et al., 2018, p. 2). In our case, this unachievable ideal was, of course, not achieved. There are several motives why this can happen—in cross-cultural research, the categories of construct, method, and item bias have been well documented (Byrne & van de Vijver, 2014a, 2014b; van de Vijver & Leung, 1997; van de Vijver & Tanzer, 1997). We consider that in our case, construct bias is unlikely, as metric invariance (loading invariance) is present to a very large degree for almost all the analyzed variables. Method bias could be an issue in our analysis, especially sample bias, i.e., the lack of comparability of the samples used for each country. Differences in sample characteristics are visible in terms of volume, gender and composition, although we consider that the (for the present study) more important differences of education and occupation are not large (i.e., all the participants are active in higher education), thus making method bias less likely. Finally, item bias could also be a possible source of this non-equivalence. In this case, we consider the most current sources of item bias, such as blatantly incorrect item translation (wrong translation), poor item translation (shift in meaning due to new connotations), or inadequate item formulation, to be less likely, given the attentive translation of all the instruments by the experienced research team. Items with significant non-invariance (e.g., item 1 of the Job identity measure—"My job is a central part of my identity"; item 1 of the Social identity measure—"I see myself as part of the [country's name] workforce"; item 2 of the Regulatory focus measure—"-Job security is an important factor for me in any job search") should be investigated to ascertain to what degree item bias is likely in this case, but we point out that this can only be established through cognitive interviews, i.e., a supplementary phase of qualitative inquiry.

We note that invariance is not only a question of quality (an on/off decision) but also of quantity, i.e., of degree. The degree of confidence one should place on the comparisons made in our case should be guided by the conclusions in Table 3.6 and especially by the Average Invariance Index (R^2) noted in this table. Finally, the idea of partial invariance (i.e., of a better form or amount of invariance for a partial set of the items in a measure) could become attractive for the present analysis, and the easiest way to simulate this in the absence of a dedicated partial invariance analysis is by looking in each variable at the items or item with the best alignment for both loadings and intercepts.

3.9 Take home message

In light of our analysis, we suggest that the cross-cultural comparisons in this study can be operated with a reasonable degree of confidence for the variables of burnout, engagement, innovative work behaviour, in-role performance, job crafting, overall organizational justice and social identity. Comparisons on regulatory focus and social identity should be done with more prudence. None of the variables have achieved full scalar equivalence across all the ten samples, but through contrast with similar results obtained in other studies, comparability is adequate.

References

Ambrose, M. L., & Schminke, M. (2009). The role of overall justice judgments in organizational justice research: A test of mediation. *Journal of Applied Psychology, 94*(2), 491–500.

Asparouhov, T., & Muthén, B. (2014). Multiple-group factor analysis alignment. *Structural Equation Modeling, 21*, 1–14.

Benet-Martinez, V. (2007). Cross-cultural personality research: Conceptual and methodological issues. In R. W. Robins, R. C. Fraley, & R. F. Krueger (Eds.), *Handbook of research methods in personality psychology* (pp. 170–189). Guilford Press.

Byrne, B., & van de Vijver, F. J. R. (2014a). Validating factorial structure of the family values scale from a multilevel-multicultural perspective. *International Journal of Testing, 14*, 168–192.

Byrne, B. M., & Van de Vijver, F. J. (2014b). Factorial structure of the family values scale from a multilevel-multicultural perspective. *International Journal of Testing, 14*(2), 168–192.

Chen, F. F. (2008). What happens if we compare chopsticks with forks? The impact of making inappropriate comparisons in cross-cultural research. *Journal of Personality and Social Psychology, 95*(5), 1005–1018.

Cronbach, L. J. (1946). Response sets and test validity. *Educational and Psychological Measurement, 6*(4), 475–494.

De Jong, J., & Den Hartog, D. (2010). Measuring innovative work behaviour. *Creativity and Innovation Management, 19*(1), 23–36.

Doosje, B., Ellemers, N., & Spears, R. (1995). Perceived intragroup variability as a function of group status and identification. *Journal of Experimental Social Psychology, 31*(5), 410–436.

Greiff, S., & Iliescu, D. (2017). A test is much more than just the test itself: Some thoughts on adaptation and equivalence. *European Journal of Psychological Assessment, 33*(3), 145–148.

He, J., & Van de Vijver, F. J. R. (2013). A general response style factor: Evidence from a multi-ethnic study in The Netherlands. *Personality and Individual Differences, 55*, 794–800.

Iliescu, D. (2017). *Adapting tests in Linguistic and cultural situations*. Cambridge University Press.

Ion, A., & Iliescu, D. (2017). The measurement equivalence of personality measures across high- and low-stake test taking settings. *Personality and Individual Differences, 110*, 1–6.

Marsh, H. W., Guo, J., Parker, P. D., Nagengast, B., Asparouhov, T., Muthén, B., & Dicke, T. (2018). What to do when scalar invariance fails: The extended alignment method for multi-group factor analysis comparison of latent means across many groups. *Psychological Methods, 23*(3), 524–545.

Matsumoto, D., & Van de Vijver, F. J. R. (Eds.). (2011). *Culture and psychology. Cross-cultural research methods in psychology*. Cambridge University Press.

McLarnon, M. J., & Romero, E. F. (2020). Cross-cultural equivalence of shortened versions of the Eysenck Personality Questionnaire: An application of the alignment method. *Personality and Individual Differences, 163*, 110074.

Meredith, W. (1993). Measurement invariance, factor analysis and factorial invariance. *Psychometrika, 58*, 525–543.

Messick, S. (1962). Response style and content measures from personality inventories. *Educational and Psychological Measurement, 22*, 41–56.

Millsap, R. E., & Kwok, O.-M. (2004). Evaluating the impact of partial factorial invariance on selection of multiple populations. *Psychological Methods, 9*, 93–115.

Muthén, B., & Asparouhov, T. (2018). Recent methods for the study of measurement invariance with many groups: Alignment and random effects. *Sociological Methods & Research, 47*(4), 637–664.

Muthén, L. K., & Muthén, B. O. (2020). *Mplus user's guide* (6th ed.).

Neubert, M. J., Kacmar, K. M., Carlson, D. S., Chonko, L. B., & Roberts, J. A. (2008). Regulatory focus as a mediator of the influence of initiating structure and servant leadership on employee behavior. *Journal of Applied Psychology, 93*(6), 1220.

Nye, C. D., & Drasgow, F. (2011). Effect size indices for analyses of measurement equivalence: Understanding the practical importance of differences between groups. *Journal of Applied Psychology, 96*(5), 966–980.

Poortinga, Y. H. (1989). Equivalence of cross-cultural data: An overview of basic issues. *International Journal of Psychology, 24*, 737–756.

Putnick, D. L., & Bornstein, M. H. (2016). Measurement invariance conventions and reporting: The state of the art and future directions for psychological research. *Developmental Review, 41*, 71–90.

Schaufeli, W. B., Desart, S., & De Witte, H. (2020). Burnout Assessment Tool (BAT)—Development, validity, and reliability. *International Journal of Environmental Research and Public Health, 17*(24), 9495.

Schmitt, N., Golubovich, J., & Leong, F. T. (2011). Impact of measurement invariance on construct correlations, mean differences, and relations with external correlates: An illustrative example using Big Five and RIASEC measures. *Assessment, 18*(4), 412–427.
Schmitt, N., & Kuljanin, G. (2008). Measurement invariance: Review of practice and implications. *Human Resource Management Review, 18*(4), 210–222.
Van de Vijver, F. J. R., & Leung, K. (1997). Methods and data analysis of comparative research. In J. W. Berry, Y. H. Poortinga, & J. Pandey (Eds.), *Handbook of cross-cultural psychology* (2nd ed., pp. 257–300). Allyn & Bacon.
Van de Vijver, F. J., & Poortinga, Y. H. (2004). Conceptual and methodological issues in adapting tests. In *Adapting educational and psychological tests for cross-cultural assessment* (pp. 51–76). Psychology Press.
Van de Vijver, F. J. R., & Tanzer, N. K. (1997). Bias and equivalence in cross-cultural assessment: An overview. *European Review of Applied Psychology, 47*, 263–279.
Vanbelle, E. (2017). *Job crafting: An overarching approach (Unpublished doctoral thesis).* KU Leuven.
Vanbelle, E., Griep, Y., Van den Broeck, A., & De Witte, H. (2023). Development and validation of a short broad job crafting scale. *Group & Organization Management*—3 October 2023. https://doi.org/10.1177/10596011231208924.
Vandenberg, R. J. (2002). Toward a fuller understanding of and improvement in measurement invariance methods and procedures. *Organizational Research Methods, 5*, 139–158.
Widaman, K. F., & Reise, S. P. (1997). Exploring the measurement invariance of psychological instruments: Applications in the substance use domain. In K. J. Bryant, M. Windle, & S. G. West (Eds.), *The science of prevention: Methodological advances from alcohol and substance abuse research* (pp. 281–324). American Psychological Association.
Williams, L. J., & Anderson, S. E. (1991). Job satisfaction and organizational commitment as predictors of organizational citizenship and in-role behaviors. *Journal of Management, 17*(3), 601–617.

Dragos Iliescu is Professor of Psychology with the University of Bucharest. Dragos Iliescu has served in various capacities for a number of national and international professional associations; he is a Past-President (2016–2018) of the International Test Commission (ITC). He is the Editor-in-Chief for the European Journal of Psychological Assessment, and the author of over 200 scientific papers, book chapters and books, among them the co-Editor of the acclaimed ITC International Handbook of Testing and Assessment, published in 2016 by Oxford University Press, and the author of an important monography (Adapting tests in linguistic and cultural situations) published with Cambridge University Press.

Andreea Butucescu holds a doctorate in Organizational Psychology and has graduated two postdoctoral programs in the same domain. She is a lecturer at the University of Bucharest. Andreea has won several awards and scholarships for scientific and professional performance and is currently a member of the executive committee of the Romanian Association of Work and Organizational Psychology.

Andreea Corbeanu is Lecturer in Work and Organisational Psychology in the Department of Work and Employment Studies at the Kemmy Business School, University of Limerick and affiliated with the Department of Cognitive Science, Faculty of Psychology and Educational Sciences, University of Bucharest. Her research interests are currently centered around individual differences and job attitudes, in the context of employee performance. As a practitioner, Andreea has worked on numerous consulting projects. She is currently the administrative secretary of the European Association of Work and Organizational Psychology, and an active member of several research-focused endeavors.

Roxana Spinu holds a Ph.D. in Organizational Psychology and is affiliated with the Department of Cognitive Science at the Faculty of Psychology and Educational Sciences, University of Bucharest. Her research interests center on the ergonomic design of employee assessment reports and the overall efficiency of decision-making processes in human resources. As a practitioner, Roxana has worked with consulting firms like SHL and SkillTests and contributed to the ResearchCentral project. She is currently collaborating with TestCentral, where she is involved in the development and production of training programs for the administration and interpretation of psychological tests.

Chapter 4
Thriving or Depleted? Profiles of Burnout and Work Engagement in Academia

Hans De Witte and Anahí Van Hootegem

Studies on occupational stress in the general population show that the education sector (and especially teachers) reports higher levels of occupational stress (Smith et al., 2000) and lower levels of physical health and psychological well-being (Johnson et al., 2005). Large-scale studies in several countries around the globe suggest that occupational stress is also high in the specific education subsector of academia (Catano et al., 2010; Tytherleigh et al., 2005; Winefield et al., 2003). Quite a few studies have even reported that academic staff members experience lower levels of psychological well-being compared to other professional categories and community samples (Kinman, 2001; Kinman et al., 2006; Winefield et al., 2003). Several stressors have been found to explain their ill-being, such as excessive workload and inadequate resources (see, for example, Kinman, 2001). The study by Tytherleigh and her colleagues adds that occupational stress is not limited to academics (such as professors and researchers) but also extends to non-academic categories, such as administrative and clerical staff, and support roles (Tytherleigh et al., 2005; see also Winefield et al., 2003). Studies on PhD students show that this group is at particular risk (Editorial Nature Cell Biology, 2018). In Belgium, Levecque et al. (2017) reported that 39.5% of the surveyed PhD students scored

H. De Witte (✉)
Research Group Work, Organizational and Personnel Psychology (O2L-WOPP), FPPW, KU Leuven, Leuven, Belgium

Optentia Research Unit, North-West University, Vanderbijlpark, South Africa
e-mail: hans.dewitte@kuleuven.be

A. Van Hootegem
Research Group Work, Organizational and Personnel Psychology (O2L-WOPP), FPPW, KU Leuven, Leuven, Belgium

School of psychology, speech, and hearing, University of Canterbury, Canterbury, New Zealand
e-mail: anahi.vanhootegem@canterbury.ac.nz

L. C. Roll et al. (eds.), *Global Perspectives on Job Insecurity in Higher Education*, Aligning Perspectives on Health, Safety and Well-Being,
https://doi.org/10.1007/978-3-031-85772-0_4

above the cut-off point for mental disorders on the GHQ-12, a score that was even surpassed (59.3%) by PhD students in Spain (Estupiñá et al., 2024). It is, therefore, not surprising that several (systematic) literature reviews are devoted to the well-being of PhD students (Martínez-García et al., 2024; Schmidt & Hansson, 2018) and university teaching staff (Watts & Robertson, 2011).

Studies, however, also show that the experience of working in academia is not entirely negative or problematic. Academia, after all, is an environment where one can demonstrate creativity and flourish. This is well illustrated by the relatively high level of job satisfaction in the academic sector (Catano et al., 2010; Winefield et al., 2003). The large-scale study by Hakanen et al. (2019), comprising 30 European countries, even showed that respondents in the education sector scored highest on work engagement across all the industries analysed. Unfortunately, no data on academia (as part of the education sector) were reported in that study.

Taken together, the available evidence paints an ambivalent picture, suggesting that the work experience of employees in academia can be (perhaps even simultaneously) both negative and positive. This indicates that it is imperative to analyse their work experience by measuring both negative and positive conceptualisations of work related well-being. Only in this way can we truly establish whether their well-being is predominantly positive *or* negative. This will be the approach of this chapter, as we will focus on the measurement of burnout (complaints) versus work engagement.

4.1 Well-Being Operationalised as Burnout Versus Work Engagement

The introduction of the Job Demands-Resources (JDR) model in the field of occupational health psychology strongly contributed to the popularisation of burnout versus work engagement as antipole operationalisations of well-being at work (Demerouti et al., 2001; Schaufeli & Bakker, 2004). Both concepts refer to opposing experiences of work-related energy (Schaufeli & De Witte, 2017): burnout as energy depletion versus work engagement as example 'par excellence' of energy excess. The history of both concepts, however, predates their inclusion in the JDR-model.

Burnout was originally described as a syndrome with three interrelated components: emotional exhaustion, depersonalisation and reduced personal accomplishment (Maslach & Jackson, 1986). Over the years, this definition was broadened to include the work of all kinds of employees, not just those who work professionally 'with people', like workers in health care and therapists (Maslach et al., 1996). Emotional exhaustion was expanded to include mental exhaustion, depersonalisation to cynicism regarding the impact of one's work, and the third factor to a broader sense of reduced professional accomplishment. Several versions of the Maslach Burnout Inventory (MBI) were developed, including a version to measure burnout among teachers in an educational setting.

Recently, a new conceptualisation of burnout was developed, leading to the measurement of the concept via the *Burnout Assessment Tool* (BAT; see Schaufeli et al., 2020a, b). In this updated concept, burnout is defined as a syndrome encompassing four interrelated components: exhaustion (severe loss of mental and physical energy), emotional impairment (feeling unable to control one's emotions at work), cognitive impairment (attention and concentration deficits, and trouble staying focused at work) and mental distance (psychologically distancing oneself from work). In this chapter, we will measure burnout according to this newer operationalisation. For a more extensive discussion of this updated conceptualisation and its measurement via the BAT, see: Schaufeli et al. (2020a, b) and Schaufeli and De Witte (2023). Note that the assessment of 'burnout' via a questionnaire like the MBI or BAT does not refer to the diagnosis of burnout, but rather to the measurement of 'burnout complaints': negative experiences of one's work in line with the components of the burnout concept. In this chapter, the term 'burnout' will therefore always refer to 'burnout complaints'.

In the Netherlands, several large-scale studies on representative samples of the working population have been conducted over the years. These studies enable the determination of the professions and occupational sectors with high scores on burnout (complaints). Note that most studies in the Netherlands only measured exhaustion, thus limiting the concept to one core dimension only. In an overview of several samples from 2007–2012, Smulders et al. (2013) reported that the educational sector showed the highest scores on exhaustion of all occupational groups. Three categories were distinguished. Teachers in primary and secondary education scored highest, whereas lecturers and university teachers scored somewhat lower (but still higher than other non-educational categories). These findings are in line with those of a more recent study in the Netherlands (Houtman et al., 2020) and an overview of US studies where the three dimensions of the MBI were assessed (Schaufeli & Enzmann, 1998). We can conclude that academics seem to score higher on burnout compared to other professions, although their colleagues in primary and secondary education appear to score slightly higher still.

The conceptualisation (and measurement) of *work engagement* is more recent, as the concept was only introduced around the start of the new millennium (Schaufeli et al., 2002; Schaufeli & Bakker, 2010). In the wake of the positive psychology movement around that time, scholars felt that the dominant negative view of occupational well-being needed to be complemented with a positive counterpart (Schaufeli, 2014). Work engagement was defined as a "a positive, fulfilling, work related state of mind, characterised by vigour, dedication, and absorption" (Schaufeli & Bakker, 2010; Schaufeli et al. 2002, p. 74). Vigour refers to high levels of energy and mirrors the lack of exhaustion, the energy dimension of the burnout concept. Dedication refers to feelings of significance and pride, and implies a strong identification with one's work, mirroring burnout's mental distance component. The last component is not mirrored in burnout and refers to being fully engrossed in one's work (absorption). These three components are strongly intercorrelated and can be measured with the Utrecht Work Engagement Scale (UWES; Schaufeli & Bakker, 2010), for which a short 3-item version was developed and used in this study (Schaufeli et al., 2019).

A study of a representative sample in the Netherlands compared various professions based on their score on a version of the UWES (Smulders, 2006).

Interestingly, those working in education were among the categories that scored higher on work engagement, along with professions such as artists and nurses. Here again, academics scored somewhat lower than their colleagues in primary and secondary education, although academics still belonged to the category of those with the highest work engagement scores.

We can conclude that a somewhat ambivalent picture emerges: employees in the academic sector appear to score higher than many other professions in *both* burnout complaints and work engagement. However, this seemingly puzzling finding does not mean that workers in academia score equally high on both constructs. The findings mentioned above all refer to relative comparisons ("group X scores higher than group Y"), and not to their absolute scores (i.e., their absolute level of burnout or work engagement). In other words, it is still possible that academics experience more work engagement than burnout, a finding that is typical of the general population (see f.i. De Witte & Thil, 2023). This suggests that we need to combine both aspects of work-related well-being to get an overall picture of well-being in academia.

4.2 In Search of Combinations of Burnout and Work Engagement

One way to look at both burnout and work engagement is to simply compare their scores. A more thorough and comprehensive manner, however, is to analyse how both variables combine: can one distinguish various 'types', 'clusters' or 'profiles' of academics in which different combinations of burnout and work engagement can be observed? Such an analysis has several advantages. Firstly, when both dimensions are considered simultaneously, this provides a clear indication of the dominance of burnout versus work engagement in a given professional category. This finding has practical value, as it indicates the prevalence of the risk group with problematic scores (as well as of the size of the group that might flourish). Next, such an analysis is also interesting from a theoretical point of view. In the literature on burnout and work engagement, there is ongoing debate regarding their relationship (see e.g., Schaufeli & De Witte, 2017). Is burnout the 'exact reverse' of work engagement, with each concept positioned at opposite poles of a single dimension (Maslach & Leiter, 1997)? Or are they distinct yet negatively correlated forms of work-related well-being, as argued by Schaufeli and colleagues (Schaufeli & Salanova, 2014)? This means that the negative correlation between both variables will not be maximal. These views have consequences for the combinations one can observe. The idea of perfectly opposing poles suggests that one can only distinguish combinations that slide from a 'high burnout/low work engagement' pole to a 'low burnout/high work engagement' pole. In this view, one can only score high on one construct *and* low on the other, not high on both as they are antagonistic. Positions in between are obviously also possible (moderate scores on both variables). The idea of *not perfectly* negatively related constructs allows some minority combinations that score high on both variables, and combinations that score low on both, as the correlation between burnout and work engagement is not perfect (e.g. not exactly '-1.00'). Obviously, most combinations will also reflect the negative association between both variables (e.g. ranging from 'high burnout/low work engagement' to 'low burnout/high work engagement'). In other words: the spectrum of possible combinations is much larger when one assumes burnout and work engagement to be negatively related, but not perfectly antagonistic concepts.

Studies in the literature are, thus far, inconclusive. The number of types varies, firstly, between two (e.g., Innanen et al., 2014; Salmela-Aro et al., 2019) and five (e.g. Gillet et al., 2022; Moeller et al., 2018; Van der Vaart & de Beer, 2021). Next, some studies find the types to be situated on a continuum from 'high burnout/low work engagement' to 'low burnout/high work engagement' (González-Rico et al., 2022; Innanen et al., 2014; Mäkikangas et al., 2014; Salmela-Aro et al., 2019). Other studies present a more diverse and heterogeneous set of combinations, distinguishing both a 'high-high' type (Holmström et al., 2023; Lombardero-Posada et al., 2023; Moeller et al., 2018; Van der Vaart & de Beer, 2021) and a 'low-low' type (Lombardero-Posada et al., 2023; Moeller et al., 2018). The results of the extant studies are, however, difficult to compare, as the methods, samples, and measures often differ. For instance, some studies focus on a heterogeneous sample (e.g., Van der Vaart & de Beer, 2021), while others sample a specific subset of the population, such as social workers or teachers (Holmström et al., 2023; Salmela-Aro et al., 2019). Additionally, the variability in methods complicates the comparison, as some scholars use cluster analysis (Lombardero-Posada et al., 2023), whereas others prefer latent class analysis (Van der Vaart & de Beer, 2021) or latent profile analysis (e.g. Holmström et al., 2023; González-Rico et al., 2022; Innanen et al., 2014).

The inspiration for the analysis in this chapter comes from a previous study on a large-scale dataset of more than 4000 employed respondents of a big university in the Flemish part of Belgium in 2015 (De Witte 2019a, 2019b). The sample consisted of professors, PhD students, post docs and administrative personnel, thus covering the full heterogeneity of those working at a university. The online questionnaire measured various job characteristics (work related demands and resources), aspects of well-being, such as job satisfaction, burnout and work engagement, attitudes towards the organisation and demographical variables. A cluster analysis was performed on two variables: exhaustion (as indicator of burnout) and vigour (as an indicator of work engagement). The analysis identified three distinct types, who experienced their job in similar ways.

The first type scored highest on exhaustion and lowest on vigour. These respondents were rather fatigued and were consequently labelled the '*tired'*. This type comprised 19% of the respondents. Age, staff status, and language were associated with this type. Those who spoke English were overrepresented, in contrast to those who spoke Flemish, suggesting that non-native employees had a higher probability of becoming 'tired'. The respondents of this type were, on average, younger, likely because this type was also overrepresented among PhD students. The associations in terms of job characteristics were even more pronounced, showing higher scores for job demands (such as workload) and lower scores for job resources (such as autonomy and skill utilisation). These results align with the logic of the JDR-model (Demerouti et al., 2001; Schaufeli & Bakker, 2004) and suggest that this type corresponds to Karasek's 'high strain' job type (Karasek & Theorell, 1990).

The *'enthusiasts'* were the antipole of the 'tired' group. This type scored highest on vigour and lowest on exhaustion, consistently showing a high level of energy, in contrast to the consistently low energy levels of the tired group. Approximately 44% of the respondents belonged to this cluster. Two demographic variables characterised this type: age and staff status. Respondents in this cluster were, on average, older, likely because professors and post-docs were overrepresented among the enthusiasts, mirroring the pattern of the tired. The high scores on various job resources were particularly striking, including autonomy, skill utilisation, role clarity and social support. These higher levels of resources likely enabled them to become more energised by working. This finding again aligns well with the logic of the JDR-model (Demerouti et al., 2001; Schaufeli & Bakker, 2004), suggesting that especially work related resources are conductive to work engagement.

In between these two antipodal types (tired and enthusiasts), a third type emerged with moderate scores on vigour and exhaustion. This group, referred to as the '*moderates*,' comprised 37% of the respondents. Notably, their score on vigour exceeded their exhaustion score, suggesting that they were more engaged than exhausted overall. Younger respondents and administrative staff were particularly overrepresented in this group. As their label suggests, their scores on various job characteristics were also moderate.

These findings indicate that, within this Belgian academic sample, work engagement was more prevalent than burnout, as the enthusiasts (and to some extent the moderates) outnumbered the tired group. Additionally, it was striking that the three types appeared to align along a single dimension, ranging from exhausted (or burned out) to engaged, consistent with Maslach and Leiter's (1997) conceptualisation of burnout and work engagement as perfectly opposing ends of a spectrum. Notably, no type scoring high on both burnout and work engagement was identified, nor was there a type with low scores on both.

4.3 Research Questions

In this chapter, we will analyse the combination of burnout complaints and work engagement among academics by means of a latent profile analysis. In this exploratory, descriptive study, we will analyse the following research questions:

1. **How many profiles can be distinguished?** In line with the literature discussed above, one could expect between two and five profiles.
2. **What is the *content* of these profiles?** More precisely, we will analyse whether these profiles align with the antipodal one-dimensional view of Maslach and

Leiter (1997) versus the less strictly negatively correlated conceptualisation of Schaufeli and colleagues (Schaufeli & Salanova, 2014).

3. **What is the size of each profile, and what does the comparison tell us about the dominance of burnout compared to work engagement?** We will also compare the means of both variables for the total sample, as this will also answer this research question in a somewhat less sophisticated way.
4. **What are the associations between the various profiles and (a) demographic variables (e.g., country, professional position, age, gender, etc.), (b) quantitative and qualitative job insecurity, and (c) several outcome variables related to well-being and organizational behaviours?** Because the questionnaire used in this international study did not include a full set of work-related demands and resources, which limits the analysis of job characteristics, we will only focus on job insecurity. This variable is however central to this edited volume, and previous studies have identified job insecurity as a crucial risk factor for well-being in academia (Editorial, Nature Cell Biology, 2018; Tytherleigh et al., 2005).

4.4 Method

4.4.1 Dataset and Measures

The analysis will be performed on the total dataset (ten countries), as presented in Chap. 1 (n = 4743; for a description of the sample characteristics, see Chap. 1 (Roll et al., 2025)). All measures are presented in Chap. 1, and their cross-cultural equivalence was analysed and discussed in Chap. 2 (Jiang et al., 2025) and Chap. 3 (Iliescu et al., 2025). The latent profile analysis will be performed on the items for burnout (a 4-item version of the BAT; Schaufeli et al., 2020a; see also Hadžibajramović et al., 2024) and work engagement (the 3-items of the UWES-3; Schaufeli et al., 2019). Both variables were assessed with a scale from 1 ('never')—7 ('every day'). Quantitative and qualitative job insecurity were measured with Vander Elst et al. (2014) and Fischmann et al. (2022) respectively (scale range 1 ('strongly disagree')—5 ('strongly agree')). The equivalence of both job insecurity scales was analysed and discussed in Chap. 2 (Jiang et al., 2025). Job satisfaction, mental health and physical health were each measured with one item (job satisfaction on a 7-point scale from 1 ('highly dissatisfied') to 7 ('highly satisfied'), mental and physical health on a 5-point scale from 1 ('very poor' to 5 'very good')). Four aspects of organisational behaviour will be analysed. In-role performance, extra-role performance and innovative work behaviour were scored on a 5-point scale, ranging from 1 ('strongly disagree') to– 5 ('strongly agree'). Counterproductive behaviours were measured on a 7-point scale (1 = 'never'; 7 = 'daily').

4.4.2 Preliminary Analyses

The analyses were conducted using Mplus 8.3 software. We used a full information maximum likelihood estimator with robust standard errors (MLR). We first assessed the measurement invariance of burnout and work engagement across the ten countries. The configural measurement model of burnout generated an acceptable fit to the data (χ^2 (20) = 99.201, CFI = 0.977, TLI = 0.930, RMSEA = 0.091, SRMR = 0.024). When proceeding to a metric invariance model, the modification indices indicated that some adjustments needed to be made. For Romania and Croatia, we freed the item referring to exhaustion and the item referring to emotional control, respectively. This resulted in a model with an acceptable fit (χ^2 (20) = 99.201, CFI = 0.960, TLI = 0.947, RMSEA = 0.079, SRMR = 0.052). Since a scalar invariance model generated a poor fit to the data, we proceeded with a metric invariance model. The configural measurement model of work engagement resulted in a good fit after having to fix the residual variance of the dedication item in China (χ^2 (1) = 1.467, CFI = 1.000, TLI = 0.995, RMSEA = 0.031, SRMR = 0.002), due to a negative, albeit insignificant, residual variance. The modification indices of the metric invariance model also indicated that some changes needed to be implemented to obtain acceptable model fit. After freeing the dedication item in Romania and the absorption item in Belgium, the metric model generated a good fit to the data (χ^2 (17) = 50.157, CFI = 0.989, TLI = 0.981, RMSEA = 0.064, SRMR = 0.081). As a scalar invariance model resulted in a poor model fit, we advanced with a metric invariance model.

For both burnout and work engagement we saved factor scores from their respective metric invariance measurement models. We obtained one composite factor based on the four burnout items, and one based on the three work engagement items. Unlike latent factors, factor scores do not explicitly control for measurement error. However, they allow to preserve the measurement invariance structure when continuing with a pooled data set. In addition, factor scores partially take measurement error into account by assigning more weight to items with less measurement error, thereby making them a more reliable alternative than scale scores (Skrondal & Laake, 2001).

4.4.3 Latent Profile Analysis

Latent profile analysis was conducted using Mplus 8.3, and with a full information maximum likelihood estimator with robust standard errors (MLR). The factor scores of burnout and work engagement were used in one pooled dataset. We controlled for country to take into account any systematic country effects (Abadie et al., 2017) by regressing class membership on nine dummy variables, with Belgium as the reference category. The latent profile analyses were run with 5000 random sets of start values and 1000 iterations. To decide on the number of profiles, a number of fit statistics were consulted (Nylund et al., 2007). We assessed the Bayesian information criterion (BIC), for which lower values indicate a superior class solution. In addition, we evaluated the adjusted Lo-Mendell-Rubin likelihood ratio test, which examines whether a solution with k + 1 classes results in a significantly better fit than a solution with k classes. We also inspected the entropy and average posterior probabilities (AvePP), for which values closer to one indicate clearer class separation (Clark & Muthén, 2009). To conclude with, we evaluated the meaningfulness of the class solution and the proportion of the smallest class, which should contain at least 5% of the sample (Wickrama et al., 2016).

4.5 Results

4.5.1 Latent Profile Solution

The BIC continued to decrease as the number of classes increased. When this is the case, an 'elbow plot' can provide a graphical illustration of the improvement in fit per additional profile (Morin et al., 2011). The optimal number of profiles corresponds with the point after which the slope flattens in the plot (see Fig. 4.1). In the current study, the plot demonstrates that the fit gains flatten between three and four profiles. Both the three and the four-profile solution were statistically sound (see Table 4.1). However, as the entropy and AvePP indicated that the classification

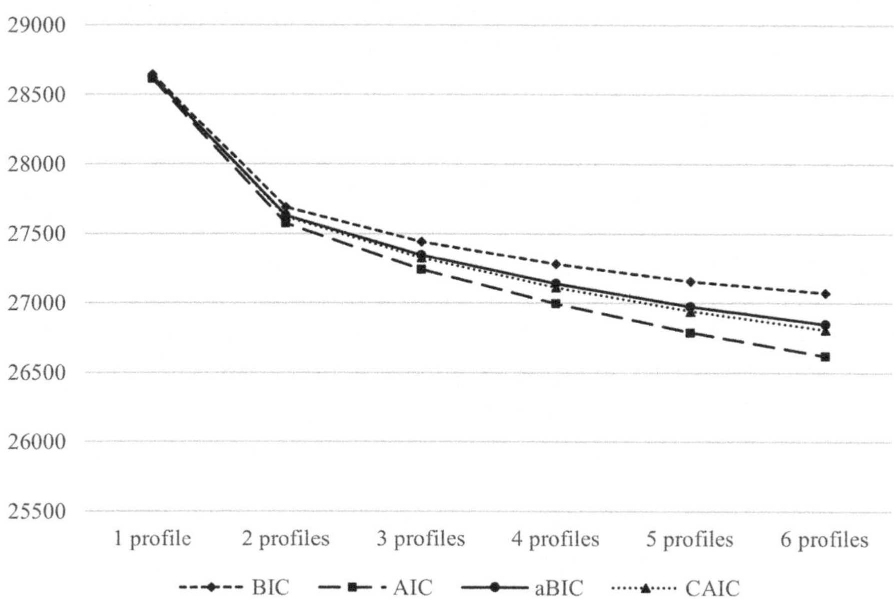

Fig. 4.1 Scores of the various latent profile solutions on fit statistics

Table 4.1 Results of the latent profile analysis

No. of trajectories	logL	No. free parameters	BIC	aLMR p value	Entropy	Latent trajectory proportions	AvePP
1	−14301.115	23	28644.538			100	
2	−13768.752	18	27689.81	.000	.822	22.3 / 77.7	.89–.97
3	−13590.345	31	27443.003	.000	.831	7.6 / 22.8 / 69.6	.82–.97
4	−13454.470	44	27281.25	.000	.783	6.5 / 13.3 / 64.4 / 15.9	.70–.94
5	−13338.145	57	27158.61	.000	.803	2.9 / 11.6 / 6.2 / 18.0 / 61.4	.71–.95
6	−13240.098	70	27072.513	.240	.746	42.3/ 4.2 / 5.9 / 22.4 / 10 / 15.2	.71–.85

Note: logL: log-likelihood value; BIC: Bayesian information criterion; aLMR: adjusted Lo-Mendel-Rubin likelihood test; AvePP: average latent class posterior probabilities

Table 4.2 Results of the latent profile analysis and scores for burnout and work engagement

	Percentage	Burnout score (1–7)	Work engagement score (1–7)
Exhausted	7.6%	4.09	2.73
Moderate	22.8%	3.20	4.26
Engaged	69.6%	2.64	6.06
Eta coefficient		.34***	.83***

accuracy of a three-profile solution was somewhat better, we retained the three-profile solution. The results of the latent profile analysis are presented in Table 4.2.[1]

The first profile consists of 7.6% of the sample ($n = 359$). These respondents have the highest burnout scores and the lowest scores for work engagement. Their scores for burnout are also higher than those for work engagement. Consequently, we refer to them as the '*exhausted*,' as their energy levels appear to be remarkably low. Assessing the exact degree of exhaustion for this profile is challenging, given that the rating scale was altered from the original BAT scale (from a 5-point to a 7-point scale). However, a score around the midpoint of the original 5-point scale indicates severe burnout (Schaufeli et al., 2023). The actual mean in Table 4.1 is slightly above the midpoint of the 7-point scale, which might be evaluated similarly. This, combined with their relatively low score on work engagement, reinforces that this type indeed appears to be exhausted. Profile 2 consists of 22.8% of the sample (n = 1080) and includes individuals with moderate burnout and work engagement scores. Consequently, we refer to them as the '*moderate*.' Notably, their work engagement scores surpass their burnout scores, suggesting that they are more engaged than burned out. The final profile includes 69.6% of the sample (n = 3291) and comprises individuals with the lowest burnout scores and the highest work engagement scores. Given these clearly high work engagement scores, these respondents seem to have a lot of energy. Consequently, we refer to them as the '*engaged*.'

Interestingly, the three profiles identified align with Maslach and Leiter's (1997) conceptualisation, as they can all be situated on the one-dimensional continuum of 'high burnout/low work engagement' versus 'low burnout/high work engagement.' Additionally, the results within academia demonstrate that work engagement is far more prevalent than burnout, as the size of the 'engaged' profile is approximately nine times larger than that of the 'exhausted' profile. Even the intermediate 'moderate' profile exhibits higher levels of work engagement than burnout. This difference is further illustrated by the mean scores of the total sample, where respondents averaged 2.88 on the 7-point burnout scale compared to 5.40 on the 7-point work engagement scale. Calculating the percentage of respondents who scored above the neutral midpoint ('4') on each scale makes this contrast even more evident: 16.2% for burnout versus 82.1% for work engagement.

---

[1] Burnout was less strongly reflected in the profiles than work engagement, as illustrated by the lower eta for burnout (.34) as compared to the eta for work engagement (.83). The profiles thus primarily reflect differences regarding work engagement rather than burnout.

4.5.2 Correlates of the Latent Profiles

A previous study conducted in Belgium suggested that specific categories of respondents can be overrepresented among specific profiles, or reversed, that specific categories of respondents can show a different distribution of the profiles (De Witte 2019a, 2019b). To examine these associations, crosstabulations were made with seven background (demographic) variables: country, professional category (professor, PhD or administrative position), gender, age, level of education, employment contract (temporary or permanent) and hours worked (full time versus part time). Surprisingly little associations were found. Only two out of these seven variables showed a significant association with the three profiles. These two significant associations were also rather weak, as illustrated by the association coefficient Cramer's V. In other words: it proved rather difficult to characterise the latent profiles based on demographic variables. Table 4.3 shows the results of the two statistically significant background variables.

Country shows a weak association with the three latent profiles (Cramer's V: .08, $p < .001$). Lithuania, Switzerland, South Africa, and Croatia show slightly more 'exhausted' respondents, whereas Belgium and especially China have fewer respondents in this category. Belgium and China also have a somewhat higher proportion of 'moderate' respondents, followed by Greece and Romania. The 'engaged' profile is slightly more prominent in the UK, US, and South Africa. The differences between countries are, however, relatively small, with the 'engaged' profile being the largest in all countries and the 'exhausted' profile being the minority in every country. In other words, the rank order by profile size is identical across all countries in this study.

Table 4.3 Crosstabulation of latent profiles with country and professional category (in %)

Country	Exhausted	Moderate	Engaged	
Belgium	3.7	27.2	69.1	
China	0.6	28.1	71.3	
Croatia	8.2	23.8	68.1	
Greece	6.9	26.3	66.7	
Lithuania	11.9	21.5	66.6	
Romania	6.9	25.4	67.6	
South Africa	8.5	19.3	72.3	
Switzerland	9.7	19.2	71.1	
UK	7.1	20.0	72.9	
US	6.8	20.8	72.4	
Cramers' V				.08***
Professional category				
Professors	6.4	23.5	70.1	
PhDs	9.5	22.6	67.9	
Administrative position	6.2	23.8	70.0	
Cramers' V				.04*

The differences according to professional category are also minimal (Cramer's V: .04, $p < .05$). The PhD student category contains a slightly higher proportion of 'exhausted' respondents, while the categories of professors and administrative positions contain somewhat more 'engaged' and 'moderate' respondents. Here too, the rank order of profile size is consistent, with the 'engaged' profile being the largest in all professional categories.

The scores of the three latent profiles on the various insecurity and outcome variables is somewhat more pronounced, as shown in Table 4.4.

The 'exhausted' show higher scores for both job insecurity dimensions than the 'engaged'. Qualitative job insecurity particularly characterises the 'exhausted' profile, as they score above the neutral midpoint on that scale. These findings align with the literature, which suggests that work-related demands, such as job insecurity, are traditionally more strongly associated with burnout (Schaufeli & Bakker, 2004). These results also corroborate the finding that job insecurity is among the core risk factors for well-being in academia (Editorial, Nature Cell Biology, 2018; Tytherleigh et al., 2005).

The associations between the latent profiles and the three aspects of health and well-being are even stronger. As expected, the 'exhausted' exhibit the lowest scores for job satisfaction, mental health, and physical health, while the 'engaged' profile shows the highest scores, and the 'moderate' profile falls in between. These associations validate the results of the latent profile analysis, confirming that the 'exhausted' have the lowest levels of health and well-being, and the 'engaged' have the highest. Notably, the differences in well-being are somewhat more pronounced than those in physical health. These findings are consistent with the existing literature in this field (Halbesleben, 2010).

The results for the four aspects of performance also align with this pattern. The 'engaged' show higher levels of in-role and extra-role performance, as well as innovative work behaviour, while the 'exhausted' have the lowest scores, with the 'moderate' again falling in between. This pattern is reversed for counterproductive behaviours, where the 'exhausted' score the highest and the 'engaged' the lowest,

Table 4.4 Mean scores of the latent profiles on various scales

	Exhausted	Moderate	Engaged	Eta coefficient
Quantitative job insecurity (1–5)	2.56	2.46	2.26	.11***
Qualitative job insecurity (1–5)	3.50	3.10	2.68	.26***
Job satisfaction (1–7)	3.52	4.60	5.33	.33***
Mental health (1–5)	3.12	3.60	4.04	.29***
Physical health (1–5)	3.42	3.71	3.97	.19***
In-role performance (1–5)	4.13	4.25	4.45	.18***
Extra-role performance (1–5)	2.82	2.94	3.18	.13***
Innovative work behaviour (1–5)	3.16	3.32	3.69	.22***
Counterproductive behaviour (1–7)	2.28	2.09	1.83	.16***

although all scores on this 7-point scale are relatively low. Also the findings regarding the associations between work engagement and performance indicators are consistent with the existing literature in this field (Halbesleben, 2010).

4.6 Discussion

In this chapter, the 10-country dataset was analysed to explore the well-being profiles of employees in academia. Burnout and work engagement were selected as indicators of well-being (versus ill-being), as these variables have been prominent in the occupational health literature since the introduction of the Job Demands-Resources model (Demerouti et al., 2001; Schaufeli & Bakker, 2004). A brief overview of the literature on well-being in academia suggests an ambivalent picture, where both burnout and work engagement appear to be prevalent. By empirically analysing the combination of these variables using latent profile analysis, we aimed to explore and clarify this puzzling finding.

The results in this chapter reveal three latent profiles, each representing a consistent combination of scores on burnout and work engagement. A small profile of 'exhausted' individuals (7.6%) combines high burnout with low work engagement. Diametrically opposed to this is the 'engaged' profile, which exhibits high work engagement and the lowest burnout scores, encompassing 69.6% of all respondents. The 'moderate' profile (22.8%) falls between these two extremes, with moderate scores on both variables, although they score higher on work engagement than burnout. Attempts to characterise these profiles based on demographic variables were not particularly successful: only country of origin and professional category showed weak associations with profile membership. However, the profiles did correlate with both quantitative and qualitative job insecurity, as well as with several outcome variables, supporting previous findings on the antecedents and consequences of burnout and work engagement (Halbesleben, 2010; Schaufeli & Bakker, 2004).

The three profiles identified in this chapter are similar to the three clusters found in a previous study conducted at a large university in Belgium (De Witte, 2019a, 2019b). This similarity is striking given the differences in sample (one country—Flanders in Belgium—versus 10 countries), method (cluster analysis versus latent profile analysis), and variables used (only one subscale of burnout and work engagement versus a more comprehensive scale covering all components). The results reported in this chapter also align with findings from previous studies, such as a study conducted among journalists in Belgium (De Witte et al., 2013). The results of the study by González-Rico et al. (2022) also appear to align with the findings in this chapter. Similar to this chapter, these scholars examined the full range of employees at a Spanish university, including both academic and administrative staff. They identified four latent profiles: in addition to the opposing poles of a 'burned-out' and an 'engaged' profile, they also found two moderate ('in between') profiles. The comparison of the results in this chapter with those from previous studies reveals that the risk group of 'burned-out' respondents was somewhat smaller in this international study. In this chapter, approximately 8% of respondents exhibited a problematic profile, compared to 19% in a previous study in a Belgian University (De Witte 2019a, 2019b), and to about 13% in the Spanish study of González-Rico et al. (2022). Conversely, the 'positive' profile of the 'engaged' covered about 70% of the respondents in this international study, compared to 44% in a previous Belgian study (De Witte 2019a, 2019b), and to 11 to 15% in the Spanish study (González-Rico et al., 2022). These differences could be due to sample, method, and measurement differences. The main conclusion, however, is that work engagement in academia appears to be significantly more prevalent than burnout—in this chapter, the ratio was approximately 9 to 1. In other words, there were about nine times more engaged respondents than those suffering from burnout complaints. This is an important finding that challenges the often negative portrayal of working in academia in the media.

Finally, the content of the three profiles identified in this chapter aligns with the conceptualisation of burnout and work engagement as opposing poles of a single dimension, consistent with the view of Maslach and Leiter (1997). Profiles showing high scores on both variables, or low scores on both, were not found in this international study. However, caution is advised when interpreting these results, as the findings might have differed if a different number of profiles had been selected. Determining the exact and "correct" number of profiles is always challenging, and pragmatic considerations also influence this decision. Consequently, this exploratory study does not definitively settle this academic debate.

4.7 Take Home Message

The image of working in academia is ambivalent. While numerous reports highlight rising levels of stress and burnout, positive perspectives also suggest that academia is an environment where individuals can develop, be creative, and thrive. Consequently, work engagement is often highlighted as a key characteristic of academia. In analysing the experience of working in an academic environment, this chapter focused on the balance between burnout and work engagement. The main conclusion is that academia is predominantly characterised by high levels of work engagement and lower levels of burnout. The group primarily experiencing burnout and low levels of work engagement comprised only about 8% of the sample. In contrast, the 'engaged' group accounted for approximately 70% of respondents. This indicates that there were about nine times more engaged respondents than those suffering from burnout. This finding challenges the predominantly negative image of the work experience in academia and was consistent across all professional categories, including professors, PhD students, postdocs, and administrative staff. While working in academia can indeed be stressful, it is also a highly engaging environment, leading to "a positive, fulfilling, work-related state of mind characterised by vigour, dedication, and absorption"—the very definition of work engagement (Schaufeli et al., 2002, p. 74).

References

Abadie, A., Athey, S., Imbens, G. W., & Wooldridge, J. (2017). When should you adjust standard errors for clustering? *The Quarterly Journal of Economics, 138*(1), 1–35.

Catano, V., Francis, L., Haines, T., Kirpalani, H., Shannon, H., Stringer, B., & Lozanzki, L. (2010). Occupational stress in Canadian universities: A national survey. *International Journal of Stress Management, 17*(3), 232–258.

Clark, S., & Muthén, B. O. (2009). *Relating latent class analysis results to variables not included in the analysis*. http://statmodel2.com/download/relatinglca.pdf

De Witte, H. (2019a). Well-being of PhD students at the KU Leuven: Some findings based on recent studies. *Lecture at a Seminar on the Mental Well-being of PhD-candidates*, Leuven, 28 June 2019.

De Witte, H. (2019b). Job characteristics and Well-Being among Academia. A tale of two stories (and datasets). *Lecture at the seminar on Healthy Universities in Italy*, Naples, Italy, November 2019.

De Witte, H., Teugels, M., & Van Hoof, E. (2013). Burnout en bevlogenheid bij Vlaamse journalisten: prevalentie, antecedenten en gevolgen. [Burnout and work engagement among Flemish journalists: Prevalence, antecedents, and consequences]. *Tijdschrift voor Arbeidsvraagstukken, 29*(3), 287–303.

De Witte, H., & Thil, L. (2023). Méér uitputting dan bevlogenheid? Een exploratie van de antecedenten, gevolgen en onderlinge samenhang van uitputting en bevlogenheid in België in 2021. [More exhaustion than engagement? Exploration of antecedents, consequences and interrelation of exhaustion and work engagement in Belgium in 2021]. In L. Thil et al. (Eds.), *Jobkwaliteit in België in 2021. Analyse aan de hand van de Europese enquête naar de arbeidsomstandigheden (Ewc(t)s) 2021* (pp. 228–247). HIVA KU Leuven.

Demerouti, E., Bakker, A. B., Nachreiner, F., & Schaufeli, W. B. (2001). The job Demands-Resources model of burn-out. *Journal of Applied Psychology, 86*(3), 499–512.

Editorial. (2018). A PhD state of mind. *Nature Cell Biology, 20*, 363. https://doi.org/10.1038/s41556-018-0085-4

Estupiñá, F. J., Santalla, Á., Prieto-Vila, M., Sanz, A., & Larroy, C. (2024). Mental health in doctoral students: Individual, academic, and organizational predictors. *Psicothema, 36*(2), 123–132. https://doi.org/10.7334/psicothema2023.156

Fischmann, G., De Witte, H., Sulea, C., Vander Elst, T., De Cuyper, N., & Iliescu, D. (2022). Validation of a short and generic qualitative job insecurity scale (QUAL-JIS). *European Journal of Career Assessment, 38*(5), 397–411. https://doi.org/10.1027/1015-5759/a000674

Gillet, N., Morin, A. J. S., & Blais, A. R. (2022). A Multilevel Person-Centered Perspective on the Role of Job Demands and Resources for Employees' Job Engagement and Burnout Profiles. *Group and Organization Management, 49*, 1–52. https://doi.org/10.1177/10596011221100893

González-Rico, P., Guerrero-Barona, E., Chambel, M. J., & Guerrero-Molina, M. (2022). Well-Being at work: Burnout and engagement profiles of university workers. *International Journal of Environmental Research and Public Health, 19*(23), 15436. https://doi.org/10.3390/ijerph192315436

Hadžibajramović, E., Schaufeli, W. B., & De Witte, H. (2024). The ultra-short version of the Burnout Assessment Tool (BAT4)—development, validation, and measurement invariance across countries, age and gender. *PLoS ONE, 19*(2), e0297843. https://doi.org/10.1371/journal.pone.0297843

Hakanen, J., Ropponen, A., De Witte, H., & Schaufeli, W. (2019). Testing demands and resources as determinants of vitality among different employment contract groups. A study in 30 European countries. *International Journal of Environmental Research and Public Health, 16*(24), 4951. https://doi.org/10.3390/ijerph16244951

Halbesleben, J. (2010). A meta-analysis of work engagement: Relationships with burnout, demands, resources, and consequences. In A. B. Bakker & M. P. Leiter (Eds.), *Work engagement: A handbook of essential theory and research* (Vol. 2010, pp. 102–117). Psychology Press.

Holmström, A., Tuominen, H., Laasanen, M., & Veermans, M. (2023). Teachers' work engagement and burnout profiles: Associations with sense of efficacy and interprofessional collaboration in school. *Teaching and Teacher Education, 132*, 104251. https://doi.org/10.1016/j.tate.2023.104251

Houtman, I., Kraan, K., Rosenkrantz, N., Bouwens, L., Van den Bergh, R., Venema, A., Teeuwen, P., Verhoeff, H., Schoone, M., van der Zwaan, J. S., & Hummel, L. (2020). *Burn-out. Oorzaken, gevolgen en risico-groepen. Eindrapport. [Burnout: Origins, consequences and risk groups. Final report]*. Leiden: TNO.

Iliescu, D., Butucescu, A., Corbeanu, A., & Spinu, R. (2025, this volume). The cross-cultural equivalence of predictor, moderator, and outcome variables related to job insecurity in academic settings: A maximum likelihood alignment approach. In L. C. Roll, H. De Witte, & S. Rothmann (Eds.), *Global perspectives on job insecurity in higher education: Precarity in the ivory tower* (pp. 67–93). Springer.

Innanen, H., Tolvanen, A., & Salmela-Aro, K. (2014). Burnout, work engagement and workaholism among highly educated employees: Profiles, antecedents and outcomes. *Burnout Research, 1*(1), 38–49. https://doi.org/10.1016/j.burn.2014.04.001

Jiang, L., Bazzoli, A., Jenkins, M. J., & Probst, T. M. (2025, this volume). Job insecurity within higher education: An assessment of measurement invariance and global trends. In L. C. Roll, H. De Witte, & S. Rothmann (Eds.), *Global perspectives on job insecurity in higher education: Precarity in the ivory tower* (pp. 37–66). Springer.

Johnson, S., Cooper, C., Cartwright, S., Donald, I., Taylor, P., & Millet, C. (2005). The experience of work-related stress across occupations. *Journal of Managerial Psychology, 20*(2), 178–187.

Karasek, R. A., & Theorell, T. (1990). *Healthy work: Stress, productivity and the reconstruction of working life*. Basic Books.

Kinman, G. (2001). Pressure points: A review of research on stressors and strains in UK academics. *Educational Psychology, 21*(4), 473–492.

Kinman, G., Jones, F., & Kinamn, R. (2006). The Well-being of the UK Academy, 1998–2004. *Quality in Higher Education, 12*(1), 15–27.

Levecque, K., Anseel, F., de Beuckelaer, A., van der Heyden, J., & Gisle, L. (2017). Work organization and mental health problems in PhD students. *Research Policy, 46*(4), 868–879. https://doi.org/10.1016/j.respol.2017.02.008

Lombardero-Posada, X. M., Murcia-Álvarez, E., Aguiar-Fernández, F. J., Méndez-Fernández, A. B., & González-Fernández, A. (2023). Burned out, engaged, both, or neither? Exploring engagement and burnout profiles among social workers in Spain. *Social Work, 68*(2), 131–140. https://doi.org/10.1093/sw/swad002

Mäkikangas, A., Kinnunen, S., Rantanen, J., Mauno, S., Tolvanen, A., & Bakker, A. B. (2014). Association between vigor and exhaustion during the workweek: A person-centered approach to daily assessments. *Anxiety, Stress and Coping, 27*(5), 555–575. https://doi.org/10.1080/10615806.2013.860968

Martínez-García, I., De Witte, H., García-Martínez, J., & Cano-García, F.J. (2024). A systematic review and a comprehensive approach to PhD students' mental Wellbeing. *Applied Psychology: Health and Well-Being,16,* 1565-1583. https://doi.org/10.1111/aphw.12541.

Maslach, C., & Jackson, S. E. (1986). *Maslach burnout inventory: Manual* (2nd ed.). Consulting Psychologists Press.

Maslach, C., Jackson, S. E., & Leiter, M. P. (1996). *Maslach burnout inventory manual* (3rd ed.). Consulting Psychologists Press.

Maslach, C., & Leiter, M. P. (1997). *The truth about burnout*. Jossey-Bass.

Moeller, J., Ivcevic, Z., White, A. E., Menges, J. I., & Brackett, M. A. (2018). Highly engaged but burned out: Intra-individual profiles in the US workforce. *Career Development International, 23*(1), 86–105. https://doi.org/10.1108/CDI-12-2016-0215

Morin, A. J. S., Maïano, C., Nagengast, B., Marsh, H. W., Morizot, J., & Janosz, M. (2011). General growth mixture analysis of adolescents' developmental trajectories of anxiety: The impact of untested invariance assumptions on substantive interpretations. *Structural Equation*

Modeling: A Multidisciplinary Journal, 18(4), 613–648. https://doi.org/10.1080/10705511.2011.607714

Nylund, K. L., Asparouhov, T., & Muthén, B. O. (2007). Deciding on the number of classes in latent class analysis and growth mixture modeling: A Monte Carlo simulation study. *Structural Equation Modeling, 14*(4), 535–569. https://doi.org/10.1080/10705510701575396

Roll, L. C., De Witte, H., & Rothmann, S. (2025, this volume). Introduction: The growing crisis of job insecurity in academia. In L. C. Roll, H. De Witte, & S. Rothmann (Eds.), *Global perspectives on job insecurity in higher education: Precarity in the ivory tower* (pp. 1–35). Springer.

Salmela-Aro, K., Hietajärvi, L., & Lonka, K. (2019). Work burnout and engagement profiles among teachers. *Frontiers in Psychology, 10*(October), 1–8. https://doi.org/10.3389/fpsyg.2019.02254

Schaufeli, W. B. (2014). What is engagement? In C. Truss, K. Alfes, R. Delbridge, A. Shantz, & E. Soane (Eds.), *Employee engagement in theory and practice* (pp. 15-35). Routledge.

Schaufeli, W., & Bakker, A. B. (2004). Job demands, job resources, and their relationships with burnout and engagement: A multi-sample study. *Journal of Organisational Behavior, 25*, 293–315.

Schaufeli, W. B., & Bakker, A. B. (2010). The conceptualisation and measurement of work engagement. In A. B. Bakker & M. P. Leiter (Eds.), *Work engagement: A handbook of essential theory and research* (Vol. 2010, pp. 10–24). Psychology Press.

Schaufeli, W., & De Witte, H. (2017). Work engagement in contrast to burnout: Real or Redundant? *Burnout Research, 5*, 1–2. https://doi.org/10.1016/j.burn.2017.06.001

Schaufeli, W., & De Witte, H. (2023). Burnout Assessment Tool (BAT). In C. U. Krägeloh, M. Alyami, & O. N. Medvedev (Eds.), *International handbook of behavioral health assessment*. Springer. https://doi.org/10.1007/978-3-030-89738-3_54-1

Schaufeli, W. B., De Witte, H., & Desart, S. (2020a). *Manual Burnout Assessment Tool (BAT)*. KU Leuven, Belgium: Unpublished internal report – online.

Schaufeli, W. B., De Witte, H., Hakanen, J. J., Kaltiainen, J., & Kok, R. (2023). How to assess severe burnout? Cutoff points for the Burnout Assessment Tool (BAT) based on three European samples. *Scandinavian Journal of Work, Environment and Health, 49*(4), 293–302. https://doi.org/10.5271/sjweh.4093

Schaufeli, W., Desart, S., & De Witte, H. (2020b). Burnout Assessment Tool (BAT)—Development, validity and reliability. *International Journal of Environmental Research and Public Health, 17*, 9495. https://doi.org/10.3390/ijerph17249495

Schaufeli, W. B., & Enzmann, D. (1998). *The burnout companion to study & practice: A critical analysis*. Taylor & Francis.

Schaufeli, W. B., & Salanova, M. (2014). Burnout, boredom and engagement in the workplace. In M. C. Peeters, J. de Jonge, & T. W. Taris (Eds.), *An introduction to contemporary work psychology* (pp. 293–320). Wiley-Blackwell.

Schaufeli, W. B., Salanova, M., González-Romá, V., & Bakker, A. B. (2002). The measurement of engagement and burnout: A two sample confirmatory factor analytic approach. *Journal of Happiness Studies, 3*, 71–92.

Schaufeli, W. B., Shimazu, A., Hakanen, J., Salanova, M., & De Witte, H. (2019). An ultra-short measure for work engagement: The UWES-3. *v*alidation across five countries. *European Journal of Psychological Assessment, 35*(4), 577–591. https://doi.org/10.1027/1015-5759/a000430

Schmidt, M., & Hansson, E. (2018). Doctoral students' well-being: A literature review. *International Journal of Qualitative Studies on Health and Well-Being, 13*(1), 1508171. https://doi.org/10.1080/17482631.2018.1508171

Skrondal, A., & Laake, P. (2001). Regression among factor scores. *Psychometrika, 66*(4), 563–575.

Smith, A., Brice, C., Collins, A., Matthews, V., & McNamara, R. (2000). The scale of occupational stress: A further analysis of the impact of demographic factors and type of job. *Report 311/2000*, School of Psychology, Cardiff University. https://eprints.lancs.ac.uk/id/eprint/59753

Smulders, P. (2006, September). *De bevlogenheid van werknemers gemeten [Assessing employee's work engagement]*. TNO-Special.

Smulders, P., Houtman, I., van Rijssen, J., & Mol, M. (2013). Burnout: trends, internationale verschillen, determinanten en effecten. [Burnout: Trends, international differences, determinants and effects]. *Tijdschrift voor Arbeidsvraagstukken, 29*(3), 258–278.

Tytherleigh, M., Webb, C., Cooper, C., & Ricketts, C. (2005). Occupational stress in UK higher education institutions: A comparative study of all staff categories. *Higher Education Research & Development, 24*(1), 41–61.

Van der Vaart, L., & de Beer, L. T. (2021). Engaged but exhausted: Work-related wellbeing profiles of South African employees. *International Journal of Wellbeing, 11*(4), 88–105. https://doi.org/10.5502/ijw.v11i4.1823

Vander Elst, T., De Witte, H., & De Cuyper, N. (2014). The job insecurity scale: A psychometric evaluation across five European countries. *European Journal of Work and Organisational Psychology, 23*(3), 364–380. https://doi.org/10.1080/1359432X.2012.745989

Watts, J., & Robertson, N. (2011). Burnout in university teaching staff: A systematic literature review. *Educational Research, 53*(1), 33–50.

Wickrama, K. A. S., Lee, T. K., O'Neal, C. W., & Lorenz, F. O. (2016). *Higher-order growth curves and mixture modeling with Mplus: A practical guide*. Routledge.

Winefield, A. H., Gillespie, N., Stough, C., Dua, J., Hapuarachchi, J., & Boyd, C. (2003). Occupational stress in Australian university staff: Results from a national survey. *International Journal of Stress Management, 10*(1), 51–63.

Hans De Witte (PhD in Psychology) was Full Professor in Work Psychology at the Faculty of Psychology and Educational Sciences of the KU Leuven, Belgium (Research Group Work, Organizational and Personnel Psychology). He is academically active since October 2023 as emeritus with assignment. He is also appointed as Extraordinary Professor at the North-West University of South Africa (Optentia Research Unit, Vanderbijlpark Campus). His research includes the study of the psychological consequences of job insecurity, unemployment, temporary employment and downsizing, as well as mobbing and burnout versus work engagement. He (co-) authored about 300 articles in English peer-reviewed journals, published 30 books (14 English and 16 in Dutch; most as co-editor) and is (co-)author of about 80 chapters in English academic books.

Anahí Van Hootegem is a lecturer at the School of Psychology, Speech and Hearing at the University of Canterbury | Te Whare Wānanga o Waitaha, New Zealand. She holds a PhD in psychology from KU Leuven, Belgium, where she specialised in the relationship between job insecurity and work-related learning. More broadly, Anahí's research explores how job insecurity influences various behavioural outcomes, such as innovative work behaviour and creativity, as well as the links between job insecurity/precarity and career-related outcomes. Following her PhD, she completed postdoctoral research on the relationship between job insecurity and broader societal and political outcomes. Anahí has a particular interest in advanced longitudinal modelling and has been involved in interdisciplinary and international projects. Her recent research efforts include an interest in Green HRM. Her work has been published in leading journals, including Work and Stress, Journal of Vocational Behavior, and the European Journal of Work and Organizational Psychology.

Chapter 5
Job Insecurity and Self-Undermining: Exploring the Mediating Effects on Counterproductive Work Behavior and In-Role Performance in Higher Education

Lara Christina Roll, Tahira M. Probst, Jurgita Lazauskaite-Zabielske, and Marius W. Stander

Amidst an atmosphere of uncertainty, university staff members from different corners of the globe are taking to the streets. In 2023, Australia, India, and the UK witnessed widespread demonstrations at their universities, with staff voicing their grievances over what they see as "unsustainable" work conditions ("Contractual teachers of Plus 2 colleges demand job security", 20 June 2023; Gibney, 2022; Duffy, 2023).

Statistics from the National Tertiary Education Union (NTEU) reveal that merely three in ten jobs in Australian universities are permanent, highlighting the sector's status as one of the most casualized in the country (Duffy, 2023). Meanwhile, tutors at some Australian universities are being instructed to offer substandard assessment, asked to "skim read" student essays in order to meet untenable marking pay rates

L. C. Roll (✉)
Research Group Work, Organizational and Personnel Psychology (O2L-WOPP), FPPW, KU Leuven, Leuven, Belgium

Optentia Research Unit, North-West University, Vanderbijlpark, South Africa
e-mail: lara.roll@kuleuven.be

T. M. Probst
Department of Psychology, Washington State University, Vancouver, WA, USA
e-mail: probst@wsu.edu

J. Lazauskaite-Zabielske
Centre for Organizational Psychology Research, Institute of Psychology, Faculty of Philosophy, Vilnius University, Vilnius, Lithuania
e-mail: jurgita.lazauskaite@fsf.vu.lt

M. W. Stander
Optentia Research Unit, North-West University, Vanderbijlpark, South Africa
e-mail: marius.stander@nwu.ac.za

L. C. Roll et al. (eds.), *Global Perspectives on Job Insecurity in Higher Education*, Aligning Perspectives on Health, Safety and Well-Being,
https://doi.org/10.1007/978-3-031-85772-0_5

(Duffy, 2020). The implications of this precarious scenario extend beyond the teaching staff; they profoundly affect the students and the quality of their education.

Recent developments in North Carolina and Texas (USA) further underscore the urgency of the situation, with bills proposed that aim to eliminate tenure, the solitary avenue available for academics to find respite from chronic job insecurity (Wood, 2023). However, job insecurity in universities is not limited to quantitative job insecurity, which refers to the fear of losing one's job. Even if university staff members do not fear losing their position, they can experience uncertainty surrounding the retention of valued job aspects (De Witte et al., 2015), such as access to research funding, career opportunities, or a certain teaching load.

The experience of job insecurity can be highly demanding and has been linked to numerous adverse health and performance outcomes, including burnout, reduced work engagement and organizational commitment, turnover, and work accidents (for meta-analyses, see Cheng & Chan, 2008; Jiang & Lavaysse, 2018; Sverke et al., 2002). Despite this understanding, there remains a need to explore the underlying mechanisms that contribute to these negative consequences. In the present study, our objective is to investigate self-undermining as a potential factor that may serve as a key explanatory element in unraveling the intricacies of these detrimental outcomes. Specifically, this study examines whether self-undermining behavior mediates the relationship between job insecurity and in-role performance as well as counterproductive work behavior.

Self-undermining behavior includes self-created stress, confusion, and conflict (Bakker & Demerouti, 2018). Employees who engage in such behavior are more likely to experience higher levels of work pressure, and exhaustion, and perform poorly on supervisor evaluations (Bakker & Wang, 2020). Ratiu and Dobre (2020) suggest that understanding the role of self-undermining can help researchers identify ways to counteract negative effects on employee well-being and performance.

To this end, we examine results across ten countries (Belgium, China, Croatia, Greece, Lithuania, Romania, South Africa, Switzerland, the U.S. and the UK). Finding similar results across these countries would support the generalizability of this mediated relationship and could lead to the development of interventions aimed at interrupting this negative cycle in the future.

5.1 Job Insecurity, In-Role Performance and Counterproductive Work Behavior

Job insecurity is the subjective experience of uncertainty about the continuity of employment or the ability to retain valued job aspects (De Witte et al., 2015). Specifically, quantitative job insecurity refers to the fear of job loss or unemployment and is often characterized by factors such as job cuts, layoffs, or the use of temporary contracts (Cheng & Chan, 2008; Sverke et al., 2002). For example, an academic working on a series of temporary contracts may experience quantitative job insecurity due to the uncertainty of future employment.

Qualitative job insecurity, on the other hand, refers to the uncertainty surrounding the availability of resources, job demands, and opportunities for career advancement (De Witte et al., 2015). This type of job insecurity can be caused by factors such as changes in the organizational structure or funding cuts that may affect job aspects such as working conditions, wages, or career opportunities (Davydova et al., 2019). For instance, a researcher who is uncertain about future funding or access to research resources may experience qualitative job insecurity.

Employee performance is of the utmost importance for any organization to grow and be competitive, with in-role performance being one of the most significant organizational outcomes (Fischmann et al., 2022). Although a minority of studies in the job insecurity literature argue that it can motivate workers to improve performance (Shoss, 2017), the majority of research suggests the opposite. Analyzing data from several studies that have investigated the impact of job insecurity on employee performance, a meta-analysis found a consistent negative relationship between job insecurity and performance (Cheng & Chan, 2008). Specifically, the researchers found that job insecurity had a moderate-to-strong negative correlation with job performance and that this relationship was present across different occupational groups and countries. Other studies have found that job insecurity is related to reduced task performance, contextual performance, and lower safety performance (Sverke et al., 2019), as well as to lower creativity performance (Probst et al., 2020).

Similarly, qualitative job insecurity has been found to be a negative predictor of in-role performance (Fischmann et al., 2022). In one of the first longitudinal studies investigating this relationship, Fischmann et al. (2022) established a negative association between qualitative job insecurity and in-role performance. Moreover, their findings revealed a reciprocal relationship, suggesting that poor in-role performance can also contribute to the emergence of qualitative job insecurity, thereby functioning as a predictor for its occurrence.

Overall, most recent research indicates that experiencing job insecurity could lead to impairment in-role performance, a trend that can impact employee's wellness and organizations' profitability. Therefore, we hypothesize:

H1: Quantitative (H1a) and qualitative (H1b) job insecurity are negatively related to in-role performance.

Job insecurity may not only impair performance, but might also promote negative performance, such as counterproductive work behavior. This includes a wide range of negative and undesirable acts that employees perform to harm the organization and its stakeholders, such as taking excessively long breaks, coming late, working slower, and putting in little effort at work (Marasi et al., 2018; Singh, 2020). Deviant behavior is a pervasive and costly phenomenon that can harm an organization's reputation and profitability (Marasi et al., 2018; Singh, 2020). Within the challenging higher educational environment, staff members may direct their frustrations and stress arising from experiencing quantitative or qualitative job insecurity toward the university by showing counterproductive work behavior.

The experience of uncertainty regarding future employment can have detrimental effects on employees' self-regulation and moral engagement (Huang et al., 2017; Shoss, 2017). When employees perceive a lack of employment security and attribute their negative emotions to the organization's inability to provide job stability (Chiu & Peng, 2008; Tian et al., 2014), they may be more inclined to engage in behaviors that violate organizational norms.

High levels of job insecurity can lead employees to engage in negative behaviors as a means to cope with the resulting strain, both directed towards the organization and their colleagues (Fox et al., 2001; Penney & Spector, 2005; Tian et al., 2014). Moreover, job insecurity can also lead employees to harm their co-workers with whom they collaborate. This can occur through behaviors such as bullying, ridiculing, offending, acting rudely, or withholding important information (Bennett & Robinson, 2000; Robinson & Bennett, 1995). In this way, job insecurity not only affects employees' relationship with the organization but also has detrimental consequences for the social dynamics and collaboration within the workplace.

While Costa and Neves (2017) found no significant direct relationship between job insecurity and deviant behavior, several other researchers have reported a positive and significant relationship between job insecurity and counterproductive work behavior (Van den Broeck et al., 2014; Tian et al., 2014; Huang et al., 2017; Ma et al., 2019; Sahi & Ahmad, 2019). Accordingly, we hypothesize that:

H2: Quantitative (H2a) and qualitative (H2b) job insecurity are positively related to counterproductive work behavior.

5.2 The Mediating Role of Self-Undermining

This study explores the concept of self-undermining as a potential mediator in the relationship between job insecurity and in-role performance and counterproductive work behavior. Self-undermining as a measurable construct has only been explored fairly recently (Bakker & Costa, 2014; Bakker & Wang, 2020) but has since gained significant research traction (e.g., Döbler et al., 2022; Golu et al., 2022; Körner et al., 2021; Rațiu & Dobre, 2020; Roczniewska & Bakker, 2021). Self-undermining is a construct that is defined as creating obstacles that may undermine one's own performance (Bakker & Costa, 2014; Bakker & Wang, 2020). This behavior arises due to reduced self-regulatory resources, which limits an individual's ability to substitute an undesirable response with a more desirable one. This limitation can cause individuals to struggle with everyday pressures and obstacles, resulting in poor communication, mistakes, and conflicts (Ratiu & Dobre, 2020). By investigating the mechanism through which self-undermining mediates the impact of job insecurity on performance outcomes, this research contributes valuable insights into understanding the underlying processes that lead to the adverse effects of job insecurity on employees.

We draw on job demands-resources (JD-R) theory to explain these underlying relationships. According to JD-R theory, job demands, such as job insecurity, can lead to negative outcomes such as burnout and job dissatisfaction, while job resources, such as job autonomy and social support, can lead to positive outcomes such as job satisfaction and engagement (Bakker & Demerouti, 2017). Further, JD-R theory proposes that job demands and resources can create either a gain cycle, in which resources lead to positive outcomes, or a loss cycle, in which demands lead to negative outcomes. In the gain cycle, employees are motivated and engaged because they feel that they have the necessary resources to meet their job demands. However, in the loss cycle, employees lack the necessary resources to manage their job demands, which can lead to negative outcomes.

Job insecurity is a significant stressor and demand that can contribute to the loss cycle (Piccoli et al., 2021). Academic professionals tend to report higher levels of job insecurity compared to the general population (Kinman et al., 2006). In the loss cycle, employees may engage in self-undermining behavior as a way to cope with the situation, which can further increase the negative impact of job insecurity. Fischmann et al. (2022) identified a loss cycle in which qualitative job insecurity and in-role performance formed a reciprocal negative relationship, adding performance as a predictor of job insecurity. Therefore, according to JD-R theory, job insecurity can lead to a negative spiral in which employees may feel overwhelmed and unable to cope with the demands of their job.

Employees experiencing high levels of job demands are more likely to engage in self-undermining behaviors (Bakker & Wang, 2020), such as poor communication, creation of problems, confusion, conflicts and mistakes. Bakker and Costa (2014) hypothesized that exhausted employees lack the concentration needed to perform well and therefore make more mistakes, indicating a direct link between self-undermining and work performance. Job insecurity should also be considered an important factor contributing to a greater risk of making mistakes (Roll et al., 2019) and experiencing cognitive failures (e.g., Roll et al., 2019; Lee et al., 2024). When job insecurity leads to mistakes, employees may compensate for their mistakes by performing additional tasks, which may lead to work overload, restarting the cycle of self-undermining (Bakker & Wang, 2020).

Self-undermining weakens employees' job performance when undesirable behaviors could harm relationships or put others' performance and safety at risk (Bakker & Wang, 2020). This creates additional job demands that employees need to cope with. Bakker and Wang's (2020) research found that self-undermining is negatively related to job performance and positively related to exhaustion, while to the best of our knowledge, the impact on counterproductive work behavior has not yet been researched.

In sum, in this study, we aim to investigate how self-undermining behavior mediates the relationship between job insecurity and in-role performance and counterproductive work behavior. Based on JD-R theory, we hypothesize that job insecurity will lead to a loss cycle, in which job insecurity increases self-undermining behavior, which in turn will further result in negative impacts on

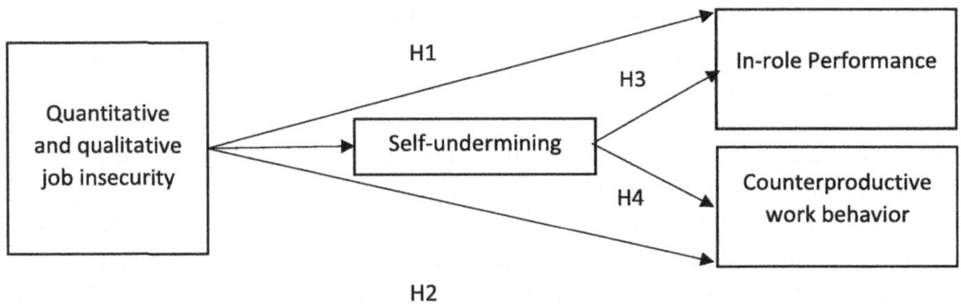

Fig. 5.1 Hypothesised relationships between quantitative and qualitative job insecurity, self-undermining, in-role performance and counterproductive work behavior. Note. Arrows indicate relationships as proposed in the respective hypotheses

employee performance and increase the likelihood of counterproductive work behavior:

H3: Self-undermining mediates the relationship between quantitative (3a) and qualitative (3b) job insecurity and in-role performance.

H4: Self-undermining mediates the relationship between quantitative (4a) and qualitative (4b) job insecurity and counterproductive work behavior.

Understanding the relationship between job insecurity and self-undermining could offer clues as to how best to mitigate adverse outcomes, such as diminished work performance and greater counterproductive work behavior, and could offer a means to positively influence insecure workers. Figure 5.1 gives an overview of the proposed theoretical model, which serves as the foundation for the empirical research.

5.3 Analyzing These Relationships Across Countries and Positions

Examining the relationships between job insecurity, in-role performance, and counterproductive work behavior within the academic context across countries is crucial to understanding the generalizability of these relationships. If the same findings are observed across different countries, it would support the argument that job insecurity is a universal stressor that has negative consequences for employees' in-role performance and increases their likelihood of engaging in counterproductive work behavior. Moreover, consistent results would indicate a shared psychological process involving self-undermining that is common despite different sociocultural and economic country contexts.

Different positions (i.e., faculty members, junior staff and support staff) within the academic context encounter unique challenges within the higher education landscape. Faculty members, for instance, often grapple with the pursuit of tenure and the acquisition of research grants to further their scholarly endeavors. On the other hand, junior staff (i.e., masters' students, doctoral students, research/teaching assistants) frequently harbor concerns regarding establishing a secure career trajectory within the higher education context. Meanwhile, support staff members may find themselves preoccupied with issues surrounding their specific types of employment contracts and working conditions. Consequently, our study examines the different ways in which these three position types are influenced by the hypothesized relationships.

5.4 Methods

5.4.1 Participants and Procedure

The study included faculty, staff, and junior staff (e.g., master's students, doctoral students, research/teaching assistants) from universities in ten countries: Belgium (N = 596), China (N = 160), Croatia (N = 722), Greece (N = 403), Lithuania (N = 530), Romania (N = 476), South Africa (N = 1096), Switzerland (N = 318), the UK (N = 70), and the U.S. (N = 372). The average age of the employees in the total sample was 41.2 years (SD = 11.29). A majority of the total sample identified as female (58,1%), 36.4% identified as male, and a small percentage identified as transgender (0.1%; 5.1% of respondents did not provide gender information). Of those who indicated their employment status, a significant portion (66%; N = 2835) worked on permanent contracts, while 1309 participants worked on temporary contracts (30.5%), and 151 reported their employment status as "other" (3.5%). The largest group in the sample included faculty members (47.4%), followed by university support staff (34.1%) and junior staff (18.5%). The majority of participants held a doctoral degree or the equivalent (38.8%), while 31.5% had a master's degree, 19.2% had a bachelor's degree, and 10.4% had post-secondary education or less. Further details on the data collection procedure can be found in Chap. 1.

5.4.2 Measures

Unless noted otherwise, participants rated their agreement with each item on a five-point Likert scale ranging from 1 (strongly disagree) to 5 (strongly agree).

Quantitative job insecurity was assessed with the four-item scale developed by Vander Elst and colleagues (2014). The scale items included "Chances are, I will soon lose my job" and "I think I might lose my job in the near future".

Qualitative job insecurity was measured using a four-item scale, which included items such as "Chances are, my job will change in a negative way" (Fischmann et al., 2022).

Self-undermining behavior was assessed with six items developed by Bakker and Wang (2020), e.g. "I make mistakes". Two items from the original scale were reworded (from "I admit that I create stress at work" to "I create stress at work" and from "I admit that I create conflicts" to "I create conflicts"). Answer options ranged from 1 (Never) to 5 (Very Often).

In-role performance was measured with four items by Williams and Anderson (1991), e.g. "I meet performance expectations."

Counterproductive work behavior was measured using the four-item workplace deviance scale by Bennett and Robinson (2000). The introductory statement to the scale reads "To what extent have you engaged in each of the following behaviors in the last year?" Participants are then asked to rate on a scale from 1 (Never) to 7 (Daily) how often they have, for example, "come in late to work without permission".

5.4.3 Data Analyses

In order to test our hypotheses, we used Mplus (Version 8, Muthén & Muthén, 2017) to conduct a series of observed variable path analyses using a maximum likelihood estimator with 10,000 bootstraps to generate 95% bias-corrected confidence intervals (CIs) for the path coefficients. In the first analysis, we tested a path analysis model using the full dataset of N = 4743 respondents specifying quantitative and qualitative job insecurity as our independent variables, self-undermining as the mediator, and in-role task performance and counterproductive work behaviors as our dependent variables. Because this is a just identified model with zero degrees of freedom, no traditional indices of model fit are available for the baseline model. In the second model, we conducted a multigroup path analysis estimating path coefficients by country. In the third model, a multigroup analysis was conducted estimating path coefficients by position. In each of these models, the hypothesized indirect effects via self-undermining were also estimated along with 95% confidence intervals. Invariance across countries and positions was assessed by comparing the model fits of the two sets of nested models (i.e., the baseline model with no constraints and the subsequent models where all paths were constrained to be invariant across groups).

5.5 Results

5.5.1 Descriptive Statistics

Using data from all participant responses, Table 5.1 presents the means and standard deviations for the variables of interest as well as their intercorrelations. As can be seen, quantitative and qualitative job insecurity were moderately positively

Table 5.1 Descriptive statistics and correlations among the full sample

	N	Mean	SD	1	2	3	4
1. Quantitative JI	4736	2.33	.95				
2. Qualitative JI	4736	2.85	.95	.51**			
3. Self-undermining	4726	1.71	.46	.05**	.15**		
4. In role performance	4733	4.38	.60	−.12**	−.02	−.20**	
5. Counterproductive work behaviors	4717	1.92	.96	.07**	.06**	.33**	−.24**

Note. **$p < .01$

correlated ($r = .51, p < .01$). Moreover, as anticipated, both forms of job insecurity were positively correlated with self-undermining ($r = .05$, $p < .01$ and $r = .15$, $p < .01$, respectively). Self-undermining, in turn, was negatively associated with in-role performance ($r = -.20$, $p < .01$) and positively associated with counterproductive work behaviors ($r = .33$, $p < .01$).

5.5.2 *Model Testing and Mediating Effects for the Full Sample*

We initially tested the hypothesized mediation model using the full sample. Because it is a just identified model, no model fit indices are available; Table 5.2 presents the standardized path coefficients and 95% bootstrapped confidence intervals, as well as the indirect effect estimates. In support of Hypothesis 1a, quantitative job insecurity was significantly negatively related to in-role task performance ($\beta = -.10$, $p < .001$). Contrary to Hypothesis 1b, however, qualitative job insecurity was positively related to in-role task performance ($\beta = .06$, $p < .001$). In support of Hypothesis 2a, quantitative job insecurity was significantly positively related to counterproductive work behaviors ($\beta = .07$, $p < .001$). However, qualitative job insecurity was unrelated to counterproductive work behaviors ($\beta = -.02$, *ns*), thus failing to support Hypothesis 2b.

In support of Hypothesis 3a, a test of the indirect effect indicated that self-undermining acts as a mediator of the relationship between quantitative job insecurity and in-role performance. However, that indirect effect was positive (.005, $p < .01$), since quantitative job insecurity was somewhat surprisingly negatively associated ($\beta = -.02$, $p < .001$) with self-undermining. On the other hand, as predicted by Hypothesis 3b, the indirect effect between qualitative job insecurity and in-role performance via undermining was significant and negative (−.022, $p < .001$), given that the relationship between qualitative job insecurity and self-undermining was positive ($\beta = .084$, $p < .001$).

Hypothesis 4 predicted that self-undermining would mediate the relationships between quantitative (4a) and qualitative (4b) job insecurity and counterproductive work behavior. In support of Hypothesis 4a, self-undermining acts as a mediator of

Table 5.2 Unstandardized path coefficients, 95% bias-corrected bootstrapped confidence intervals, and indirect effects using the full sample

Path	Estimate	S.E.	*t*	*p*	*95% CIs*	
					Lower	Upper
Self-undermining → IRP	−0.267	0.024	−11.254	.000	−0.314	−0.221
Quantitative JI → IRP	−0.100	0.011	−9.263	.000	−0.121	−0.078
Qualitative JI → IRP	0.059	0.011	5.431	.000	0.038	0.081
Self-undermining → CWB	0.688	0.042	16.377	.000	0.606	0.770
Quantitative JI → CWB	0.065	0.016	3.954	.000	0.033	0.098
Qualitative JI → CWB	−0.021	0.016	−1.296	.195	−0.053	0.012
Quantitative JI → self-undermining	−0.021	0.008	−2.570	.010	−0.036	−0.005
Qualitative JI → self-undermining	0.084	0.008	9.870	.000	0.067	0.100
Indirect effects						
Quantitative JI → self-undermining → IRP	0.005	0.002	2.436	0.015	0.001	0.010
Qualitative JI → self-undermining → IRP	−0.022	0.003	−8.395	0.000	−0.028	−0.018
Quantitative JI → self-undermining → CWB	−0.014	0.006	−2.567	0.010	−0.025	−0.004
Qualitative JI → self-undermining → CWB	0.058	0.007	7.816	0.000	0.044	0.073

Note. N = 4743; missing data were treated using FIML estimation. IRP = In role performance; CWB = counterproductive work behaviors; JI = job insecurity. Bootstrap estimates based on N = 10,000 samples

the relationship between quantitative job insecurity and counterproductive work behavior (−.014, p < .01); however, again, the direction of that effect is somewhat surprising in that quantitative job insecurity appears to reduce counterproductive work behaviors due to its negative relationship with self-undermining. On the other hand, as anticipated and in support of Hypothesis 4b, the indirect effect between qualitative job insecurity and counterproductive work behaviors via undermining was significant and positive (.058, $p < .001$).

5.5.3 Multiple Group Path Analysis Across Countries

Constraining the structural parameters to be equal across all ten countries indicated a statistically significant worse overall model fit, $\chi^2(72) = 282.77$, $p < .001$, suggesting non-invariance of the previously reported effects from the full sample across individual countries. The largest contributor to the model misfit was Romania (108.11) with all other countries contributing 33 or less to the overall chi-square. Other model indices likewise indicated a poor fit (RMSEA = .079; CFI = .835; TLI = .793). While the full output from these country-specific results are available upon request from the first author, Table 5.3 presents a summary of the extent to which each of the tested effects were replicated across the ten countries.

Table 5.3 Summary of multigroup analysis effect replications across positions and countries compared to full sample results

	Replications across positions			Replications across countries									
Hypothesized structural path	Faculty	Staff	Junior staff	USA	UK	Switzerland	S. Africa	Romania	Lithuania	Greece	Croatia	China	Belgium
Quantitative JI → self-undermining	X							X					
Qualitative JI → self-undermining	X	X	X	X	X	X	X	X		X	X		X
Quantitative JI → IRB (H1a)	X	X						X		X	X	X	X
Qualitative JI → IRB (H1b)	X							X					
Quantitative JI → CWB (H2a)							X						X
Qualitative JI → CWB* (H2b)	X		X	X	X	X	X	X	X	X	X	X	X
Self-undermining → IRB	X	X	X	X	X	X	X	X	X	X	X	X	X
Self-undermining → CWB	X	X	X	X	X	X	X	X	X	X	X	X	X
Quantitative JI → self-undermining → IRB (H3a)	X							X					
Quantitative JI → self-undermining → CWB (H4a)	X							X					X
Qualitative JI → self-undermining → IRB (H3b)	X	X	X	X			X	X		X	X		

(continued)

Table 5.3 (continued)

Hypothesized structural path	Replications across positions			Replications across countries									
	Faculty	Staff	Junior staff	USA	UK	Switzerland	S. Africa	Romania	Lithuania	Greece	Croatia	China	Belgium
Qualitative JI → self-undermining → CWB (H4b)	X	X	X	X		X	X	X		X	X		X

Note. X = replication of effect found in full sample; *replication of the *non-significant* effect found in the full sample

As can be seen, in all countries, the significant and adverse effects of self-undermining on in-role performance and counterproductive work behaviors were replicated. In other words, in all countries, self-undermining was significantly associated with lower in-role performance and greater reports of counterproductive work behaviors. Additionally, the failure to find support for Hypothesis 2b (i.e., the anticipated relationship between qualitative job insecurity and counterproductive work behaviors) was observed in each of the countries as well. A majority of countries (8) found support for a positive relationship between qualitative job insecurity and self-undermining, as well as the predicted (H4b) indirect effect of undermining between qualitative job insecurity and counterproductive work behaviors. Half of the countries found support for Hypothesis 1a, indicating a significant relationship between quantitative job insecurity and in-role performance. Additionally, half of the countries found support for H3b which predicted that self-undermining would mediate the relationship between qualitative job insecurity and in-role performance. Support for the hypothesized: (1) direct effects between qualitative job insecurity and in-role performance (H1b); (2) direct effects between quantitative job insecurity and counterproductive work behaviors (H2a); and (3) mediating effect of self-undermining for the relationship between quantitative job insecurity and in-role performance (H3a) or counterproductive work behaviors (H4a) were not consistently found. Thus, to recap, the most consistent support across countries was found for Hypotheses 1a, 3b, and 4b.

5.5.4 Multiple Group Path Analysis Across Positions

Constraining the structural parameters to be equal across the three positions of faculty, support staff, and junior staff indicated a statistically significant worse overall model fit, $\chi^2(16) = 44.861$, $p < .001$, suggesting non-invariance of the previously reported effects from the full sample across the three positions. All three groups contributed approximately equally to model misfit, ranging from 12.831 to 17.308. However, while the chi-square test indicated that the fit of the constrained model was worse compared to the baseline model, the other model indices nevertheless indicated adequate model fit (RMSEA = .036; CFI = .970; TLI = .949). As before, complete outputs from these position-specific results are available upon request from the first author, whereas Table 5.3 presents a summary of the extent to which each of the tested effects was replicated across the faculty, support staff, and junior staff groups.

Five of the tested effects were replicated across all positions. This included the hypothesized mediating effect of self-undermining between qualitative job insecurity and in-role performance (H3b) and counterproductive work behaviors (H4b), as well as the paths between (1) qualitative job insecurity and self-undermining, (2) self-undermining and in-role performance, and (3) self-undermining and counterproductive work behaviors. Similar to the analyses by country, the non-significant path between qualitative job insecurity and counterproductive work behaviors was found in two of the three positions. However, the originally predicted positive relationship (H2b) was observed among the support staff participants. Similarly, H3a and H4a (predicting indirect effects between quantitative job insecurity and the dependent variables via undermining) were only supported among the faculty participants. Thus, to recap, the most consistent support across positions was found for Hypotheses 3b and 4b, with H1a also finding support among faculty and support staff, but not junior staff.

5.6 Discussion

The study presented in this chapter aimed to investigate the mediating role of self-undermining behavior in the relationship between job insecurity, in-role performance, and counterproductive work behavior. Based on JD-R theory, we expected job insecurity to be associated with increased self-undermining behavior, which would subsequently be associated with reduced employee performance and an increased likelihood of counterproductive work behavior. Examining these relationships across ten countries and three positions and considering both types of job insecurity allowed us to test their generalizability. Therefore, we will discuss those results that gained consistent support across countries and positions while also considering areas of interest where the results diverged.

5.6.1 Summary of Results

5.6.1.1 Relationship Between Job Insecurity and In-Role Performance

Quantitative job insecurity was negatively related to in-role performance, thereby supporting the results found by previous studies and several meta-analyses (e.g., Cheng & Chan, 2008; Chirumbolo & Areni, 2010; Fischmann et al., 2022; Gilboa et al., 2008). More precisely, employees' concerns about losing their jobs were related to poorer performance of their tasks. This result is congruent with social exchange theory and the norm of reciprocity (Blau, 1964; Gouldner, 1960), which posits that any social exchange involves a series of interactions that generate obligations. Moreover, these interactions are considered interdependent and contingent upon the actions of another party (Cropanzano & Mitchell, 2005). Therefore, when organizations fail to provide their employees with employment security, they are tempted to respond likewise and, consequently, lower their work efforts. Psychological contract theory and justice theory illustrate social exchange in organizations. In the former case, job insecurity appears as a breach of psychological contract (De Cuyper & De Witte, 2006), while in the latter, job insecurity constitutes an unfair change in the rewards for their efforts (Piccoli & De Witte, 2015), resulting in a decrease in employees' work efforts that are valuable for their organizations.

Interestingly, when looking at the consistency of results across positions, the significant effect between quantitative job insecurity and in-role task performance appears to be driven by the faculty and staff respondents rather than the junior staff sample. This may be because junior staff usually occupy transitional positions with fixed-term contracts, such as research assistants, enabling them to predict the nature and duration of their employment. As demonstrated by some empirical studies (e.g., De Cuyper & De Witte, 2006, 2007), temporary employees have lower expectations about job security and experience less severe outcomes of job insecurity.

When considering these results across countries, while statistical replication of the negative relationship between quantitative job insecurity and in-role performance in the whole sample was only found in Romania, Greece, Croatia, China, and Belgium, it is essential to note that the direction of the effect was consistent (albeit not reaching statistical significance) in the remaining five countries, adding to the generalizability of the results.

On the other hand, although a minor positive relationship between qualitative job insecurity and in-role performance was found in the full sample, it was replicated only in one country (i.e., Romania) and one occupational group (i.e., the faculty staff). The existing empirical evidence regarding the relationship between insecurity and performance is mixed (Lee et al., 2018), and this inconsistency also persists in the current study. Although a minority of studies in the job insecurity literature suggest it can motivate workers to enhance performance (Shoss, 2017), other research has found either a negative relationship (e.g., Piccoli et al., 2021) or no significant relationship (e.g., Loi et al., 2011) between job insecurity and performance.

5.6.1.2 Relationship Between Job Insecurity and Counterproductive Work Behavior

Overall, quantitative job insecurity was positively related to counterproductive work behavior, indicating that the fear of losing one's employment might turn into destructive organization-oriented behaviors. However, this effect was replicated only in two out of ten countries and was not found among any of the occupational positions, offering low support for its consistency. On the contrary, qualitative job insecurity was not related to counterproductive work behavior in the overall sample. This result was consistently replicated in all ten countries and two out of three occupational positions, adding to its generalizability. In other words, our study does not support the relationship between job insecurity and counterproductive work behavior. Presumably, even in the face of changing working conditions and the associated uncertainty, employees might refrain from any behavior that would make their situation even worse (Probst et al., 2007).

5.6.1.3 Relationship Between Job Insecurity and Self-Undermining

Qualitative job insecurity predicted self-undermining behaviors in the overall sample, in eight out of ten countries and all occupational positions. Thus, the uncertainty about the future of valued job features such as working conditions, wages (which could worsen), or career opportunities (which could become lacking) appears to prompt the creation of problems, mistakes, conflicts, and confusion. These results are in line with JD-R theory, which states that a lack of resources and an abundance of job demands might lead to strain that in turn leads to more job demands, forming the so-called "loss cycle" (Bakker & Demerouti, 2017) with self-undermining being an integral part of this cycle (Bakker & Wang, 2020). In other words, self-undermining behavior is a response to a stressor (Bakker & Costa, 2014) in this case—job insecurity. As previously demonstrated by some studies (e.g., Fischmann et al., 2022; Piccoli et al., 2021), job insecurity is a stressor that might reduce self-regulatory resources and impair self-control (Vohs & Faber, 2007), resulting in employees creating obstacles for themselves. However, this negative relationship was observed only with qualitative job insecurity and self-undermining behavior, not with quantitative job insecurity. In fact, quantitative job insecurity was associated with a reduction in self-undermining behavior across the full sample, though this effect was predominantly driven by the data from Romania. Therefore, it appears that, in general, quantitative job insecurity does not lead to self-undermining behavior. This is a positive finding, as individuals experiencing quantitative job insecurity already face significant challenges.

5.6.1.4 Relationship Between Self-Undermining, In-Role Task Performance, and Counterproductive Work Behavior

The results of our study showed self-undermining to be negatively related to in-role task performance and positively related to counterproductive work behaviors, indicating that creating obstacles for oneself is related to poorer performance and more intense deviant behaviors. Importantly, these relationships were consistent across all ten countries and all three occupational groups, offering solid support for their generalizability. Although the positive relationship between self-undermining and performance has been confirmed by previous studies (e.g., Bakker & Wang, 2020), our study is the first to empirically support the positive relationship between self-undermining and counterproductive work behaviors.

5.6.1.5 Self-Undermining as a Mediator of the Relationship Between Qualitative Job Insecurity, In-Role Task Performance, and Counterproductive Work Behavior

Self-undermining mediated the relationship between qualitative (but not quantitative) job insecurity, in-role performance, and counterproductive work behavior. In other words, self-undermining acts as a mechanism that explains the relationship between job insecurity and performance outcomes. As previously mentioned, the relationships between job insecurity, self-undermining, in-role performance, and counterproductive work behavior might be explained using JD-R theory (Bakker & Demerouti, 2017). To elaborate, the uncertainty that employees experience about their working conditions drains self-regulatory resources, resulting in undesirable behaviors that undermine their own effective functioning, which in turn hinders employees' performance and fosters engaging in a broader range of harmful acts that are aimed at the organization and its stakeholders, such as taking excessively long breaks, coming late, working slower, and putting in little effort at work. This mediating effect was supported in seven out of ten countries in case of in-role performance and five countries in case of counterproductive behavior, confirming its generalizability.

To summarize, our study provides support for job insecurity being a hindrance stressor in academia that tampers with self-regulatory resources, resulting in problems, conflicts, and mistakes that lead to poorer performance and more organization-directed counterproductive behavior.

5.6.2 Limitations and Future Research

The undoubted strength of our study is that we examined the mediating role of self-undermining behavior in the relationship between job insecurity and in-role performance and counterproductive work behavior across ten countries, thereby confirming their generalizability and answering the call by Piccoli et al. (2021). However, at the same time, we should note that some of the studied relationships failed to gain support across countries. For example, we found that qualitative job insecurity was positively related to in-role performance in the general sample—a relationship previously confirmed by other studies (e.g., Staufenbiel & König, 2010). However, this relationship was replicated only in two out of ten countries and one of three occupational groups. The positive relationship between insecurity and performance supports the job preservation motivation theory (Shoss, 2017), which, in contrast to the social exchange theory that gained support in our study, argues that when employees perceive a threat to their valued job features, they may try to preserve them by engaging in a wide range of behaviors that could prove their worth to the employer.

A positive relationship between quantitative job insecurity and counterproductive work behavior was identified in only two out of ten countries. Notably, our study's results were most consistently replicated in the U.S., South Africa, Romania, Greece, Croatia, and Belgium. Discrepancies in results may stem from sample size issues, such as insufficient statistical power, or substantive cross-cultural differences. The variation in sample sizes suggests that some inconsistent results may indeed be due to insufficient power. However, significant unmeasured country-level differences likely account for most of the variation. For example, social safety nets and legislative job protections that guard against job loss may reduce quantitative job insecurity but do not address qualitative job insecurity. Therefore, future studies should investigate specific country-level characteristics, such as higher education policies, social safety nets, and legislative job protections, to provide additional insights into the relationships between job insecurity, performance, and counterproductive work behavior.

Second, our study also provides insights into possibly different ways in which job insecurity is experienced across various occupational groups in academia. For example, the positive relationship between qualitative job insecurity and counterproductive work behavior was observed only among support staff participants. At the same time, the indirect effects between quantitative job insecurity and the dependent variables via self-undermining were only supported among the faculty participants. Some empirical (although scarce) evidence suggests that job insecurity might have different outcomes among various academic staff categories. For example, Urbanaviciute et al. (2021) found qualitative job insecurity to predict lower work engagement and job satisfaction and higher burnout among administrative and support staff and junior research staff, while in the group of permanent academic staff, job insecurity was related only to burnout. Moreover, the same study found that job crafting moderated the relationship between qualitative job insecurity and work engagement only among permanent academic staff. On the contrary, participative decision-making was effective in counteracting the adverse effects of insecurity on job satisfaction across all staff categories. Therefore, future studies might provide more detailed insights into how job insecurity is experienced across different staff categories.

Finally, the current study was based on a cross-sectional design. Therefore, no causal implications can be drawn from these findings. Although our study offers preliminary support for self-undermining as a mediator between qualitative job insecurity, in-role performance, and counterproductive work behaviors, extending the current analysis into a longitudinal design to inspect whether the mediational effect holds over time would be essential. For example, the study by Fischmann and colleagues (2022) showed job insecurity and performance to be reciprocally related. Presumably, poorer performance might lead to more self-undermining and even more job insecurity.

5.6.3 Practical Implications

Job insecurity is a pervasive academic reality and is worthy of continued study. More precisely, to understand the underlying processes that lead to these effects, organizations can get suggestions to design strategies and manage outcomes of job insecurity.

First of all, academic institutions might eliminate or reduce insecurity as such. Although preventing employees from feeling insecure might seem complicated, it is nevertheless possible to minimize employees' exposure to job insecurity through communication about future organizational plans. Communication is indeed a valuable resource that increases the predictability of the situation and makes it more understandable (Jiang & Probst, 2014). Moreover, uncertainty about the continuance of one's employment or its conditions prompts employees to seek information about their work situation. Consequently, employees who receive explicit and realistic communication not only have more information about their future in the organization but can also gain more resources to cope with the adverse consequences of job insecurity. Furthermore, participative decision-making might also be a strategy that managers can adopt to reduce job insecurity, as it increases control over the situation (Urbanaviciute et al., 2021). Sharing organizational decisions with employees may enhance the information circulation rate across the organization, improve employee work incentives, and increase a sense of belonging to an organization (Piccoli et al., 2021).

Furthermore, organizations might develop interventions to buffer the negative consequences of job insecurity. Based on the results of our study, the adverse effects of job insecurity on in-role performance and counterproductive work behaviors run through increased self-undermining. Therefore, monitoring and reducing self-undermining may be a crucial intervention to interrupt the negative cycle, preventing impairment in job performance and increasing counterproductive work behaviors. By monitoring observable self-undermining behaviors, managers may be able to correct them promptly. They could intervene by providing the needed individual consideration and sufficient job resources, such as social support, skill discretion, performance feedback, and autonomy (Breevaart et al., 2014). This top-down approach was shown to help prevent exhaustion and improve employees' performance as well as overall organizational performance (Bakker & Wang, 2020).

Additionally, organizations could monitor employee self-undermining and encourage employees to optimize their job design by engaging in job crafting. Job crafting is a bottom-up strategy aimed at optimizing job demands and resources so that the job fits better with the employee's preferences and abilities (Tims et al., 2013). Job crafting was shown to counteract the adverse effects of job insecurity on employee well-being (Urbanaviciute et al., 2021).

5.7 Take Home Message

This study highlights the importance of addressing job insecurity and self-undermining behaviors to improve employee performance and reduce harmful actions in higher education. When employees feel insecure about their jobs, they are more likely to engage in self-undermining behaviors that lower their productivity and increase counterproductive actions, such as taking long breaks or working slower. Organizations can help by fostering a supportive environment, improving communication about job security, and providing resources to help employees manage stress. By doing so, institutions can enhance overall employee well-being and performance, benefiting both staff and the organization as a whole.

References

Bakker, A. B., & Costa, P. L. (2014). Chronic job burnout and daily functioning: A theoretical analysis. *Burnout research, 1*(3), 112–119.

Bakker, A. B., & Demerouti, E. (2017). Job demands–resources theory: Taking stock and looking forward. *Journal of Occupational Health Psychology, 22*(3), 273–285.

Bakker, A. B., & Demerouti, E. (2018). Multiple levels in job demands-resources theory: Implications for employee Well-being and performance. In *Handbook of Well-being*.

Bakker, A. B., & Wang, Y. (2020). Self-undermining behavior at work: Evidence of construct and predictive validity. *International Journal of Stress Management, 27*(3), 241–251.

Bennett, R. J., & Robinson, S. L. (2000). Development of a measure of workplace deviance. *Journal of Applied Psychology, 85*(3), 349.

Blau, P. M. (1964). Justice in social exchange. *Sociological inquiry, 34*(2).

Breevaart, K., Bakker, A. B., & Demerouti, E. (2014). Daily self-management and employee work engagement. *Journal of vocational behavior, 84*(1), 31–38.

Cheng, G. H. L., & Chan, D. K. S. (2008). Who suffers more from job insecurity? A meta-analytic review. *Applied Psychology, 57*(2), 272–303.

Chirumbolo, A., & Areni, A. (2010). Job insecurity influence on job performance and mental health: Testing the moderating effect of the need for closure. *Economic and Industrial Democracy, 31*(2), 195–214.

Chiu, S. F., & Peng, J. C. (2008). The relationship between psychological contract breach and employee deviance: The moderating role of hostile attributional style. *Journal of Vocational Behavior, 73*(3), 426–433.

Costa, S., & Neves, P. (2017). Job insecurity and work outcomes: The role of psychological contract breach and positive psychological capital. *Work & Stress, 31*(4), 375–394.

Cropanzano, R., & Mitchell, M. S. (2005). Social exchange theory: An interdisciplinary review. *Journal of management, 31*(6), 874–900.

Davydova, I., De Witte, H., & Job Insecurity. (2019). In E. K. Kelloway, J. Barling, & M. R. Frone (Eds.), *Handbook of work stress* (pp. 109–128). Sage Publications.

De Cuyper, N., & De Witte, H. (2006). The impact of job insecurity and contract type on attitudes, well-being and behavioural reports: A psychological contract perspective. *Journal of occupational and organizational psychology, 79*(3), 395–409.

De Cuyper, N., & De Witte, H. (2007). Job insecurity in temporary versus permanent workers: Associations with attitudes, well-being, and behaviour. *Work & Stress, 21*(1), 65–84.

De Witte, H., Vander Elst, T., & De Cuyper, N. (2015). Job insecurity, health, and Well-being. In *Sustainable working lives* (pp. 109–128). Springer.

Döbler, A. S., Emmermacher, A., Richter-Killenberg, S., Nowak, J., & Wegge, J. (2022). New insights into selfinitiated work design: The role of job crafting, self-undermining and five types of job satisfaction for employee's health and work ability. *German Journal of Human Resource Management, 36*(2), 113–147.

Duffy, C. (2020, August 24). University underpayment so rampant tutors "instructed to do a poor job" to avoid unpaid hours, former staff say. ABC News. https://www.abc.net.au/news/2020-08-18/rmit-uq-now-among-universities-accused-of-underpaying-staff/12565528

Duffy, C. (2023, May 4). University staff strike across Australia over pay and conditions. ABC News. https://www.abc.net.au/news/2023-05-04/university-unions-strike-across-australia-over-pay-work/102298204

Fischmann, G., De Witte, H., Sulea, C., Vander Elst, T., De Cuyper, N., & Iliescu, D. (2022). Validation of a short and generic qualitative Job insecurity scale (QUAL-JIS). *European Journal of Career Assessment, 38*, 397–411.

Fox, S., Spector, P. E., & Miles, D. (2001). Counterproductive work behavior (CWB) in response to job stressors and organizational justice: Some mediator and moderator tests for autonomy and emotions. *Journal of Vocational Behavior, 59*(3), 291–309.

Gibney, E. (2022). Massive strikes at UK universities over "unsustainable" working conditions. *Nature*. https://doi.org/10.1038/d41586-022-00525-5

Gilboa, S., Shirom, A., Fried, Y., & Cooper, C. (2008). A meta-analysis of work demand stressors and job performance: Examining main and moderating effects. *Personnel Psychology, 61*(2), 227–271.

Golu, F., Cotel, A., Sava, N. I., Oprea, B., & Condrea, S. (2022, July). The link between job demands, burnout, and the self-undermining of healthcare employees during the COVID-19 pandemic: an underestimated threat?. In Healthcare (Vol. 10, No. 8, p. 1408). MDPI.

Gouldner, A. W. (1960). The norm of reciprocity: A preliminary statement. *American Sociological Review, 25*, 161–178.

Huang, G. H., Wellman, N., Ashford, S. J., Lee, C., & Wang, L. (2017). Deviance and exit: The organizational costs of job insecurity and moral disengagement. *Journal of Applied Psychology, 102*(1), 26.

Jiang, L., & Lavaysse, L. M. (2018). Cognitive and affective job insecurity: A meta-analysis and a primary study. *Journal of Management, 44*(6), 2307–2342.

Jiang, L., & Probst, T. M. (2014). Organizational communication: A buffer in times of job insecurity? *Economic and Industrial Democracy, 35*, 557–579.

Kinman, G., Jones, F., & Kinman, R. (2006). The Well-being of the UK academy 1998–2004. *Quality in Higher Education, 12*(1), 15–27.

Körner, L. S., Rigotti, T., & Rieder, K. (2021). Study crafting and self-undermining in higher education students: a weekly diary study on the antecedents. *International journal of environmental research and public health, 18*(13), 7090.

Lee, C., Huang, G. H., & Ashford, S. J. (2018). Job insecurity and the changing workplace: Recent developments and the future trends in job insecurity research. *Annual Review of Organizational Psychology and Organizational Behavior, 5*, 335–359.

Lee, H. J., Tomas, J., Probst, T. M., & Lindgren, R. J. (2024). Production pressure, cognitive failures, and injuries under an insecure job climate. *International Journal of Stress Management, 31*(2), 174.

Loi, R., Hang-Yue, N., & Foley, S. (2011). Linking employees' justice perceptions to organizational commitment and intention to leave: The mediating role of perceived organizational support. *Journal of Occupational and Organizational Psychology, 79*(1), 101–120.

Ma, B., Liu, S., Lassleben, H., & Ma, G. (2019). The relationships between job insecurity, psychological contract breach, and counterproductive workplace behavior. *Personnel Review, 48*(2), 595–610.

Marasi, S., Bennett, R. J., & Budden, H. (2018). The structure of an organisation: Does it influence workplace deviance and its dimensions? And to what extent? *Journal of Managerial Issues, 30*(1), 8–27.

Muthén, B., & Muthén, L. (2017). Mplus. In *Handbook of item response theory* (pp. 507–518). Chapman and Hall/CRC.

Penney, L. M., & Spector, P. E. (2005). Job stress, incivility, and counterproductive work behavior (CWB): The moderating role of negative affectivity. *Journal of Organizational Behavior: The International Journal of Industrial, Occupational and Organizational Psychology and Behavior, 26*(7), 777–796.

Piccoli, B., & De Witte, H. (2015). Job insecurity and emotional exhaustion: Testing psychological contract breach versus distributive injustice as indicators of lack of reciprocity. *Work & Stress: An International Journal of Work, Health & Organisations, 29*, 246–263.

Piccoli, B., Reisel, W. D., & De Witte, H. (2021). Understanding the relationship between job insecurity and performance: Hindrance or challenge effect? *Journal of Career Development, 48*(2), 150–165.

Probst, T., Chizh, A., Hu, S., Jiang, L., & Austin, C. (2020). Explaining the relationship between job insecurity and creativity: A test of cognitive and affective mediators. *Career Development International, 25*(3), 247–270.

Probst, T. M., Stewart, S. M., Gruys, M. L., & Tierney, B. W. (2007). Productivity, counterproductivity and creativity: The ups and downs of job insecurity. *Journal of Occupational and Organizational Psychology, 80*(3), 479–497.

Rațiu, L., & Dobre, A. M. (2020). Job demands when exhausted: The relationship between exhaustion and the perception of job demands mediated by self-undermining. *Psihologia Resurselor Umane, 18*(1), 38–50.

Robinson, S. L., & Bennett, R. J. (1995). A typology of deviant workplace behaviors: A multidimensional scaling study. *Academy of Management Journal, 38*(2), 555–572.

Roczniewska, M., & Bakker, A. B. (2021). Burnout and self-regulation failure: A diary study of self-undermining and job crafting among nurses. *Journal of Advanced Nursing, 77*(8), 3424–3435.

Roll, L. C., Siu, O. L., Li, S. Y., & De Witte, H. (2019). Human error: The impact of job insecurity on attention-related cognitive errors and error detection. *International Journal of Environmental Research and Public Health, 16*(13), 2427.

Sahi, Q. B., & Ahmad, M. (2019). Impact of job insecurity and moral disengagement on counterproductive work behavior. *City University Research Journal, 9*(2).

Singh, Y. (2020). Workplace deviance: A conceptual framework. In *Analyzing workplace deviance in modern organizations* (pp. 1–22). IGI Global.

Shoss, M. K. (2017). Job insecurity: An integrative review and agenda for future research. *Journal of Management, 43*(6), 1911–1939.

Staufenbiel, T., & König, C. J. (2010). A model for the effects of job insecurity on performance, turnover intention, and absenteeism. *Journal of occupational and organizational psychology, 83*(1), 101–117.

Sverke, M., Hellgren, J., & Näswall, K. (2002). No security: A meta-analysis and review of job insecurity and its consequences. *Journal of Occupational Health Psychology, 7*(3), 242.

Sverke, M., Låstad, L., Hellgren, J., Richter, A., & Näswall, K. (2019). A meta-analysis of job insecurity and employee performance: Testing temporal aspects, rating source, welfare regime, and union density as moderators. *International Journal of Environmental Research and Public Health, 16*(14), 2536.

Tian, Q., Zhang, L., & Zou, W. (2014). Job insecurity and counterproductive behavior of casino dealers–the mediating role of affective commitment and moderating role of supervisor support. *International Journal of Hospitality Management, 40*, 29–36.

Tims, M., Bakker, A. B., Derks, D., & Van Rhenen, W. (2013). Job crafting at the team and individual level: Implications for work engagement and performance. *Group & Organization Management, 38*(4), 427–454.

Urbanaviciute, I., Roll, L. C., Tomas, J., & De Witte, H. (2021). Proactive strategies for countering the detrimental outcomes of qualitative job insecurity in academia. *Stress and Health, 37*(3), 557–571.

Van den Broeck, A., Sulea, C., Vander Elst, T., Fischmann, G., Iliescu, D., & De Witte, H. (2014). The mediating role of psychological needs in the relation between qualitative job insecurity and counterproductive work behavior. *Career Development International, 19*(5), 526–547.

Vander Elst, T., De Witte, H., & De Cuyper, N. (2014). The Job Insecurity Scale: A psychometric evaluation across five European countries. *European Journal of Work and Organizational Psychology, 23*(3), 364–380.

Vohs, K. D., & Faber, R. J. (2007). Spent resources: Self-regulatory resource availability affects impulse buying. *Journal of consumer research, 33*(4), 537–547.

Williams, L. J., & Anderson, S. E. (1991). Job satisfaction and organizational commitment as predictors of organizational citizenship and in-role behaviors. *Journal of management, 17*(3), 601–617.

Wood, O. (2023, April 28). North Carolina and Texas bills would eliminate long-term Job security in higher education. Left Voice. https://www.leftvoice.org/north-carolina-and-texas-bills-would-eliminate-long-term-job-security-in-higher-education

Lara Christina Roll is a Senior Associate at PwC Belgium, an External Researcher at KU Leuven (Belgium) and an Extraordinary Professor with the Optentia Research Unit at North-West University (South Africa). Her primary research focuses on workplace insecurity, particularly on how employees perceive the impact of technological advancements on their occupations. From 2022 until 2024 she has served as vice-chair of Algorigth e.V., a think tank comprised of young scholars to support research exchange and good digitalisation in Germany (https://algoright.de/). Furthermore, from 2023 to 2024, she served as an expert panel member for the Flemish Minister for Economy, Innovation, Work, Social Economy, and Agriculture, contributing to the development of future scenarios on the role of technology in creating an inclusive job market.

Tahira M. Probst is a Professor of Psychology at Washington State University (USA) where she directs the Coalition for Healthy and Equitable Workplaces lab. Her research focuses on the health, safety and performance-related outcomes of economic stressors (including job insecurity, financial strain, and underemployment), as well as multilevel contextual variables that influence these relationships. She is past Editor of *Stress & Health* and sits on the Editorial Boards of the *Journal of Occupational Health Psychology*, *Occupational Health Science*, *International Journal of Workplace Health Management*, *Military Psychology*, *International Journal of Environmental Research and Public Health*, and the *Journal of Business and Psychology*.

Jurgita Lazauskaitė-Zabielskė is a Professor and Head of the Center for Organizational Psychology Research at Vilnius University, Lithuania. Her primary research interests include employee well-being and performance within flexible working arrangements, with a specific emphasis on psychosocial working conditions, work engagement, burnout, work–life balance, organizational justice, and job (in)security. She has co-authored numerous articles and several books on psychosocial factors and employee well-being.

Marius W. Stander is a professor at North-West University, South Africa, and a management consultant specialising in the assessment and optimisation of talented individuals and teams. He is a Life-Long Honorary member of the Society for Industrial and Organisational Psychology of South Africa (SIOPSA) and a registered Industrial Psychologist with the Health Professions Council of South Africa (HPCSA). Additionally, he serves as a Mentor and Master Human Resource Practitioner with the South African Board for People Practices (SABPP). Dr. Stander has actively contributed to numerous professional organisations, including SIOPSA, SABPP, the Institute of People Management (IPM), the Psychological Society of South Africa (PsySSA), and the Black Management Forum. He has also served as an Executive Committee member of the Convocation of North-West University. In the realm of academic publishing, Dr. Stander has held positions as a Section Editor and member of the Editorial Board for the South African Journal of Industrial Psychology. He is an active reviewer for academic journals and conferences, an evaluator for the National Research Foundation (NRF), and an examiner for master's and doctoral theses at various universities. Throughout his career, he has presented over 34 scientific papers at national conferences and more than 33 at international conferences.

Chapter 6
Afraid of Losing Who You Are? Job Insecurity Among Academics Can Become an Identity Threat

Eva Selenko

6.1 Introduction

Work is part of who we are. It can give us a sense of purpose, of contributing to something larger than ourselves, of belonging to a collective. It also conveys a sense of status and standing in society; it can give meaning and associates us with each other. Most importantly, it provides an important identity-forming function (Hulin, 2002; Jahoda, 1982; Joelson & Wahlquist, 1987). This is likely to be particularly the case in academia, where academic freedom and intellectual creativity are encouraged and where incentives circle very much around peer recognition and public status (Rosewell & Ashwin, 2019). These favourable aspects of the job are often in stark contrast to the precarious working conditions many academics face: in many countries, academic employees find themselves on short-term, temporary contracts, with an uncertain employment future in the university sector (Pruvot et al., 2021). This is likely to threaten people's self-understandings in multiple ways. This chapter will present data from the multi-country job insecurity project to provide empirical evidence for these claims.

6.2 An Introduction to Work-Related Social Identities

What is identity? Identity is a multifaced, dynamic construct. We are many people at once—parents and children, citizens of certain countries and foreigners in most others, employed and not employed at different times, members of organisations,

E. Selenko (✉)
Loughborough University, Loughborough, UK
e-mail: E.Selenko@lboro.ac.uk

L. C. Roll et al. (eds.), *Global Perspectives on Job Insecurity in Higher Education*, Aligning Perspectives on Health, Safety and Well-Being,
https://doi.org/10.1007/978-3-031-85772-0_6

groups, teams, families, neighbourhoods. All these different groups can provide an answer to the question "who are you" and indicate a person's identity (Ashforth et al., 2008). The social identity approach (Tajfel & Turner, 1986; Turner et al., 1987) calls these group memberships 'social self-categorisations' that can together form a person's identity. These social self-categorisations offer the opportunity to fulfil several fundamental motives or needs for people—e.g., they provide an esteem function and the opportunity to feel good about oneself (e.g., if one's own group is better than the other) (see, e.g., Ashforth & Schinoff, 2016 for an overview of identity motives), but they also have an informative function by offering guidance for appropriate behavior, values, and attitudes. These identity categories are fluid—a person is not aware of all of their social category memberships all the time, but depending on the context, different categories will be more salient and hence relevant for identity than others. For example, when picking up their kids from kindergarten, a person will be less aware of their own occupation, whereas when they are talking to a client at work, they will be less aware of their family role. The same person will show different motivations, different attitudes and even different tastes depending on the current social self-categorisation that was made salient by the context (e.g., Oyserman, 2009). In other words, while it is true that we are multiple people at once, we are not all of them simultaneously.

The work arena offers a wealth of social group memberships that lend themselves to provide an answer to the question of who one is. For example, people can define themselves as members of certain organisations, they can define themselves as members of a certain occupation, and as holders of a certain position, the possibilities are endless. If nothing else, most broadly, employed people can define themselves as 'I am part of the employed workforce of this country' (as opposed to people who are unemployed or out of work).

In theory, there are limitless possibilities for positive social self-identifications at work, as literally, almost everything can be psychologically perceived as a social group. In reality, there are factors that make certain social self-categorisations more likely than others (Ashforth & Schinoff, 2016; Stryker & Serpe, 1994). Particularly, aspects such as whether there is competition plays a role, the time and opportunity a person has to enact group prototypical behavior, the type of group prototypical behavior itself (e.g., whether it enables the experience of autonomy and competence), the social validation someone receives for a certain group membership and the social status and esteem gained from a certain group membership play a crucial role (Turner et al., 1987; Ashforth & Schinoff, 2016).

For example, groups that are difficult to get into, that offer an elaborate socialisation process ensure that people will value their group membership once they made it into those groups and became 'official' members. Similarly, high-status groups that lend themselves for self-enhancement and growth are more likely to generate a feeling of social identification (Ellemers et al., 1988). Social contexts that offer the opportunity to enact particular work-related identities further strengthen those identities. For example, a threat or competition situation will make identification more likely. Eventually, if there are enough other people who positively validate their respective identities and encourage group membership, then identity formation is more likely to happen (see, e.g., Ashforth & Schinoff, 2016).

6.3 Work Is Part of Who We Are in Academia

According to the premises of social identity theory, work in academia would lend itself particularly well for strong social self-identifications. This is because of the long and competitive pathway that accompanies a job in academia, the nature of the job itself (and its elements of discovery and autonomy), the tight-knit social system of academia with its set of rules and rewards, and the status an academic may encounter in wider society.

First, it takes time and effort to get a job in academia in the first place, be that as lecturer, professor, or post-doc. A candidate often has to prove themselves against an impressive list of competitors in a multi-stage selection process (see, e.g., academicpositions.com). Not only does an academic career require a specialist PhD level education, it often also demands a certain number of publications and funding successes. Often, additional hurdles are in place as well, such as supportive references or closed networks. Meeting all these requirements takes many years of laborious work (under often precarious conditions). The time spent on these activities alone implies the learning of associated cognitive schemas, learned thought-action patterns, that get activated more easily (Stryker & Serpe, 1994). The longer someone 'does' academic work, the more easily this schema becomes activated and the more likely someone will also 'be' an academic, i.e., see themselves as such. In other words, the more someone does research, the more likely this activity will form a prominent part of their self-understanding, something that is likely to inform behaviors, attitudes, and self-definitions in other areas too. Additionally, passing these hurdles to get into an academic job is not simply a matter of time but involves a substantial amount of competition, and there will be multiple set-backs on the way. With rejection rates of over 80% in world-leading journals and diminishing public research funds, successfully publishing and landing grant funding is increasingly difficult (e.g., Bloch et al., 2014; Horn, 2016). Publication and funding successes require focus and determination to a level that can only be achieved through intrinsic or at least identified motivation that is self-concordant (Sheldon & Elliot, 1999). In other words, people have to strongly believe in what they are doing to keep on being persistent in an uncertain educational and academic career trajectory. This identified motivation is more likely to fortify identities.

Secondly, also the specific person-ascribed nature of research work is likely to foster self-identification. Academic research by its nature involves an element of discovering and working on new knowledge. The result of this labour is closely associated with the person themselves; for example through authorships. This aspect of growth and discovery and its intertwined nature with people's ownership is likely to inform identity. Experiences of personal growth lend themselves particularly well to seeing them as part of one's self (Ashforth & Schinoff, 2016). Furthermore, despite a growing culture of managerialism and formalisation, working in academia still provides a substantial amount of autonomy and freedom, perhaps more so than in other professions (e.g., Hyde et al., 2013). This makes it easier for a person to express their own interests and values in their work. For example, the research focus and procedures one chooses are closely intertwined with a person's own epistemology and ontology, their way of understanding the nature of knowledge and their interests. This close alignment between work and own values will foster a close alignment with identity.

A third factor that is contributing to identification with the job lies in the tight-knit social context of the 'academic world'. Most research work relies on collaborations with others, as large-scale research efforts can rarely be achieved by a single person. This creates groups and disciplinary niches that offer opportunities for self-definition and identification. Working collaboratively with equals often also allows for the observation of role models and further confirms one's own role as academic. Much research work often happens under pressure of deadlines and under scrutiny from reviewers and funding bodies. The combination of working together closely while being exposed to a competitive environment is likely to strengthen identification with one's own group of collaborators. International conferences and specialised meetings are offering an arena to foster a feeling of shared identity and belonging. Moreover, social identification in academia is enhanced by social validation by others, which is a central part of an academic's career. Some even go thus far to call academia a 'prestige economy' (Blackmore & Kandiko, 2011), where recognition by reviewers, journal editors, and funding bodies is confirming arduously developed ideas and intertwined identities. Indeed, academia mostly strives for prestige awards, which denote value within a circumferenced social system: while relatively unimportant to the wider public, publication counts and citation rates act as indicators of standing and influence in the discipline, further enhancing identification with that discipline. However, as much as getting published and recognised by academic peers can foster academic self-understanding, getting repeated rejections, being without a network (as is often the case at the beginning of an academic career) are likely to undermine it. Social validation by peers can hence be a double-edged sword.

Finally, there is also the status that working in academia can earn in the wider society, which could foster identification with the job. In many countries, working in academia—e.g., in an academic or research position—is highly valued and associated with high status, which is an indicator of occupational prestige (e.g., Zhou, 2005). Most research-related jobs fall within the ISCO-88 classification 2 'professionals' or 1 'legislators, senior officials', which correlates with perceived occupational prestige. The high skill and education, as well as responsibility and autonomy that characterise academic jobs, are factors that are also associated with the attribution of prestige. When discussed favourably, research is often deemed of being of value to society. Therefore, it is likely that in the eyes of others, working in academia is viewed as having prestige and high status. In social identity terms, because academic jobs are viewed as positive by others, they can easily serve as a source for self-esteem and feeling good about oneself (Ashforth & Schinoff, 2016).

In sum, there is good reason to purport that people working in academia will be highly identified with their job. Hypothesis 1 (H1) consequently states that people who work on academic contracts at universities will be more strongly identified with their job and the working population than people who work as support staff or as PhD students.

6.4 Precarious Work in Academia—Job Insecurity as Identity Threat

Unfortunately, despite the relatively high prestige of academic jobs, many job positions in academia are rather precarious. Cuts to public financial budgets for higher education have led to an underfunding of universities in many European countries of the south and east (Pruvot et al., 2021). This led to a hollowing out of academic institutions, with posts removed or not re-filled, leading to an acute shortage of permanent positions in institutions that could not compensate for public financial cuts with private funding.

Indeed, there exists an unhealthy, socially unjust divide in university contracts (Batterbury, 2008): On the one side, there are the 'lucky' few (often older) people on permanent contracts, enjoying the benefits associated with working in academia outlined above; on the other side, there are many (often younger) people in precariously temporary job contracts, project bound, financially more precarious with limited autonomy or opportunity to be themselves and express their values. Given the plausible entanglement of identity and work in academia, the fear of losing one's job, or *quantitative* job insecurity, is likely to threaten various aspects of a person's academic-related identity. The nature of temporary, project-based employment means that people have to change employers and project positions frequently, sometimes at high personal costs, should they want to stay employed in academia. This comes with a level of *qualitative* job insecurity on what a specific job will look like in the future, where it will be conducted and under which conditions.

Perceived job insecurity (quantitative and qualitative) will threaten the enactment and meaning of academics' work-related identity. Identifying as an academic meets several identity motives (Ashforth & Schinoff, 2016): it provides certainty about one's role and status in society, affords belonging and self-esteem and indicates competence. Being job insecure threatens these aspects of identity: where else would one's place in society be, if not as lecturer, professor, post-doc or PhD student? Where does one belong professionally if one will work on a different project at a different institution with a different focus in the future? What does job insecurity say about one's competence as academic (where a meritocratic narrative prevails, Kinman & Jones, 2008)? These questions are threatening identity.

This hence leads to two hypotheses: job insecurity (quantitative and qualitative) in academia will threaten a person's identification with the academic job (H2a) but also with the wider working population (H2b). This threat to identities will result in a weaker identification with these two groups.

6.5 Consequences of Identity Threat for Well-being

Threats to work-related identities are important, as they can have serious consequences in the workplace (see Petriglieri, 2011 for an overview): threats to important work-related identities (from various causes) have been found to reduce well-being and health (e.g., Wegge et al., 2006) and job performance (Logel et al., 2009) and even affect political attitudes (Selenko & De Witte, 2021). The ten-country study offers a unique opportunity to investigate these mechanisms in the context of academic jobs and across different country settings. Questioning core assumptions about oneself and feeling less part of the working population or less identified with one's job will affect well-being in a number of ways.

First of all, a weaker identification with the working population indicates less belonging to general society and less clarity about one's place in society, which is one of the core functions of social identity (Tajfel & Turner, 1986). Feeling disconnected from society, which is often reported by unemployed people, has been associated with lowered mental health (Blustein et al., 2013; De Witte et al., 2012). Also, a lower identification with society or one's profession also weakens support networks associated with those groups. This lack of social connectedness and support can then cause mental health problems, as social relationships are deemed core to health (Haslam et al., 2018). Eventually, feeling confused in one's self-understanding as a member of the working population or a job holder will make it more difficult to appraise whether a work demand poses a challenge or hindrance for oneself, potentially leading to less effective coping strategies (see Haslam et al., 2005, for the relationship between identification and stress appraisal).

In sum, there is reason to expect that people who feel threatened in their identity as members of the working population and who also feel threatened in their identification with their job will respond with more mental health problems, as expressed in a higher likelihood of burnout. Hypothesis 3 (H3) consequently states that people who feel threatened in (a) their identification with the working population and (b) their identification with their job will report more burnout.

Furthermore, because of the link between job insecurity and identity threat, it is plausible to expect that part of the negative effect of job insecurity on mental health among academics could be explained by a threat to identity. Hypothesis 4 (H4) hence states that the effect of quantitative and qualitative job insecurity on burnout will be partly mediated by identity threat. Figure 6.1 gives an overview of the proposed theoretical model that will inform the empirical part.

6.6 Evidence from the Study

The ten-country study offers a unique opportunity to explore the close entanglement of identity, job insecurity and burnout among academics and other people working at universities. The present study assessed two aspects of identity: personal

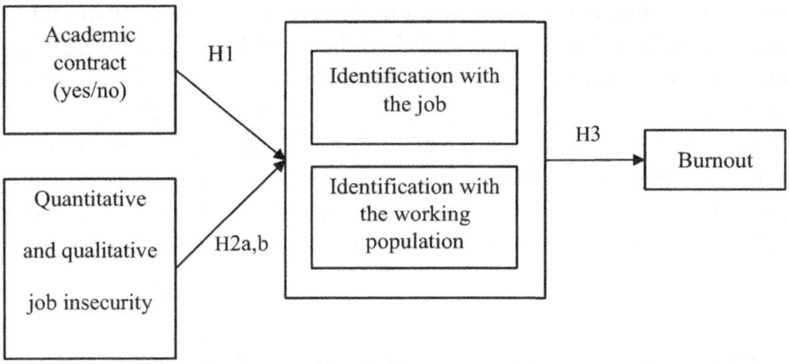

Fig. 6.1 Hypothesised relationships between academic position, job insecurity, identity threat and burnout. Note. Arrows indicate relationships as proposed in the respective hypotheses. Hypothesis 4 (mediation hypotheses) is not shown

identification with the job and social identification with the wider working population. It will employ quantitative and qualitative job insecurity, as well as the 4-item measure of burnout (see contributions in Chaps. 2 and 3 in this book for the scales used and on measurement equivalence between the samples of this study).

Personal identification with the job was measured with three items: "My job is a central part of my identity", "My job defines who I am" and "My personal identity is defined by my job". These items were based on the social identity scale developed by Doosje et al. (1995) and reworded to measure the extent to which participants identified with their job. People could indicate their agreement and disagreement on a 5-point Likert scale, with higher values indicating higher identity. Reliability for this measurement ranged between Cronbach's alpha = 0.77 and 0.92.

Social identification with the working population was measured with four items which were developed in a similar way and previously used by Selenko et al. (2017): "I see myself as part of [country's] workforce", "I am pleased to be part of [country's] workforce", "I feel strong ties with [country's] workforce" and "I identify with others who are part of [country's] workforce. Reliability for this scale was also good, with Cronbach's alpha values ranging between 0.80 and 0.91 across the countries.

In addition to the main constructs of interest, this analysis will also include other aspects that can potentially influence people's job insecurity, their identification with their job and the working population and their health: financial strain (single item, "I am stressed by my financial situation", 5-point Likert scale answering format) and previous unemployment experience (single item, "Have you been involuntarily unemployed in the last 2 years", yes/no answering format). Together with job insecurity, financial strain is part of the experience of precarity, which is related to identity and health (e.g., Allan et al., 2021; Creed et al., 2020). Next to financial strain, people's own unemployment experience will also be included to control for potentially scarring unemployment histories.

To compare differences in identification between different occupational groups at university, the entire sample of the study will be considered, consisting of people in academic positions (as a lecturer, researcher, teacher) and people in non-academic positions (e.g., academic support staff, or PhD students). In addition, age and gender will be investigated as control variables. Table 6.1 shows the correlations between the variables of interest and the control variables across all countries. Age, gender, academic role, and unemployment experience are all correlated with two or more of the variables of interest, which is why they will be included in further analysis.

6.6.1 Evidence for the Identity-Fostering Effect of Academic Position and the Threatening Effect of Job Insecurity

To test the hypotheses, hierarchical linear regression analyses were carried out on the overall sample and for each country separately to allow for a robustness check of the results across different samples. Age, gender, academic role, financial strain and unemployment experience served as control variables in all analyses and were added in the first step together with the academic position variable. Qualitative and quantitative job insecurity were then added in a second step. To test Hypothesis 1 (that people in academic positions would report more identification with the job, as well as a higher identification with the working population) and Hypothesis 2 (that job insecurity (quantitative and qualitative) would threaten identity (with the job and the working population)), two regression analyses were carried out for the two different aspects of identity. While the following text will provide detail on and explanations of the results, please also refer to Fig. 6.2 for a convenient summary of the significant relationships that were found.

When inspecting the results in Tables 6.2 and 6.3 (in which unstandardised coefficients are reported), an interesting picture emerges. There is strong support for Hypothesis 1 (see Table 6.3): academic role significantly predicted identification with the job in the combined sample as well as in almost every of the separate country samples (except for in the Chinese sample). In all countries, the pattern of difference was the same: People who were academic members of staff identified more strongly with their job than people who were in administrative support roles or PhD students. This supports the notion that academic work lends itself particularly well for personal identification. Interestingly, it did not predict identification with the working population (except for in Romania, see Table 6.2).

The results regarding Hypothesis 2 are less strongly supportive: if the combined sample results are considered, there is partial support for Hypotheses 2a and b. Qualitative job insecurity was negatively related to identification with the working population as well as to identification with the job. Quantitative job insecurity, however, did not significantly predict the two identification measures in the expected way (it even affected identification with the job *positively* once it was controlled for qualitative job insecurity—a curious finding, perhaps indicating a suppressor effect).

When inspecting the individual country results, it appears that in five countries, job insecurity (quantitative and qualitative) significantly mattered for identification with

Table 6.1 Correlations of job insecurity, identity and burnout with control variables for the combined sample (n = 3684–4740)

	M	SD	1	2	3	4	5	6	7	8	9
1. Age	41.21	11.29	–								
2. Gender	0.61	0.49	−.07**	–							
3. Academic role	0.48	0.50	.34**	−.08**	–						
4. Unemployment	0.06	0.24	−.17**	−.03	−.11**	–					
5. Financial strain	3.03	1.31	−.09**	.01	−.07**	.08**	–				
6. Job insecurity (quant.)	2.33	0.95	−.19**	.04*	−.18**	.09**	.19**	–			
7. Job insecurity (qual.)	2.85	0.95	−.01	.04*	.00	.03*	.22**	.51**	–		
8. Identification w. working population	3.93	0.82	.11**	−.04*	.04*	−.02	−.09**	−.10**	−.13**	–	
9. Identification w. job	3.48	0.96	.10**	−.03*	.20**	−.01	−.01	−.01	−.05**	.27**	–
10. Burnout	2.88	1.23	−.19**	.01	−.10**	.03*	.14**	.21**	.36**	−.17**	−.07**

Note. Gender (0 = male, 1 = female), academic role (0 = non academic, 1 = academic), unemployment (1 = was involuntarily unemployed in the last 2 years, 0 = was not)

$^{*}p < .05$, $^{**}p < .01$

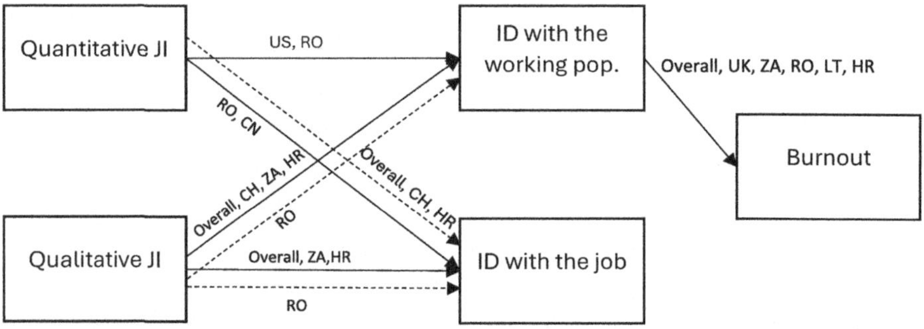

Fig. 6.2 Summary of the relationships between job insecurity, identity threat and burnout for the overall sample as well as individual countries. *Note:* The straight lines show significant effects as hypothesized. The broken lines indicate unexpected positive effects. No effect was found between identification with the job and burnout in any of the samples. CH = Switzerland, CN = China, HR = Croatia, LT = Lithuania, RO = Romania, UK = United Kingdom, US = United States of America, ZA = South Africa

the working population (US, Switzerland, South Africa, Romania, Croatia) and the job (South Africa, Romania, Croatia, China) (see Tables 6.2 and 6.3 for further details). Most of the significant effects were in the expected direction; however, rather unexpectedly, there were also positive effects. In the Romanian sample, qualitative (but not quantitative) job insecurity had a *positive* effect on both identification with the working population and identification with the job. These effects are likely to be spurious; when looking at the Pearson correlations in the Romanian sample (not shown here), qualitative job insecurity correlates either negatively or non-significantly with both aspects of identity. In the Swiss and Croatian samples, quantitative job insecurity had a *positive* effect on identification with the job (but not on identification with the working population). In the Croatian sample, spurious effects may have been at work again, as quantitative job insecurity did not correlate with identification with the job. In the Swiss sample, however, there truly seemed to have been a positive relationship between quantitative job insecurity and identification with the job, as they even correlated positively before performing the regressions.

6.6.2 *Evidence for the Health Damaging Effect of Identity Threat and the Mediation Effect*

To test Hypothesis 3 (identity threat will be negatively related to mental well-being) and Hypothesis 4 (the effect of job insecurity on mental health will be mediated by identity threat), the 2020 PROCESS macro 3.5 by Hayes (2017) was employed, using 5000 bootstrapping samples. Again, the analysis was conducted for the combined (overall) sample and for each country separately, and the same control variables were used as for the test of Hypotheses 1 and 2.

Table 6.4 shows a detailed overview of the results; please refer also to Fig. 6.2, which gives an overview of the significant results per country and in the combined

Table 6.2 Regression of qualitative and quantitative job insecurity on identification with the working population

	overall	US	UK	Switzerland	South Africa	Romania	Lithuania	Greece	Croatia	China	Belgium
	B (SEB)	B (SEB)	B (SEB)	B (SEB)	B (SEB)	B (SEB)	B (SEB)	B (SEB)	B (SEB)	B (SEB)	B (SEB)
Age	.01 (.00)**	.01 (.00)	.02 (.01)*	.02 (.01)**	.01 (.00)**	.00 (.00	.02 (.00)**	.02 (.01)*	.01 (.00)	.00 (.01)	.02 (.00)**
Gender	−.04 (.03)	.10 (.09)	.54 (.20)*	−.05 (.10)	−.02 (.05)	−.13 (.07)	.40 (.09)**	.01 (.09)	−.05 (.09)	−.15 (.10)	.32 (.10)**
Acad. Role	−.02 (.03)	−.02 (.10)	−.09 (.21)	−.22 (.15)	.02 (.06)	.53 (.08)**	.00 (.08)	−.14 (.11)	−.07 (.09)	−.01 (.10)	.07 (.13)
Unemployment	−.01 (.06)	−.18 (.25)	−.64 (.31)*	−.10 (.20)	.16 (.10)	−.08 (.21)	.15 (.18)	−.35 (.20)	.01 (.15)	.07 (.31)	.05 (.15)
Financial strain	−.02 (.01)*	.01 (.04)	−.04 (.07)	.09 (.05)*	−.06 (.02)*	−.02 (.03)	−.03 (.03)	.00 (.04)	−.04 (.03)	.14 (.05)**	−.15 (.04)*
Job ins. (quant.)	−.01 (.02)	−.13 (.06)*	−.06 (.09)	−.07 (.05)	−.05 (.04)	−.29 (.06)**	−.08 (.07)	−.06 (.07)	.03 (.05)	−.16 (.12)	.06 (.04)
Job ins. (qual.)	−.10 (.02)**	−.04 (.05)	−.10 (.10)	−.15 (.07)*	−.12 (.04)**	.12 (.04)**	−.03 (.07)	−.07 (.06)	−.12 (.05)**	−.04 (.10)	−.03 (.05)
R^2	.031	.049	.242	.119	.076	.220	.111	.056	.029	.095	.155
R^2change	.014	.032	.026	.044	.031	.051	.010	.010	.016	.032	.008
Fchange	25.430	5.287	1.078	7.578	12.920	13.469	1.960	2.139	3.535	2.668	1.351
p	<.001	.006	.346	.001	<.001	<.001	.142	.119	.030	.073	.261

Note. Acad. Role (1 = academic, 0 = non academic), Unemployment (1 = previous unemployment experience, 0 = no previous unemployment experience)
$^{*}p < .05$, $^{**}p < .001$

Table 6.3 Regression of qualitative and quantitative job insecurity on identification with the job

	overall	US	UK	Switzerland	South Africa	Romania	Lithuania	Greece	Croatia	China	Belgium
	B (SEB)	B (SEB)	B (SEB)	B (SEB)	B (SEB)	B (SEB)	B (SEB)	B (SEB)	B (SEB)	B (SEB)	B (SEB)
Age	.00 (.00)*	.00 (.00)	.00 (.01)	.00 (.01)	.01 (.00)	.01 (.00)	.01 (.00)	.00 (.01)	.00 (.01)	.01 (.01)	.01 (.01)
Gender	.01 (.03)	.04 (.10)	.19 (.25)	.13 (.11)	−.02 (.07)	.06 (.08)	.09 (.11)	.04 (.09)	−.14 (.10)	−.17 (.11)	.27 (.12)
Acad. Role	.42 (.03)**	.45 (.11)**	.95 (.25)**	.62 (.17)**	.19 (.07)*	.41 (.09)**	.29 (.10)**	.65 (.11)**	.54 (.11)**	−.04 (.12)	.51 (.16)**
Unemployment	.05 (.07)	−.35 (.29)	−.06 (.37)	−.11 (.22)	.32 (.13)*	−.26 (.23)	.20 (.22)	−.28 (.21)	.23 (.18)	.07 (.35)	−.06 (.19)
Financial strain	.02 (.01)	.03 (.04)	.17 (.09)	.05 (.05)	−.01 (.03)	−.05 (.03)	−.03 (.04)	.05 (.04)	−.02 (.04)	.07 (.06)	.02 (.05)
Job ins. (quant.)	.04 (.02)*	.05 (.06)	−.13 (.11)	.21 (.06)**	−.07 (.05)	−.32 (.06)**	.01 (.08)	.05 (.07)	.17 (.06)**	−.27 (.13)*	.02 (.05)
Job ins. (qual.)	−.08 (.02)**	.01 (.06)	−.03 (.13)	−.06 (.07)	−.09 (.05)*	.17 (.05)**	.10 (.08)	−.08 (.06)	−.13 (.06)*	.01 (.11)	.01 (.06)
R^2	.056	.062	.259	.080	.038	.162	.075	.109	.092	.082	.070
R^2change	.004	.003	.023	.048	.017	.056	.007	.003	.020	.045	.001
Fchange	8.011	0.484	0.972	7.918	6.713	13.887	1.385	0.753	4.653	3.715	0.221
p	<.001	.617	.384	<.001	.001	<.001	.252	.472	.010	.027	.801

Note. Acad. Role (1 = academic, 0 = non academic), Unemployment (1 = previous unemployment experience, 0 = no previous unemployment experience)
$^{*}p < .05$, $^{**}p < .001$

Table 6.4 Regression of job insecurity and identification on burnout

	overall	US	UK	Switzerland	South Africa	Romania	Lithuania	Greece	Croatia	China	Belgium
	B (SEB)	B (SEB)	B (SEB)	B (SEB)	B (SEB)	B (SEB)	B (SEB)	B (SEB)	B (SEB)	B (SEB)	B (SEB)
Age	−0.02 (0.00)**	−0.02 (0.01)**	−0.01 (0.01)	−0.02 (0.01)*	0.00 (0.00)	−0.04 (0.01)**	−0.04 (0.01)**	−0.01 (0.01)	−0.01 (0.00)**	−0.01 (0.01)	−0.03 (0.01)**
Gender	−0.02 (0.04)	0.20 (0.12)	0.05 (0.34)	−0.20 (0.14)	0.01 (0.09)	0.38 (0.11)**	−0.01 (0.14)	0.03 (0.11)	−0.41 (0.09)**	−0.08 (0.15)	0.02 (0.17)
Acad. Role	−0.05 (0.04)	−0.01 (0.13)	0.23 (0.37)	−0.05 (0.21)	0.08 (0.09)	0.03 (0.13)	−0.08 (0.12)	0.04 (0.14)	−0.06 (0.10)	−0.16 (0.15)	0.14 (0.23)
Unemployment	−0.06 (0.08)	0.01 (0.33)	−0.74 (0.51)	0.21 (0.27)	−0.10 (0.16)	−0.33 (0.32)	−0.19 (0.27)	0.83 (0.25)**	−0.25 (0.16)	−0.06 (0.47)	−0.04 (0.26)
Financial strain	0.03 (0.01)*	0.10 (0.05)*	0.08 (0.12)	0.00 (0.06)	0.08 (0.03)*	0.00 (0.04)	−0.07 (0.05)	0.02 (0.05)	0.06 (0.03)	0.08 (0.08)	0.09 (0.07)
Job ins. (quant.)	−0.03 (0.02)	−0.16 (0.08)*	0.14 (0.15)	0.03 (0.07)	−0.23 (0.06)**	−0.51 (0.09)**	−0.08 (0.10)	0.02 (0.08)	0.05 (0.05)	0.41 (0.18)*	−0.03 (0.07)
Job ins. (qual.)	0.44 (0.02)**	0.46 (0.07)**	0.44 (0.16)*	0.53 (0.09)**	0.60 (0.06)**	0.47 (0.06)**	0.45 (0.10)**	0.52 (0.07)**	0.41 (0.05)**	−0.01 (0.15)	0.41 (0.08)**
Ident. Work pop.	−0.15 (0.02)**	−0.09 (0.08)	−0.54 (0.20)*	−0.05 (0.08)	−0.28 (0.06)**	−0.27 (0.08)**	−0.22 (0.08)*	−0.11 (0.06)	−0.14 (0.06)*	−0.21 (0.15)	−0.16 (0.10)
Ident. Job	−0.01 (0.02)	0.04 (0.07)	0.05 (0.17)	−0.04 (0.07)	−0.03 (0.05)	0.11 (0.07)	−0.02 (0.07)	0.03 (0.06)	0.01 (0.05)	0.10 (0.13)	0.12 (0.08)
R^2	0.17	0.27	0.34	0.23	0.20	0.29	0.20	0.22	0.25	0.11	0.16
F	95.08	12.50	3.45	9.87	21.43	18.29	9.40	12.43	15.73	2.10	6.46
p	<.001	<.001	0.002	<.001	<.001	<.001	<.001	<.001	<.001	0.033	<.001

Note. Acad. Role (1 = academic, 0 = non academic), Unemployment (1 = previous unemployment experience, 0 = no previous unemployment experience)
$^{*}p < .05$, $^{**}p < .001$

sample. When combining the data of all samples, evidence for a negative effect of identification as a member of the working population on burnout can be found. Looking at country samples individually, in five out of ten countries, this relationship was significant. People who identified less with the workforce or their country reported more burnout. No effect of identification with the job on burnout could be found. Hypothesis 3 can hence only be regarded as partially supported.[1]

Regarding mediation, only support for one specific type of indirect effect could be found, but not for the others. When taking the data of the combined sample, the effect of qualitative job insecurity on burnout was partially mediated by threatened identity as member of the working population ($B_{bootstrap} = 0.12$, SEB = .00, CIlo/up = .01/.02). This exact pattern of results was also found in the South African sample ($B_{bootstrap} = 0.02$, SEB = .01, CIlo/up = .01/.05). In the Romanian sample, quantitative job insecurity had an indirect effect on burnout via identification with the working population ($B_{bootstrap} = 0.06$, SEB = .03, CIlo/up = .02/.12). In the UK, Lithuanian, Romanian and Croatian samples, a negative relationship between identification with the workforce and exhaustion could also be found, but there was no significant indirect effect. In all other samples, there also seemed to be a negative trend, but the effect was not significant. In the Romanian sample, due to the positive effect of qualitative job insecurity on identification with the working population, even a negative indirect effect was found. The combined sample indicates support for one specific form of mediation (of qualitative job insecurity, through identification with the working population) but not the others. There is hence only weak support for Hypothesis 4.

6.7 Discussion

The ten-country study offers interesting evidence for the role of identity threat in the academic context. As predicted, the results clearly show that academics identify more strongly with their job than people working in other roles at university, a finding that was consistent across all samples of this study. Also, the results show that there is a case to be made for *precarity*, as a broader concept, more so than for just job insecurity on its own, as being a threat to people's work-related identities. Precarity is a situation arising from high financial strain, low job security, and low status (Creed et al., 2020)—all factors that were found to predict identity threat in this study.

[1] A potential factor influencing this finding could be that the items intended to measure burnout exhibited cross-loading on qualitative job insecurity, and vice versa (see Chap. 7).

Taken together, this study delivers interesting new evidence for the relationship between job insecurity and identity. It seems that working in an academic position (as lecturer, professors, university teacher, or on a research position) lends itself much better to becoming part of a person's identity than other job roles (university support staff or PhD students), independent of the country. Why this is the case needs further investigation. Perhaps academic jobs are better able to fulfil core identity motives, such as the experience of self-esteem, meaning, competence and autonomy (Ashforth & Schinoff, 2016), than other job roles at university. Perhaps also the uncertainty of academic careers plays a role—which can create anxiety and motivate people to highly identify with their own group (Van den Bos, 2009). Interestingly, this identification with one's job did not relate to burnout in any of the countries, at least not linearly. This seems to disconfirm the initial assumption that being highly identified might render someone particularly vulnerable to burnout. Perhaps a nonlinear effect is plausible: Exhaustion and burnout often follow from an *over*commitment to the job (Siegrist, 1996). So, while some people might have overidentified and experienced exhaustion, others might have underidentified with the same result. These two opposing effects might have led to the overall nil effect in this study.

Another interesting finding of this study is that although identity threat was clearly related to markers of precarity (financial strain, academic status, job insecurity), the effect of job insecurity on identity was less consistent. Specifically, only qualitative job insecurity affected identification with the job and the working population. This resonates with studies showing that qualitative changes to a job can lead to a questioning of one's own professional identity (e.g., Strich et al., 2021). Furthermore, the more people felt their job would change in the future, the less they felt part of the workforce of their country. Work serves an important self-referential function; it helps to define a person's place in society to 'be someone' (Tajfel & Turner, 1986). If core work components become uncertain, apparently people question their place in society. This threat can have far-reaching consequences: in this and other studies, threat to identification with the working population relates to worse health, and other studies also found worse job performance (see also Selenko et al., 2017) and even less tolerance towards others to follow from that (Selenko & De Witte, 2021). In the context of academia, a threatened identity might affect commitment to publications, persistence in research and teaching, and perhaps undermine the egalitarian, tolerant mindset that working at universities should entail.

What was curious was that *quantitative* job insecurity did not relate to *any* of the identity measures once qualitative job insecurity, financial strain, academic status and demographic variables were controlled for. This is surprising, as previous studies (e.g., Selenko et al., 2017; Selenko & De Witte, 2021) show a robust negative relationship between quantitative job insecurity and identification with the working population. However, these previous studies did not control for those other variables. A closer inspection of the results shows that quantitative job insecurity not only correlated fairly strongly positively with qualitative job insecurity but also moderately (positively) with financial strain and (negatively) with age and academic status, which had their own independent effect on identification with the working population and the job. This suggests that the effect of quantitative job insecurity on identification with the working population was partly affected by age, financial strain and qualitative job insecurity, and its effect on identification with the job was partly explained by age, academic status and qualitative job insecurity. People who were younger, who experienced more financial strain, who were not in an academic role, and who felt their job content was insecure felt less identified. From an identity perspective, this is not surprising: younger people usually had less opportunity to enact their work-related identity and get recognition for it, which are factors that affect identification. Financial deprivation also reduces the chances of seeing oneself as a high-status member of a particular job or even more generally of the working population. In short, including these aspects might have overshadowed the effect of quantitative job insecurity.

It needs to be clarified that the samples in this study were collected through convenience sampling, they are not representative of their country, nor do they allow for a matched comparison. Any country-sample comparison needs hence to be done with the greatest caution. Still, we need to acknowledge the variation in findings between the samples (see Fig. 6.2 for a visual summary). While in most countries some effect of job insecurity on one or both of the identity aspects could be found, in the Greek, Belgian, and Lithuanian samples, job insecurity did not seem to matter for identity at all; only age, gender and financial strain or academic role seemed to matter. In the Greek and Belgian samples, identity threat also did not matter for burnout. Does this indicate that identity threat (to these two aspects of identity) is not relevant in these countries? What differentiates the Greek, Belgian and Lithuanian sample from the other samples? Furthermore, there were some unexpected *positive* effects of quantitative job insecurity on identification with the job (in the overall sample and the Swiss and Croatian samples) and of qualitative job insecurity on identification with the working population (in the Romanian sample). While the effects in the Croatian and Romanian samples might have been spurious (they only appear in the regression equation but not the individual correlations) and some of nil-effects might be due to the small sample sizes, they still raise interesting questions: Does this suggest that there are conditions when job insecurity is regarded as an important aspect of identification with the job? Is job insecurity perhaps a prototypical feature that is expected of an academic career by some people? Or is the positive effect on identity perhaps even the result of identity management? In laboratory studies, people have been found to react with *even stronger* identification upon identity threat to re-establish their threatened ingroup status (Branscombe et al., 1999). Further research is needed to answer these questions.

6.7.1 *Where to Go from Here? Novel Questions for Research*

The results of the 10-country study clearly show that academics identify highly with their job and that precarity (job insecurity but also financial strain) can threaten identity, with consequences for health. Including the broader, identity-related meaning of work in explanations of job insecurity is an under-explored avenue in job insecurity research (for exceptions see Piccoli et al., 2017; Selenko et al., 2017; Selenko & De Witte, 2021).

This chapter argues that identity threat is particularly relevant in the context of academia because an academic job lends itself well for self-identification, and the empirical results seem to support this notion. The factors that might foster identification with an academic job (the long socialisation, the experience of competence, autonomy and social validation) however are not unique to academia alone: other professions (e.g., entrepreneurship, the medical profession) might offer similar job features. A systematic exploration of the job and occupational characteristics that foster (or undermine) identification would be important to be better able to predict who might have difficulties adjusting once these job characteristics change or become lost. Such an exploration should also include individual factors: people to whom their job is personally more important, who are more involved in their work (e.g., Kanungo, 1982), will probably experience this job as more central to their identity.

The identity-threatening effect of job insecurity also points to the risk of high identification. Generally, high identification with a job or a profession is desirable for organisations. It is associated with a better accomplishment of tasks, more motivation and more willingness to support the organisational, social and psychological environment in an organisation (Van Knippenberg, 2000). The social identity approach to job insecurity, however, shows that this identification can easily be threatened—for example, by changes to the job. Such changes are increasingly likely, as technological developments in machine learning and data processing are predicted to affect how cognitive tasks will be carried out (Lanzolla et al., 2020). There is evidence that those dramatic changes to work and workers' roles have serious consequences for workers' identities (e.g., Lee et al., 2018; Strich et al., 2021). Given the evidence, more knowledge on interventions and on what can be done to assist people through those identity changes would be needed.

In general, there are several avenues to pursue this research further: while the international robustness of some of the associations is promising, the longitudinal nature and the causality order of the proposed relationships need to be verified. What these results clearly suggest is that identity threat is a worthwhile mechanism to explore further in relation to job insecurity. Initial research in this area already points to the validity of identity as a bridge between job insecurity and a variety of work-related, well-being-related and even political outcomes (e.g., Piccoli et al., 2017; Selenko et al., 2017; Selenko & De Witte, 2021). Seen from a wider angle, the results confirm the context-identity interaction: how people define themselves (as members of the working population or as identified with their job) is not just a matter of personal choice but depends on their specific job context: job insecurity and precarity will affect identity negatively, while certain job positions (e.g., being an academic) can affect identity positively.

6.7.2 Concluding Remarks

Working in academia offers multiple ways for a person to feel good about themselves—to feel belonging, prestige, meaning. Due to the chronic underfunding of academic institutions, working in academia can also be rather precarious. This stands in stark contrast to the high prestige and identity function of academic work. The results from the 10-country study show that across almost all samples, academics are more strongly identified with their job than any other group working at university. High identification with a job is something positive—it is beneficial for well-being and facilitates people going the extra mile in their work. University managers as well as public funders need to recognise that job changes, job insecurity and precarity can undermine this specific academic dedication and need to be mitigated if society wants to benefit from healthy academics dedicated to teaching and research for the greater good.

6.8 Take Home Message

Academics are more identified with their job than any other group at the university, according to data from nine out of ten countries. Universities need to be cautious if there is an onslaught of job insecurity or job changes, as this can negatively affect identification with their job and the working population and ultimately lead to burnout among staff.

References

Allan, B. A., Autin, K. L., & Wilkins-Yel, K. G. (2021). Precarious work in the 21st century: A psychological perspective. *Journal of Vocational Behavior, 126*, 103491. https://doi.org/10.1016/j.jvb.2020.103491

Ashforth, B. E., Harrison, S. H., & Corley, K. G. (2008). Identification in organizations: An examination of four fundamental questions. *Journal of Management, 34*(3), 325–374.

Ashforth, B. E., & Schinoff, B. S. (2016). Identity under construction: How individuals come to define themselves in organizations. *Annual Review of Organizational Psychology and Organizational Behavior, 3*, 111–137.

Batterbury, S. (2008). Tenure or permanent contracts in north American higher education? A critical assessment. *Policy Futures in Education, 6*(3), 286–297.

Blackmore, P., & Kandiko, C. B. (2011). Motivation in academic life: A prestige economy. *Research in Post-Compulsory Education, 16*(4), 399–411.

Bloch, C., Graversen, E. K., & Pedersen, H. S. (2014). Competitive research grants and their impact on career performance. *Minerva, 52*(1), 77–96.

Blustein, D. L., Kozan, S., & Connors-Kellgren, A. (2013). Unemployment and underemployment: A narrative analysis about loss. *Journal of Vocational Behavior, 82*(3), 256–265.

Branscombe, N. R., Ellemers, N., Spears, R., & Doosje, B. (1999). The context and content of social identity threat. In N. Ellemers, R. Spears, & B. Doosje (Eds.), *Social identity: Context, commitment, content*. Blackwell.

Creed, P. A., Hood, M., Selenko, E., & Bagley, L. (2020). The development and initial validation of a self-report job precariousness scale suitable for use with young adults who study and work. *Journal of Career Assessment, 28*(4), 636–654.

Doosje, B., Ellemers, N., & Spears, R. (1995). Perceived intragroup variability as a function of group status and identification. *Journal of experimental social psychology, 31*(5), 410-436.

De Witte, H., Rothmann, S., & Jackson, L. T. (2012). The psychological consequences of unemployment in South Africa. *South African Journal of Economic and Management Sciences, 15*(3), 235–252.

Ellemers, N., Van Knippenberg, A., De Vries, N., & Wilke, H. (1988). Social identification and permeability of group boundaries. *European Journal of Social Psychology, 18*(6), 497–513.

Haslam, S. A., McMahon, C., Cruwys, T., Haslam, C., Jetten, J., & Steffens, N. K. (2018). Social cure, what social cure? The propensity to underestimate the importance of social factors for health. *Social Science & Medicine, 198*, 14–21.

Haslam, S. A., O'Brien, A., Jetten, J., Vormedal, K., & Penna, S. (2005). Taking the strain: Social identity, social support, and the experience of stress. *British Journal of Social Psychology, 44*(3), 355–370.

Hayes, A.F. (2017). Introduction to mediation, moderation and conditional process analysis. A regression-based approach (2nd ed.). New York: Guildford Press.

Horn, S. A. (2016). The social and psychological costs of peer review: Stress and coping with manuscript rejection. *Journal of Management Inquiry, 25*(1), 11–26.

Hulin, C. L. (2002). Lessons from industrial and organizational psychology. In J. M. Brett & F. Drasgow (Eds.), *The psychology of work: Theoretically based empirical research* (pp. 3–22). Lawrence Erlbaum Associates Publishers.

Hyde, A., Clarke, M., & Drennan, J. (2013). The changing role of academics and the rise of managerialism. In *The academic profession in Europe: New tasks and new challenges* (pp. 39–52). Springer.

Jahoda, M. (1982). *Employment and unemployment: A social-psychological analysis* (Vol. 1). Cambridge University Archive.

Joelson, L., & Wahlquist, L. (1987). The psychological meaning of job insecurity and job loss: Results of a longitudinal study. *Social Science & Medicine, 25*(2), 179–182.

Kanungo, R. N. (1982). Measurement of job and work involvement. *Journal of Applied Psychology, 67*(3), 341–349.

Kinman, G., & Jones, F. (2008). A life beyond work? Job demands, work-life balance, and wellbeing in UK academics. *Journal of Human Behavior in the Social Environment, 17*(1–2), 41–60.

Lanzolla, G., Lorenz, A., Miron-Spektor, E., Schilling, M., Solinas, G., & Tucci, C. L. (2020). Digital transformation: What is new if anything? Emerging patterns and management research. *Academy of Management Discoveries, 6*(3), 341–350.

Lee, C., Huang, G. H., & Ashford, S. J. (2018). Job insecurity and the changing workplace: Recent developments and the future trends in job insecurity research. *Annual Review of Organizational Psychology and Organizational Behavior, 5*, 335–359.

Logel, C., Walton, G. M., Spencer, S. J., Iserman, E. C., von Hippel, W., & Bell, A. E. (2009). Interacting with sexist men triggers social identity threat among female engineers. *Journal of Personality and Social Psychology, 96*(6), 1089–1103.

Oyserman, D. (2009). Identity-based motivation: Implications for action-readiness, procedural-readiness, and consumer behavior. *Journal of Consumer Psychology, 19*(3), 250–260.

Petriglieri, J. L. (2011). Under threat: Responses to and the consequences of threats to individuals' identities. *Academy of Management Review, 36*(4), 641–662.
Piccoli, B., Callea, A., Urbini, F., Chirumbolo, A., Ingusci, E., & De Witte, H. (2017). Job insecurity and performance: The mediating role of organizational identification. *Personnel Review, 46*(7), 1508–1522.
Pruvot, E. B., Estermann, T., & Stoyanova, H. (2021). EUA public funding observatory. Report 2020/21. Part 2. Downloaded from: http://efficiency.eua.eu/public-funding-observatory
Rosewell, K., & Ashwin, P. (2019). Academics' perceptions of what it means to be an academic. *Studies in Higher Education, 44*(12), 2374–2384.
Selenko, E., & De Witte, H. (2021). How job insecurity affects political attitudes: Identity threat plays a role. *Applied Psychology: An International Review, 70*(3), 1267–1294.
Selenko, E., Mäkikangas, A., & Stride, C. B. (2017). Does job insecurity threaten who you are? Introducing a social identity perspective to explain Well-being and performance consequences of job insecurity. *Journal of Organizational Behavior, 38*(6), 856–875.
Sheldon, K. M., & Elliot, A. J. (1999). Goal striving, need satisfaction, and longitudinal Well-being: The self-concordance model. *Journal of Personality and Social Psychology, 76*(3), 482–497.
Siegrist, J. (1996). Adverse health effects of high-effort/low-reward conditions. *Journal of Occupational Health Psychology, 1*(1), 27–41.
Strich, F., Mayer, A. S., & Fiedler, M. (2021). What do I do in a world of artificial intelligence? Investigating the impact of substitutive decision-making AI systems on employees' professional role identity. *Journal of the Association for Information Systems, 22*(2), 304–324.
Stryker, S., & Serpe, R. T. (1994). Identity salience and psychological centrality: Equivalent, overlapping, or complementary concepts? *Social Psychology Quarterly, 57*(1), 16–35.
Tajfel, H. T., & Turner, J. J. C. (1986). The social identity theory of intergroup behavior. In S. Worchel (Ed.), *Psychology of intergroup relations* (pp. 7–24). Nelson-Hall.
Turner, J. C., Hogg, M. A., Oakes, P. J., Reicher, S. D., & Wetherell, M. S. (1987). *Rediscovering the social group: A self-categorization theory*. Basil Blackwell.
Van den Bos, K. (2009). Making sense of life: The existential self trying to deal with personal uncertainty. Psychological Inquiry, 20(4), 197-217.
Van Knippenberg, D. (2000). Work motivation and performance: A social identity perspective. *Applied Psychology: An International Review, 49*(3), 357–371.
Wegge, J., Van Dick, R., Fisher, G. K., Wecking, C., & Moltzen, K. (2006). Work motivation, organisational identification, and Well-being in call Centre work. *Work & Stress, 20*(1), 60–83.
Zhou, X. (2005). The institutional logic of occupational prestige ranking: Reconceptualization and reanalyses. *American Journal of Sociology, 111*(1), 90–140.

Eva Selenko is a Professor in Work Psychology at Loughborough University, United Kingdom. She is lucky enough to hold a permanent position but well aware of the job insecurity other colleagues face. Eva is interested in work and identity research and how situations of insecurity and crisis affect people's understanding of themselves. She has published numerous articles in well-regarded academic journals. In this project she was responsible for collecting the UK dataset.

Chapter 7
How Can Job Insecurity Lead to Poor In-role Performance and Innovative Work Behavior in Academia? The Mediating Role of Burnout

Darja Maslić Seršić and Jasmina Tomas

7.1 Introduction

The last several decades have brought significant changes to work in the higher education sector, which have resulted in increased work demands, greater time pressure, and intensified work uncertainty. Already by the late 1980s and 1990s, studies examining occupational stress among employees in higher education demonstrated that an occupation in academia had lost the characteristics traditionally considered to be its perks (e.g., job security, flexible time schedule), a trend that was especially evident in certain groups, such as women and academics with temporary contracts (Aisenberg & Harrington, 1988; Hensel, 1991; Kinman, 1998; Thorsen, 1996). To illustrate, Kinman (1998, p. 20), based on survey data collected with a wide sample of higher education employees in the UK, concluded that "*It is evident that a substantial number of academic and academic related staff working in higher education institutions in the UK are experiencing a high degree of pressure at work from a number of different sources. They report that the impact of the changing nature of their work has led to work overload, long working hours, job insecurity and a range of other problems, causing stress for many.*"

In more recent years, there is a growing body of literature that has confirmed the growing work pressure experienced by higher education staff, which makes working conditions in academia more similar to those in the business sector (Kinman, 2014; Kinman & Wray, 2016). The highly demanding and ever-changing context of higher education has brought increased work stress, lower job satisfaction, and impaired

D. Maslić Seršić (✉) · J. Tomas
Faculty of Humanities and Social Sciences, Department of Psychology, University of Zagreb, Zagreb, Croatia
e-mail: darja.maslic@ffzg.hr; jasmina.tomas@ffzg.hr

L. C. Roll et al. (eds.), *Global Perspectives on Job Insecurity in Higher Education*, Aligning Perspectives on Health, Safety and Well-Being,
https://doi.org/10.1007/978-3-031-85772-0_7

work-related health to members of the academic community (Catano et al., 2010; Kinman, 2008; Opstrup & Pihl-Thingvad, 2016; Shin & Jung, 2014; Slišković & Maslić Seršić, 2011; Tytherleigh et al., 2005; Winefield et al., 2003). Examples of the most detrimental sources of stress that are becoming increasingly salient in the higher education sector are work intensification, reduced work control and decreased job security – in other words, the loss of positive job characteristics that have been traditionally associated with employment in higher education (Kinman, 2001; Kinman & Jones, 2003). In the first study that included all categories of employees of UK higher education institutions (HEI) and compared the findings with established normative data, Tytherleigh et al. (2005) found that levels of occupational stress for higher education staff were significantly higher than the normative data. Importantly, the source of stress that most bothered respondents was job insecurity, and in particular employees' perception that their jobs would change for the worse in the future.

Taken together, the results of these studies indicate that employees working in the higher education sector worldwide need to simultaneously cope with increasing levels of job insecurity and increasing pressure to perform. This combination of working conditions may be particularly deleterious for employees and HEIs, where a growing number of empirical findings indicate that employees who are more insecure about their jobs tend to perform worse (for meta-analyses, see Jiang & Lavaysse, 2018; Sverke et al., 2019). In the long run, this may undermine not only employees' chances for career advancement but also the prosperity of entire HEIs, which strongly depend on the performance of their individual members. For this reason, gaining a deeper understanding of the relationship between job insecurity and employee performance in the higher education sector is essential for guiding effective interventions that aim to ameliorate the detrimental effects of job insecurity on employees and HEIs. To this end, the present study aims to add to existing knowledge on the job insecurity-performance relationship in four ways.

The first research aim of this study concerns the conceptualization of job insecurity. In this regard, most previous studies have examined the relationship between *quantitative* job insecurity (i.e., the perceived threat of losing the job itself; Probst, 2003) and employee performance (e.g., Piccoli et al., 2021; Probst et al., 2007; Staufenbiel & König, 2010). In contrast, comparatively fewer studies have addressed the relationship between performance and *qualitative* job insecurity (i.e., the perceived threat of losing the valued features of one's job such as opportunities for career advancement and flexible working hours; Hellgren et al., 1999) (but see Fischmann et al., 2018). However, the reality of working in the higher education sector often includes unpredictable and comprehensive changes to one's job that stem from organizational restructuring, privatization, and curriculum reforms (Dolenec & Doolan, 2013; Kinman & Jones, 2003; Marginson, 2000; Trow, 1994). Because these circumstances give rise to qualitative job insecurity, the focus of this study is placed on this work stressor specifically.

The second contribution of the present study relates to the conceptualization of employee performance. As demonstrated by the recent meta-analysis by Sverke et al. (2019), the majority of previous studies have examined the relationship between job insecurity and in-role performance, i.e., behaviors that are expected from employees based on their job description and that are consequently subjected to a formal organizational reward system (Williams & Anderson, 1991). In contrast, comparably fewer studies have addressed other types of job performance, with the fewest number of studies focusing on creative and innovative employee performance (see Niesen et al., 2018a, b; Probst et al., 2019; Van Hootegem et al., 2019 for notable exceptions). A high level of individual in-role performance is considered essential for organizational success (Sonnentag & Frese, 2002). However, to thrive in today's unpredictable, volatile and highly competitive market environments, organizations also depend on innovation, which is determined by the innovative work behavior (IWB) of its individual members (De Jong & Den Hartog, 2010). This may be particularly true for highly innovation-driven sectors such as the higher education sector. IWB encompasses intentional behaviors oriented towards the introduction and application of new and useful ideas, processes, products and procedures that are intended to benefit the individual, the group or the wider society (West & Farr, 1990). Accordingly, in addition to in-role performance, which encompasses performance in job tasks that are central to one's work role, organizations strongly benefit from behaviors that fall outside one's work role, including thinking "outside the box" and aiming to improve the status quo. For this reason, in this study, we examine the relationship between qualitative job insecurity and both in-role performance and IWB.

Third, we investigate the explanatory mechanism of the relationship between job insecurity and performance, a research agenda that has thus far been scarcely pursued. Existing studies on this topic have predominantly tested work attitudes (Piccoli et al., 2021), psychological contract breach (Niesen et al., 2018a, b), cognitive manifestations of psychological strain (Probst et al., 2019) and organizational identification (Callea et al., 2016) as mediators of the job insecurity-performance relationship. In this study, we aim to expand this list by departing from the well-established finding that job insecurity leads to strain (De Witte et al., 2016). Specifically, we have applied job demands—resources (JD-R) theory (Bakker & Demerouti, 2017) to frame qualitative job insecurity as a job demand that instigates a health-impairment process leading to burnout and, in turn, impaired performance. This theoretical perspective has been relatively understudied in research investigating reasons why job insecurity relates to poorer performance (but see Darvishmotevali et al., 2017; Roll et al., 2019). Yet, it might provide informative, theoretically driven guidelines for designing effective organizational interventions.

Fourth, to determine whether our findings can be replicated across higher education sectors in different cultural settings, we test the hypothesized mediation model across eight countries on four continents (USA, Switzerland, South Africa, Lithuania, Greece, Croatia, China, and Belgium). In doing so, we aim to increase the generalizability of our findings beyond the cultural contexts in which the relationship between job insecurity and performance has been predominantly examined to date (i.e., western Europe and the USA).

7.1.1 Job Insecurity and Employee Performance

Job insecurity has been framed as a work stressor, which implies the anticipation of a stress event that could be more stressful than the event itself (e.g., loss of a valuable job feature) (De Witte, 2005; Sverke & Hellgren, 2002). In addition, the experience of job insecurity is strongly associated with a sense of powerlessness because it implies ambiguity in maintaining the desired continuity of the current work situation (Greenhalgh & Rosenblatt, 1984). As such, job insecurity is an undesirable experience that should be negatively associated with work-related well-being and work motivation and ultimately should negatively affect work commitment and employee performance. While existing research confirms these general assumptions (for meta-analyses, see Jiang & Lavaysse, 2018; Sverke et al., 2002; Sverke et al., 2019), the association between job insecurity and IWB is still rarely investigated.

Probst et al. (2007) conducted a laboratory experiment in which they manipulated the experience of quantitative job insecurity and tested its effects on creative problem solving and productivity. Compared to the control group, participants who were exposed to the threat of job loss exhibited a significant increase in productivity, while creative problem solving decreased. In a second field study, the same authors confirmed these results: the experience of quantitative job insecurity predicted lower levels of creativity but had no negative effects on counterproductive work behavior. These results have important practical implications because they indicate that managements' efforts to increase employees' flexibility and innovation through organizational restructuring and downsizing may have unexpected and undesirable consequences for employee creativity.

It seems theoretically plausible that job insecurity, as a stressful experience, would have a greater negative impact on performance in more cognitively demanding tasks (such as those involving creative solutions) than on routine behaviors (Lazarus & Folkman, 1984). In a recent meta-analysis, Sverke et al. (2019) demonstrated that quantitative job insecurity was negatively associated with task performance and contextual performance and positively associated with counterproductive work behavior. With regards to creative work behavior, the study found no evidence of a significant negative association. Furthermore, this meta-analysis revealed significant methodological and macro factors that moderated the negative relationship between quantitative job insecurity and task performance. Namely, cross-sectional studies and research based on self-perceived task performance showed higher negative correlations in comparison to longitudinal studies and studies utilizing supervisor-rated performance measures. Interestingly, the study also revealed significant intercultural differences; the lowest negative associations were found in Scandinavian countries, while the highest associations were found in countries of Southern Europe, suggesting that the relationship between quantitative job insecurity and performance is weaker in countries with stronger social protection systems.

Despite its increasing prevalence in academia, the experience of job insecurity and its effect on the performance of higher education staff has not yet received sufficient research attention. In one of the few studies on this topic, Benson et al.

(2017) collected data with a sample of US public university faculty experiencing repeated budget cuts and found that both quantitative job insecurity and pay stagnation were indirectly related to lower performance via job satisfaction. As discussed previously, we argue that the academic context creates conditions in which not only quantitative but also qualitative job insecurity may function as salient precursors of employee performance. Both permanent staff, who represent the majority of employees in HEIs, and employees with temporary contracts are exposed to rapid and fundamental work-related changes. The resulting experience of qualitative job insecurity may affect their well-being and performance, a notion further elaborated upon in the following section.

7.1.2 The Mediating Role of Burnout in the Job Insecurity-Performance Relationship

In line with JD-R theory (Bakker & Demerouti, 2017), we propose that qualitative job insecurity predicts impaired in-role performance and IWB through burnout (see Fig. 7.1). We frame job insecurity as a job demand that has the potential to instigate a health-impairment process—a psychological process in which job demands are responsible for the development of burnout because they drain employees' psychological and physical resources (Bakker & Demerouti, 2017; Schaufeli & Taris, 2014). In particular, job demands represent "*those physical, psychological, social or organizational aspects of the job that require sustained physical and/or psychological effort and are therefore associated with certain physiological and/or psychological costs*" (Bakker & Demerouti, 2017, p. 274). In a similar fashion, we argue that qualitative job insecurity represents a work stressor that requires substantial effort to cope with and, as a result, may lead to the loss of abundant employee

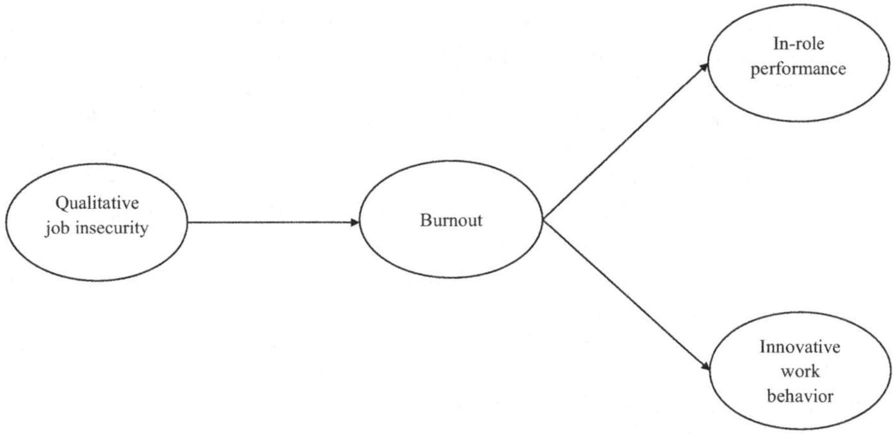

Fig. 7.1 Hypothesized research model

resources. Job-insecure employees anticipate the loss of important job features but do not know whether, when and under which circumstances this loss will actually occur (Vander Elst et al., 2014a). The uncertainty and uncontrollability inherent to job insecurity make it difficult for employees to take concrete actions to prevent losses from happening. Consequently, any coping efforts are likely to be in vain and lead to a depletion of employee resources (Vander Elst et al., 2014b). This may be particularly true in the higher education sector, which is characterized by ongoing unpredictable alterations that require constant adaptation. Prolonged exposure to such a stressful work environment is likely to lead to burnout (Demerouti et al., 2001).

In the current study, burnout is conceptualized as a syndrome encompassing four components: exhaustion (i.e., inability to exert effort on work tasks due to severe energy depletion associated with feelings of physical and mental exhaustion), mental distance (i.e., unwillingness to exert effort on work tasks due to a lack of interest and increased aversion to work), and cognitive and emotional impairment (i.e., reduced functional capacity to regulate one's cognitive and emotional processes, respectively) (Schaufeli et al., 2020a, b). This conceptualization and the corresponding Burnout Assessment Tool (BAT) are the result of extensive validation studies that aimed to provide a novel, theoretically grounded measure of burnout that would overcome the deficiencies inherent to the most frequently used Maslach Burnout Inventory (MBI; Maslach & Jackson, 1981) (for a more detailed comparison of BAT and MBI, see de Beer et al., 2020; Schaufeli et al., 2020a, b). We suggest that employees who perceive a threat to the important characteristics of their job are more likely to develop burnout, manifested in high levels of exhaustion and resistance to work and an impaired ability to regulate their emotional (e.g., feeling angry and irritated) and cognitive (e.g., experiencing impaired memory and attention) processes. Consistent with the presented theoretical arguments, previous research has demonstrated a positive correlation between qualitative job insecurity and burnout (De Witte et al., 2010; Roll et al., 2019).

According to JD-R theory, burnout further leads to impaired employee performance (Bakker & Demerouti, 2017). Employees experiencing burnout feel both unable and unwilling to invest effort in work tasks (Schaufeli et al., 2019). In other words, they are not only tired and worn out, but they also feel an aversion to work (de Beer et al., 2020). As such, they are less likely to perform successfully. Based on this proposition of JD-R theory, we propose that burnout will predict lower levels of in-role performance and IWB. With regards to in-role performance, high levels of burnout may result in less successful completion of task assignments because employees do not have adequate energy resources and feel an aversion towards those assignments. Moreover, cognitive and emotional impairment may interfere with employees' focus on accomplishing work goals.

Behaviors conceptualized as IWB can be described along four dimensions that describe an innovation process—idea exploration, idea generation, idea championing and idea implementation (De Jong & Den Hartog, 2010). Idea exploration and idea generation include exploring methods and generating novel ideas according to which the current status quo at work can be improved, whereas idea championing and idea implementation include the promotion and realization of these ideas. Idea exploration and generation are considered crucial for innovative employee behavior (Anderson et al., 2014). Therefore, the focus of the current study is on these dimensions of IWB (cf. Niesen et al., 2018a, b). To accurately assess areas for improvement and produce novel ideas, employees need to invest considerable effort in their work. Furthermore, idea generation is usually oriented towards producing solutions to identified problems (De Jong & Den Hartog, 2010). For this reason, employees need to be able to "keep their eyes on the prize" by remaining motivated, focused and resilient in the face of potential obstacles and by successfully regulating emotions such as frustration and disappointment. Accordingly, when employees suffer from burnout, they are less likely to possess the ability and willingness to think about how current products, processes and procedures can be improved. In line with arguments outlined in JD-R theory, the negative correlation between burnout and both in-role performance and IWB has been empirically supported in previous studies (Bakker & Heuven, 2006; Roll et al., 2015).

The assumptions presented here form the basis for a mediation model in which burnout underlies the relationship between qualitative JI and two types of employee performance. Accordingly, we hypothesize:

Hypothesis 1: Burnout mediates the relationship between qualitative job insecurity and in-role job performance.

Hypothesis 2: Burnout mediates the relationship between qualitative job insecurity and IWB.

7.2 Method

7.2.1 Participants and Procedure

For this study, we used data from eight countries, as we were not able to test the hypothesized model in the UK and Romanian samples.[1] Therefore, the total effective sample consisted of 4194 employees from US (N = 372 (54.2% female); M_{age} = 47.31 years; SD_{age} = 13.17 years), Swiss (N = 318 (62.3% female); M_{age} = 41.48 years; SD_{age} = 10.42 years), South African (N = 1096 (54.1% female); M_{age} = 38.93 years; SD_{age} = 12.26 years), Lithuanian (N = 530 (54.6%

[1]The sample from the UK was not large enough to test the hypothesized model ($N = 70$). The measurement model in the Romanian sample did not fit well to the data according to commonly accepted cut-of criteria ($\chi^2 = 760.185$, $df = 98$, $p < .001$, SRMR = .089, CFI = .820, RMSEA = .119). Furthermore, the fit could not be improved by introducing any theoretically or methodologically justifiable modification (e.g., by adding covariance between items measuring the same construct that have similar wording). A plausible explanation for the inadequate model fit in the Romanian sample is the presence of numerous item cross-loadings (e.g., the item that was intended to measure burnout had a cross-loading on qualitative job insecurity and vice versa), which were revealed after closer inspection of modification indices.

female); $M_{age} = 40.66$ years; $SD_{age} = 11.13$ years), Greek ($N = 403$ (54.6% female); $M_{age} = 46.88$ years; $SD_{age} = 8.91$ years), Croatian ($N = 719$ (67.3% female); $M_{age} = 40.47$ years; $SD_{age} = 9.98$ years), Chinese ($N = 160$ (58.8% female); $M_{age} = 36.50$ years; $SD_{age} = 7.49$ years) and Belgian ($N = 596$ (72.2% female); $M_{age} = 39.24$ years; $SD_{age} = 11.26$ years HEIs.

7.2.2 *Data Analyses*

In the first step of the analyses, we verified the discriminant validity of the study constructs by conducting a series of confirmatory factor analyses (CFAs). Specifically, we tested the hypothesized four-factor measurement model (Model 1 encompassing qualitative job insecurity, burnout, in-role performance and IWB) and compared it to two plausible alternative models: a three-factor model in which indicators intended to measure in-role performance and IWB loaded onto one factor and the remaining indicators loaded onto their respective factor (Model 2) and a single-factor model in which all items loaded onto one factor (Model 3).

To address the study hypotheses, we specified a structural model including direct and indirect paths from qualitative job insecurity to both performance outcomes and tested it with each sample. The statistical significance of the direct and indirect effects was tested by means of a bootstrap method (with 10,000 resamples and 95% bias-corrected confidence intervals (CI)). This method is particularly convenient for testing indirect effects because it does not impose normality assumptions of their sampling distributions (MacKinnon et al., 2007). The effect is considered statistically significant if its CI does not contain zero (Preacher & Hayes, 2008).

To estimate measurement and structural models, we employed the full information maximum likelihood (FIML) method using Mplus, version 8.4 (Muthén & Muthén, 2017). This estimation procedure enabled us to use all available information in the dataset without listwise deletion to produce less biased parameter estimates and more accurate standard errors (Newman, 2014). The acceptability of the fitted models was evaluated based on the following goodness-of-fit indices: standardized root mean square residual (SRMR; with values below. 08 indicating acceptable model fit), comparative fit index (CFI; with values above .90 indicating acceptable model fit) and root mean square error of approximation (RMSEA; with values below. 08 indicating acceptable model fit).

7.2.3 *Measures*

All constructs were measured using internationally validated measures. Measurement equivalence was established in Chaps. 2 and 3. In addition, we collected data on the demographic and work-related characteristics of employees.

Qualitative job insecurity. Qualitative job insecurity was measured using four items validated by Fischmann et al. (2022). A sample item was *"I feel insecure about the characteristics and conditions of my job in the future."* Participants provided responses on a scale ranging from 1 (*strongly disagree*) to 5 (*strongly agree*). Cronbach's alpha coefficients ranged from .73 (Chinese sample) to .90 (US sample).

Burnout. To measure burnout, we used the short four-item version of the Burnout Assessment Tool (BAT; Schaufeli et al., 2020a, b). Each item measured one of the four core dimensions of burnout (exhaustion, mental distance, emotional and cognitive impairment). A sample item was "*At work, I feel mentally exhausted.*" Responses were recorded on a scale ranging from 0 (*never*) to 6 (*every day*). Cronbach's alpha coefficients ranged from .69 (Swiss sample) to .81 (Lithuanian sample).

In-role performance. In-role performance was measured with four items from the Williams and Anderson (1991) In-role Behavior Scale. A sample item was *"I fulfil responsibilities specified in my job description."* Participants provided responses on a scale ranging from 1 (*strongly disagree*) to 5 (*strongly agree*). Cronbach's alpha coefficients ranged from .66 (Chinese sample) to .92 (Greek sample).

Innovative work behavior. We measured IWB using four items from De Jong and Den Hartog's (2010) scale of innovative work behavior. One item assessed the idea exploration component (*"In your job, how often do you wonder how things can be improved?"*), whereas three items assessed the idea generation component of IWB (sample item: *"In your job, how often do you generate original solutions for problems?"*). De Jong and den Hartog (2010) questioned the distinctiveness of these dimensions due to their high intercorrelation. In this study, we also found that the four items loaded onto one factor (as confirmed by the confirmatory factor analyses (CFAs) described below). Therefore, we used all four items to operationalize the construct of IWB. To assess their IWB, participants were asked to estimate how often in their job they exhibited behaviors corresponding to idea generation and implementation on a scale ranging from 1 (*never*) to 5 (*daily*). Cronbach's alpha coefficients ranged from .81 (South African sample) to .88 (Lithuanian and Chinese samples).

Control variables. Among the collected demographics and work-related characteristics, we controlled for age, gender (treated as a binary variable due to the small number of participants who self-identified as transgender or "other") and staff category (i.e., permanent academic staff, support and administrative staff and junior research staff, which were dummy recoded with permanent academic staff as a reference group).

7.3 Results

7.3.1 Measurement Model

The results of the CFAs are presented in Table 7.1. In each sample, the hypothesized four-factor model fit the data acceptably well and significantly better than the two alternative nested models. Moreover, all indicators were significantly related to the hypothesized factor in each sample (see Table 7.1). It should be noted that each tested measurement model included two correlated measurement errors, one between the items measuring qualitative JI (i.e., items "I think my job will change for the worse" and "Chances are, my job will change in a negative way") and one between the items measuring in-role performance ("I fulfill the responsibilities specified in my job description" and "I perform the tasks that are expected as part of my job"). These correlations were retained in the structural models described below. Taken together, the results of the conducted CFAs demonstrated the discriminant validity of the constructs examined in this study.

7.3.2 Descriptive Statistics

Table 7.2 reports the means, standard deviations, Cronbach's alpha coefficients and correlations between the core study variables in all eight samples. In most countries, the relationships between qualitative job insecurity and both forms of employee work behavior were not statistically significant. More specifically, qualitative JI was negatively related to in-role performance among participants from Switzerland, Croatia and China. A statistically significant relationship between qualitative job insecurity and IWB was also found in three countries—the USA, Greece and China. While qualitative job insecurity was negatively related to IWB in the Chinese sample, higher levels of job insecurity were unexpectedly related to higher scores on the measure of IWB in the US and Greek samples.

The relationship between qualitative JI and burnout was statistically significant and positive in all samples, indicating that the more concerned employees were about losing valued aspects of their job, the more burnout they experienced. Furthermore, burnout was negatively related to in-role performance in all eight countries. In contrast, the relationships between burnout and IWB were statistically significant in only three samples—the US, South Africa and Lithuania. More specifically, burnout was related to lower levels of IWB in South Africa and Lithuania, while contrary to expectations, the relationship between burnout and IWB in the US sample was positive.

Table 7.1 Goodness-of-fit indices in measurement and structural models (in eight samples)

Model	χ^2	*df*	SRMR	CFI	RMSEA	Model comparison	$\Delta\chi^2$	Δdf	Range of standardized factor loadings
USA									
4-factor MM (Model 1)	252.96***	96	.053	.952	.066	–			.53–.92
3-factor MM (Model 2)	984.99***	99	.139	.731	.155	M2 – M1	732.03***	3	
1-factor MM (Model 3)	1731.80***	102	.177	.505	.207	M3 – M1	1478.84***	6	
Structural model	353.88***	144	.049	.939	.063	–			
Switzerland									
4-factor MM (Model 1)	192.59***	96	.076	.950	.056	–			.33–.91
3-factor MM (Model 2)	642.99***	99	.126	.716	.131	M2 – M1	450.40***	3	
1-factor MM (Model 3)	1066.03***	102	.146	.496	.172	M3 – M1	873.44***	6	
Structural model	334.96***	144	.073	.884	.065	–			
South Africa									
4-factor MM (Model 1)	347.40***	96	.043	.968	.049	–			
3-factor MM (Model 2)	1850.28***	99	.107	.779	.127	M2 – M1	1502.88***	3	.46–.88
1-factor MM (Model 3)	4400.25***	102	.173	.457	.196	M3 – M1	4052.85***	6	
Structural model	442.43***	144	.038	.963	.043	–			
Lithuania									
4-factor MM (Model 1)	304.76***	96	.039	.954	.064	–			.62–.94
3-factor MM (Model 2)	1399.34***	99	.119	.716	.157	M2 – M1	1094.58***	3	
1-factor MM (Model 3)	3056.57***	102	.215	.355	.234	M3 – M1	2751.81***	6	
Structural model	434.87***	144	.041	.939	.062	–			
Greece									
4-factor MM (Model 1)	319.04***	96	.075	.937	.076	–			
3-factor MM (Model 2)	1005.89***	99	.127	.744	.151	M2 – M1	686.85***	3	.38–92
1-factor MM (Model 3)	2037.84***	102	.188	.454	.217	M3 – M1	1718.80***	6	
Structural model	445.41***	144	.068	.918	.072	–			

(continued)

Table 7.1 (continued)

Model	χ^2	*df*	SRMR	CFI	RMSEA	Model comparison	$\Delta\chi^2$	Δdf	Range of standardized factor loadings
Croatia									
4-factor MM (Model 1)	314.54***	96	.050	.966	.056	–			.30–93
3-factor MM (Model 2)	1705.48***	99	.122	.751	.150	M2 – M1	1390.94***	3	
1-factor MM (Model 3)	3282.15***	102	.191	.508	.208	M3 – M1	2967.61***	6	
Structural model	438.79***	144	.048	.955	.053	–			
China									
4-factor MM (Model 1)	189.73***	96	.073	.895	.078	–			.44–.89
3-factor MM (Model 2)	250.94***	99	.095	.829	.098	M2 – M1	61.21***	3	
1-factor MM (Model 3)	486.93***	102	.143	.568	.154	M3 – M1	297.20***	6	
Structural model	246.31***	144	.066	.886	.067	–			
Belgium									
4-factor MM (Model 1)	252.68***	96	.050	.963	.052	–			.56–.88
3-factor MM (Model 2)	1137.77***	99	.117	.757	.133	M2 – M1	885.09***	3	
1-factor MM (Model 3)	2727.69***	102	.187	.385	.208	M3 – M1	2475.01***	6	
Structural model	449.11***	144	.052	.933	.060	–			

Table 7.2 Descriptive statistics, reliabilities (in parentheses) and inter-correlations between study variables (in eight samples)

		M	*SD*	1	2	3	4
USA	1. Qualitative JI	2.99	1.13	(.90)			
	2. Burnout	3.10	1.29	.45***	(.78)		
	3. In-role performance	4.81	0.38	−.07	−.18***	(.86)	
	4. IWB	3.71	0.82	.21***	.14**	.13*	(.86)
Switzerland	1. Qualitative JI	2.74	0.90	(.78)			
	2. Burnout	3.20	1.26	.44***	(.69)		
	3. In-role performance	4.22	0.65	−.33***	−.25***	(.79)	
	4. IWB	3.31	0.86	.05	.01	.13*	(.82)
South Africa	1. Qualitative JI	2.81	0.92	(.85)			
	2. Burnout	3.00	1.36	.40***	(.78)		
	3. In-role performance	4.38	0.58	−.002	−.15***	(.88)	
	4. IWB	3.80	0.90	−.06	−.06*	.19***	(.81)
Lithuania	1. Qualitative JI	3.06	0.87	(.86)			
	2. Burnout	2.99	1.24	.19***	(.81)		
	3. In-role performance	4.27	0.56	−.001	−.22***	(.89)	
	4. IWB	3.22	0.89	−.04	−.09*	.26***	(.88)
Greece	1. Qualitative JI	3.16	0.87	(.85)			
	2. Burnout	2.86	1.19	.41***	(.76)		
	3. In-role performance	4.43	0.57	−.05	−.16**	(.92)	
	4. IWB	3.75	0.83	.10*	.06	.19***	(.82)
Croatia	1. Qualitative JI	3.04	0.97	(.88)			
	2. Burnout	2.70	1.05	.40***	(.70)		
	3. In-role performance	4.52	0.54	−.07*	−.23***	(.90)	
	4. IWB	3.80	0.86	−.01	−.04	.19***	(.86)
China	1. Qualitative JI	2.47	0.67	(.73)			
	2. Burnout	2.65	0.94	.20*	(.77)		
	3. In-role performance	3.97	0.50	−.17*	−.19*	(.66)	
	4. IWB	3.28	0.92	−.21**	−.03	.34***	(.88)
Belgium	1. Qualitative JI	2.70	0.90	(.85)			
	2. Burnout	2.73	1.14	.27***	(.76)		
	3. In-role performance	4.30	0.58	−.06	−.23***	(.89)	
	4. IWB	3.29	0.73	.04	−.01	.15***	(.83)

*$p < .05$, **$p < .01$, ***$p < .001$. *JI* job insecurity, *IWB* innovative work behavior

7.3.3 Structural Model: Indirect and Direct Effects of Qualitative JI on In-role Performance and IWB

Goodness-of-fit indices for each structural model are presented in Table 7.1, whereas standardized path coefficients are presented in Table 7.3. With few detected differences, we observed a relatively similar pattern of relationships among constructs in all eight samples. In the first instance, qualitative JI was predictive of higher levels of

Table 7.3 Direct and indirect standardized path coefficients (in eight samples)

	Coefficient	*SE*	*p*	Bootstrap 95% CI
USA				
Direct effect				
Qualitative JI on burnout	.50	0.05	<.001	[.40; .60]
Burnout on in-role performance	−.14	0.09	n.s.	[−.31; .02]
Burnout on IWB	−.002	0.09	n.s.	[−.17; .17]
Qualitative JI on in-role performance	−.01	0.07	n.s.	[−.14; .13]
Qualitative JI on IWB	.16	0.07	< .05	[.02; .30]
Indirect effect				
Qualitative JI on in-role performance	−.07	0.04	n.s.	[−.17; .01]
Qualitative JI on IWB	−.001	0.05	n.s.	[−.09; .09]
$R^2_{(burnout)} = .39^{***}$; $R^2_{(in\text{-}role\ performance)} = .18^{*}$; $R^2_{(IWB)} = .06^{*}$				
Switzerland				
Direct effect				
Qualitative JI on burnout	.56	0.08	<.001	[.39; .71]
Burnout on in-role performance	−.26	0.11	<.05	[−.46; −.04]
Burnout on IWB	−.16	0.11	n.s.	[−.37; .08]
Qualitative JI on in-role performance	−.09	0.11	n.s.	[−.31; .14]
Qualitative JI on IWB	.20	0.11	n.s.	[−.01; .42]
Indirect effect				
Qualitative JI on in-role performance	−.15	0.06	<.05.	[−.28; −.03]
Qualitative JI on IWB	−.09	0.07	n.s.	[−.22; .04]
$R^2_{(burnout)} = .34^{***}$; $R^2_{(in\text{-}role\ performance)} = .11^{*}$; $R^2_{(IWB)} = .05^{n.s.}$				
South Africa				
Direct effect				
Qualitative JI on burnout	.46	0.03	<.001	[.39; .53]
Burnout on in-role performance	−.22	0.05	<.001	[−.31; −.13]
Burnout on IWB	−.12	0.05	<.01	[−.20; −.03]
Qualitative JI on in-role performance	.10	0.04	<.05	[.02; .18]
Qualitative JI on IWB	−.02	0.04	n.s.	[−.10; .07]
Indirect effect				
Qualitative JI on in-role performance	−.10	0.02	<.001	[−.15; −.06]
Qualitative JI on IWB	−.05	0.02	<.001	[−.10; −.01]
$R^2_{(burnout)} = .22^{***}$; $R^2_{(in\text{-}role\ performance)} = .08^{***}$; $R^2_{(IWB)} = .04^{*}$				
Lithuania				
Direct effect				
Qualitative JI on burnout	.33	0.05	<.001	[.23; .42]
Burnout on in-role performance	−.38	0.06	<.001	[−.50; −.25]
Burnout on IWB	−.18	0.07	<.01	[−.30; −.04]
Qualitative JI on in-role performance	.12	0.05	<.05	[.01; .22]
Qualitative JI on IWB	.02	0.06	n.s.	[−.10; .17]

(continued)

Table 7.3 (continued)

	Coefficient	*SE*	*p*	Bootstrap 95% CI
Indirect effect				
Qualitative JI on in-role performance	−.12	0.03	<.001	[−.19; −.08]
Qualitative JI on IWB	−.06	0.02	<.05	[−.11; −.02]
$R^2_{(burnout)} = .29^{***}$; $R^2_{(in\text{-}role\ performance)} = .12^{**}$; $R^2_{(IWB)} = .04^{n.s.}$				
Greece				
Direct effect				
Qualitative JI on burnout	.46	0.05	<.001	[.35; .56]
Burnout on in-role performance	−.18	0.08	<.05	[−.32; −.02]
Burnout on IWB	−.07	0.08	n.s.	[−.23; .08]
Qualitative JI on in-role performance	.03	0.07	n.s.	[−.10; .16]
Qualitative JI on IWB	.03	0.08	n.s.	[−.12; .18]
Indirect effect				
Qualitative JI on in-role performance	−.07	0.03	< .05	[−.16; −.01]
Qualitative JI on IWB	−.02	0.02	n.s.	[−.11; .04]
$R^2_{(burnout)} = .28^{***}$; $R^2_{(in\text{-}role\ performance)} = .08^{*}$; $R^2_{(IWB)} = .01^{n.s.}$				
Croatia				
Direct effect				
Qualitative JI on burnout	.50	0.04	<.001	[.42; .57]
Burnout on in-role performance	−.27	0.07	<.001	[−.40; −.13]
Burnout on IWB	−.11	0.06	n.s.	[−.23; .02]
Qualitative JI on in-role performance	.01	0.05	n.s.	[−.09; .11]
Qualitative JI on IWB	.002	0.06	n.s.	[−.11; .11]
Indirect effect				
Qualitative JI on in-role performance	−.14	0.04	<.001	[−.21; −.07]
Qualitative JI on IWB	−.05	0.03	n.s.	[−.12; .01]
$R^2_{(burnout)} = .30^{***}$; $R^2_{(in\text{-}role\ performance)} = .09^{**}$; $R^2_{(IWB)} = .03^{n.s.}$				
China				
Direct effect				
Qualitative JI on burnout	.13	0.12	n.s.	[−.10; .38]
Burnout on in-role performance	−.33	0.11	<.01	[−.54; −.13]
Burnout on IWB	−.04	0.11	n.s.	[−.24; .19]
Qualitative JI on in-role performance	−.17	0.15	n.s.	[−.48; .14]
Qualitative JI on IWB	−.25	0.11	<.05	[−.47; −.05]
Indirect effect				
Qualitative JI on in-role performance	−.04	0.04	n.s.	[−.15; .02]
Qualitative JI on IWB	−.005	0.02	n.s.	[−.08; .02]
$R^2_{(burnout)} = .07$; $R^2_{(in\text{-}role\ performance)} = .18^{*}$; $R^2_{(IWB)} = .09^{n.s.}$				
Belgium				
Direct effect				
Qualitative JI on burnout	.36	0.05	<.001	[.26; .46]
Burnout on in-role performance	−.27	0.07	<.001	[−.40; −.14]
Burnout on IWB	−.07	0.07	n.s.	[−.21; .07]
Qualitative JI on in-role performance	.06	0.06	n.s.	[−.06; .17]
Qualitative JI on IWB	.04	0.06	n.s.	[−.07; .15]

(continued)

Table 7.3 (continued)

	Coefficient	*SE*	*p*	Bootstrap 95% CI
Indirect effect				
Qualitative JI on in-role performance	−.10	0.03	<.01	[−.16; −.05]
Qualitative JI on IWB	−.03	0.03	n.s.	[−.08; .02]
$R^2_{(\text{burnout})} = .29^{***}$; $R^2_{(\text{in-role performance})} = .10^{*}$; $R^2_{(\text{IWB})} = .02^{\text{n.s.}}$				

*$p < .05$, **$p < .01$; ***$p < .001$. *JI* job insecurity; *IWB* innovative work behavior

burnout in each country except China, where this effect was non-significant. As expected, we also found that burnout was related to lower levels of in-role performance with only one exception (the effect in the US sample was non-significant). In contrast, the effect of burnout on IWB was non-significant in all samples except in the South African and Lithuanian samples, where we found that employees experiencing higher levels of burnout reported lower levels of IWB, as expected.

Consistent with this pattern of direct effects, the indirect effect of qualitative JI on in-role performance through burnout was negative in almost all samples. As hypothesized, qualitative JI predicted higher levels of burnout in six samples, which was in turn predictive of lower levels of in-role performance. In two samples—the US and Chinese samples—this indirect effect did not reach statistical significance. In contrast, we did not find empirical support for the hypothesized mediation effect of burnout on the relationship between qualitative job insecurity and IWB. This was predominantly due to the non-significant effect of burnout on IWB. The only two exceptions were found in the South African and Lithuanian samples, where burnout emerged as a significant explaining mechanism of the qualitative job insecurity–IWB relationship. In sum, the pattern of indirect effects found across six samples implies that burnout does have a salient role in explaining why job-insecure employees exhibit lower in-role performance. In contrast, burnout did not serve as the explaining mechanism in the relationship between qualitative job insecurity and IWB.

Finally, we found a non-significant direct effect of qualitative job insecurity on in-role performance across almost all samples. Two exceptions were found in the South African and Lithuanian samples, where this effect was unexpectedly positive, indicating that higher levels of qualitative job insecurity predicted higher levels of in-role performance. The direct effect of qualitative job insecurity on IWB was also predominantly non-significant. Two exceptions to this result were obtained in the USA and China. In the Chinese sample, higher levels of qualitative job insecurity were associated with lower levels of IWB. However, in the US sample, this effect was positive, indicating that the more threat employees perceived to valued features of their job, the more innovative they rated their work behavior.

7.4 Discussion

The present study examined the relationship between job insecurity and employee performance among higher education staff, a group of employees who must cope with both the growing threat of losing valued job features and increasing workload. In doing so, we aimed to contribute to the extant literature in four ways. First, we focused on qualitative job insecurity instead of on the more extensively examined quantitative job insecurity. Second, we examined two types of employee performance—in-role performance and IWB. Third, the study utilized JD-R theory and advanced burnout as the mechanism underlying the relationships between qualitative job insecurity and both performance indicators. Fourth, we tested the generalizability of the hypothesized mediation effects across eight different cultural settings. With few exceptions, the results of the current study are generally consistent: employees who perceived a greater threat to valued job features reported higher levels of burnout. In turn, burnout was predictive of poorer in-role performance and had a non-significant effect on employees' IWB. In most samples, burnout mediated the relationship between qualitative job insecurity and in-role performance but not between qualitative job insecurity and IWB.

Our first hypothesis concerned the explanatory role of burnout in the relationship between qualitative job insecurity and in-role performance. This assumption was supported in almost all samples: we found that qualitative job insecurity has a negative indirect effect on in-role performance in the Swiss, South African, Lithuanian, Greek, Croatian and Belgian samples. The two exceptions to this finding were the US and Chinese samples, a result that will be further discussed below. We also found that qualitative job insecurity was related to higher levels of employee burnout, as predicted by JD-R theory. Importantly, this finding was found in all samples except one, attesting to the universally harmful nature of qualitative job insecurity in the higher education sector. Although also positive, this effect did not reach statistical significance in the Chinese sample, potentially due to a relatively small sample size and the lack of statistical power (Cohen et al., 2003). In the current study, we utilized a recently developed model of burnout that conceptualizes this construct as a higher-order factor comprising four dimensions (exhaustion, mental distance, emotional and cognitive impairment) (Schaufeli et al., 2020a). Accordingly, our first finding aligns with the suggestion that perceiving a threat to one's valued job characteristics (and most often not knowing whether or when this might occur) drains employees' psychological and physical resources, leaving them exhausted, indifferent, or even cynical and unable to successfully regulate emotional and cognitive processes. In other words, qualitative job insecurity has the potential to instigate a health impairment process, a notion outlined in JD-R theory and empirically supported by previous research (e.g., Roll et al., 2019) and the current study.

As expected, we found that burnout was, in turn, predictive of lower levels of self-reported in-role performance. Again, this finding applied to all samples except one (it was non-significant in the US sample). According to JD-R theory, employees suffering from burnout are unable to successfully function at work (Bakker &

Demerouti, 2017; Schaufeli et al., 2019). This impairment in function can take many forms, with impaired in-role performance as one of the most obvious forms because it encompasses task assignments that are formally expected from employees. In the academic context, examples of impaired in-role performance are a reduced number of high-quality publications (academic staff) or unmet deadlines for financial reports (non-academic staff). We have argued that burnout, as a syndrome, may undermine employees' efforts to successfully perform their formal job duties due to a lack of energy and psychological detachment from work accompanied by unpleasant emotions and diminished cognitive capacities (Schaufeli et al., 2019). Our results conform with these theoretical assumptions as well as with previous studies (Bakker & Heuven, 2006).

The second hypothesis stated that burnout mediates the relationship between qualitative job insecurity and IWB. In addition to in-role performance, IWB has been advanced as essential for individual and organizational success, particularly in dynamic business environments characterized by rapid organizational change and intensive competition (e.g., Janssen et al., 2004; West & Farr, 1990). In line with this notion, we argue that IWB among higher education staff may be particularly relevant for HEIs for two main reasons. First, in recent decades, the higher education sector has undergone major structural reforms that require an innovative response from employees. Reform processes aimed at making higher education more inclusive, attractive, and competitive worldwide have required innovative changes in the work context. Furthermore, innovative work behavior at all levels has helped employees adapt to the changes introduced. Second, creativity and innovation are part of the very nature of scientific and educational work and have traditionally been linked to the context of higher education. However, the results of our analyses did not confirm Hypothesis 2. Although, as discussed above, we almost unequivocally confirmed a positive association between qualitative job insecurity and burnout across all samples, we found a non-significant effect of burnout on IWB in all samples except two (the effects in the South African and Lithuanian samples were statistically significant and negative, as expected). As a result, except for the South African and Lithuanian samples, burnout was not a statistically significant mediator of the relationship between qualitative job insecurity and IWB.

A plausible explanation for these unexpected results can be found in models that assume opposing cause-and-effect relationships between burnout and IWB. Namely, IWB can also be framed as an antecedent of impaired work-related well-being, such as burnout. In this regard, the consequences of IWB can vary depending on the organizational context (Huhtala & Parzefall, 2007). In a situation where employees fail to realize their innovative ideas due to situational constraints or when these ideas provoke negative reactions from colleagues and managers, well-being may be impaired. In this case, IWB will be positively associated with burnout. On the other hand, in a situation where the organization nurtures a positive climate and managers encourage innovation, IWB will be negatively associated with burnout. In other words, the association between IWB and burnout in our study may have been moderated (i.e., positive in some cases and negative in others) by variables that were not accounted for in the study, such as organizational context. Consistent with this assumption, Janssen et al. (2004) demonstrated that IWB was positively related to burnout only when levels of distributive and procedural organizational justice were low. Recently, Hammond et al. (2019) demonstrated that the perceived costs of speaking up moderate the association between IWB and burnout. Contrary to the authors' expectations, engagement in IWB was negatively related to burnout when employees perceived that they had little influence within the organization. Accordingly, future studies examining the relationship between IWB and burnout might account for its boundary conditions related to the organizational context.

Overall, burnout emerged as a salient explaining mechanism of the negative effects of qualitative job insecurity on in-role performance but not on employee IWB. The indirect effect on in-role performance aligns with the process described by Bakker and Demerouti (2017), according to which job demands cause strain, which in turn has a negative impact on employee performance. As such, it complements the extant theoretical perspectives that were predominantly used to explain the negative effects of qualitative job insecurity on employee performance, such as psychological contract theory (Niesen et al., 2018a, b), social identity theory (Callea et al., 2016) and threat rigidity theory (Probst et al., 2019). To the best of our knowledge, only two studies have utilized JD-R theory to examine burnout (or any of its subdimensions) as the mechanism underlying the relationship between job insecurity and performance-related indicators. Specifically, Darvishmotevali et al. (2017) demonstrated that anxiety, but not emotional exhaustion, mediated the relationship between a perceived threat of losing one's job (i.e., quantitative job insecurity) and in-role performance among frontline employees in the hospitality industry. Roll et al. (2019) found that burnout mediated the negative effects of both quantitative and qualitative job insecurity on the attention-related cognitive errors made by employees working in schools, banks, and hospitals. In addition to these two studies, the results of the current study portray burnout as the relevant precursor to poor in-role performance in the higher education sector. In contrast, the relationship between burnout and IWB seems slightly less straightforward and conditional upon the context of HEIs.

In addition to indirect effects, we found a non-significant direct effect of qualitative job insecurity on in-role performance across almost all samples (note that both the direct and indirect effects of qualitative job insecurity on in-role performance were non-significant in the US and Chinese samples). This finding indicates that burnout fully mediated the relationship between qualitative job insecurity and in-role performance in four samples (the Swiss, Greek, Croatian and Belgian samples) and partially in two samples (the South African and Lithuanian samples). Contrary to our expectations, the direct effect in the South African and Lithuanian samples was positive. The pattern of findings obtained in these two samples corresponds to the model proposed by Staufenbiel and König (2010). According to these authors, job insecurity can simultaneously exert both a negative indirect and positive direct effect on employee performance, which cancel each other out and thus result in a non-significant total effect (corresponding to the non-significant zero-order correlations between qualitative job insecurity and in-role performance found in both countries in the present study). In this case, the positive direct effect reflects the idea that job insecurity not only hinders but also has the potential to simultaneously enhance in-role performance as a form of job preservation strategy. We discuss the latter effect in greater detail when addressing the direct effect of job insecurity on IWB below.

With regards to the direct effects of qualitative job insecurity on IWB, we found non-significant effects in six samples (i.e., Swiss, South African, Lithuanian, Greek, Croatian and Belgian samples), a negative effect in the Chinese sample and a positive effect in the US sample. These findings indicate that burnout fully mediated the effect of qualitative job insecurity on IWB in the South African and Lithuanian samples and that qualitative job insecurity, although not through burnout, exerted the expected harmful effect on IWB in the Chinese sample. This set of findings conforms with the dominant perspective that job insecurity represents a hindrance job demand that negatively affects employee performance (Van Laethem et al., 2019). However, the direct effects of qualitative job insecurity on IWB were non-significant in most of the samples and positive in the US sample (it should be noted that these effects were consistent with the positive zero-order correlation). These findings call for additional explanation because it is difficult to find a theoretical argument for a non-significant or positive association between qualitative job insecurity and IWB among higher education staff. For example, the results contradict the well-known threat rigidity theory, which implies a positive relationship between anxiety and the tendency to persist in well-learned courses of action, which certainly does not include IWB (Staw et al., 1981). Furthermore, the positive effect found in the US sample is consistent with studies that have discussed the possibility that job insecurity can trigger employees' effort as a form of job preservation strategy (Shoss, 2017). In this latter case, qualitative job insecurity may trigger preservation strategies used by employees to prevent losing valued job characteristics. IWB can represent such a strategy if job-insecure employees believe that this kind of work behavior might portray them as valuable employees. Consistent with these assumptions, several other studies have reported positive relationships between work stressors and IWB. For example, in a sample of health professionals, Bunce and West (1994) demonstrated that IWB can represent a plausible strategy for coping with various sources of occupational stress. In their study, IWB was defined as coping behavior "*… occurring when: an individual perceives him or herself intentionally to introduce and apply, alone or within a group, new skills or procedures, designed significantly to benefit self, the group or the organization, with the result that recognized external demands appraised as taxing or exceeding resources are actually reduced or alleviated.*" (Bunce & West, 1994, p. 320). In a more recent cross-sectional study with Chinese employees, Ren and Zhang (2015) found a positive link between several work stressors and IWB (i.e., idea generation). However, it is also worth mentioning that the positive effect of qualitative job insecurity on in-role performance was not obtained in the US sample, which would substantiate the suggested designation of IWB as a preservation strategy. Our proposed explanation is therefore tentative and should be considered with caution.

Finally, the non-significant direct effects observed in our findings may be the result of boundary conditions that cancel each other out. However, this study did not account for these boundary conditions. Arguments for this assumption are evident in stress theories, as well as in the higher education reform process. Specifically, the goals of structural reforms in higher education are usually defined at the national and global levels, whether it is the internationalization of higher education (e.g., in Europe through the *Bologna reform*) or a heightened focus on performance and increasing student employability. The implementation of these reforms implies organizational changes carried out autonomously by HEIs. Scientific and teaching work should be adapted to goals often defined outside the institutions themselves. In such a situation, employees in higher education experience qualitative job insecurity as a hindrance job demand that negatively impacts their well-being. However, at the same time, they may perceive innovativeness as a job requirement. Yuan and Woodman (2010) demonstrated that when perceiving innovativeness as a component of one's job requirements, employees will exhibit IWB. Here, the authors have proven that these employees, when they exhibit IWB, expect positive work outcomes and strive to achieve a positive image in their organization. As such, two job demands—qualitative job insecurity and innovativeness—can interactively impact IWB. In a situation when qualitative job insecurity is paired with innovativeness as a perceived job demand, engagement in IWB is more likely than in a situation when innovativeness is not perceived as a job demand.

7.4.1 Limitations and Directions for Future Research

The research presented in this chapter has a few methodological shortcomings that might have affected the results and their interpretation. Specifically, we see three main sources of limitations in this study: (1) application of a cross-sectional design, (2) non-representative research sample and (3) measurements of the variables. In the following paragraphs, we discuss the possible impacts of these limitations on our findings and suggest future research directions.

Based on JD-R theory, our mediation model implies causal relationships between variables. However, the cross-sectional study design used in our study does not allow us to draw causal inferences. In this regard, the negative indirect effects of qualitative job insecurity on in-role performance via burnout may also be interpreted in the direction opposite to that hypothesized. For example, employees suffering from burnout may feel a greater threat of losing valued job features due to drained resources, and poor in-role performance may facilitate the development of burnout due to accumulated assignments and a bad relationship with one's supervisor. Moreover, poor in-role performance may also directly increase the perceived threat of losing valued job features, as demonstrated in the longitudinal study by Fischmann et al. (2018). Therefore, the results of this study should be interpreted as preliminary, and the conclusions should be limited to the established relationships between the studied variables. In the future, cross-lagged panel designs with a minimum of three measurement occasions are needed for sound testing of the mediation model proposed in the current study (Burkholder & Harlow, 2003).

Secondly, the samples used in this study were not representative of higher education staff in each country, thus limiting the external validity of our findings. In addition, the response rates varied across countries (from 6% in the USA to 58.8% in China) and could not be precisely calculated in some cases. These sample distortions may have affected the obtained results. As such, future studies may benefit from testing the hypothesized research model on more representative samples.

Finally, the measures used to operationalize the core study concepts have several limitations. First, the concept of burnout was defined by a four-item measure in which only one item operationalized each of the four burnout dimensions proposed by Schaufeli et al. (2019). Second, IWB was measured using a four-item scale that encompassed components of idea exploration and generation components, but not idea championing and implementation, as originally proposed by De Jong and Den Hartog (2010). Therefore, future research may include more comprehensive measures of both burnout and IWB. Additionally, low internal reliabilities of the burnout and in-role work behavior scales obtained in some samples (i.e., Cronbach's alphas below .70) may have distorted the correlations obtained in this study.

7.4.2 Conclusions and Practical Implications

Our study aligns with JD-R theory by demonstrating that qualitative job insecurity positively relates to burnout among higher education staff, indicating that the more concerned employees were about losing what is valuable in their jobs, the more burnout they experienced. It seems that the experience of qualitative job insecurity limits the physical and psychological resources necessary for coping with the high job demands present in academia. In addition, coping daily with qualitative job insecurity may also increase other job demands, such as workload and interpersonal conflicts. Importantly, our finding was invariant across almost all national samples with different cultural backgrounds (one exception was the Chinese sample). It was also found in heterogeneous samples encompassing all categories of higher education staff (academic and non-academic) and various job positions (e.g., permanent academic staff and junior research staff). As such, the results of the current study attest to the importance of implementing organizational interventions aimed at reducing qualitative job insecurity and/or its negative effects in order to promote well-being and prevent health deterioration of higher education staff.

With the exception of the US sample, we also found that burnout related negatively to in-role performance in each country. As a result, burnout fully mediated the relationship between qualitative job insecurity and in-role performance in six countries. We believe that these findings additionally strengthen the argument to policymakers regarding the importance of dealing with qualitative job insecurity in the higher education sector and delineate more precise guidelines for organizational interventions that might target burnout symptoms when dealing with the negative effects of this work stressor on in-role performance.

In contrast to in-role performance, the results concerning the mediating role of burnout in the relationship between qualitative job insecurity and IWB are less clear. The mediation effect of burnout was proven only in the South African sample. In all other countries, burnout was non-significantly related to IWB. As such, these results call for an investigation of the potential moderators of the link between burnout and IWB that might determine conditions under which this relationship is negative or, in some cases, even positive.

In sum, the pattern of indirect effects found across six samples implies that burnout does have a salient role in explaining why job-insecure employees in higher education exhibit lower in-role performance. In contrast, burnout did not serve as the explaining mechanism in the relationship between qualitative job insecurity and IWB.

7.5 Take Home Message

By exploring whether burnout can explain why employees who perceive more threat to valued features of their jobs tend to perform worse, this study moves the current understanding of the detrimental effects of qualitative job insecurity on employee performance one step forward. Using data collected in eight countries across four continents from employees working in the higher education sector, we found that burnout has substantial explanatory power in the relationship between qualitative job insecurity and in-role performance. These findings demonstrate that job-insecure employees do not perform their core task duties well because experiencing job insecurity exhausts their physical and psychological resources, making them unable and unwilling to do so. In contrast, burnout did not serve as a convincing explanation for the relationship between qualitative job insecurity and innovative work behavior, thus highlighting the need for additional studies that would identify and test alternative psychological explanations of this relationship.

References

Aisenberg, N., & Harrington, M. (1988). *Women of Academia: Outsiders in the sacred grove.* University of Massachusetts Press.

Anderson, N., Potočnik, K., & Zhou, J. (2014). Innovation and creativity in organizations: A state-of-the-science review, prospective commentary, and guiding framework. *Journal of Management, 40*(5), 1297–1333. https://doi.org/10.1177/0149206314527128

Bakker, A. B., & Demerouti, E. (2017). Job Demands–Resources theory: Taking stock and looking forward. *Journal of Occupational Health Psychology, 22*(3), 273–285. https://doi.org/10.1037/ocp0000056

Bakker, A. B., & Heuven, E. (2006). Emotional dissonance, burnout, and in-role performance among nurses and police officers. *International Journal of Stress Management, 13*(4), 423–440. https://doi.org/10.1037/1072-5245.13.4.423

Benson, W. L., Probst, T. M., Jiang, L., Olson, K. J., & Graso, M. (2017). Insecurity in the Ivory Tower: Direct and indirect effects of pay stagnation and job insecurity on faculty performance. *Economic and Industrial Democracy*, 1–16. DOI: https://doi.org/10.1177/0143831X17734297.

Bunce, D., & West, M. (1994). Changing work environments: innovative coping responses to occupational stress. *Work and Stress, 8*(4), 319–331. https://doi.org/10.1080/02678379408256539

Burkholder, G. J., & Harlow, L. L. (2003). An illustration of a longitudinal cross-lagged design for larger structural equation models. *Structural Equation Modeling, 10*, 465–486. https://doi.org/10.1207/S15328007SEM1003_8

Callea, A., Urbini, F., & Chirumbolo, A. (2016). The mediating role of organizational identification in the relationship between qualitative job insecurity, OCB and job performance. *Journal of Management Development, 35*(6), 735–746. https://doi.org/10.1108/JMD-10-2015-0143

Catano, V., Francis, L., Haines, T., Kirpalani, H., Shannon, H., Stringer, B., & Lozanzki, L. (2010). Occupational stress in Canadian universities: A national survey. *International Journal of Stress Management, 17*(3), 232–258. https://doi.org/10.1037/a0018582

Cohen, J., Cohen, P., West, S. G., & Aiken, L. S. (2003). *Applied multiple regression/correlation analysis for the behavioral sciences* (3rd ed.). Lawrence Erlbaum Associates.

Darvishmotevali, M., Arasli, H., & Kilic, H. (2017). Effect of job insecurity on frontline employee's performance. Looking through the lens of psychological strains and leverages. *International Journal of Contemporary Hospitality Management, 29*(6), 1724–1744. https://doi.org/10.1108/IJCHM-12-2015-0683

de Beer, L. T., Schaufeli, W. B., De Witte, H., Hakanen, J. J., Shimazu, A., Glaser, J., Seubert, C., Bosak, J., Sinval, J., & Rudnev, M. (2020). Measurement Invariance of the Burnout Assessment Tool (BAT) Across Seven Cross-National Representative Samples. *International Journal of Environmental Research and Public Health, 17*(15), 5604. https://doi.org/10.3390/ijerph17155604

De Jong, J. P. J., & Den Hartog, D. (2010). Measuring innovative work behavior. *Creativity and Innovation Management, 19*(1), 23–36. https://doi.org/10.1111/j.1467-8691.2010.00547.x

De Witte, H. (2005). Job insecurity: Review of the international literature on definitions, prevalence, antecedents and consequences. *Scandinavian Journal of Industrial Psychology, 31*, 1–6. https://doi.org/10.4102/sajip.v31i4.200

De Witte, H., De Cuyper, N., Handaja, Y., Sverke, M., Näswall, K., & Hellgren, J. (2010). Associations between quantitative and qualitative job insecurity and well-being: A test in Belgian banks. *International Studies of Management and Organization, 40*, 40–56. https://doi.org/10.2753/IMO0020-8825400103

De Witte, H., Pienaar, J., & De Cuyper, N. (2016). Review of 30 years of longitudinal studies on the association between job insecurity and health and well-being: Is there causal evidence? *Australian Psychologist, 51*(1), 18–31. https://doi.org/10.1111/ap.12176

Demerouti, E., Bakker, A. B., Nachreiner, F., & Schaufeli, W. B. (2001). The Job Demands – Resources model of burnout. *Journal of Applied Psychology, 86*(3), 499–512. https://doi.org/10.1037/0021-9010.86.3.499

Dolenec, D., & Doolan, K. (2013). Reclaming the role of higher education in Croatia: Dominant and oppositional framings. In P. Zgaga, U. Teichler, & J. Brennan (Eds.), *The Globalization Challenge for European Higher Education: Convergence, and Diversity, Centres and Peripheries*. Peter Lang.

Fischmann, G., De Witte, H., Sulea, C., & Iliescu, D. (2018). Qualitative job insecurity and in-role performance: A bidirectional longitudinal relationship? *European Journal of Work and Organizational Psychology, 27*(5), 603–615. https://doi.org/10.1080/1359432X.2018.1504769

Fischmann, G., De Witte, H., Sulea, C., Vander Elst, T., De Cuyper, N., & Iliescu, D. (2022). Validation of a Short and Generic Qualitative Job Insecurity Scale (QUAL-JIS). *European Journal of Career Assessment, 38*(5), 397–411. https://doi.org/10.1027/1015-5759/a000674

Greenhalgh, L., & Rosenblatt, Z. (1984). Job insecurity: Toward conceptual clarity. *Academy of Management Review, 3*, 438–448. https://doi.org/10.2307/258284

Hammond, M., Cross, C., Farrell, C., & Eubanks, D. (2019). Burnout and innovative work behaviour for survivors of downsizing: An investigation of boundary conditions. *Creativity and Innovation Management, 28*(3), 306–317. https://doi.org/10.1111/caim.12327

Hellgren, J., Sverke, M., & Isaksson, K. A. (1999). Two-dimensional approach to job insecurity: Consequences for employee attitudes and well-being. *European Journal of Work and Organizational Psychology, 8*, 179–195. https://doi.org/10.1080/135943299398311

Hensel, N. (1991). *Realizing gender equality in higher education: The need to integrate work-family issues. ASHE-ERIC Higher Education Report No. 2*. The George Washington University, School of Education and Human Development.

Huhtala, H., & Parzefall, M.-R. (2007). A review of employee well-being and innovativeness: An opportunity for a mutual benefit. *Creativity and Innovation Management, 16*(3), 299–306. https://doi.org/10.1111/j.1467-8691.2007.00442.x

Janssen, O., Van de Vliert, E., & West, M. (2004). The bright and dark sides of individual and group innovation: A special issue introduction. *Journal of Organizational Behavior, 25*, 129–145. https://doi.org/10.1002/job.242

Jiang, L., & Lavaysse, L. M. (2018). Cognitive and affective job insecurity: A meta-analysis and a primary study. *Journal of Management, 44*(6), 2307–2342. https://doi.org/10.1177/0149206318773853

Kinman, G. (1998). *Pressure points: A survey into the causes and consequences of occupational stress in UK academic and related staff*. London: Association of University Teachers [displayed 25 March 2011]. Available from http://www.ucu.org.uk/media/pdf/pressurepoints.pdf

Kinman, G. (2001). Pressure points: A review of stressors and strains in UK academics. *Educational Psychology, 21*(4), 474–492. https://doi.org/10.1080/01443410120090849

Kinman, G. (2008). Work stressors, health and sense of coherence in UK academic employees. *Educational Psychology: An International Journal of Experimental Educational, 28*(7), 823–835. https://doi.org/10.1080/01443410802366298

Kinman, G. (2014). Doing more with less? Work and wellbeing in academics. *Somatechnics, 4*, 219–235. https://doi.org/10.3366/soma.2014.0129

Kinman, G., & Jones, F. (2003). 'Running up the down escalator': Stressors and strains in UK academics. *Quaility in Higher Education, 9*(1), 22–38. https://doi.org/10.1080/13538320308162

Kinman, G., & Wray, S. (2016). *Work-related wellbeing in UK higher education*. University and College Union.

Lazarus, R. S., & Folkman, S. (1984). *Stress, appraisal, and coping*. Springer Publishing.

MacKinnon, D. P., Fairchild, A. J., & Fritz, M. S. (2007). Mediation analysis. *Annual Review of Psychology, 58*, 593–614. https://doi.org/10.1146/annurev.psych.58.110405.085542

Marginson, S. (2000). Rethinking academic work in the global era. *Journal of Higher Education Policy and Management, 22*(1), 23–35. https://doi.org/10.1080/713678133

Maslach, C., & Jackson, S. E. (1981). The measurement of experienced burnout. *Journal of Organizational Behavior, 2*, 99–113. https://doi.org/10.1002/job.4030020205

Muthén, L. K., & Muthén, B. O. (1998–2017). *Mplus user's guide*. 8: Muthén & Muthén.

Newman, D. A. (2014). Missing data: Five practical guidelines. *Organizational Research Methods, 17*(4), 372–411. https://doi.org/10.1177/1094428114548590

Niesen, W., Van Hootegem, A., Handaja, Y., Battistelli, A., & De Witte, H. (2018a). Quantitative and qualitative job insecurity and idea generation: The mediating role of psychological contract breach. *Scandinavian Journal of Work and Organizational Psychology, 3*(1), 1–14. https://doi.org/10.16993/sjwop.36

Niesen, W., Van Hootegem, A., Vander Elst, T., Battistelli, A., & De Witte, H. (2018b). Job insecurity and innovative work behaviour: A psychological contract perspective. *Psychologica Belgica, 57*(4), 174–189. https://doi.org/10.5334/pb.381

Opstrup, N., & Pihl-Thingvad, S. (2016). Stressing academia? Stress-as-offence-to-self at Danish universities. *Journal of Higher Education Policy and Management, 38*(1), 39–52. https://doi.org/10.1080/1360080X.2015.1126895

Piccoli, B., Reisel, W. D., & De Witte, H. (2021). Understanding the relationship between job insecurity and performance: Hindrance or challenge effect? *Journal of Career Development, 48*(2), 150–165. https://doi.org/10.1177/0894845319833189

Preacher, K. J., & Hayes, A. F. (2008). Asymptotic and resampling strategies for assessing and comparing indirect effects in multiple mediator models. *Behavior Research Methods, 40*(3), 879–891. https://doi.org/10.3758/BRM.40.3.879

Probst, T. M. (2003). Development and validation of the Job Security Index and the Job Security Satisfaction scale: A classical test theory and IRT approach. *Journal of Occupational and Organizational Psychology, 76*(4), 451–467.

Probst, T. M., Stewart, S. M., Gruys, M. L., & Tierney, B. W. (2007). Productivity, counterproductivity and creativity: The ups and downs of job insecurity. *Journal of Occupational and Organizational Psychology, 80*, 479–497. https://doi.org/10.1348/096317906X159103

Probst, T., Chizh, A., Hu, S., Jiang, L., & Austin, C. (2019). Explaining the relationship between job insecurity and creativity. A test of cognitive and affective mediators. *Career Development International*, 1362–0436. doi:https://doi.org/10.1108/CDI-04-2018-0118.

Ren, F., & Zhang, J. (2015). Job stressors, organizational innovation climate, and employees' innovative behavior. *Creativity Research Journal, 27*(1), 16–23. https://doi.org/10.1080/10400419.2015.992659

Roll, L. C., Siu, O., Li, S. Y. W., & De Witte, H. (2015). Job insecurity: Cross-cultural comparison between Germany and China. *Journal of Organizational Effectiveness: People and Performance, 2*(1), 36–54. https://doi.org/10.1108/JOEPP-01-2015-0002

Roll, L. C., Siu, O. L., Li, S. Y. W., & de Witte, H. (2019). Human error: The impact of job insecurity on attention-related cognitive errors and error detection. *International Journal of Environmental Research and Public Health, 16*(13). https://doi.org/10.3390/ijerph16132427

Schaufeli, W. B., & Taris, T. W. (2014). A critical review of the Job Demands-Resources Model: Implications for improving work and health. In G. Bauer & O. Hämmig (Eds.), *Bridging occupational, organizational and public health* (pp. 43–68). Springer. https://doi.org/10.1007/978-94-007-5640-3_4

Schaufeli, W. B., De Witte, H., & Desart, S. (2019). *Burnout assessment Tool – Test Manual.* KU Leuven. Retrieved from: https://www.burnoutassessmenttool.be

Schaufeli, W., Desart, S., & De Witte, H. (2020a). Burnout assessment tool (BAT) – Development, validity and reliability. *International Journal of Environmental Research and Public Health, 17*(24), 9495. https://doi.org/10.3390/ijerph17249495

Schaufeli, W. B., De Witte, H. & Desart, S. (2020b). *Manual Burnout Assessment Tool (BAT) – Version 2.0.* KU Leuven. Unpublished internal report. https://burnoutassessmenttool.be/project_eng/

Shin, J. C., & Jung, J. (2014). Academics job satisfaction and job stress across countries in the changing academic environments. *Higher Education, 67*(5), 603–620. https://doi.org/10.1007/s10734-013-9668-y

Shoss, M. K. (2017). Job insecurity: An integrative review and agenda for future research. *Journal of Management, 43*(6), 1911–1939. https://doi.org/10.1177/0149206317691574

Slišković, A., & Maslić, S. D. (2011). Work stress among university teachers. *Arhiv za Higijenu Rada i Toksikologiju, 62*, 299–307.

Sonnentag, S., & Frese, M. (2002). Performance concepts and performance theory. In S. Sonnentag (Ed.), *Psychological management of individual performance* (pp. 3–25). Wiley.

Staufenbiel, T., & König, C. J. (2010). A model for the effects of job insecurity on performance, turnover intention and absenteeism. *Journal of Occupational and Organizational Psychology, 83*(1), 101–117. https://doi.org/10.1348/096317908X401912

Staw, B. M., Sandelands, L. E., & Dutton, J. E. (1981). Threat rigidity effects in organizational behavior: A multilevel analysis. *Administrative Science Quarterly*, 501–524.

Sverke, M., & Hellgren, J. (2002). The nature of job insecurity: Understanding employment uncertainty on the brink of a new millennium. *Applied Psycholohy, 51*, 23–42. https://doi.org/10.1111/1464-0597.0077z

Sverke, M., Hellgren, J., & Naswall, K. (2002). No security: A review and meta-analysis of job insecurity and its consequences. *Journal of Occupational Health Psychology, 7*, 242–264. https://doi.org/10.1037/1076-8998.7.3.242

Sverke, M., Låstad, L., Hellgren, J., Richter, A., & Näswall, K. (2019). A meta-analysis of job insecurity and employee performance: Testing temporal aspects, rating source, welfare regime, and union density as moderators. *International Journal of Environmental Research and Public Health, 16*(14), 2536. https://doi.org/10.3390/ijerph16142536

Thorsen, E. J. (1996). Stress in academia: What bothers professors? *Higher Education, 31*, 471–489. https://doi.org/10.1007/BF00137127

Trow, M. (1994). Managerialism and the academic profession: The case of England. *Higher Education Policy, 7*(2), 11–18. https://doi.org/10.1057/hep.1994.13

Tytherleigh, M. Y., Webb, C., Cooper, C., & Ricketts, C. (2005). Occupational stress in UK higher education institutions: A comparative study of all staff categories. *Higher Education Research and Development, 24*(1), 41–61. https://doi.org/10.1080/0729436052000318569

Van Hootegem, A., Niesen, W., & De Witte, H. (2019). Does job insecurity hinder innovative work behaviour? A threat rigidity perspective. *Creativity and Innovation Management, 28*, 19–29. https://doi.org/10.1111/caim.12271

Van Laethem, M., Beckers, D. G. J., de Bloom, J., Sianoja, M., & Kinnunen, U. (2019). Challenge and hindrance demands in relation to self-reported job performance and the role of restoration, sleep quality, and affective rumination. *Journal of Occupational and Organizational Psychology, 92*(2), 225–254. https://doi.org/10.1111/joop.12239

Vander Elst, T., Richter, A., Sverke, M., Näswall, K., De Cuyper, N., & De Witte, H. (2014a). Threat of losing valued job features: The role of perceived control in mediating the effect of qualitative job insecurity on job strain and psychological withdrawal. *Work & Stress: An International Journal of Work, Health & Organisations, 28*(2), 143–164. https://doi.org/10.1080/02678373.2014.899651

Vander Elst, T., Van den Broeck, A., De Cuyper, N., & De Witte, H. (2014b). On the reciprocal relationship between job insecurity and employee well-being: Mediation by perceived control? *Journal of Occupational and Organizational Psychology, 87*, 671–693. https://doi.org/10.1111/joop.12068

West, M. A., & Farr, J. L. (1990). *Innovation and creativity at work: Psychological and organisational strategies*. Wiley.

Williams, L. J., & Anderson, S. E. (1991). Job satisfaction and organizational commitment as predictors of organizational citizenship and in-role behaviors. *Journal of Management, 17*, 601–617. https://doi.org/10.1177/014920639101700305

Winefield, A. H., Gillespie, N. A., Stough, C., Dua, J., Hapuarachchi, J., & Boyd, C. (2003). Occupational stress in Australian university staff: Results from a national survey. *International Journal of Stress Management, 10*(1), 51–63. https://doi.org/10.1037/1072-5245.10.1.51

Yuan, F., & Woodman, R. W. (2010). Innovative behavior in the workplace: The role of performance and image outcome expectations. *Academy of Management Journal, 53*(2), 323–342. https://doi.org/10.5465/AMJ.2010.49388995

Darja Maslić Seršić is Professor of Psychology at the Department of Psychology, Faculty of Humanities and Social Sciences, University of Zagreb. Her research interests are in the area of Occupational Health Psychology and include unemployment, stress at work and well-being. She teaches courses in quantitative research methods, vocational behavior and organizational psychology.

Jasmina Tomas is an Assistant Professor at the Faculty of Humanities and Social Sciences, University of Zagreb. In her research, she mainly focuses on topics of work stressors (with an emphasis on economic stressors such as job insecurity) and occupational well-being. She teaches courses in the realm of W/O psychology and research methods.

Chapter 8
Insecurity and Justice in Academia: Exploring the Interplay

Jurgita Lazauskaitė-Zabielskė and Ieva Urbanavičiūtė

Insecurity and justice have gained particular relevance in the academic context, which the current book is focused on. A number of factors have contributed to substantial shifts in the way faculty life has been organised over recent decades. They include, for example, technological and organisational change, the evolution of university management regimes, pressures related to redefinition and broadening of the role of academia in society (Alexander & Manolchev, 2020; Shin & Jung, 2014), as well as the need to be highly adaptive to unexpected shocks, such as the global COVID-19 pandemic (Savic, 2020). Arguably, all of them have their share in perceived job insecurity and fairness of treatment at work that is ultimately reflected in higher education employees' job attitudes, in-role performance, and occupational health.

Indeed, research on the quality of work in higher education consistently points to the expected or actual increase in job demands and obstacles to gaining promotion as a key risk for academic employees' well-being (e.g., Biron et al., 2008; Bryson, 2004; Kinman & Court, 2010), which underlines the presence of qualitative job insecurity in their psychosocial work environment. Furthermore, many academics face precarious job contracts, with quantitative job insecurity not only marking early careers but often extending into a prolonged pattern (Alexander & Manolchev, 2020; Brechelmacher et al., 2015). The aspect of fairness has an essential resonance in these uncertainties and draws attention to a broad range of issues related to perceived effort-reward imbalance (Kinman, 2019), academic freedom and participation in decision-making (Silvernail et al., 2021), and equity practices (Kjeldal et al., 2005) that may be a deciding factor in the way academic employees respond to their career challenges.

J. Lazauskaitė-Zabielskė (✉) · I. Urbanavičiūtė
Center for Organizational Psychology Research, Institute of Psychology, Faculty of Philosophy, Vilnius University, Vilnius, Lithuania
e-mail: jurgita.lazauskaite@fsf.vu.lt; ieva.urbanaviciute@fsf.vu.lt

L. C. Roll et al. (eds.), *Global Perspectives on Job Insecurity in Higher Education*, Aligning Perspectives on Health, Safety and Well-Being,
https://doi.org/10.1007/978-3-031-85772-0_8

We start this chapter by presenting the notion of overall justice and its role in the organisation. We explore the relationship between perceived justice and job insecurity, starting from (in)justice as the antecedent of job (in)security. We then focus on perceived justice as an explanatory mechanism (i.e., mediator) for the job insecurity–outcomes relationship. Finally, we explore the interaction between overall justice and job insecurity. Drawing on empirical data from a large cross-sectional study of academia in 10 countries, we demonstrate that perceptions of an organisation's fairness provide a basis for the effect of job insecurity on employees' performance and well-being. We conclude the chapter by giving practical implications and guidelines for future research.

8.1 Organisational Justice and Its Role in the Organisation

Organisational justice—a term coined a few decades ago by Greenberg (1987)—refers to the extent to which people perceive organisational events as fair. It is widely regarded to take three forms: the perceived fairness of decision outcomes (i.e., distributive justice), the perceived fairness of decision-making procedures (i.e., procedural justice), and the perceived fairness of interpersonal treatment (i.e., interactional justice). In this chapter, we shall take the holistic approach to justice and focus on overall justice, the interest in which has grown considerably in recent decades (Ambrose et al., 2015).

Overall justice refers to individuals' global assessment of the fairness of a social entity, for example, supervisor or organisation (Ambrose & Schminke, 2009). Although the focus on facet-specific justice judgements has been shown to help understand the justice phenomenon in organisations, some scholars (e.g., Greenberg, 2001) have suggested that overall justice perceptions capture individuals' justice experiences more accurately, and it may indeed help to overcome some limitations in the existing examinations of justice (e.g., Lind, 2001; Shapiro, 2001). More precisely, the literature maintains that although individuals may distinguish between different types of justice, they experience justice in a holistic manner (Ambrose & Schminke, 2009; Ambrose et al., 2015). Hence, by focusing on overall justice, one may grasp the entire justice experience better. Secondly, focusing on justice facets may underrepresent the total impact of justice in a given situation (Ambrose & Arnaud, 2005; Ambrose & Schminke, 2009). Therefore, researchers should focus on overall justice when interested in the effects of justice (Hauenstein et al., 2001). Thirdly, as noted by Ambrose et al. (2015), researchers often predict the same antecedents and/or outcomes for different types of justice (e.g., DeConinck, 2010; Holtz & Harold, 2013; Hulland et al., 2012), suggesting that they are indeed more interested in the general judgement of fairness than in particular types of it.

Fourthly, overall justice predicts outcomes above and beyond particular justice types and a composite measure of justice facets and, therefore, increases the predictability of justice judgements in relation to outcomes (Ambrose et al., 2015). Thus, when one is interested in the effects of perceived fairness in the organisation, measurement of overall justice would be advantageous. As explained by Colquitt and Shaw (2005), researchers should match the specificity of the justice dimension being investigated to the outcomes of interest. Consequently, global attitudes towards a job or organisation should be examined together with a global measure of justice. Finally, as noted in seminal works on justice (e.g., Lind, 2001), fairness constitutes only one among the many motivational forces influencing behaviour. Therefore, studying overall justice helps assess the relative importance of justice compared to other motivational forces. Moreover, while studies on organisational fairness usually focus on justice types, which reflect fairness assessments of finite, time- and situation-bound events, entities (e.g., organisations) exist beyond individual events and may, in fact, be associated with numerous and conflicting events (Hollensbe et al., 2008). Indeed, previous theoretical as well as empirical research suggests that individuals form overall justice perceptions when exposed to different justice cues in the workplace and that these overall justice perceptions influence employee behaviour in organisations. In the following parts of the chapter, we highlight the relationship between job insecurity and perceived overall justice, mainly focusing on their role in higher education employees' well-being. As a result of various transformations of the higher education sector worldwide, individuals pursuing academic careers are often subject to a considerable amount of uncertainty and precarisation that may be highly detrimental to the quality of their working life (Brechelmacher et al., 2015; Catano et al., 2010). Thus, it is crucial to increase our understanding of the role of institutional aspects in shaping or alleviating these stressors. Fairness in the organisation is one such important aspect that has been shown to contribute to the quality of the organisational climate for academia (McMurray & Scott, 2013) and has long-term effects on faculty members' commitment (Ambrose & Cropanzano, 2003). Yet, it is under-researched in the context of job insecurity in academia.

8.2 Injustice as the Antecedent of Job Insecurity

Although most of the existing research focuses on the outcomes of job insecurity, its far-reaching detrimental effects on employees' attitudes, well-being, and job performance (e.g., see meta-analysis and reviews by Cheng & Chan, 2008; Sverke et al., 2002) urge us to better understand the antecedents of job insecurity because it can inform about how job insecurity occurs in the first place. As a perceptual phenomenon, job insecurity may result from contextual and individual factors. In their review on the nature of job insecurity, Sverke and Hellgren (2002) suggested that in addition to environmental factors (e.g., economic fluctuations, labour market characteristics, organisational changes, and employment contracts), job insecurity may also depend upon employees' individual characteristics (e.g., family responsibilities, employability) and subjective perceptions, such as perceived fairness. As noted in seminal works on justice, employees seek fair treatment for two reasons. According to the instrumental model (Thibaut & Walker, 1975), fairness helps to control economic outcomes, while the relational model posits that fair treatment indicates the value of employees' membership in the organisation (Lind & Tyler, 1988). In either case, being fairly treated by the organisation can be expected to promote employees' perceptions of situational control and make the future more predictable, consequently reducing the uncertainty about one's employment and/or its conditions. As has been previously demonstrated by some studies, the perceived fairness of employee treatment during organisational changes in the past helps to maintain employee positive attitudes and diminishes perceived insecurity. For example, Brockner et al. (1992) have found that layoff survivors, who believed that the layoff implementing procedures and layoff outcomes were fair, were less worried and distressed. Ito and Brotheridge (2007) conceptualised organisational justice as perceived fairness of an important change that the organisation had recently experienced and hypothesised that employees might expect that previously experienced fairness would continue and that their contributions would be considered, and interests would be taken into account when layoff decisions are made, consequently leading to lower levels of job insecurity. A cross-sectional study among 600 full-time employees of the federal civil service confirmed their predictions and showed perceived fairness to negatively predict job insecurity. Finally, a study by Loi et al. (2012) showed that procedural justice was negatively related to job insecurity, with the effect being stronger under the condition of ethical leadership and among employees with low power distance orientation. While such studies are scarce and most focus on perceived procedural fairness in the context of layoffs, they nevertheless demonstrate the potential of perceived justice to prevent job insecurity from occurring.

8.3 Justice as an Explanatory Mechanism for the Job Insecurity Effects

One of the lenses to view the relationship between job insecurity and fairness is offered by the social exchange perspective that posits job insecurity as an imbalance in the exchange relationship between the employee and employer and suggests perceived justice to act as a mediational mechanism for the job insecurity-outcomes relationship (Lee et al., 2018; Shoss, 2017).

Social Exchange Theory (SET; Blau, 1964) posits that any social exchange involves a series of interactions that generate obligations. Moreover, these interactions are considered interdependent and contingent on the actions of another party (Cropanzano & Mitchell, 2005). Resources in exchange situations may be particular or universal, tangible or symbolic (Foa & Foa, 1980). In the organisational context, resources translate into economic and socio-emotional outcomes (Blau, 1964; Cropanzano & Mitchell, 2005). In academic settings, the organisational part of this social exchange relationship is strongly based on esteem (e.g., through recognition of achievements), career progression, and security, which are seen as rewards for the time and effort academic employees invest in their work (e.g., Hamilton, 2019; Kinman, 2019). This in turn reflects individual-level outcomes, such as job satisfaction, engagement, and further commitment, to name just a few (Ambrose & Cropanzano, 2003; Mudrak et al., 2018; Shin & Jung, 2014). Arguably, organisational fairness perceptions are an essential linking element in these social exchange dynamics because they serve as a basis for employees' interpretations about 'what is right'.

From this perspective, employment and its conditions may be regarded as a type of crucial resource (Hobfoll, 2001) that is reciprocated by employees' investments. When employees experience job insecurity (i.e., a threat of losing valuable job features or the job itself), it may signal that there is a change in the exchange relationship on the part of the organisation. As the anticipated changes are unwanted and imply a possible loss of resources, they inevitably invoke fairness judgments, as posited by organisational justice theory (Ambrose, 2002). In other words, failure to provide employees with job security presumably leads employees to interpret the situation as unfair, creating an imbalance in the social exchange relationship (Folger & Cropanzano, 2001; Schumacher et al., 2016) and resulting in employees' perception that their organisation has failed to meet its reciprocal exchange obligations (Rosen et al., 2009).

The mediating role of perceived justice in the job insecurity-outcomes relationship is also consistent with the arguments of Fairness Heuristic Theory (FTH; Lind, 2001; Van den Bos et al., 2001) and Uncertainty Management Theory (UMT, Lind & Van den Bos, 2002). According to FHT, employees rather quickly develop judgments about the fairness of a given work context, which they use as a cognitive shortcut to guide their behavior and regulate emotional involvement in that context. More precisely, FHT states that there are two phases of fairness heuristic formation and use. The first phase—the judgmental phase—occurs at the beginning of the relationship or in times of uncertainty when employees feel insecure about the future. During this phase, justice-relevant information is processed to create a general justice judgment. Once general justice judgments are formed, the use phase starts. In this second phase, justice judgments act as heuristics influencing attitudes, and they guide subsequent social decisions, turning into a more stable and more general justice judgment. FHT posits that employees seek to form judgments about fairness because fairness acts as a readily available indicator that signals safety from being excluded from the group or exploited by its members. In other words, fairness judgments help solve what Lind (2001) called the "fundamental social dilemma", arising from the tension between the advantages and risks of being a group member. The fairness heuristic helps to solve this dilemma by allowing employees to evaluate whether they are safe as they move from personal interests and follow the interests of the group or the organisation.

FHT offers two theoretical ideas that were new at the time and are still relevant today. Firstly, instead of underlining the differential effects of specific types of justice, it posits that different types of justice form an overall judgment of fairness, the so-called fairness heuristic, that subsequently influences employees' attitudes and behaviours. Secondly, FTH suggests that employees' interest in fairness might be episodic because once formed, the fairness heuristic acts as a relatively stable lens through which subsequent organisational events are interpreted. However, while FHT argues that fairness heuristics remain quite stable, it also states that the perceiver may re-enter the judgmental phase under certain circumstances. Any actual (e.g., shifts in organisational structure, fundamental changes in the organisation) or symbolic evidence (e.g., feelings of individual job insecurity resulting from the anticipated negative change in the working conditions or the job contract) indicating that the relationship between the individual and organisation is changing may prompt employees to revisit existing fairness judgements (Proudfoot & Lind, 2015). Not surprisingly, longitudinal studies (e.g., Holtz & Harold, 2009) have shown significant variability in overall justice perceptions over time.

UMT extended many of the propositions of FTH and argued that fairness judgements serve a particular function in helping manage feelings of uncertainty. Therefore, employees are more likely to consider fairness in times of uncertainty, and uncertainty plays an important role in fairness judgements. Employees will be more sensitive to fairness in highly uncertain situations, and when uncertainty is low, employees will be less sensitive. UMT also posits that being in a state of uncertainty or insecurity may prompt people to gather new information and revisit their existing fairness judgments in order to predict whether they can expect fair treatment in the future. In terms of FHT, uncertainty might induce one to leave the use phase and re-enter the judgmental phase where new fairness judgments are established.

The assumptions of the above-presented theories are beautifully illustrated in the research findings. Drawing on SET (Cropanzano & Mitchell, 2005), Piccoli and De Witte (2015) suggested distributive injustice as a measure of an unfair social exchange relationship and tested whether perceived imbalance might constitute a mediational mechanism through which job insecurity relates to workers' well-being. Using a sample of blue-collar workers, they found distributive injustice to mediate the relationship between job insecurity and emotional exhaustion. In another study, Piccoli et al. (2017) showed procedural and interactional justice to act as mediators in the relationship between job insecurity and citizenship behaviour. Similarly, Schumacher et al. (2016) showed that procedural justice mediates the relationship between job insecurity and affective commitment.

Furthermore, Haynie et al. (2016) expected job insecurity to undermine the social exchange relationship held with the organisation by lowering overall justice, which in turn was expected to reduce satisfaction with pay and incentives. They found overall justice to mediate the relation between job insecurity and pay satisfaction but not incentive satisfaction. A recent study by Lazauskaite-Zabielske et al. (2019) built on FHT and SET and found qualitative job insecurity to be related to affective organisational commitment, satisfaction with the organisation, and turnover intention via perceived overall organisation-focused justice.

To sum up, existing empirical studies confirm the role of organisational justice as a potential explanatory mechanism in the job insecurity-outcomes relationship. Having a tangible, practical aspect, it definitely merits more research attention in the future. However, the above-discussed mediation scheme is not the only way of investigating justice judgements in job-insecure contexts. Interestingly, the mechanisms relating organisational justice and job insecurity may be quite multi-faceted, and in this chapter, we aim to provide a glimpse of their variety.

8.4 Justice and Insecurity as Interacting Variables

In this section, we turn to the interaction between perceived justice and job insecurity. An interaction, or otherwise moderation, offers a range of interesting possibilities for investigating the nature of both organisational justice and job insecurity as well as the relationship between the two in predicting well-being outcomes. When testing an interaction, the moderator is often considered a rather stable variable, to some extent representing situational or individual differences between the employees. Hence, this approach offers an entirely different insight into justice and/or job insecurity as established phenomena in the organisation. We will overview the underlying implications in more detail below.

8.4.1 Organisational Justice as a Buffer of the Job Insecurity Effects

One way of exploring the interaction effects is to test organisational justice as a buffer, or a boundary condition, that potentially determines the strength of the negative job insecurity outcomes. Here, we encounter a major conceptual difference between the earlier described mediation and the current moderation hypotheses. Whereas in the mediation model one would expect justice to be quite dynamic and malleable perception (i.e., fairness judgments can be affected by job insecurity), when testing a moderation, we are treating perceived justice as a relatively static, established organisational characteristics that one can rely on and that can act as a resource for counteracting the detrimental effects of job insecurity.

The moderating role of organisational justice in the job insecurity-outcomes relationship can be investigated using the same theoretical framework, comprising of Fairness Heuristic Theory (FTH; Lind, 2001; Van den Bos et al., 2001) and Uncertainty Management Theory (UMT, Lind & Van den Bos, 2002). As described in the previous section of this chapter, employees are likely to seek information about fairness to help manage their feelings of uncertainty. Hence, established justice judgements may be seen as an essential condition determining how employees will eventually react to job insecurity cues.

Several empirical studies have taken this approach, testing organisational justice as a moderator. For example, a study by Silla et al. (2010) investigated the relationship between quantitative job insecurity and employee attitudes. Their study provided some support for the claim that fairness may buffer the detrimental effects of job insecurity, and these effects were found to be weaker when fairness was present in the organisation. Another study by Sora et al. (2010) took a step further by applying multilevel analyses to better capture contextual effects. Their findings revealed that both organisational justice and organisational justice climate buffered the relationship between quantitative job insecurity and employee attitudes. However, notably, no such effects were found for affective well-being as an outcome.

At this point, one may wonder whether the buffering role of organisational justice could depend on the type of outcome. Even though still scarce, existing findings hint at it, showing quite mixed and contradictory evidence when the investigation of job insecurity outcomes shifts from employee attitudes to more tangible aspects, such as job performance. To illustrate that, Wang et al. (2015), using 2-wave and 3-wave data, found that when employees perceived low levels of overall justice, job insecurity was significantly negatively related to job performance based on company records and supervisor ratings, while under conditions of high levels of overall justice, job insecurity was not related to job performance. Moreover, in the same study, a mediated moderation analysis revealed job insecurity to be negatively related to job performance through work engagement when organisational justice was low. In other words, Wang et al.'s (2015) findings suggest that the negative effect of job insecurity appears to be first manifested in reduced positive affect at work and then poorer job performance when overall justice is low. Quite on the contrary, a study by Piccoli et al. (2011), conducted among blue-collar workers in two Italian organisations, demonstrated that high organisational justice might exacerbate the negative impact of job insecurity on some performance aspects. They found that while the adverse effects of job insecurity on affective commitment and citizenship behaviour were more pronounced under low procedural and interactional justice, the interaction pattern for self-rated job performance was just the opposite, that is, justice perceptions exacerbated the negative effect of job insecurity. Whereas yet another research adds even more complications to the story. According to Koen et al. (2020), in times of job insecurity, demonstrating good job performance may be seen as a strategy for preserving one's job, but obviously, it would be reasonable only if the organisation is perceived as fair by the employee. Interestingly, however, their findings did not support this premise, showing that job insecurity was associated with enhanced performance only in extremely vulnerable situations (i.e., when distributive justice was perceived as low and employees could not rely on their organisation to reward their performance fairly, thus reflecting high person-at-risk threat).

Such equivocal results call for a better understanding of the ways in which job insecurity and organisational justice interact in predicting different outcomes, thus opening several potential research lines that we discuss below and further illustrate with our data in the second part of this chapter.

8.5 Justice and Insecurity in Academia: An Empirical Study

In this section, we will empirically illustrate the interaction between job insecurity and organisational justice in academia. Following the recommendations in the literature (e.g., Shoss, 2017), we shall examine both types of job insecurity, that is, qualitative and quantitative job insecurity, to better take into account the full scope of job insecurity as a phenomenon. Furthermore, we will focus on the moderating role of overall justice rather than its distinct types when investigating the outcomes of job insecurity. Based on FHT (Lind, 2001) and UMT (Lind & van den Bos, 2002), employees rely on a general judgement of justice instead of specific types of justice when encountering uncertain situations. Hence, overall justice is particularly relevant here. Finally, we explore a range of outcome variables, including attitudinal, performance-related, and well-being outcomes of job insecurity, to unravel the potentially differential moderator effects.

8.6 Method

8.6.1 *Participants and Procedure*

Employees from various universities across ten countries (Belgium, China, Croatia, Greece, Lithuania, Romania, South Africa, Switzerland, United Kingdom, and the United States) were invited to complete an online questionnaire. Participants in all countries were informed about the purpose of the study, were assured that their participation was voluntary and anonymous, and that their data would be treated confidentially.

The final sample included 4669 employees (36.5% male, 58.5% female, 5.1% did not indicate their gender), with a mean age of 41.15 ($SD = 11.24$) years. Regarding position, 41% of the participants were academic staff (i.e., professors, lecturers), 29.4% were administrative staff, and 16.1% were PhD students and postdoc researchers. The majority of the sample (72%) held full-time jobs and were highly educated (6.5% had obtained a bachelor's degree, 29.7% a master's degree, and 59.5% had a doctoral degree or another equivalent). Below, we describe in more detail the sample in each country.

8.6.2 *Measures*

Quantitative job insecurity was assessed with the 4-item JI scale developed by De Witte (2000) and validated by Vander Elst et al. (2014). A sample item is "I feel insecure about the future of my job". Items were assessed on a 5-point scale, ranging from (1) "strongly disagree" to (5) "strongly agree".

Qualitative job insecurity was measured with four validated by Fischmann et al. (2022). A sample item is "I think my job will change for the worse". Items were assessed on a 5-point scale, ranging from (1) "strongly disagree" to (5) "strongly agree".

Overall justice was measured with the 3-item scale developed by Ambrose and Schminke (2009). Sample item: "Overall, I'm treated fairly by my (HE institution)". Items were assessed using a 5-point scale, ranging from (1) "strongly disagree" to (5) "strongly agree".

Work engagement was measured with the ultra-short version of the Utrecht Work Engagement Scale (UWES-3; Schaufeli et al., 2017). The UWES-3 measures three dimensions of work engagement: vigor ("At my work I feel bursting with energy"), dedication ("I am enthusiastic about my job") and absorption ("I am immersed in my work") with the use of a 7-point scale, ranging from (0) "never" to (6) "always".

Burnout was assessed with four items from the Burnout Assessment Tool (BAT) (Schaufeli et al., 2019). Example item: "At work, I feel mentally exhausted". Items were scored on a 7-point scale, ranging from (0) "never" to (6) "always".

In-role performance was measured with four items from Williams and Anderson (1991). Example item: "I fulfil the responsibilities specified in my job description". Items were assessed on a 5-point scale, ranging from (1) "strongly disagree" to (5) "strongly agree".

Job satisfaction was measured with one item from Quinn and Shepard (1974). The respondents were asked to indicate how satisfied they were with their job, considering everything, based on a 7-point scale, from 1 (highly dissatisfied) to 7 (highly satisfied).

8.6.3 Strategy of Analysis

We performed hierarchical linear regression analyses using the PROCESS macro for SPSS (Model 1) developed by Hayes (2013) to test the proposed moderating effects across the entire sample. Work engagement, burnout, in-role performance, and job satisfaction were modelled as outcome variables one at a time. The main and interaction effects for quantitative and qualitative job insecurity were tested separately. Thus, hypothesised effects were tested in two sets of analyses for each dependent variable. The control variables (i.e., age, gender) did not change the results in a significant way; hence, they were not included in the final output. Predictor and moderating variables were mean centered prior to calculating the interactions (Aiken & West, 1991). Significant interaction effects were plotted at +/− 1SD of the moderator (Preacher et al., 2006). For measurement equivalence, please see Chaps. 2 and 3.

8.7 Results

8.7.1 *Descriptive Statistics*

Means, standard deviations, Cronbach's alphas, and correlations between the variables are presented in Table 8.1.

8.7.2 *Main and Moderating Effects*

Table 8.2 shows the results of regression analyses, where job insecurity and overall justice interactively predict work engagement, burnout, in-role performance, and job satisfaction. Quantitative and qualitative job insecurity were found to negatively predict job satisfaction and positively predict burnout. Quantitative job insecurity was also weakly although significantly negatively related to job performance. Moreover, overall justice positively predicted work engagement, job performance, and job satisfaction and negatively predicted burnout. Furthermore, out of eight tested interactions between quantitative and qualitative job insecurity and overall justice, seven appeared significant. However, except for job satisfaction, the significant interactions between the two types of job insecurity and overall justice in predicting outcome variables showed the opposite pattern: high overall justice exacerbated the negative impact of job insecurity on perceived performance, work engagement, and burnout. More precisely, under the condition of low overall justice, quantitative job insecurity was unrelated to work engagement ($B = .01$, 95%CI [–.05, .06], $t = .26$, $p = .79$). Nevertheless, when overall justice was high, quantitative job insecurity negatively predicted work engagement ($B = -.15$, 95%CI [–.20, –.10], $t = -6.33$, $p < 0.01$). Moreover, the negative relationship between qualitative

Table 8.1 Means, Standard deviations, Alpha Coefficients and Correlations between the study variables ($n = 4669$)

		Mean	*SD*	*α*	1	2	3	4	5	6
1	Quantitative JI	2.33	.95	.85	–					
2	Qualitative JI	2.84	.95	.86	.51**	–				
3	Overall justice	3.44	.96	.92	–.30**	–.50**	–			
4	Work engagement	5.39	1.28	.82	–.13**	–.27**	.25**	–		
5	Burnout	2.87	1.23	.76	.21**	.36**	–.25**	–.34**	–	
6	In-role performance	4.37	.60	.88	–.12**	–.02	.08**	.25**	–.16**	–
7	Job satisfaction	5.02	1.59	–	–.29**	–.39**	.47**	.34**	–.33**	.12*

JI job insecurity. $^{**}p < .01$, $^{*}p < .05$

Table 8.2 Interactions of qualitative and quantitative job insecurity and overall justice ($n = 4669$)

	Work engagement			Burnout			In-role performance			Job satisfaction		
Predictors	*B* (SE)	R^2	*F*	*B* (SE)	R^2	*F*	*B* (SE)	R^2	*F*	*B* (*SE*)	R^2	*F*
Constant	3.78(.18)**			2.89(.02)**			4.35(.01)**			5.04(.02)**		
Quantitative JI	.22(.06)			.20(.02)**			−.07(.01)*			−.28(.02)**		
Overall Justice	.53(.49)**			−.27(.02)**			.04(.01)**			.69(.02)**		
Quantitative JI ⊆ Over-all Justice	−.09(.02)**	.07	114.86**	.06 (.02)**	.08	142.27**	−.07(.01)**	.03	47.84**	.06(.02)**	.25	515.19**
Constant	4.52(.24)**			2.88(.02)**			4.31(.01)**			5.08(.02)**		
Qualitative JI	.03(.07)			.41(.02)**			.03(.01)			−.36(.022)**		
Overall Justice	.45(.06)**			−.12(.02)**			.09(.01)**			.58(.02)**		
Qualitative JI ⊆ Overall Justice	−.08(.02)**	.09	155.49**	.01(.02)	.14	245.93**	−.13(.01)**	.05	82.98**	.13(.02)**	.26	551.35**

JI job insecurity. $^*p < .05$, $^{**}p < .01$, $^{***}p < .001$

job insecurity and work engagement was weaker ($B = -.16$, 95%CI [−.22, −.10], $t = -5.24$, $p < .01$) when overall justice was low than when overall justice was high ($B = -.29$, 95%CI [−.34, −.25], $t = -12.63$, $p < .01$). Furthermore, quantitative job insecurity was unrelated to in-role job performance under low levels of overall justice ($B = .01$, 95%CI [−.02, .03], $t = .32$, $p = .75$), but negatively predicted job performance when overall justice was high ($B = -.11$, 95%CI [−.13, −.09], $t = -10.00$, $p < .01$). Qualitative job insecurity was positively related to in-role performance ($B = .17$, 95%CI [.14, .19], $t = 11.44$, $p < .01$) when overall justice was low, and it negatively predicted performance ($B = -.04$, 95%CI [−.06, −.02], $t = -3.85$, $p < .01$) under high levels of overall justice. Similarly, quantitative job insecurity was more strongly related to burnout when overall justice was high ($B = .23$, 95%CI [.19, .28], $t = 10.67$, $p < .01$) than when it was low ($B = .13$, 95%CI [.07, .18], $t = 4.78$, $p < .01$), while the interaction between qualitative job insecurity and overall justice when predicting burnout was non-significant. The illustration of the interaction effects is presented in Figs. 8.1, 8.2, 8.3 and 8.4.

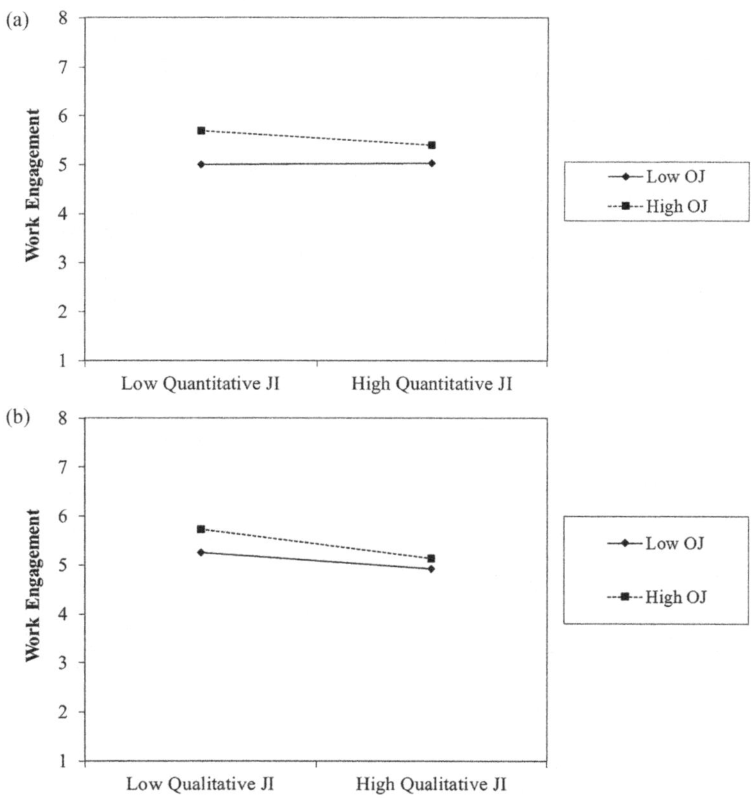

Fig. 8.1 Interaction between quantitative (model A) and qualitative job insecurity (model B) and overall justice in predicting work-engagement. *JI* job insecurity, *OJ* overall justice

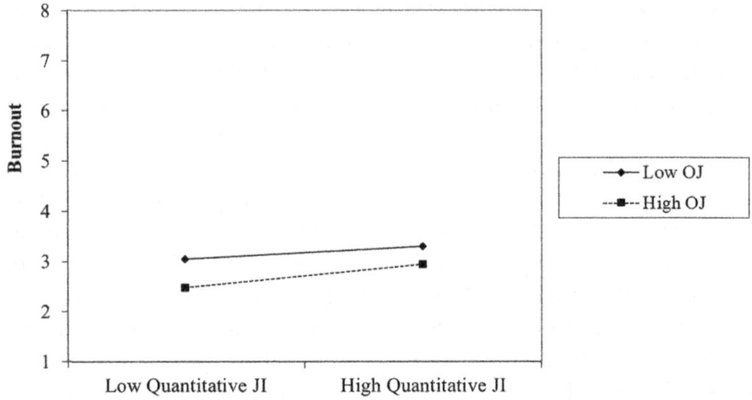

Fig. 8.2 Interaction between quantitative job insecurity (model A) and overall justice in predicting burnout. *JI* job insecurity, *OJ* overall justice. The interaction between qualitative job insecurity and overall justice was non-significant and is not illustrated here

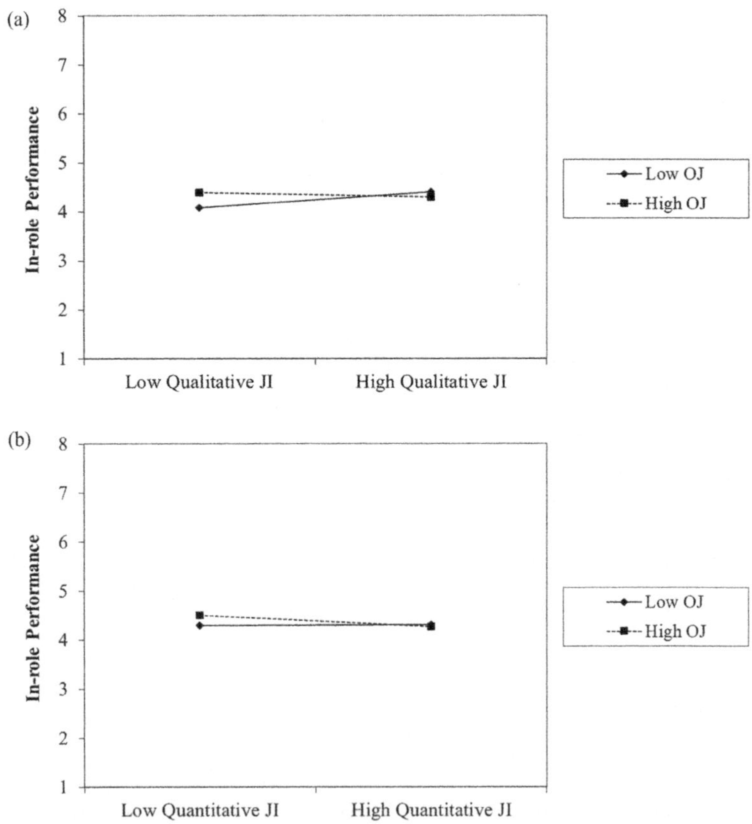

Fig. 8.3 Interaction between quantitative (model A) and qualitative job insecurity (model B) and overall justice in redicting in-ole performance. *JI* job insecurity, *OJ* overall justice

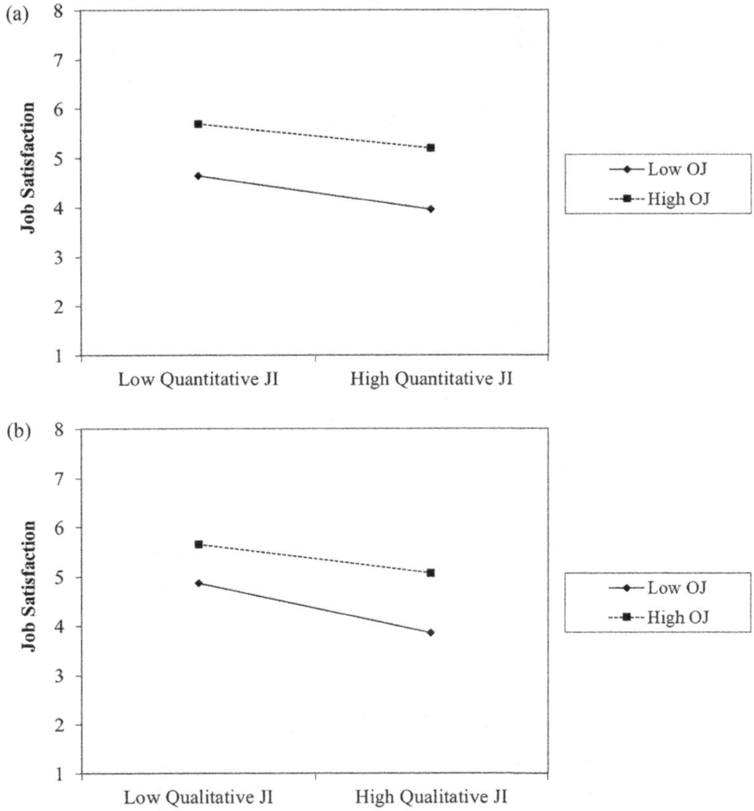

Fig. 8.4 Interaction between quantitative (model A) and qualitative job insecurity (model B) and overall justice in predicting job satisfaction. *JI* job insecurity, *OJ* overall justice

In contrast to other outcomes, the interaction effects between job insecurity and overall justice showed the expected pattern when job satisfaction was tested as an outcome. Specifically, the adverse effects of quantitative and qualitative job insecurity on job satisfaction were weaker when overall justice was high ($B = -.24$, 95%CI [−.29, −.19], $t = -9.47$, $p < .01$; $B = -.29$, 95%CI [−.34, −.24], $t = -11.07$, $p < .01$ respectively) in comparison to than when it was low ($B = -.35$, 95% CI[−.41, −.29], $t = -11.24$, $p < .01$; $B = -.51$, 95%CI [−.58, −.44], $t = -14.89$, $p < .01$ respectively).

To rule out the possibility of different moderation patterns across countries, we also performed a separate analysis in each country. A summary of the results is presented in Table 8.3. Notably, the results were quite the same across all countries. More precisely, high overall justice exacerbated the negative impact of qualitative and quantitative job insecurity on perceived performance, work engagement, and burnout. In the case of job satisfaction, overall justice buffered the negative effects of qualitative and quantitative job insecurity.

Table 8.3 Overall justice as a moderator for qualitative and quantitative job insecurity effects across different countries

	N	In-role performance		Work engagement		Exhaustion		Job satisfaction	
		Quantitative JI	Qualitative JI	Quantitative JI	Qualitative JI	Quantitative JI	Qualitative JI	Quantitative JI	Qualitative JI
Belgium	596	ns	TNE	ns	ns	ns	ns	ns	PE
China	160	TNE	TNE	TNE	TNE	ns	TNE	ns	ns
Croatia	709	TNE	TNE	TNE	TNE	ns	ns	ns	PE
Greece	398	TNE	TNE	ns	TNE	ns		ns	PE
Lithuania	530	TNE	TNE	ns	TNE	TNE	TNE	PE	PE
Romania	476	TNE	TNE	TNE	TNE	TNE	TNE	ns	PE
South Africa	1088	TNE	TNE	ns	ns	TNE	ns	PE	PE
Switzerland	318	ns	ns	ns	ns	ns	ns	ns	PE
UK	68	ns	ns	ns	ns	ns	ns	ns	ns
USA	326	ns	ns	ns	ns	TNE	ns	ns	PE

TNE triggering negative effect, *PE* preventive effect; *ns* non-significant moderation effect, *JI* job insecurity

8.8 Discussion

In this part of the chapter, we aimed to empirically demonstrate the buffering role of overall justice in the negative relationship between qualitative and quantitative job insecurity and its attitude-, performance-, and well-being-related outcomes among higher education sector employees in various countries. In doing so, we replicated previous research on the negative correlates of job insecurity, providing additional evidence on the interplay of job insecurity and overall justice in the academic context.

Following our expectations, both types of job insecurity were negatively related to job satisfaction. Moreover, overall justice buffered the negative relationship between quantitative and qualitative job insecurity and job satisfaction. This result is consistent with the findings of previous studies that show the detrimental effects of job insecurity on job satisfaction (e.g., Sverke et al., 2002) and demonstrate organisational justice to buffer the relationships between job insecurity and its negative correlates (e.g., Silla et al., 2010; Sora et al., 2010). It is also in line with the assumptions of FHT (Lind, 2001) and UMT (Lind & van den Bos, 2002). Based on these theories, fairness judgments become more salient when employees confront job insecurity. Furthermore, as demonstrated by some laboratory studies, perceived fairness appears crucial when uncertainty is high (e.g., van den Bos, 2001; van den Bos & Miedema, 2000). Thus, high overall justice seems to act as a buffer in alleviating the negative relationship between job insecurity and job satisfaction.

Moreover, qualitative and quantitative job insecurity negatively predicted job performance and work engagement. Both types of job insecurity were positively related to burnout, thereby confirming the previously demonstrated performance-impairing and energy-draining effects of insecurity (De Cuyper et al., 2008; De Witte et al., 2010; Mauno et al., 2005). However, the results concerning the remaining outcomes were contrary to our assumptions. Instead of buffering the negative associations between job insecurity and job performance and work engagement, overall justice exacerbated job insecurity's negative effect on these outcomes. Moreover, the positive relationship between job insecurity and burnout was stronger when overall justice was high. Notably, these results were consistent across both types of job insecurity among academic employees in different countries. Although such findings seem contrary to conventional wisdom and some empirical evidence (e.g., Wang et al., 2015), they were also observed in some previous studies. For example, Piccoli et al. (2011) found organisational justice to strengthen the negative relationship between job insecurity and in-role performance. According to Piccoli et al. (2011), this result can be explained by Group Value Theory (Lind & Tyler, 1988) and Relational Theory (Tyler & Lind, 1992). According to these theories, individuals use information about the fairness of the decision-making process to make inferences about how other group members regard them. Fair decision-making procedures and enactment indicate that individuals are viewed favourably, resulting in more positive self-evaluations (Tyler et al., 1996).

Moreover, when employees receive an unfavourable outcome, the perceived fairness of the decision-making process might result in lower self-evaluation (Schroth & Shah, 2000). According to Brockner et al. (2003), low justice allows externalising the reasons for the outcomes, while high justice prompts making internal attributions. Therefore, receiving negative outcomes under conditions of high fairness might lead to lower self-evaluations (Brockner et al., 2003), which may be the case with self-rated job performance.

Furthermore, as job insecurity carries feelings of powerlessness, it might threaten employees' self-esteem (Kinnunen et al., 2003). Consequently, experiencing job insecurity might lead to lower self-esteem that, under conditions of high perceived justice, would likely prompt employees to make internal attributions and lead to lower levels of self-rated performance (Piccoli et al., 2011). The explanation for these results can also be drawn from the Relational model of Authority (Tyler & Lind, 1992). According to this model, people need the security of believing that they will be treated fairly; therefore, they are likely to be particularly sensitive to any disconfirmation of this belief on behalf of an authority. In their experimental study, Lind and Lissak (1985) demonstrated that unethical behaviour coming from an authority violated expectations and impaired procedural justice judgements even when individuals were granted a voice, that is, even when they were assigned to a fair process condition. As noted by the authors themselves, when people expect procedures to be enacted fairly, the unexpected appearance of impropriety leads to a more intensive cognitive analysis. Some scholars have previously explored the notion of justice expectations and the reactions to their violation. For example, Shapiro and Kirkman (2001) noted that justice expectations are based on existing general fairness judgments and, when violated, lead to adverse reactions even if violations allow individuals more input into the decision-making process. Moreover, Bell et al. (2004) noted that fairness expectations serve as a point of reference when evaluating the outcomes received. Similarly, Gilliland and Steiner (2001) suggested that inexperienced applicants will be more tolerant of justice violations in the selection process because their expectations are less likely to be strong. As has been accurately noted by Lind and Van den Bos (2002, p. 216), "people use fairness to manage their reactions to uncertainty, finding comfort in related or even unrelated fair experiences and finding additional distress in unfair experiences." Presumably, when employees judge their organisation to be fair, they expect to receive fair treatment. As a major stressor, job insecurity is obviously an unfavourable experience, implying adverse outcomes. One may infer that in high justice conditions, the occurrence of job insecurity is experienced as particularly stressful because it contradicts the very idea of a fair organisation, which may consequently drain employees' energetic resources when coping with it. This might serve as an explanation for why in our study, higher education sector employees were likely to react more negatively to job insecurity when justice was high, leading to lower work engagement and higher levels of burnout.

8.8.1 Practical Implications

The theoretical overview and empirical data presented in this chapter offer several valuable insights for managerial practices in academia and beyond. Firstly, considering the individual and organisational costs of job insecurity, organisations would benefit from using clear procedures and explicit communication about future corporate plans (see De Witte et al., 2015) and offering employment security (Pfeffer, 2007). Second, according to the results of our study, employees' fairness judgments were positively related to work engagement, job satisfaction, and in-role performance and negatively related to burnout. Moreover, overall fairness perceptions might also alleviate the negative effect of job insecurity on job satisfaction. Therefore, to prevent job insecurity from resulting in poor attitudes and behaviours, managers of higher education institutions may take actions that have been proven fruitful in terms of enhancing employees' fairness perceptions, such as voice and participative decision making, equitable compensation, and respectful interpersonal treatment (see Ambrose et al., 2015). Although specific types of organisational justice might be relevant to particular organisational attitudes and behaviours, the study by Ambrose and Schminke (2009) strongly implies that managers should pay heed to all forms of justice, seeking to better understand in which area they are lacking and may need improvement. While justice is considered an organisational-level variable, it must be kept in mind that everyday fairness practices permeate every aspect of working life and can be implemented at both the corporate level (e.g., transparent academic career advancement system, ethical HRM policies) and the supervisor level (e.g., fair junior faculty treatment from their supervisors). Hence, promoting justice through better communication and participation should target these different levels as well. Finally, it is crucial to note that managerial practices such as clear communication and participative decision-making have been shown to effectively enhance fairness and diminish job insecurity, which may bring a double benefit in the turbulent and changing world of academia.

8.8.2 Directions for Future Studies

Given the diversity of approaches for studying the relationship between justice and job insecurity presented in this chapter, it is not surprising that a clear picture of their interplay has not emerged. As demonstrated by our theoretical overview and empirical study, organisational justice may be seen either as an antecedent factor that prevents job insecurity from occurring or might attenuate (hence, moderate) the adverse effects of job insecurity on specific employee outcomes. In addition, some previous findings also suggest the reverse model, where job insecurity is thought to impair justice perceptions and even prevent its positive effects on employee well-being. Given so many alternative viewpoints, there is undoubtedly a need for greater clarity in this field to unravel the dynamic relationship between justice and insecurity. Below, we outline the guidelines for further research based on both the empirical study and theoretical overview presented in this chapter.

Firstly, we believe it would be essential to test a broader range of outcomes when investigating the interplay between job insecurity and organisational justice. Only then can we state that differential moderation effects are due to the nature of the relationships between the variables and not because of the study design. As shown in our empirical illustration, justice buffered the negative relationship between job insecurity and job satisfaction, but this was not true for the outcomes outside of the attitudinal variable category. Hence, future research may focus on expanding the list of attitudinal outcomes and cross-validating the moderation patterns with regard to them. Furthermore, additional research is needed to unravel the delicate nuances of the interactive effects of insecurity and justice regarding a broader range of work performance and well-being indicators.

Moreover, as has been demonstrated by previous studies, the relationship between job insecurity and its outcomes might not be linear. For example, Selenko et al. (2013) found the relationship between quantitative job insecurity and self-reported job performance to be U-shaped. At lower and extremely high degrees of job insecurity, employees reported better job performance than at moderate job insecurity degrees. Importantly, this effect was demonstrated cross-sectionally as well as longitudinally. Therefore, future studies might test the very nature of the relationship between job insecurity and its behavioural outcomes.

Thirdly, most insecurity and justice moderation studies still refer to quantitative job insecurity as the main predictor. While both quantitative and qualitative forms of job insecurity have been shown to trigger similar detrimental outcomes (De Witte et al., 2010), this holds for direct but not for interaction effects. Hence, a focus on qualitative versus quantitative job insecurity may bring interesting additional insights into the contradictory moderation results found in previous studies (cf., Koen et al., 2020; Piccoli et al., 2011). Whether job insecurity prompts a transient increase in performance (because of the intention to preserve the job) or a decrease in performance (due to stress-withdrawal reactions), it is crucial to check if these effects are equally applicable in the case of qualitative job insecurity, which refers to the loss of valued parts of the job but not the job itself. If so, what implications can we eventually draw about organisational justice as a regulatory factor in coping with (anticipated) changes at work?

Furthermore, we advocate for future longitudinal research to examine the relationship between job insecurity, perceived fairness, and attitudinal and behavioural outcomes so that not only can causality be addressed but also the temporal order of the variables can be inspected. Well-documented empirical evidence on the negative outcomes of job insecurity (e.g., De Witte et al., 2016; Sverke et al., 2002) imperatively suggests directing more efforts at preventing it from occurring (De Witte et al., 2015). Hence, it is crucial to test whether organisational justice serves such a preventive role in job insecurity. In other words, does organisational justice predict lower job insecurity, or does job insecurity impair fairness perceptions over the course of time? Alternatively, are job insecurity and justice perceptions intertwined in a reciprocal relationship, mutually affecting each other? This knowledge is very much needed for practitioners and leaders seeking to counteract job insecurity in practice.

The theoretical perspectives discussed in the first part of this chapter provide ample directions for investigating even more complex aspects of this relationship. For example, FHT suggests a seemingly contradictory role of justice in the insecurity-outcomes relationship, treating it either as a buffer of the negative effects of job insecurity or as an explanatory mechanism for the detrimental outcomes of job insecurity. If we assume that all the variations in the insecurity-justice relationship proposed by various theoretical perspectives are reasonable, they most likely hold true at different points of time and in different organisational contexts. For example, we might expect employees to re-evaluate their existing fairness judgments (in terms of FHT, employees re-enter the judgmental phase, where the fairness heuristic is formed) when they encounter organisational change, during which the levels of job insecurity are high. In contrast, in ‘normal’ working conditions, when the levels of job insecurity are much lower, existing fairness judgments might help alleviate the possible negative effects of job insecurity. In terms of FHT, the use phase occurs in this case, where a previously established fairness heuristic is being used. Hence, capturing the dynamics of the interplay between job insecurity and overall justice is a highly relevant yet very under-researched aspect. With our empirical illustration in mind, one possible explanation for the counterintuitive moderation patterns observed in the current study is that they may reflect an instant reaction to an unexpected situation that potentially changes over time. In other words, high job insecurity and high organisational justice are antitheses of each other. Thus, when job insecurity happens, people may instantly not interpret it as “unjust” but rather try to increase their effort to remedy the situation. The question is how long this reaction lasts and how durable the high insecurity-high justice situation can be in general. For this reason, further research may be interested in disentangling the temporal dynamics of employees’ reactions to job insecurity against the backdrop of organisational (in)justice in the first place.

Another benefit of longitudinal research is that it would also allow us to evaluate the cumulative effect of unjust events, as previously demonstrated by Gilliland et al. (1998). These authors found justice judgments to accumulate in a way that there was a threshold at which just events could no longer compensate for the unjust ones. Similarly, Taylor (2001) argued that there is a threshold effect associated with the accumulation of unfair events. In the context of job insecurity, the accumulation of job insecurity-related events or decisions could help determine the conditions for the moderating and mediating role of overall justice more precisely. This opens up an exciting research perspective for future studies trying to incorporate mediator and moderator effects: presumably, to a certain extent, overall justice perceptions act as a moderator for the adverse effects of job insecurity, as has been demonstrated by previous studies (e.g., Silla et al., 2010). However, under certain conditions, it may also act as a mediator, as other empirical studies show (e.g., Lazauskaite-Zabielske et al., 2019; Piccoli et al., 2017).

Finally, when examining the relationship between insecurity and justice, we would also advise a careful selection of the organisational justice type for a few reasons. Firstly, different types of justice can originate from various sources (Blader & Tyler, 2003; Colquitt et al., 2001; Rupp & Cropanzano, 2002), namely, from a human decision-making agent or formal organisational system. Blader and Tyler (2003) distinguished between "formal justice" that originates from the organisation and "informal justice" that originates from the supervisor. Similarly, Byrne and Cropanzano (2000) used the term "multifoci" when referring to various sources from which justice perceptions originate. It may be useful to differentiate between them in empirical studies. Secondly, it is crucial to consider the context in which justice is being formed. From this perspective, one might examine the co-called context-specific fairness of one particular event, such as layoffs (Brockner et al., 1993). Perceived fairness might also be examined across multiple events. For example, Sweeney and McFarlin (1997) studied distributive and procedural justice across various performance management practices. Eventually, one may choose the so-called entity measure that appraises the organisation or the supervisor as a whole (Cropanzano et al., 2001). In the context of job insecurity, it is relevant to consider the fairness of certain changes and their implementation procedures and the general fairness of decision-making processes or decision-making agents in the organisation (for an exhaustive analysis of justice measures, see Colquitt and Shaw 2005). Importantly, specifying the source and context of justice also suggests the choice of outcomes to be examined. Following the target similarity model (Lavelle et al., 2007), justice perceptions concerning a given target best reflect the exchange quality with that target and, consequently, predict reciprocation toward it. Thus, when employees are treated fairly by the organisation, they reciprocate the organisation with positive attitudes and behaviours, while being fairly treated by the supervisor would result in favourable reactions towards the supervisor himself/herself. Although there is some evidence for so-called spillover effects when supervisory-focused justice results in organisationally directed outcomes (Rupp & Cropanzano, 2002), the reverse is unlikely to happen. The choice of justice type and outcome might also depend upon the theoretical framework that one selects. For example, FHT and UMT rest on the global impression of fair treatment rather than on one type of fairness. They state that fairness indicates the other party's trustworthiness in the relationship, suggesting that the most appropriate outcome for analysis would be trust and reciprocation in the relationship with authorities. Moreover, SET refers to the relationships in quid pro quo terms, where one party offers some benefits in exchange for reciprocation from the other party. Hence, according to this theory, the reciprocation of fair treatment may result in "extra mile" efforts on the part of an employee, such as citizenship behaviour and task performance (for an extensive overview, see Colquitt & Zipay, 2015).

As illustrated in this section, organisational justice is bound to quite complex objective and subjective conditions determining its formation and use. In its own right, job insecurity entails a number of psychological mechanisms that may shape the magnitude of its effects. Thus, the list of the above-mentioned future research suggestions is not exhaustive. However, we hope that it provides some direction for achieving a better understanding of the dynamics of the insecurity-justice relationship and encourages a more substantial reliance on the justice theoretical framework in doing so.

8.9 Take Home Message

This study investigated the relationship between job insecurity and organisational justice in higher education institutions. It highlights that perceived fairness in organisations can significantly influence how job insecurity affects employees' well-being and job performance. Surprisingly, while overall justice helps mitigate the negative impact of job insecurity on job satisfaction, it may exacerbate its adverse effects on work engagement and burnout. These findings suggest that while fostering a fair work environment is crucial, the dynamics between justice and insecurity are complex and warrant further investigation to better support academic staff facing job insecurity.

References

Aiken, L. S., & West, S. G. (1991). *Multiple regression: Testing and interpreting interactions*. Sage.

Alexander, A., & Manolchev, C. (2020). The future of university or universities of the future: a paradox for uncertain times. *International Journal of Educational Management, 34*(7), 1143–1153.

Ambrose, M. L. (2002). Contemporary justice research: a new look at familiar questions. *Organizational Behavior and Human Decision Processes, 89*(1), 803–812.

Ambrose, M. L., & Arnaud, A. (2005). Distributive and procedural justice: Construct distinctiveness, construct interdependence, and overall justice. In R. Cropanzano & M. L. Ambrose (Eds.), *The Oxford handbook of justice in the workplace* (pp. 59–84). Oxford University Press.

Ambrose, M. L., & Cropanzano, R. (2003). A longitudinal analysis of organisational fairness: An examination of reactions to tenure and promotion decisions. *Journal of Applied Psychology, 88*(2), 266–275.

Ambrose, M. L., & Schminke, M. (2009). The role of overall justice judgments in organisational justice research: A test of mediation. *Journal of Applied Psychology, 94*(2), 491–500.

Ambrose, M. L., Wo, D. X. H., & Griffith, M. D. (2015). Overall justice: Past, present, and future. In R. Cropanzano & M. L. Ambrose (Eds.), *The Oxford handbook of justice in the workplace* (pp. 109–135). Oxford University Press.

Bell, B. S., Ryan, A. M., & Wiechmann, D. (2004). Justice expectations and applicant perceptions. *International Journal of Selection and Assessment, 12*(1/2), 24–38.

Biron, C., Brun, J. P., & Ivers, H. (2008). Extent and sources of occupational stress in university staff. *Work, 30*(4), 511–522.

Blader, S. L., & Tyler, T. R. (2003). What constitutes fairness in work settings? A four-component model of procedural justice. *Human Resource Management Review, 13*, 107–126.

Blau, P. M. (1964). *Exchange and power in social life*. Wiley.

Brechelmacher, A., Park, E., Ates, G., & Campbell, D. F. (2015). The rocky road to tenure–Career paths in academia. In T. Fumasoli, G. Goastellec, & B. M. Kehm (Eds.), *Academic work and careers in Europe: Trends, challenges, perspectives* (pp. 13–40). Springer.

Brockner, J., Grover, S., Reed, T. F., & DeWitt, R. L. (1992). Layoffs, job insecurity, and survivors' work effort: evidence of an inverted-U relationship. *Academy of Management Journal, 35*(2), 413–425.

Brockner, J., Wiesenfeld, B. M., Reed, T., Grover, S., & Martin, C. (1993). Interactive effect of job content and context on the reactions of layoff survivors. *Journal of Personality and Social Psychology, 64*(2), 187–197.

Brockner, J., Heuer, L. B., Magner, N., Folger, R., Umphress, E., & Van den Bos, K. (2003). High procedural fairness heightens the effect of outcome favorability on selfevaluations: An attributional analysis. *Organisational Behavior and Human Decision Processes, 91*, 51–68.

Bryson, C. (2004). What about the workers? The expansion of higher education and the transformation of academic work. *Industrial Relations Journal, 35*(1), 38–57.

Byrne, Z. S., & Cropanzano, R. (2000, April). To which source do I attribute this fairness? Differential effects of multi-foci justice on organizational work behaviors. In 15th annual conference of the Society for Industrial and Organizational Psychology, New Orleans, LA

Catano, V., Francis, L., Haines, T., Kirpalani, H., Shannon, H., Stringer, B., & Lozanzki, L. (2010). Occupational stress in Canadian universities: A national survey. *International Journal of Stress Management, 17*(3), 232–258.

Cheng, G. H.-L., & Chan, D. K.-S. (2008). Who suffers more from job insecurity? A meta-analytic review. *Applied Psychology: An International Review, 57*(2), 272–303.

Colquitt, J. A., & Shaw, J. C. (2005). How should organisational justice be measured. In J. Greenberg & J. A. Colquitt (Eds.), *Handbook of organisational justice* (pp. 113–152). Psychology Press.

Colquitt, J. A., & Zipay, K. P. (2015). Justice, fairness, and employee reactions. *Annual Review of Organizational Psychology and Organizational Behaviour, 2*(1), 75–99.

Colquitt, J. A., Conlon, D. E., Wesson, M. J., Porter, C. O., & Ng, K. Y. (2001). Justice at the millennium: A meta-analytic review of 25 years of organizational justice research. *Journal of Applied Psychology, 86*(3), 425–445.

Cropanzano, R., & Mitchell, M. S. (2005). Social exchange theory: An interdisciplinary review. *Journal of Management, 31*(6), 874–900.

Cropanzano, R., Byrne, Z. S., Bobocel, D. R., & Rupp, D. R. (2001). Moral virtues, fairness heuristics, social entities, and other denizens of organisational justice. *Journal of Vocational Behavior, 58*, 164–209.

De Cuyper, N., Bernhard-Oettel, C., Berntson, E., De Witte, H., & Alarco, B. (2008). Employability and employees' well-being: Mediation by job insecurity. *Applied Psychology: An International Review, 57*(3), 488–509.

De Witte, H. (2000). Arbeidsethos en jobonzekerheid: Meting en gevolgen voor welzijn, tevredenheid en inzet op het werk [Work ethic and job insecurity: Assessment and consequences for well-being, satisfaction and performance at work]. In R. Bouwen, K. De Witte, H. De Witte, & T. Taillieu (Eds.), *Van groep naar gemeenschap [From group to community]. Liber Amicorum Prof. Dr. Leo Lagrou* (pp. 325–350). Garant.

De Witte, H., De Cuyper, N., Handaja, Y., Sverke, M., Näswall, K., & Hellgren, J. (2010). Associations between quantitative and qualitative job insecurity and well-being: A test in Belgian banks. *International Studies of Management & Organization, 40*(1), 40–56. https://doi.org/10.2753/IMO0020-8825400103.

De Witte, H., Vander Elst, T., & De Cuyper, N. (2015). Job insecurity, health and well-being. In Vuori, J., Blonk, R. and Price, R.H. (Eds), Sustainable Working Lives: Managing Work Transitions and Health Throughout the Life Course (pp. 109–128), Springer, New York, NY.

De Witte, H., Pienaar, J., & De Cuyper, N. (2016). Review of 30 years of longitudinal studies on the association between job insecurity and health and well-being: Is there causal evidence?. *Australian Psychologist, 51*(1), 18–31. https://doi.org/10.1111/ap.12176

DeConinck, J. B. (2010). The effect of organisational justice, perceived organisational support, and perceived supervisor support on marketing employees' level of trust. *Journal of Business Research, 63*(12), 1349–1355.

Fischmann, G., De Witte, H., Sulea, C., Vander Elst, T., De Cuyper, N., & Iliescu, D. (2022). Validation of a short and generic qualitative job insecurity scale (QUAL-JIS). *European Journal of Career Assessment, 38*(5), 397–411. https://doi.org/10.1027/1015-5759/a000674

Foa, U. G., & Foa, E. B. (1980). Resource theory: Interpersonal behavior as exchange. In K. J. Gergen, M. S. Greenberg, & R. H. Willis (Eds.), *Social exchange: Advances in theory and research* (pp. 77–94). Plenum Press.

Folger, R., & Cropanzano, R. (2001). Fairness theory: Justice as accountability. In J. Greenberg & R. Cropanzano (Eds.), *Advances in organizational justice* (Vol. 1, pp. 89–118). Stanford University Press.

Gilliland, S. W., & Steiner, D. D. (2001). Causes and consequences of applicant perceptions of unfairness. *Justice in the Workplace: From Theory to Practice, 2*, 175–195.

Gilliland, S. W., Benson, L., & Schepers, D. H. (1998). A rejection threshold in justice evaluations: effects on judgment and decision-making. *Organisational Behavior and Human Decision Processes, 76*(2), 113–131.

Greenberg, J. (1987). A taxonomy of organisational justice theories. *Academy of Management Review, 12*, 9–22.

Greenberg, J. (2001). Setting the justice agenda: Seven unanswered questions about "what, why, and how". *Journal of Vocational Behavior, 58*(2), 210–219.

Hamilton, J. E. (2019). Cash or kudos: Addressing the effort-reward imbalance for academic employees. *International Journal of Stress Management, 26*(2), 193–203.

Hauenstein, N. M. A., McGonigle, T., & Flinder, S. W. (2001). A meta-analysis of the relationship between procedural justice and distributive justice: Implications for justice research. *Employee Responsibilities and Rights Journal, 13*(1), 39–56.

Hayes, A. F. (2013). *Introduction to mediation, moderation, and conditional process analysis: A regression-based approach*. Guilford Press.

Haynie, J. J., Svyantek, D. J., Mazzei, M. J., & Varma, V. (2016). Job insecurity and compensation evaluations: the role of overall justice. *Management Decision, 54*(3), 630–645.

Hobfoll, S. E. (2001). The influence of culture, community, and the nested self in the stress process: Advancing conservation of resources theory. *Applied Psychology: An International Review, 50*, 337–370. https://doi.org/10.1111/1464-0597.00062

Hollensbe, E. C., Khazanchi, S., & Masterson, S. S. (2008). How do I assess if my supervisor and organisation are fair? Identifying the rules underlying entity-based justice perceptions. *Academy of Management Journal, 51*(6), 1099–1116.

Holtz, B. C., & Harold, C. M. (2009). Fair today, fair tomorrow? A longitudinal investigation of overall justice perceptions. *Journal of Applied Psychology, 94*(5), 1185–1199.

Holtz, B. C., & Harold, C. M. (2013). Effects of leadership consideration and structure on employee perceptions of justice and counterproductive work behavior. *Journal of Organizational Behavior, 34*(4), 492–519.

Hulland, J., Nenkov, G. Y., & Barclay, D. W. (2012). Perceived marketing–sales relationship effectiveness: A matter of justice. *Journal of the Academy of Marketing Science, 40*(3), 450–467.

Ito, J. K., & Brotheridge, C. M. (2007). Exploring the predictors and consequences of job insecurity's components. *Journal of Managerial Psychology, 22*, 40–64. https://doi.org/10.1108/02683940710721938

Kinman, G. (2019). Effort-reward imbalance in academic employees: Examining different reward systems. *International Journal of Stress Management, 26*(2), 184–192.

Kinman, G., & Court, S. (2010). Psychosocial hazards in U. K. universities: Adopting a risk assessment approach. *Higher Education Quarterly, 64*(4), 413–428.

Kinnunen, U., Felt, T., & Mauno, S. (2003). Job insecurity and self-esteem: Evidence from cross-lagged relations in a 1-year longitudinal sample. *Personality and Individual Differences, 35*, 617–632.

Kjeldal, S. E., Rindfleish, J., & Sheridan, A. (2005). Deal-making and rule-breaking: Behind the façade of equity in academia. *Gender and Education, 17*(4), 431–447.

Koen, J., Low, T. H. J., & Van Vianen, A. (2020). Job preservation efforts: when does job insecurity prompts performance? *Career Development International, 25*(3), 287–305.

Lavelle, J. J., Rupp, D. E., & Brockner, J. (2007). Taking a multifoci approach to the study of justice, social exchange, and citizenship behavior: The target similarity model. *Journal of Management, 33*(6), 841–866.

Lazauskaite-Zabielske, J., Urbanaviciute, I., Vander Elst, T., & De Witte, H. (2019). Explaining the link between qualitative job insecurity and attitudes: The role of perceived overall justice. *Baltic Journal of Management, 14*(2), 330–344.

Lee, C., Huang, G.-H., & Ashford, S. (2018). Job insecurity and the changing workplace: Recent developments and the future trends in job insecurity research. *Annual Review of Organizational Psychology and Organizational Behaviour, 5*, 335–359.

Lind, E. A. (2001). Fairness heuristic theory: Justice judgments as pivotal cognitions in organisational relations. In J. Greenberg & R. Cropanzano (Eds.), *Advances in organizational justice* (pp. 56–88). Stanford University Press.

Lind, E. A., & Lissak, R. (1985). Apparent impropriety and procedural fairness judgments. *Journal of Experimental Social Psychology, 21*, 19–29.

Lind, E. A., & Tyler, T. R. (1988). *The social psychology of procedural justice*. Springer Science & Business Media.

Lind, E. A., & Van den Bos, K. (2002). When fairness works: Toward a general theory of uncertainty management. In B. M. Staw & R. M. Kramer (Eds.), *Research in organisational behavior* (Vol. 24, pp. 181–224). JAI.

Loi, R., Lam, L. W., & Chan, K. W. (2012). Coping with job insecurity: The role of procedural justice, ethical leadership and power distance orientation. *Journal of Business Ethics, 108*(3), 361–372.

Mauno, S., Kinnunen, U., Makikangas, A., & Natti, J. (2005). Psychological consequences of fixed-term employment and perceived job insecurity among health care staff. *European Journal of Work and Organizational Psychology, 14*(3), 209–237.

McMurray, A., & Scott, D. (2013). Determinants of organisational climate for academia. *Higher Education Research and Development, 32*(6), 960–974.

Mudrak, J., Zabrodska, K., Kveton, P., Jelinek, M., Blatny, M., Solcova, I., & Machovcova, K. (2018). Occupational well-being among university faculty: A job demands-resources model. *Research in Higher Education, 59*(3), 325–348.

Pfeffer, J. (2007). Human resources from an organisational behavior perspective: some paradoxes explained. *Journal of Economic Perspectives, 21*(4), 115–134.

Piccoli, B., & De Witte, H. (2015). Job insecurity and emotional exhaustion: Testing psychological contract breach versus distributive injustice as indicators of lack of reciprocity. *Work & Stress, 29*(3), 246–263.

Piccoli, B., De Witte, H., & Pasini, M. (2011). Job insecurity and organisational consequences: How justice moderates this relationship. *Romanian Journal of Applied Psychology, 13*(2), 37–49.

Piccoli, B., De Witte, H., & Reisel, W. D. (2017). Job insecurity and discretionary behaviors: Social exchange perspective versus group value model. *Scandinavian Journal of Psychology, 58*(1), 69–79. https://doi.org/10.1111/sjop.12340

Preacher, K. J., Curran, P. J., & Bauer, D. J. (2006). Computational tools for probing interactions in multiple linear regression, multilevel modeling, and latent curve analysis. *Journal of Educational and Behavioral Statistics, 31*(4), 437–448.

Proudfoot, D., & Lind, E. A. (2015). Fairness heuristic theory, the uncertainty management model, and fairness at work. In I. R. Cropanzano & M. L. Ambrose (Eds.), *The Oxford handbook of justice in the workplace* (pp. 371–385). Oxford University Press.

Quinn, R. P., & Shepard, L. G. (1974). *The 1972–1973 quality of employment survey*. University of Michigan, Institute for Social Research.

Rosen, C. C., Chang, C. H., Johnson, R. E., & Levy, P. E. (2009). Perceptions of the organisational context and psychological contract breach: Assessing competing perspectives. *Organisational Behavior and Human Decision Processes, 108*(2), 202–217.
Rupp, D. E., & Cropanzano, R. (2002). The mediating effects of social exchange relationships in predicting workplace outcomes from multifoci organisational justice. *Organisational Behavior and Human Decision Processes, 89*(1), 925–946.
Savic, M. (2020). The dawn of the academic revolution: An individual contribution to shaping the future of universities. *World Futures Review, 12*(4), 385–395.
Schaufeli, W. B., Shimazu, A., Hakanen, J., Salanova, M., & De Witte, H. (2017). An ultra-short measure for work engagement: The UWES-3 validation across five countries. *European Journal of Psychological Assessment.* Advance online publication.
Schaufeli, W. B., De Witte, H. & Desart, S. (2019). *Manual Burnout Assessment Tool (BAT).* KU Leuven. Unpublished internal report.
Schroth, H., & Shah, P. (2000). Procedures, do we really want to know them? *Journal of Applied Psychology, 85*, 462–471.
Schumacher, D., Schreurs, B., Van Emmerik, H., & De Witte, H. (2016). Explaining the relation between job insecurity and employee outcomes during organisational change: a multiple group comparison. *Human Resource Management, 55*(5), 809–827.
Selenko, E., Mäkikangas, A., Mauno, S., & Kinnunen, U. (2013). How does job insecurity relate to self-reported job performance? Analysing curvilinear associations in a longitudinal sample. *Journal of Occupational and Organizational Psychology, 86*(4), 522–542. https://doi.org/10.1111/joop.12020.
Shapiro, D. L. (2001). The death of justice theory is likely if theorists neglect the "wheels" already invented and the voices of the injustice victims. *Journal of Vocational Behavior, 58*(2), 235–242.
Shapiro, D. L., & Kirkman, B. L. (2001). Anticipatory injustice: The consequences of expecting injustice in the workplace. *Advances in Organizational Justice, 32*(5), 152–178.
Shin, J. C., & Jung, J. (2014). Academics job satisfaction and job stress across countries in the changing academic environments. *Higher Education, 67*(5), 603–620.
Shoss, M. K. (2017). Job insecurity: An integrative review and agenda for future research. *Journal of Management, 43*(6), 1911–1939.
Silla, I., Gracia, F. J., Mañas, M. A., & Peiró, J. M. (2010). Job insecurity and employees' attitudes: the moderating role of fairness. *International Journal of Manpower, 31*(4), 449–465.
Silvernail, K. D., Graso, M., Salvador, R. O., & Miller, J. K. (2021). Perceived fairness of faculty governance: A study of 51 countries. *Higher Education*, 1–19.
Sora, B., Caballer, A., Peiró, J. M., Silla, I., & Gracia, F. J. (2010). Moderating influence of organisational justice on the relationship between job insecurity and its outcomes: A multilevel analysis. *Economic and Industrial Democracy, 31*, 613–637.
Sverke, M., & Hellgren, J. (2002). The nature of job insecurity: Understanding employment uncertainty on the brink of a new millennium. *Applied Psychology, 51*(1), 23–42.
Sverke, M., Hellgren, J., & Näswall, K. (2002). No security: A meta-analysis and review of job insecurity and its consequences. *Journal of Occupational Health Psychology, 7*, 242–264.
Sweeney, P. D., & McFarlin, D. B. (1997). Process and outcome: Gender differences in the assessment of justice. *Journal of Organizational Behavior, 18*, 83–98.
Taylor, M. S. (2001). Reflections on fairness: Continuing the progression of justice research and practice. *Journal of Vocational Behavior, 58*(2), 243–253.
Thibaut, J. W., & Walker, L. (1975). *Procedural justice: A psychological analysis*. Erlbaum.
Tyler, T. R., & Lind, E. A. (1992). A relational model of authority in groups. In M. Zanna (Ed.), *Advances in experimental social psychology* (Vol. 25, pp. 115–192). Academic.
Tyler, T. R., DeGoey, P., & Smith, H. J. (1996). Understanding why the justice of group procedures matters: A test of the psychological dynamics of the group-value model. *Journal of Personality and Social Psychology, 70*, 913–930.

van den Bos, K. (2001). Uncertainty management: The influence of uncertainty salience on. *Journal of Personality and Social Psychology, 80*(6), 931–941.

Van den Bos, K., & Miedema, J. (2000). Toward understanding why fairness matters: The influence of mortality salience on reactions to procedural fairness. *Journal of Personality and Social Psychology, 79*(3), 355–366.

Van den Bos, K., Lind, E. A., & Wilke, H. A. M. (2001). The psychology of distributive and procedural justice viewed from the perspective of fairness heuristic theory. In J. Greenberg (Ed.), *Justice in the workplace – From theory to practice* (Vol. 2, pp. 49–66). Lawrence Erlbaum.

Vander Elst, T., De Witte, H., & De Cuyper, N. (2014). The Job Insecurity Scale: A psychometric evaluation across five European countries. *European Journal of Work and Organizational Psychology, 23*(3), 364–380.

Wang, H. J., Lu, C. Q., & Siu, O. L. (2015). Job insecurity and job performance: The moderating role of organisational justice and the mediating role of work engagement. *Journal of Applied Psychology, 100*(4), 1249–1258.

Williams, L. J., & Anderson, S. E. (1991). Job satisfaction and organisational commitment as predictors of organisational citizenship and in-role behaviors. *Journal of Management, 17*, 601–617.

Jurgita Lazauskaitė-Zabielskė is a Professor and Head of the Center for Organizational Psychology Research at Vilnius University, Lithuania. Her primary research interests include employee well-being and performance within flexible work arrangements, with a specific emphasis on psychosocial working conditions, work engagement, burnout, work-life balance, organizational justice and job (in)security. She has co-authored numerous articles and several books on psychosocial factors and employee well-being.

Ieva Urbanavičiūtė is a former Senior Research Fellow at the Swiss National Center of Competence in Research LIVES (University of Lausanne) where she conducted research on career development and workplace well-being. She is currently a Chief Investigator and Associate Professor at Vilnius University, Lithuania. Her research interests include the dynamics of job insecurity, occupational vulnerabilities, sustainable careers, and resources for the future world of work. Ieva Urbanavičiūtė has co-authored a number of scientific articles and several book chapters on these topics.

Chapter 9
Job Insecurity, Temporary Contracts and Their Interaction: Associations with a Variety of Performance Indicators in Academia

Hans De Witte, George Gunnesch-Luca, and Dragos Iliescu

9.1 Introduction

Literature reviews on job insecurity documented its detrimental consequences for health and well-being, also in academia [e.g. De Cuyper & De Witte, 2021; De Witte, 2024; De Witte et al., 2015, 2016; Klug et al., 2024; Probst et al., 2018; Sverke & Hellgren, 2002; Vander Elst & De Witte, 2024; see also Chap. 4 (De Witte & Van Hootegem, 2025, this volume)]. Meta-analyses for instance reported lower levels of mental and physical health, less satisfaction with work and life, and higher levels of burnout and strain (e.g. Cheng & Chan, 2008; Jiang & Lavaysse, 2018; Sverke et al., 2002). The consequences of job insecurity for organisational outcomes

H. De Witte (✉)
Research Group Work, Organizational and Personnel Psychology (O2L-WOPP), FPPW, KU Leuven, Leuven, Belgium

Optentia Research Unit, North-West University, Potchefstroom, South Africa
e-mail: hans.dewitte@kuleuven.be

G. Gunnesch-Luca
Faculty of Psychology and Educational Sciences, Psychology and Cognitive Science Department, University of Bucharest, Bucharest, Romania

Chair of Psychology, especially Business and Social Psychology, University of Erlangen-Nuremberg, Erlangen, Germany
e-mail: george.gunnesch-luca@fpse.unibuc.ro

D. Iliescu
Faculty of Psychology and Educational Sciences, Psychology and Cognitive Science Department, University of Bucharest, Bucharest, Romania

Department of Industrial Psychology, Stellenbosch University, Stellenbosch, South Africa
e-mail: dragos.iliescu@fpse.unibuc.ro

L. C. Roll et al. (eds.), *Global Perspectives on Job Insecurity in Higher Education*, Aligning Perspectives on Health, Safety and Well-Being,
https://doi.org/10.1007/978-3-031-85772-0_9

are well documented too. Reviews and meta-analyses showed organisational attitudes to be negatively affected, resulting in lower levels of organisational commitment (Jiang & Lavaysse, 2018), trust in management (Cheng & Chan, 2008), job involvement (Cheng & Chan, 2008), and work motivation and morale (Jiang & Lavaysse, 2018; Sparks et al., 2001). Results on various performance indicators show that organisational behaviours are also affected, resulting in impaired task, contextual and safety performance and increased counterproductive work behaviour (Jiang & Lavaysse, 2018; Sverke et al., 2019).

A similar research stream has been focussing on the associations of temporary employment contracts with health, well-being and organisational outcomes (De Cuyper & De Witte, 2024; De Cuyper et al., 2008; Guest et al., 2010; Quinlan et al., 2001; Virtanen et al., 2005). Temporary employment contracts are a dimension of flexibility ('contractual flexibility', see e.g. De Cuyper et al., 2018), and are often considered as an objective indicator of job insecurity (Pearce, 1998). Overviews highlight the precarious nature of temporary employment contracts, as indicated by lower job quality and less advantageous job characteristics (De Cuyper & De Witte, 2024). These precarious characteristics tend to be mirrored in lower scores for indicators of health, well-being and organisational outcomes, even though mixed findings are also reported in the literature (Guest et al., 2010; Guest & Isaksson, 2019).

Despite the evidence regarding the negative consequences of job insecurity, especially the job insecurity-performance link has been subject to some debate in the literature. Next to the dominant stream of evidence on the detrimental consequences of job insecurity for performance (as documented in various meta-analyses, see Cheng & Chan, 2008; Jiang & Lavaysse, 2018; Sverke et al., 2019), a smaller current of studies maintains that job insecurity can (also) be positively associated with work behaviours (for a critical overview and discussion, see: De Witte & Van Hootegem, 2021). This idea was already advanced by Repenning (2000), but really became renowned when Shoss framed this view as 'job preservation motivation' in her *Journal of Management* review (Shoss, 2017). Similarly, the link between employment contracts and performance has raised some controversy, as the results regarding the outcomes of temporary contracts are often mixed, as stated above (e.g. De Cuyper et al., 2008).

In this chapter, we will focus on two operationalisations of insecurity: the subjective perception of job insecurity versus the objective operationalisation thereof in the employment contract. We will examine their associations with various performance indicators, and will test contrasting hypotheses: is insecurity associated with decreased or increased performance? Additionally, we will also examine contrasting hypotheses regarding the interaction of job insecurity with the employment contract in associating with performance indicators. Academia is an interesting context to examine these contrasting views. As evidenced in Chap. 1 (Roll et al., 2025, this volume), governmental cutbacks and the need to reduce expenses have increased job insecurity in many countries. Governmental policies also introduced and expanded the use of various temporary contracts among academics. Additionally, performance demands are reported to be high in academia (Roll et al., 2025, this volume), as illustrated in the saying "publish or perish". In other words, performing well under circumstances of increased insecurity seems typical for the academic sector. This is not necessarily limited to researchers (like professors and PhD-students), but could also apply to administrative workers in academia. The latter are also affected by governmental cutbacks and staff reductions. Consequently, the question whether insecurity is associated with (increased versus decreased) performance becomes an important issue to analyse, from the viewpoint of theory as well as practice and policy. Does insecurity jeopardises the creation and accumulation of scientific knowledge? Or is it on the contrary conducive to the development of knowledge in science?

9.2 Focussing on a Broad Spectrum of Insecurity and Performance Indicators

Insecurity can take different forms, and various conceptualisations have been advanced in the literature. In this volume, job insecurity is first of all defined from a psychological point of view as "the subjective perception that the existence and continuity of the actual job (or its features) are threatened" (De Witte, 2024, p. 342). One can typically distinguish two kinds (Hellgren et al., 1999). *Quantitative job insecurity* refers to the perception that one might lose the actual job. Here, the comparison is with unemployment: will one continue to have a job or become unemployed? *Qualitative job insecurity* refers to the perceived threat to the continuation of valued job characteristics, such as income, colleagues, and the content of the job. Respondents experiencing qualitative job insecurity do not fear to lose their job but are uncertain about its future characteristics.

Secondly, insecurity is sometimes also framed in an objective way, by referring to the employment contract. Here, a permanent contract (secure employment) is contrasted with a *temporary contract*, indicating insecurity. The latter can come in many forms, varying from fixed term contracts of limited duration over temporary agency work, to daily, on call contracts (De Cuyper et al., 2018). In this chapter, we will examine these three kinds of insecurity, as all three are relevant in the academic context (see Chap. 1; Roll et al., 2025, this volume). Both quantitative and qualitative job insecurity can be a reality among academics, and the increase of temporary contracts in the academic sector in many countries also shows that this kind of insecurity is pertinent in academia. By examining these three indicators, we aim to cover a broad spectrum of insecurity indicators.

Work performance also comes in many forms (Griffin, 2024). In this chapter, we aim to analyse four different kinds of performance, in order to cover a large variety of work related behavioural outcomes of insecurity. Spector distinguished productive versus counterproductive work behaviours (Spector, 2003). *Productive* behaviours are acts performed to reach the goals of the job and organization. Typical examples are in-role and extra-role behaviours. *In-role behaviours* or 'task performance' refer to fulfilling the responsibilities specified in one's job description.

Examples in academia could be teaching, publishing and performing administrative tasks. *Extra-role behaviours* or 'contextual performance' refer to 'doing something additional'—thus performing something that is not strictly specified in the job description. Acting this way, however, also helps reaching the goals of the organization. Consequently, these extra-role behaviours are often framed as 'organisational citizenship behaviours' (Anderson & Brough, 2024). Typical examples are altruism (helping colleagues—individual-directed OCB) or promoting company image (organization-directed OCB). In this study, only altruism was measured as indicator of individual-directed extra-role behaviours. Altruism is obviously a relevant OCB dimension for all professional categories working in an academic sector.

In academia, one could also add *innovative work behaviour* to the list of productive behaviour. This kind of performance can be defined as "the intentional introduction and application, within a role, group or organization of ideas, processes, products or procedures, new to the relevant unit of adoption, designed to significantly benefit the individual, the group or wider society" (West & Farr, 1989, p. 23). One typically distinguishes two dimensions (West, 2002): idea generation and idea implementation. In academia, the generation and implementation of new ideas is obviously 'core business'.

Finally, *counterproductive* behaviour refers to acts that impede reaching the goals of the job or organisation, either by withdrawing from the tasks at hand (e.g. absenteeism and coming in late) or by deliberately intending to harm the organization or its members (e.g. aggression, sabotage, theft and mobbing at work). In this study, we measured an aspect of withdrawal, related to intentionally working slower or taking longer breaks than one should, framed 'workplace deviance' (Bennett & Robinson, 2000). Because of its 'milder' content, this form of counterproductive work behaviour can be relevant for all categories of employees at universities.

9.3 How Is Insecurity Related to Performance? Developing Contrasting Hypotheses

9.3.1 The Negative Path: Insecurity Is Related to Reduced Productive and Increased Counterproductive Behaviour

Quantitative and qualitative *job insecurity* are found to be *hindrance* stressors in the literature: work related obstacles that are difficult to overcome and thus deplete energy and increase exhaustion (De Witte & Van Hootegem, 2021). As a consequence, hindrance stressors are also associated with reduced performance, and increased counterproductive behaviours (Lepine et al., 2005; Podsakoff et al., 2007; Van den Broeck et al., 2013). This empirical finding can be explained by a variety of theories (De Cuyper & De Witte, 2021; De Witte, 2024; Tomas & Maslić Seršić, 2023; Vander Elst & De Witte, 2024).

Both kinds of job insecurity first of all frustrate specific needs. Having a job allows satisfying a variety of needs, due to the manifest and latent functions offered by work (Jahoda, 1982; Selenko et al., 2020; Vander Elst et al., 2016b). Insecurity deprives workers from the opportunity to satisfy these needs, which is experienced as stressful. Secondly, the strain resulting from this deprivation is the focus of various stress theories. They have in common that they emphasise the *inability* of workers to perform due to insecurity: stress impairs their capacity to perform (Tomas & Maslić Seršić, 2023). One of the (many) stress theories explaining why insecure workers 'are not *able* to perform' (Tomas & Maslić Seršić, 2023) is conservation of resources theory (COR; Hobfoll et al., 2018). COR theory states that employment is a valuable resource, much in line with Jahoda's elaboration of its various manifest and latent functions. These resources are threatened by job insecurity. This creates strain, which consumes energy. Respondents also react by consuming additional energy and resources (e.g. by ruminating), which further reduces their level of energy and exhausts. The increase in strain levels due to the experienced threat and the reduction of energy due to the consumption of resources in order to deal with this threat, are conductive to a reduction in productive behaviours.

Thirdly, social exchange theory explains why insecurity impairs the *willingness* of employees to perform (Tomas & Maslić Seršić, 2023). Psychological contract theory is an example of such a theory (Robinson & Rousseau, 1994). This theory suggests that employees and employers develop mutual expectations regarding their reciprocal rights and duties in what is called a 'psychological contract'. Especially the relational psychological contract implies that employees expect job security from their employer in return for their inputs, like effort and loyalty (De Cuyper & De Witte, 2006, 2008; Vander Elst et al., 2016a). When they perceive their jobs to be insecure, they experience a breach of the psychological contract with the employer. This imbalance between what they perceive to give and what they perceive to get, leads to a reduction of productive behaviours in order to restore the balance. Additionally, counterproductive behaviours increase, in an attempt to retaliate.

Empirical findings are in line with these theoretical explanations. Several meta-analyses and literature reviews underpin the negative associations of both kinds of job insecurity with indicators of in-role and extra-role behaviours (Cheng & Chan, 2008; De Cuyper & De Witte, 2021; De Witte, 2024; De Witte & Van Hootegem, 2021; Jiang & Lavaysse, 2018; Klug et al., 2024; Probst et al., 2018; Sverke et al., 2019; Vander Elst & De Witte, 2024). A similar stream of empirical evidence underpins the positive associations of both kinds of job insecurity with counterproductive behaviours (for meta-analytic evidence see e.g. Jiang & Lavaysse, 2018; Sverke et al., 2019). The results regarding the association of job insecurity with (dimensions of) innovative work behaviours are, however, less convincing. This association was observed in several studies for quantitative and/or qualitative job insecurity (Niesen et al., 2018; Probst et al., 2020; Roll et al., 2015; Van Hootegem et al., 2019). However, in the meta-analysis of Sverke et al. (2019), focussing on the subdimension of creativity, no significant link with job insecurity could be found.

Research on the associations of *temporary contracts* with outcomes mainly focussed on its association with health and well-being (see e.g. Quinlan et al.,

2001; Virtanen et al., 2005). Fewer studies have been analysing the link with performance. The various theories mentioned above can however also be applied to this phenomenon, suggesting a negative association of temporary work with various performance indicators. Temporary work can first of all be considered as an objective indicator of insecurity, thus referring to the possibility that one might lose the actual job in the near future (Klandermans et al., 2010; Pearce, 1998). Hence, a temporary contract also threatens the satisfaction of the manifest and latent needs highlighted in Jahoda's (1982) latent deprivation model. Secondly, several literature reviews documented the less advantaged job quality of temporary workers (e.g. De Cuyper et al., 2008, 2010; De Cuyper & De Witte, 2024; De Graaf-Zijl, 2005). Workers tend to have a disadvantaged position in their organization, and their organisation treats them differently, with fewer investments in their position and job characteristics compared to permanents workers. As a consequence, the quality of their work is generally poorer. Temporary workers typically experience more job demands and less job resources in their job. A large amount of empirical evidence in the realm of the job demands-resources model (Bakker et al., 2023; Schaufeli & Bakker, 2004; Van den Broeck et al., 2013) has documented that this combination of job characteristics is associated with more strain and burnout and less work engagement, resulting in lower productive work behaviours and increased counterproductive behaviours. Thirdly, also social exchange theory suggests that temporary workers might be less willing to perform well, compared to workers with a permanent contract (De Cuyper et al., 2008). Here, perceptions of fairness and reciprocity play a core role. Temporary workers are often treated differently by their organisation, which might induce a sense of deprivation. Additionally, they might perceive an imbalance between their efforts and rewards, especially in comparison to permanent workers. Both can strengthen the perception of not being treated fairly, leading to lower health and well-being and poorer performance.

Empirical findings regarding the association between temporary contracts and performance are, however, rather mixed and inconclusive (De Cuyper et al., 2008; De Graaf-Zijl, 2005). Studies based on large databases, for instance, quite often do not find a significant association between temporary work and in-role behaviours (De Cuyper et al., 2010; Ellingson et al., 1998; van Vuuren et al., 2020). Results regarding extra-role behaviours are mixed, and other kinds of work behaviours have rarely been examined (De Cuyper et al., 2008).

To summarise, based on the predictions of stress theories and psychological contract theory, we hypothesise that the three indicators of insecurity (quantitative job insecurity, qualitative job insecurity and a temporary employment contract) will be associated with a reduction of productive work behaviours (in-role, extra-role and innovative work behaviours) and an increase in counterproductive work behaviours. We call this 'negative path' the *hindrance hypothesis* (hypothesis 1).

9.3.2 *The Positive Path: Insecurity Is Related to Increased Productive and Decreased Counterproductive Behaviour*

A minority stream in the job insecurity literature maintains that *job insecurity* is not necessarily negative for performance and can even lead to more and better productive work behaviours. This view aligns with the *challenge* stressor viewpoint (De Witte & Van Hootegem, 2021; Lepine et al., 2005; Podsakoff et al., 2007; Van den Broeck et al., 2010). Hindrance stressors are negative for well-being and performance. Challenge stressors, by contrast, are ambivalent in nature. They share the demanding, negative side of hindrance stressors, as exposure to this kind of stressors is also experienced as stressful. Sustained exposure risks to exhaust workers on the long run. However, contrary to hindrance stressors, the obstacles involved in challenge stressors can be overcome. This requires the investment of energy, which is demanding and potentially exhausting, but can at the same time also stimulate the development and growth of the employee and his/her capacities. Because of the latter, challenge stressors are also considered to be motivating, and to lead to goal achievement. Hindrance stressors are supposed to interfere with task accomplishment and will thus reduce performance. Challenge stressors, by contrast, are supposed to create opportunities for better work achievements. Hence, they are expected to increase performance.

The challenge stressor view of job insecurity has been concretised into what Shoss coined as '*job preservation motivation*' (Shoss, 2017). In this view, Shoss integrated a variety of ideas that were raised earlier on in the literature. As such, the job preservation motivation view is not a coherent theoretical framework, but rather a junction of assumptions suggesting that job insecurity might increase performance. The core idea is that insecurity could motivate workers to act "in ways that they believe might keep job or job feature loss from occurring" (Shoss, 2017, p. 17). Such a job preservation strategy could take two forms (Shoss, 2017). First, it might result in work intensification and extra effort, resulting in enhanced task performance. This especially applies to in-role behaviours, as these are most likely to be noticed and valued by employers, and as such are instrumental in keeping the job. One could also add extra-role behaviours and innovative work behaviours to this list, given that these acts are equally relevant for the organisation, also in academia. Note that 'putting in extra effort' not necessarily refers to quantitatively or qualitatively better performance but could also refer to creating an image of oneself as ideal employee, without creating the expected positive behavioural outcomes for the organisation ('impression management'). Second, the job preservation strategy might also lead to refraining from work behaviours that put the employee and his/her job at greater risk to be dismissed, like counterproductive behaviours.

The empirical evidence in favour of this view is however rather scarce and at most mixed (De Cuyper & De Witte, 2021; De Witte, 2024). As noted above, the results in the literature are dominantly in line with the 'negative hindrance' hypothesis developed earlier on. However, a limited amount of studies have been reporting positive associations of job insecurity with performance indicators, often in specific conditions (for an overview and detailed discussion see: De Witte & Van Hootegem, 2021). In a recent study, Shoss and her colleagues report on two studies testing her assumptions (Shoss et al., 2022). In the first, longitudinal study, they found job insecurity to be positively related to subsequent organisation-directed counterproductive work behaviours, evasive knowledge hiding, and an aspect of impression management – but not with job performance. They conclude that "the finding of a nonsignificant relationship between job insecurity and subsequent performance and a positive relationship between job insecurity and organisational counterproductive work behaviours, however, raise questions about whether employees, on average, tend to put forth effort for job performance and refrain from counterproductive work behaviour as potential job preservation strategies" (Shoss et al., 2022, p. 12). In their second study, they found that only for a segment of their respondents, and under specific conditions, signs of a job preservation strategy could be found. In this chapter, we will examine whether academia is a such a context, conductive to job preservation acts.

The job preservation strategy could also be relevant for employees on a *temporary contract*. Research suggests that temporary employment can be a stepping stone to a permanent contract (De Cuyper et al., 2018; De Cuyper & De Witte, 2021). First of all, a majority of workers in the European large scale Psycones-study motivated accepting a temporary contract because they hoped to gain a permanent contract (De Cuyper et al., 2010). Employers often use temporary employment as a selection method to screen workers, to find out whether they could be given a permanent contract later on. Good performance probably plays a key role in this assessment process. As a consequence, one could assume that temporary workers who would like to get a permanent contract will invest in performing well. At the same time, they might be inclined to avoid counterproductive behaviours that might jeopardise their chances of being offered a permanent contract. Applied to temporary workers, 'job preservation strategies' get the meaning of 'aiming to *achieve* a permanent contract in the future', rather than 'to maintain the actual job'.

The empirical evidence for the link between temporary contracts and performance is rather inconclusive, as stated above (De Cuyper et al., 2008; De Graaf-Zijl, 2005). Most studies did not find a significant association with in-role work behaviours (De Cuyper et al., 2010; Ellingson et al., 1998; van Vuuren et al., 2020). Some studies, however, found indications that temporary workers perform more than permanent workers. Engellandt and Riphahn (2005) for instance reported that workers on a temporary contract more often performed unpaid overwork compared to workers with a permanent contract.

To summarise this contrasting set of hypotheses, we hypothesise that the three indicators of insecurity (quantitative job insecurity, qualitative job insecurity and a temporary employment contract) will be associated with an increase of productive work behaviours (in-role, extra-role and innovative work behaviours) and an decrease in counterproductive work behaviours. We call this 'positive path' the *challenge hypothesis* (hypothesis 2), which is based on the 'job preservation motivation' view of Shoss (2017).

9.4 Contrasting Hypotheses on the Interaction Between Job Insecurity and the Employment Contract

The inclusion of indicators of both subjective and objective insecurity in this study offers the unique opportunity to additionally examine the *interaction* between both insecurity operationalisations. Again, contrasting hypotheses can be developed and tested.

First of all, it is possible that job insecurity and the employment contract *strengthen* each other when associating with performance indicators. This means that both variables combine in a multiplicative rather than additive way ('interaction'). In this view, the combination of both operationalisations of insecurity with performance outcomes results in a stronger effect than the 'mere' addition of the effects of both kinds of insecurity separately. We call this hypothesis the '*intensification*' hypothesis (hypothesis 3), because (subjective) job insecurity is supposed to strengthen or 'boost' the association of the temporary employment contract with performance (De Witte & Näswall, 2003; see also Mauno et al., 2005). This view aligns with the assumption that it is specifically the subjective side of insecurity that is relevant for outcomes (Klandermans & van Vuuren, 1999): temporary employment will especially be associated with outcome variables when the employee subjectively experiences his/her job as insecure. In this 'intensification' hypothesis, one thus expects the association of (two kinds of) job insecurity with performance to be stronger for workers with a temporary contract compared to those with a permanent contract.

Intensification can relate to both effects hypothesised above. The *hindrance intensification* hypothesis (hypothesis 3a) assumes that the negative association of (both quantitative and qualitative) job insecurity with productive work behaviours will be stronger for workers with a temporary contract compared to workers with a permanent contract. For counterproductive work behaviours one assumes a stronger positive association for temporary compared to permanent workers. In other words, the lowest level of productive work behaviours (and the highest for counterproductive work behaviours) is expected for those respondents who work on a temporary contract *and* perceive their job as (quantitatively or qualitatively) insecure, as these workers experience the highest levels of e.g. need deprivation and strain.

The *challenge intensification* hypothesis (hypothesis 3b) assumes that the positive association of (both quantitative and qualitative) job insecurity with productive work behaviours will be stronger for workers with a temporary contract compared to workers with a permanent contract. For counterproductive work behaviours one assumes a stronger negative association for temporary compared to permanent workers. In other words, the highest level of productive work behaviours (and the lowest for counterproductive work behaviours) is expected for those respondents who work on a temporary contract *and* perceive their jobs as (quantitatively or qualitatively) insecure. Stated yet another way, this combination is expected to result in the highest level of job preservation behaviour.

The ‘*violation*’ hypothesis (hypothesis 4; De Witte & Näswall, 2003; see also Mauno et al., 2005) contrasts the intensification hypotheses. This violation hypothesis is based on psychological contract theory. Here, one assumes that the temporary employment contract *buffers* the impact of job insecurity on outcomes like performance. This hypothesis builds on the idea that temporary and permanent workers developed different psychological contracts with their employer (De Witte & Näswall, 2003; De Cuyper & De Witte, 2006, 2008). Employees with a permanent contract expect job security in return for their efforts and loyalty. Job insecurity is therefore experienced as a violation of their psychological contract with their employer (‘psychological contract breach’), which typically leads to higher strain reactions and lower performance. Employees with a temporary contract do not necessarily expect their job to be secure, as they were not offered a permanent (hence ‘secure’) employment contract. Job security is only to a lesser extent part of their psychological contract, if at all. As a consequence, the perception of job insecurity is not experienced as a breach of their psychological contract (or to a lesser extent). In this ‘violation’ hypothesis, one thus expects the association of job insecurity with performance to be less strong (or even absent) for workers with a temporary contract compared to those with a permanent contract. This could apply to both the hindrance and challenge hypothesis developed above (respectively hypothesis 4a and 4b).

Empirical studies examining the proposed interaction are scarce. The available evidence however points towards the violation hypothesis (De Cuyper & De Witte, 2006; De Witte & Näswall, 2003; Mauno et al., 2005; van Vuuren et al., 2020). Illustrative in this regard is the large scale study of van Vuuren et al. (2020) in the Netherlands. These authors find a negative association of subjective job insecurity with in-role performance (in line with the hindrance hypothesis). This association was weaker for specific categories of temporary workers (agency and on-call workers) compared to permanent workers, in line with the (hindrance) violation hypothesis. Interestingly, however, no difference in interaction was observed between workers on a fixed-term contract and their colleagues working with a permanent contract. In other words, none of the interaction hypotheses assumed above were found to be statistically significant when focussing on workers with a temporary contract (rather than temporary agency and on call contracts).

9.5 Method

9.5.1 Dataset and Sample

For a description of the sampling procedures and sample characteristics, see Chap. 1 (Roll et al., 2025, this volume). The total dataset will be used for the analyses (all ten countries combined). There were some missing values for the two core variables in this chapter: professional position (654 respondents did not indicate their position, or positions were classified in another way), and employment contract (442 respondents failed to fill in the contract question). As a consequence, the total sample size was 3715. Temporary contracts ($n = 1310$) and 'other non-permanent' contracts ($n = 151$) were combined, resulting in 1461 respondents with a temporary contract versus 2840 respondents with a permanent contract. We will perform all analyses separately for the three core professional categories: Professors ($n = 1938$), PhD-students ($n = 756$) and Administrative staff ($n = 1395$). These categories will be analysed separately, as they occupy a particular position in academia, with different tasks and responsibilities and large differences in job characteristics. Additionally, these categories are differently composed when one looks at their demographic variables, such as age, educational level and employment contract. To give an example, there was a rather strong association between the professional position and the employment contract (Cramer's $V = .55$, $p < .001$), with 79.1% of the professors and 81.6% of the administrative staff holding a permanent contract versus 86.3% of the PhD-students holding a temporary contract. This strong overlap made controlling for most demographic or work related background variables difficult. The three professional groups are rather homogeneous regarding demographic variables, suggesting that controlling for demographic variables within each professional category is perhaps less relevant. Note that we did not develop differential hypotheses for the three professional categories. Their results will be exploratively compared. One could however assume that professors and PhD-students are somewhat different from the administrative staff. Members of the administrative staff are perhaps more similar to the general working population, whereas especially for professors and PhD-students promotion might to a larger degree be conditional on performance. In other words, specifically professors and PhD-students might be prototypical categories to expect a positive association between insecurity and performance.

9.5.2 Measures

All variables and measures are detailed in Chap. 1 (Roll et al., 2025, this volume). The cross-cultural equivalence of the two job insecurity measures was analysed and discussed in Chap. 2 (Jiang et al., 2025, this volume). The cross-cultural equivalence of in-role and innovative work behaviours was analysed and discussed in Chap. 3 (Iliescu et al., 2025, this volume).

Quantitative job insecurity was measured with the four item scale of Vander Elst et al. (2014). A sample item is "Chances are, I will soon lose my job". The 4 items of the scale of Fischmann et al. (2022) were used to measure *qualitative job insecurity* (sample item: "I think my job will change for the worse"). All items were assessed on a 5-point scale, ranging from 1 ('strongly disagree') to 5 ('strongly agree'). The scale means were $M = 2.30$; SD $= 0.94$, with internal consistency (α) .85 for the quantitative aspect, with $M = 2.80$; SD $= 0.95$ and internal consistency (α) .86 for the qualitative dimension respectively.

In-role behaviour was assessed using self-reports with four items adapted and modified from Williams and Anderson (1991). The scale measures how well one executes the core-tasks required for the job. An item example includes "*I fulfil the responsibilities specified in my job description*" with response range possibilities between 1 (*Strongly Disagree*) to 5 (*Strongly Agree*). The scale mean value was $M = 4.38$, with $SD = 0.59$ and an internal consistency of $\alpha = .88$.

Extra-role behaviour or '*Organisational Citizenship Behaviour'* (OCB) was measured with four items modified and adapted from earlier studies (see Morrison, 1994; Podsakoff et al. 1990). The instrument measures the frequency of altruistic behaviours on the individual level, such as helping with heavy workloads or lending a hand on work related issues. Respondents were specifically asked to rate how often they have enacted work-related helping behaviours during the last 6 months with response range varying between 1 (*Never*) and 5 (*Daily*). The scale mean was 3.08 with $SD = 0.94$. Coefficient alpha was a good .83.

Innovative work behaviour was measured with four items from De Jong and Den Hartog (2010). Respondents were for instance asked how often one wondered how things could be improved in their job, with responses ranging from 1 (*Never*) to 5 (*Daily*). The scale mean was $M = 3.55$ with $SD = 0.88$. Coefficient alpha was a very good .92.

Counterproductive work behaviour was measured with a scale focusing on mild 'deviant behaviours'. Four items were used, that are a subset of a larger scale (Bennet & Robinson, 2000). The items tap into the frequency of voluntary workplace behaviour that is contrary to the legitimate interest of the organization by violating organisational norms. Example items include: How often did you "*... intentionally work slower than you could work*?" or "*... put little effort into your work*?". Response range for these questions is between 1 (*Never*) and 7 (*Daily*). Psychometric properties of the scale include $M = 1.90$; $SD = 0.94$, with the internal consistency value of alpha at .69.

A table with the means, SD and intercorrelations of all variables for each professional category separately has been added as appendix to this chapter (Tables 9.4, 9.5, and 9.6).

9.5.3 Data Analysis

Data analysis was run under RStudio and R, version 4.4.1. We fitted several multiple linear regression models to analyse the relationships between quantitative job insecurity, qualitative job insecurity, employment contract, and their interactions on the various dimensions of overall job performance: in-role behaviour (task performance), innovative work behaviour, organisational citizenship behavior and counterproductive work behaviour (workplace deviance).

The primary goal of the models was to assess whether the two types of job insecurity together with employment contract are related to the individual performance dimensions, and whether the employment contract moderates the relationship between the job insecurity aspects and performance outcomes. As both dimensions of subjective job insecurity showed a considerable correlation in each of the professional categories (ranging from .50 to .55, $p < .001$), factor scores for both job insecurity variables were calculated after performing a principal components analysis in SPSS. That way, the correlation between quantitative and qualitative job insecurity was reduced to .00 (SD = 1.00) in all analyses, which avoids creating suppression effects. The correlation within each professional category between subjective job insecurity and the employment contract was rather limited (ranging from .21 to .37, $p < .001$ for quantitative job insecurity, and from −.02 to .03, *n.s.* for qualitative job insecurity), which means that multicollinearity was not a problem.

To avoid overcomplexity due to added interactions, the analyses were conducted on the unpooled data, for each professional category separately (i.e., for professors, PhD-students, and administrative staff). As we did not consider the geographic source of the data (country), the age or gender of the participant as potentially confounding our estimates, we did not use them as covariates in our analysis. The unstandardised regression coefficients will be reported in the tables. For all coefficients, 95% confidence intervals were calculated. A coefficient will only be considered statistically significant when .00 was not included in the confidence interval.

9.6 Results

The results of the various regression analyses are reported in Table 9.1 for the professors, Table 9.2 for the PhD-students and Table 9.3 for the administrative staff. To simplify the discussion of the results, we will first of all focus on the direct

Table 9.1 Results of regression analyses for professors (unstandardized coefficients)

	In-role behaviour	Innovative work behaviour	Organisational citizenship behaviour	Counterproductive work behaviour
Quantitative job insecurity	−.25***	−.17**	.01	−.12
Qualitative job insecurity	.03	−.05	−.02	−.04
Contract°	−.01	−.21**	−.25***	.00
Interaction term QN JI * contract	.13***	.15**	.01	.07
Interaction term QL JI * contract	−.01	.07	.05	.06
F-value	9.31***	4.39***	5.00***	1.57
df	(5, 1851)	(5, 1851)	(5, 1847)	(5, 1845)
R	.16	.11	.12	.065
R^2	.025	.01	.01	.00

° Dummy-variable: high = temporary employment contract; * $p < .05$; ** $p < .01$; *** $p < .001$

Table 9.2 Results of regression analyses for PhD-students (unstandardized coefficients)

	In-role behaviour	Innovative work behaviour	Organisational citizenship behaviour	Counterproductive work behaviour
Quantitative job insecurity	−.48**	−.47	−.47	.76*
Qualitative job insecurity	.15	−.29	−.04	−.13
Contract°	.17	.21	.05	−.26
Interaction term QN JI * contract	.23*	.21	.22	−.38*
Interaction term QL JI * contract	−.10	.15	.03	.09
F-value	2.42*	1.98(*)	.93	1.42
df	(5658)	(5658)	(5658)	(5, 658)
R	.13	.12	.08	.10
R^2	.02	.015	.01	.01

° Dummy-variable: high = temporary employment contract; *$p < .05$; **$p < .01$; ***$p < .001$

Table 9.3 Results of regression analyses for administrative staff (unstandardized coefficients)

	In-role behaviour	Innovative work behaviour	Organisational citizenship behaviour	Counterproductive work behaviour
Quantitative job insecurity	−.31***	.00	.15	−.00
Qualitative job insecurity	−.17**	.09	.09	.26**
Contract°	−.06	−.05	−.12	.14
Interaction term QN JI * contract	.18**	.04	−.06	−.02
Interaction term QL JI * contract	.11*	−.08	−.02	−.13
F-value	10.47***	.77	2.88*	4.66***
df	(5, 1182)	(5, 1183)	(5, 1185)	(5, 1184)
R	.21	.06	.11	.14
R^2	.04	.00	.01	.02

° Dummy-variable: high = temporary employment contract; * $p < .05$; ** $p < .01$; *** $p < .001$

associations per professional category, followed by an overall synthesis across categories. Only afterwards, we will discuss the results regarding the interactions per professional category, followed by a synthesis of the interaction results across categories.

9.6.1 Direct Associations Between Insecurity and Performance

Among the *professors*, one third (4/12) of the direct associations between the insecurity indicators and aspects of performance are significant (see Table 9.1). All significant associations with productive work behaviours have a negative sign, corroborating the hindrance hypothesis. More specifically, quantitative job insecurity is significantly negatively associated with in-role work behaviour and innovative work behaviour in this professional category. At the same time, professors on a temporary contract score significantly lower for innovative work behaviour and organisational citizenship behaviour. Qualitative job insecurity is not significantly associated with any of the performance measures, after controlling for the other insecurity indicators. When looking at the various performance indicators, especially innovative work behaviour seems to be negatively affected in this professional category, whereas no significant association with counterproductive behaviour was observed.

The results regarding the *PhD-students* show a somewhat different picture (see Table 9.2). Here, only 16.7% (2/12) of the direct effects are significant. The significant associations are again in line with the hindrance hypothesis. More specifically, quantitative job insecurity is significantly negatively associated with in-role behaviour and positively with counterproductive work behaviour. So, PhD-students perform less well regarding task performance, and show more mild counterproductive behaviour when they feel quantitatively insecure. Among the PhD-students, qualitative job insecurity again did not show a significant association with the performance indicators, nor did the employment contract. Only in-role work behaviour and counterproductive work behaviour were affected by insecurity among PhD-students, whereas no significant associations were found for innovative work behaviour or organisational citizenship behaviour. Note that several regression coefficients did not reach significance in this professional category, even with high numerical values, due to the large uncertainty around the estimate (large standard error).

Table 9.3 shows the results for the *administrative staff*. Here again, the results are somewhat different, suggesting that the picture is partly specific for each professional category. Again 25% (3/12) of all direct associations are significant, and all again corroborate the hindrance hypothesis. More specifically, quantitative job insecurity is negatively associated with in-role behaviour, in line with the results of the other professional categories. This time, however, also qualitative job insecurity plays a role, exhibiting a negative association with in-role behaviour and a positive association with counterproductive work behaviour. For the administrative staff, the employment contract does not show significant associations with performance. At the same time, no significant associations are observed for innovative work behaviour or organisational citizenship behaviour.

Taken together, the results are in line with the hindrance hypothesis, suggesting that insecurity is associated with less productive and more counterproductive work behaviour. This is the case for subjectively measured job insecurity as well as for a temporary employment contract ('objective operationalisation'): all significant associations with productive work behaviours are negative, and those with counterproductive work behaviours are positive. In total, 9 out of 36 direct effects are statistically significant (25%), suggesting that not all possible associations were found. Significant associations were especially found for quantitative job insecurity, and less so for the employment contract or qualitative job insecurity. Of the four indicators of performance, especially in-role behaviour seems to be associated with insecurity, whereas organisational citizenship behaviour was least associated. Strikingly, particularly the combination of quantitative job insecurity and in-role work behaviour did stand out, as this relationship was significant for every professional category under scrutiny. Finally, it is noteworthy that there were also category specific patterns in the results. For professors, especially innovative work behaviour was associated with insecurity. Qualitative job insecurity was only associated with aspects of performance among the administrative staff. Professors and PhD-students were only affected by quantitative job insecurity, not by qualitative job insecurity.

9.6.2 Testing Interactions Between Job Insecurity and Temporary Employment

Returning to the tests of the *interaction* hypotheses, Table 9.1 shows the results for the *professors*. For this professional category, 2 out of 8 possible interactions were found to be significant (25%). Only quantitative job insecurity was relevant, and interacted with the employment contract in determining in-role and innovative work behaviour. Also among *PhD-students* (Table 9.2) 2 out of 8 possible interactions were found to be significant (25%). Again, only quantitative job insecurity showed a significant interaction with the employment contract. This time the interactions related to in-role and counterproductive work behaviour. The results for the *administrative staff* are reported in Table 9.3. Here again 2 out of 8 possible interactions were significant (25%). This time both quantitative and qualitative job insecurity interacted significantly with the employment contract in determining in-role behaviour.

Taken together, 6 out of 24 possible interactions were statistically significant (25%). For each significant interaction, a figure was made in which the mean score of the relevant performance indicator (vertical axis) was plotted for the combination of the relevant job insecurity scale (horizontal) and the employment contract (moderator). Five out of the 6 significant interactions showed a pattern consistent with the *'hindrance violation'* hypothesis. There was no significant association between job insecurity and the performance indicator concerned for those on a temporary employment contract. This association was however statistically significant *and* in

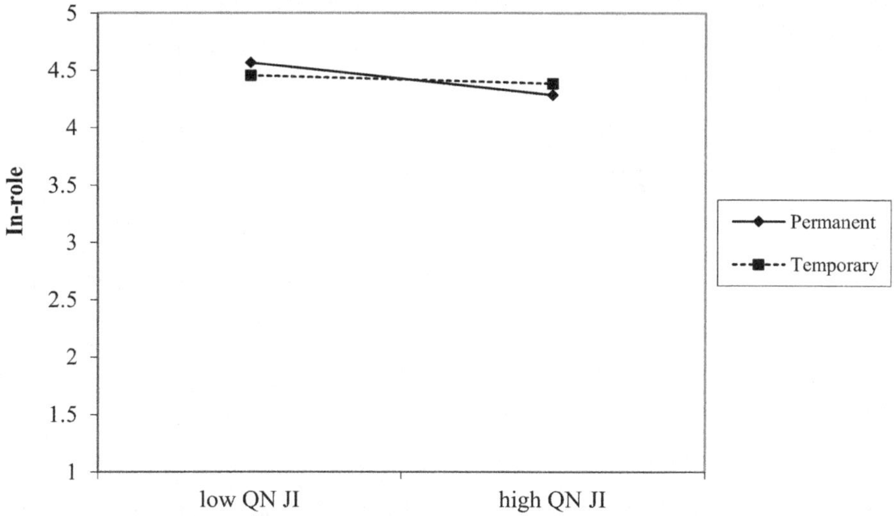

Fig. 9.1 Interaction between quantitative job insecurity and the employment contract with in-role work behaviour as dependent variable (Professors)

line with the hindrance hypothesis for those on a permanent contract. In other words, a temporary employment contract *buffered* the association of job insecurity with performance, whereas workers with a permanent contract showed a clear hindrance pattern when experiencing job insecurity. Figure 9.1 illustrates this 'hindrance violation' pattern for the interaction between quantitative job insecurity and the employment contract in relation to in-role work behaviour. This figure refers to the results of the professors, but is virtually identical for the results concerning PhD-students and administrative staff.

Figure 9.1 shows the expected buffer effect for professors working on a temporary contract, and the expected hindrance effect for those working on a permanent contract. Only among the permanent workers did in-role behaviour decrease when quantitative job insecurity increased. This is illustrated by the respective b-coefficients for both categories ($b = .01$, *n.s.* for temporary contracts versus $-.12$, $p < .001$ for permanent contracts). This pattern is repeated for PhD-students ($b = -.02$, *n.s.* for temporary contracts versus $-.25$, $p < .001$ for permanent contracts) and administrative staff ($b = .05$, *n.s.* for temporary contracts versus $-.13$, $p < .001$ for permanent contracts). For the administrate staff, a significant 'hindrance violation' pattern was also found for the interaction between qualitative job insecurity and the employment contract regarding in-role work behaviour. Here again, the association between qualitative job insecurity and in-role behaviour was not statistically significant among those with a temporary contract ($b = .04$, *n.s.*), whereas qualitative job insecurity was negatively associated with in-role behaviour among those with a permanent contract ($b = -.06$, $p < .01$). Finally, a significant 'hindrance violation' pattern was also found among PhD-students for the interaction between quantitative job insecurity and the employment contract when looking at

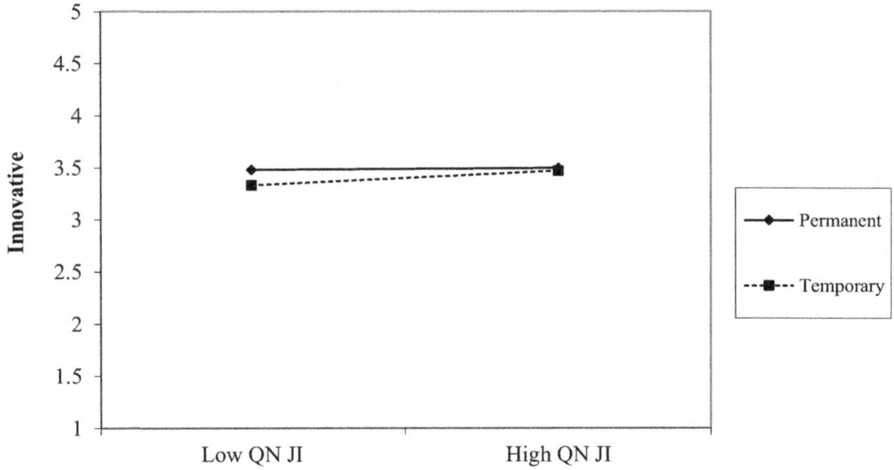

Fig. 9.2 Interaction between quantitative job insecurity and the employment contract with innovative work behaviour as dependent variable (Professors)

counterproductive behaviour. Here, the sign of the association among the permanent workers is positive, as expected: PhD-students with a permanent contract showed an increase in counterproductive behaviour when they experienced more quantitative job insecurity ($b = .38$, $p < .001$). This relationship was absent for those PhD-students who were working on a temporary contract ($b = .00$, *n.s.*).

One significant interaction deviates from the 'hindrance violation' pattern. This pattern is visualised in Fig. 9.2. Among professors a *challenge intensification* pattern could be observed when looking at innovative work behaviour. For professors on a permanent contract, there was no significant association between quantitative job insecurity and innovative work behaviour ($b = -.02$, *n.s.*). For their colleagues on a temporary contract, an increase in quantitative job insecurity was associated with an increase in innovative work behaviour ($b = .13$, $p < .001$). This pattern matches the expectations from the challenge stressor view, in which insecurity is associated with higher performance. Figure 9.2 also shows that professors with a temporary contract score somewhat lower on innovative work behaviour when they score low on quantitative job insecurity. When quantitative job insecurity increases among this group, they reach the same level of innovative work behaviour as their colleagues with a permanent contract. In other words: they are not outperforming their colleagues on a permanent contract, but rather seem to 'catch up their backlog'.

The analysis of the interactions shows that one can mainly observe 'hindrance violation': workers on a permanent contract seem to react more strongly to job insecurity by reducing their productive performance and increasing their counter productive work behaviour. For workers with a temporary contract, the relationship between job insecurity and performance seems to be absent. There was one notable exception: professors on a temporary contract seemed to increase their innovative work behaviour somewhat when they experienced (quantitative) job insecurity.

When analysing interactions, we once again found that quantitative (and not qualitative) job insecurity played a prominent role. Again, most interactions concerned in-role behaviour, suggesting that job insecurity mainly affects this performance indicator. The combination of both variables resulted in most significant interactions, as we observed a hindrance violation pattern between the employment contract and quantitative job insecurity regarding in-role behaviour for *each* professional category. Interactions with organisational citizenship behaviour were absent.

9.7 Discussion

9.7.1 Summary of Results and Discussion

In this chapter, we tested contrasting hypotheses regarding the association between insecurity and performance in academia. The academic sector is an interesting context to explore this association, as especially for professors and PhD-students, staying within academia might be conditional on performance ('publish or perish'). Additionally, this sector has been subjected to large scale changes over the year, due to governmental cut backs. As a consequence, job demands have been increasing for many, and insecurity has been on the rise. Analysing the insecurity-performance relationship in academia is not just a relevant scientific endeavour, but also an important societal pursuit, as it touches the core of scientific activity: does insecurity hinder or stimulate the development of scientific knowledge? In order to thoroughly explore this issue, a broad spectrum of insecurity and performance indicators were analysed. Insecurity was operationalised as subjective job insecurity, both quantitative and qualitative, and as the employment contract, sometimes referred to as 'objective' job insecurity. Performance was analysed by looking at three aspects of productive work behaviour: in-role, extra-role and innovative work behaviour. Counterproductive behaviour was operationalised as withdrawal, a milder form of counterproductivity related to deliberately working slower.

We used the combined database of the ten countries to test our hypotheses. Two contrasting hypotheses were developed regarding the direct relationship between insecurity and performance. The negative, *hindrance* path relates to reduced productive and increased counterproductive behaviour when experiencing insecurity. This hypothesis was based upon stress and social exchange theories, leading to the expectation that stress hinders the ability to perform, whereas a lack of reciprocity undermines the willingness to perform (Tomas & Maslić Seršić, 2023). The positive, *challenge* path relates to the expectation that workers will increase their productive behaviour (and decrease counterproductive behaviour) in order to preserve their job (Shoss, 2017). The results of our various regression analyses only corroborated the hindrance hypothesis, when looking at the direct associations. When significant associations were found, insecurity was associated with less productive and more counterproductive work behaviour. These findings are in line with the empirical evidence resulting from literature reviews and meta-analyses (Cheng & Chan, 2008;

De Cuyper & De Witte, 2021; De Witte, 2024; De Witte & Van Hootegem, 2021; Jiang & Lavaysse, 2018; Klug et al., 2024; Probst et al., 2018; Sverke et al., 2019; Vander Elst & De Witte, 2024). Interestingly, quantitative job insecurity and a temporary employment contract were both negatively associated with innovative work behaviour among professors. This suggests that insecurity might reduce their capacity to generate and implement new ideas in their work – a core activity for scientists. This finding aligns with studies showing that insecurity hinders innovative work behaviour in other professions (Niesen et al., 2018; Probst et al., 2020; Roll et al., 2015; Van Hootegem et al., 2019). Another core finding was that especially *quantitative job insecurity* seemed relevant: especially the fear of losing the actual job was associated with reduced performance. Qualitative job insecurity did not play an important role, and its relevance was restricted to the administrative staff only. Finally, of all performance indicators, especially *in-role behaviour* was affected by insecurity. Organisational citizenship behaviour was least affected by insecurity, perhaps due to its specific operationalisation. These citizenship behaviours were measured as individual-directed acts: altruism or helping colleagues. It is possible that stronger associations could have been observed when organisation-directed OCB had been measured. Taken together, the results clearly point towards a hindrance effect of quantitative job insecurity on in-role behaviour, as this association was found in each of the three professional categories. This is an important finding, as it suggests that the fear of losing the actual job hinders core task performance for everyone working in the academic sector.

Next to direct effects, we also tested hypotheses regarding potential interactions between the employment contract and subjective job insecurity. Two contrasting sets of hypotheses were advanced. The intensification hypothesis suggested that both indicators of insecurity could strengthen each other, resulting in the assumption that there could be 'hindrance intensification' or 'challenge intensification'. This would result in a stronger negative association (hindrance intensification) or stronger positive association (challenge intensification) with productive work behaviours among those on a temporary employment contract. The contrasting hypothesis assumed that especially workers on a permanent contract would show stronger effects due to the violation of their psychological contract. This could result in a stronger negative association (hindrance violation) or stronger positive association (challenge violation) with productive work behaviours among permanent workers. The pattern of significant interactions dominantly corroborated the 'hindrance violation' view. Especially those on a permanent contract reacted more negatively to insecurity, showing a stronger negative association between insecurity and (productive work) performance. This finding aligns with the literature in the field, in which one typically observes a similar interaction effect (De Cuyper & De Witte, 2006; De Witte & Näswall, 2003; Mauno et al., 2005; van Vuuren et al., 2020). Here again, quantitative job insecurity played a prominent role, especially in combination with in-role behaviour. The hindrance violation pattern was observed for each of the three professional categories separately, once again suggesting that specifically quantitative job insecurity results in reduced in-role behaviours once one perceives a breach of the psychological contract.

Only one of the six significant interactions was in line with the challenge intensification hypothesis. Interestingly, this interaction related to innovative work behaviour among professors. Professors with a temporary contract showed an increase in innovative work behaviour when they experienced more quantitative job insecurity. Note, however, that this group did not outperform their colleagues on a permanent contract, but rather managed to increase their level of innovative work behaviour to the same level of their permanent colleagues when they experienced higher levels of quantitative job insecurity.

9.7.2 Limitations

As usual, several limitations of this study should be mentioned. The *data* stem from a large variety of countries all over the globe. That is obviously an advantage. The sampling procedures in every country, however, do not guarantee a representative sample in each country separately, and not all countries across the globe are represented. Additionally, the analyses were performed on the combined dataset, without differentiating between the various countries. A country specific analysis is obviously relevant, as all countries differ to some extend regarding their context, legislation, governmental policy, history and labour market, as highlighted in the first chapter (see Roll et al., 2025, this volume). Future research should focus on collecting representative samples from a larger set of countries, and on a cross-country comparison of our hypotheses. The meta-analysis of Sverke et al. (2019) suggests that welfare regimes with strong social protection result in weaker associations between job insecurity and performance indicators (see also Klug et al., 2024). Whether this also applies to academia has yet to be analysed.

The specific *operationalisation* of the various *performance* indicators might also have influenced the results. Especially extra-role behaviours and counterproductive work behaviours were operationalised in a specific, and therefore limited way. For extra-role behaviours, only person-directed altruism was measured. Other, more organisation-directed measurements might have resulted in a different picture. Additionally, only mild counterproductive behaviours related to withdrawal were measured. Aspects intending to harm the organisation were not measured. Adding organisation-directed measures seems relevant in future research, as employees in universities might blame their organisation for being insecure, which might result in stronger effects. In the last chapter of this edited volume, results are presented on the causal attribution of job insecurity. These show that poor managerial decision making, next to governmental policies and the national economy, are held responsible for insecurity in academia. This makes stronger negative reactions towards the organisation likely.

This comment can also be expanded to the measurement of insecurity in this study. Whereas (subjective) job insecurity was measured with validated questionnaires (see also Chap. 2; Jiang et al., 2025, this volume), qualitative job insecurity could have been measured with a more differentiated questionnaire in which various relevant dimensions are distinguished (Brondino et al., 2020). Other aspects like career insecurity and its various dimensions (Spurk et al., 2022) or occupation insecurity (Roll et al., 2023) are also relevant aspects of insecurity to be analysed in future research. Finally, the merger of various kinds of temporary contracts in just one category is probably rather simplistic, as previous research has documented the impact of the type of temporary contract on outcomes (De Cuyper et al., 2008, 2010; van Vuuren et al., 2020). Also the motivation to accept a temporary contract can make a difference, and was not measured in this study (De Cuyper et al., 2010).

The data used are *cross-sectional*, which obviously limits conclusions regarding causality. Reversed causation could also explain many of the reported associations, as some studies have shown that reduced performance can also increase insecurity (e.g. Fischmann et al., 2018). The association between quantitative job insecurity and innovative work behaviour among professors could also mean that not performing well increases the risk of being dismissed in the future, thus increasing the perception of job insecurity. Note however that reversed causality is perhaps less likely when looking at the association between temporary employment and innovative work behaviour. It seems less probable that professors on a permanent contract will be offered a temporary contract when they are not innovative. Longitudinal designs with several waves are needed to further explore this issue.

Finally, recent studies have been suggesting that the association between insecurity and performance could be curvilinear (Jiang et al., 2022; Selenko et al., 2013). Such associations have not been explored in this chapter. The focus was on operationalisations of subjective and objective insecurity and their potential interaction. Given the complexity of these research questions and the extensive amount of independent and dependent variables, testing non-linear associations was beyond the scope of the focus of this chapter.

9.8 Take Home Message

The association between job insecurity and performance has been subject to some debate in the literature. Academia is probably a good context to test such a relationship, as the employment of many academics is (partly) dependent on their performance. This association was tested in academia using the total dataset of 10 countries covering four different continents. The results of these tests suggest that assumptions regarding the positive impact of insecurity on performance are overstated, and even appear as an urban myth. The core finding in this chapter is that insecurity is associated with a decrease in productive work behaviour and an increase in counterproductive work behaviour. This was especially the case for quantitative job insecurity and in-role performance. Academics who fear to lose their job perform less and show more negative work behaviour. These findings speak against the view that insecurity will increase performance in order to preserve the actual job. Applied to the academic sector and stated in yet another way: job insecurity in academia is not conductive to the development and accumulation of scientific knowledge, but rather jeopardises its creation and dissemination.

Appendices

Table 9.4 Means, standard deviations, and correlations with confidence intervals for professors

Variable	*M*	*SD*	1	2	3	4	5	6
1. QNJI	−0.00	1.00						
2. QLJI	0.00	1.00	.00					
			[−.04, .04]					
3. Contract	1.21	0.41	.37**	.03				
			[.33, .41]	[−.02, .07]				
4. IR	4.44	0.58	−.12**	.03	−.01			
			[−.16, −.07]	[−.01, .08]	[−.06, .03]			
5. IWB	3.52	0.86	.02	.03	−.06**	.28**		
			[−.03, .06]	[−.01, .08]	[−.11, −.01]	[.24, .32]		
6. OCB	2.95	0.89	−.02	.04	−.10**	.14**	.43**	
			[−.07, .02]	[−.01, .08]	[−.15, −.06]	[.10, .19]	[.39, .46]	
7. CWB	1.73	0.84	−.01	.04	.00	−.26**	−.09**	.04
			[−.06, .03]	[−.01, .08]	[−.04, .05]	[−.30, −.21]	[−.14, −.05]	[−.01, .08]

Note: *M* and *SD* are used to represent mean and standard deviation, respectively. *QNJI* quantitative job insecurity, *QLJI* qualitative job insecurity, Contract: temporary employment contract (dummy), *IR* in-role behaviour, *IWB* innovative work behaviour, *OCB* organisational citizenship behaviour, *CWB* counterproductive work behaviour. Values in square brackets indicate the 95% confidence interval for each correlation. The confidence interval is a plausible range of population correlations that could have caused the sample correlation (Cumming, 2014). * indicates $p < .05$. ** indicates $p < .01$

Table 9.5 Means, standard deviations, and correlations with confidence intervals for PhD-students

Variable	*M*	*SD*	1	2	3	4	5	6
1. QNJI	−0.00	1.00						
2. QLJI	0.00	1.00	−.00					
			[−.07, .07]					
3. Status	1.86	0.34	.21**	−.01				
			[.14, .28]	[−.08, .07]				
4. IR	4.24	0.62	−.05	−.03	.02			
			[−.12, .02]	[−.10, .04]	[−.05, .10]			
5. IWB	3.54	0.82	−.07	.03	.03	.13**		
			[−.14, .00]	[−.04, .10]	[−.05, .10]	[.06, .20]		
6. OCB	2.99	0.94	−.06	.05	−.03	.06	.48**	
			[−.13, .01]	[−.03, .12]	[−.11, .05]	[−.01, .13]	[.42, .53]	
7. CWB	2.24	1.14	.01	.05	−.02	−.23**	−.12**	.03
			[−.06, .08]	[−.02, .12]	[−.10, .05]	[−.30, −.16]	[−.19, −.05]	[−.05, .10]

Note: *M* and *SD* are used to represent mean and standard deviation, respectively. *QNJI* quantitative job insecurity, *QLJI* qualitative job insecurity, Contract: temporary employment contract (dummy), *IR* in-role behaviour, *IWB* innovative work behaviour, *OCB* organisational citizenship behaviour, *CWB* counter-productive work behaviour. Values in square brackets indicate the 95% confidence interval for each correlation. The confidence interval is a plausible range of population correlations that could have caused the sample correlation (Cumming, 2014). * indicates $p < .05$. ** indicates $p < .01$

Table 9.6 Means, standard deviations, and correlations with confidence intervals for administrative staff

Variable	*M*	*SD*	1	2	3	4	5	6
1. QNJI	0.00	1.00						
2. QLJI	−0.00	1.00	.00					
			[−.05, .05]					
3. Status	1.18	0.39	.36**	−.02				
			[.31, .41]	[−.08, .03]				
4. IR	4.36	0.59	−.14**	−.07*	−.03			
			[−.19, −.09]	[−.12, −.01]	[−.08, .03]			
5. IWB	3.63	0.94	.04	.01	.01	.23**		
			[−.01, .09]	[−.04, .06]	[−.05, .06]	[.17, .27]		
6. OCB	3.33	0.97	.06*	.07**	−.03	.14**	.45**	
			[.01, .11]	[.02, .13]	[−.09, .02]	[.09, .20]	[.41, .49]	
7. CWB	2.05	0.95	.00	.13**	.05	−.19**	−.08**	−.05
			[−.05, .05]	[.08, .18]	[−.01, .10]	[−.24, −.14]	[−.13, −.03]	[−.10, .00]

Note. *M* and *SD* are used to represent mean and standard deviation, respectively. *QNJI* quantitative job insecurity, *QLJI* qualitative job insecurity, Contract: temporary employment contract (dummy), *IR* in-role behaviour, *IWB* innovative work behaviour, *OCB* organisational citizenship behaviour, *CWB* counterproductive work behaviour. Values in square brackets indicate the 95% confidence interval for each correlation. The confidence interval is a plausible range of population correlations that could have caused the sample correlation (Cumming, 2014). * indicates $p < .05$. ** indicates $p < .01$

References

Anderson, V., & Brough, P. (2024). Organizational citizenship behaviour. In C. Cooper & P. Brough (Eds.), *Elgar encyclopedia of occupational health psychology* (pp. 118–121). Edward Elgar Publishing Limited.

Bakker, A., Demerouti, E., & Sanz-Vergel, A. (2023). Job demands–resources theory: Ten years later. *Annual Review of Organizational Psychology and Organizational Behavior, 10*, 13.1–13.29. https://doi.org/10.1146/annurev-orgpsych-120920-053933

Bennett, R. J., & Robinson, S. L. (2000). Development of a measure of workplace deviance. *Journal of Applied Psychology, 85*, 349–360.

Brondino, M., Bazzoli, A., Vander Elst, T., De Witte, H., & Pasini, M. (2020). Validation and measurement invariance of the multidimensional qualitative job insecurity scale. *Quality and Quantity, 54*, 925–942. https://doi.org/10.1007/s11135-020-00966-y

Cheng, G. H. L., & Chan, D. K. S. (2008). Who suffers more from job insecurity? A meta-analytic review. *Applied Psychology-an International Review, 57*(2), 272–303.

Cumming, G. (2014). The new statistics: Why and how. *Psychological Science, 25*(1), 7–29. https://doi.org/10.1177/0956797613504966

De Cuyper, N., & De Witte, H. (2006). The impact of job insecurity and contract type on attitudes, well-being and behavioural reports: A psychological contract perspective. *Journal of Occupational and Organizational Psychology, 79*, 395–409.

De Cuyper, N., & De Witte, H. (2008). Job insecurity and employability among temporary workers: A theoretical approach based on the psychological contract. In K. Näswall, J. Hellgren & M. Sverke (Red.), *The individual in the changing working life* (pp. 88–107). Cambridge University Press.

De Cuyper, N., & De Witte, H. (2021). Job insecurity. In *Oxford research encyclopedia of psychology*. Oxford University Press. https://doi.org/10.1093/acrefore/9780190236557.013.17.

De Cuyper, N., & De Witte, H. (2024). Temporary employment. In F. Maggino (Ed.), *Encyclopedia of quality of life and well-being research* (2nd ed., pp. 7169–7172). Springer.

De Cuyper, N., de Jong, J., De Witte, H., Isaksson, K., Rigotti, T., & Schalk, R. (2008). Literature review of theory and research on the psychological impact of temporary employment: Towards a conceptual model. *International Journal of Management Reviews, 10*, 25–51. https://doi.org/10.1111/j.1468-2370.2007.00221.x

De Cuyper, N., De Witte, H., Krausz, M., Mohr, G. & Rigotti, T. (2010). Chapter 4. Individual and organizational outcomes of employment contracts. In: Guest, D. E., Isaksson, K. & De Witte, H. (2010) (Eds.). *Employment contracts, psychological contracts & employee well-being. An international study* (pp. 65–87). Oxford University Press.

De Cuyper, N., Fontinha, R., & De Witte, H. (2018). Non-traditional employment: The careers of temporary workers. In U.-C. Klehe & E. A. J. van Hooft (Eds.), *Oxford handbook on job loss and job search* (pp. 465–480). Oxford University Press. https://doi.org/10.1093/oxfordhb/9780199764921.013.016

De Graaf-Zijl, M. (2005). *The economic and social consequences of temporary employment: A review of the literature*. Discussion paper N° 7. Universiteit van Amsterdam.

De Jong, J., & Den Hartog, D. (2010). Measuring innovative work behavior. *Creativity and Innovation Management, 19*, 23–36.

De Witte, H. (2024). Job insecurity. In M. Bal (Ed.), *Encyclopedia of organizational psychology* (pp. 342–347). Edward Elgar Publishing Limited. https://doi.org/10.4337/9781803921761

De Witte, H., & Näswall, K. (2003). Objective versus subjective job insecurity: Consequences of temporary work for job satisfaction and organizational commitment in four European countries. *Economic and Industrial Democracy, 24*, 149–188.

De Witte, H., & Van Hootegem, A. (2021). Job insecurity: Challenge or hindrance stressor? Review of the evidence and empirical test on entrepreneurs. In C. Korunka (Ed.), *Flexible working practices and approaches: Psychological and social implications of a multifaceted phenomenon* (pp. 213–229). Springer. https://doi.org/10.1007/978-3-030-74128-0_11

De Witte, H., & Van Hootegem, A. (2025). Thriving or depleted? Profiles of burnout and work engagement in academia. In L. C. Roll, H. De Witte, & S. Rothmann (Eds.), *Global perspectives on job insecurity in higher education: Precarity in the Ivory Tower* (pp. 95–113). Springer.

De Witte, H., Vander Elst, T., & De Cuyper, N. (2015). Job insecurity, health and well-being. In J. Vuori, R. Blonk, & R. H. Price (Eds.), *Sustainable working lives: Managing work transitions and health throughout the life course* (pp. 109–128). Springer.

De Witte, H., Pienaar, J., & De Cuyper, N. (2016). Review of 30 years of longitudinal studies on the association between job insecurity and health and well-being. Is there causal evidence? *Australian Psychologist, 51*(1), 18–31.

Ellingson, J. E., Gruys, M. L., & Sackett, P. R. (1998). Factors related to the satisfaction and performance of temporary employees. *Journal of Applied Psychology, 83*(6), 913–921. https://doi.org/10.1037/0021-9010.83.6.913

Engellandt, A., & Riphahn, R. T. (2005). Temporary contracts and employee effort. *Labour Economics, 12*(3), 281–299.

Fischmann, G., De Witte, H., Sulea, C., & Iliescu, D. (2018). Qualitative job insecurity and in-role performance: A bidirectional longitudinal relationship? *European Journal of Work and Organizational Psychology, 27*(5), 603–615. https://doi.org/10.1080/1359432X.2018.1504769

Fischmann, G., De Witte, H., Sulea, C., Vander Elst, T., De Cuyper, N., & Iliescu, D. (2022). Validation of a Short and Generic Qualitative Job Insecurity Scale (QUAL-JIS). *European Journal of Career Assessment, 38*(5), 397–411. https://doi.org/10.1027/1015-5759/a000674

Griffin, M. (2024). Work performance. In C. Cooper & P. Brough (Eds.), *Elgar encyclopedia of occupational health psychology* (pp. 227–229). Edward Elgar Publishing Limited.

Guest, D., & Isaksson, K. (2019). Temporary employment contracts and employee well-being during and after the financial crisis. Introduction to the special issue. *Economic and Industrial Democracy, 40*, 165–172. https://doi.org/10.1177/0143831X18804706

Guest, D., Isaksson, K., & De Witte, H. (2010). *Employment contracts, psychological contracts, and employee well-being. An international study*. Oxford University Press.

Hellgren, J., Sverke, M., & Isaksson, K. (1999). A two-dimensional approach to job insecurity: consequences for employee attitudes and well-being. *European Journal of Work and Organizational Psychology, 8*, 179–195.

Hobfoll, S., Halbesleben, J., Neveu, J.-P., & Westman, M. (2018). Conservation of resources in the organizational context: The reality of resources and their consequences. *Annual Review of Organizational Psychology and Organizational Behavior, 5*, 103–128. https://doi.org/10.1146/annurev-orgpsych-032117-104640

Iliescu, D., Butucescu, A., Corbeanu, A., & Spinu, R. (2025). The cross-cultural equivalence of predictor, moderator, and outcome variables related to job insecurity in academic settings: A maximum likelihood alignment approach. In L. C. Roll, H. De Witte, & S. Rothmann (Eds.), *Global perspectives on job insecurity in higher education: Precarity in the Ivory Tower* (pp. 67–93). Springer.

Jahoda, M. (1982). *Employment and unemployment. A social-psychological analysis*. University Press.

Jiang, L., & Lavaysse, L. M. (2018). Cognitive and affective job insecurity: A meta-analysis and a primary study. *Journal of Management, 44*(6), 2307–2342. https://doi.org/10.1177/0149206318773853

Jiang, L., Lawrence, A., & Xu, X. (2022). Does a stick work? A meta-analytic examination of curvilinear relationships between job insecurity and employee workplace behaviors. *Journal of Organizational Behavior, 43*(8), 1410–1445. https://doi.org/10.1002/job.2652

Jiang, L., Bazzoli, A., Jenkins, M., & Probst, T. (2025). Job insecurity within higher education: An assessment of measurement invariance and global trends. In L. C. Roll, H. De Witte, & S. Rothmann (Eds.), *Global perspectives on job insecurity in higher education: Precarity in the Ivory Tower* (pp. 37–66). Springer.

Klandermans, B., & van Vuuren, T. (1999). Job insecurity: Introduction. *European Journal of Work and Organizational Psychology, 8*(2), 145–153.

Klandermans, B., Klein Hesselink, J., & van Vuuren, T. (2010). Employment status and job insecurity: On the subjective appraisal of an objective status. *Economic and Industrial Democracy, 31*(4), 557–577.

Klug, K., Selenko, E., Van Hootegem, A., Sverke, M., & De Witte, H. (2024). A lead article to go deeper and broader in job insecurity research: Understanding an individual perception in its social and political context. *Applied Psychology: International Review, 73*(4), 1960-1993. https://doi.org/10.1111/apps.12535

Lepine, J. A., Podsakoff, N. P., & LePine, M. A. (2005). A meta-analytic test of the challenge Stressor-hindrance stressor framework: An explanation for inconsistent relationships among Stressors and performance. *Academy of Management Journal, 48*(5), 764–775. https://doi.org/10.5465/AMJ.2005.18803921

Mauno, S., Kinnunen, U., Mäkikangas, A., & Nätti, J. (2005). Psychological consequences of fixed-term employment and perceived job insecurity among health care staff. *European Journal of Work and Organizational Psychology, 14*(3), 209–237.

Morrison, E. W. (1994). Role definitions and organizational citizenship behavior: The importance of the employee's perspective. *Academy of Management Journal, 37*, 1543–1567.

Niesen, W., Van Hootegem, A., Handaja, Y., Battistelli, A., & De Witte, H. (2018). Quantitative and qualitative job insecurity and idea generation: The mediating role of psychological contract breach. *Scandinavian Journal of Work and Organizational Psychology, 3*(1), 1–14. https://doi.org/10.16993/sjwop.36

Pearce, J. L. (1998). Job insecurity is important, but not for the reason you might think: The example of contingent workers. In C. L. Cooper & D. M. Rousseau (Eds.), *Trends in organizational behavior* (Vol. 5, pp. 31–46). Wiley.

Podsakoff, P. M., MacKenzie, S. B., & Fetter, R. (1990). Organizational citizenship behavior and objective productivity as determinants of managerial evaluations of employee performance. *Organizational Behavior and Human Decision Processes, 50*, 123–150.

Podsakoff, N. P., LePine, J. A., & LePine, M. A. (2007). Differential challenge stressor-hindrance stressor relationships with job attitudes, turnover intentions, turnover, and withdrawal behavior: A meta-analysis. *Journal of Applied Psychology, 92*(2), 438. https://doi.org/10.1037/0021-9010.92.2.438

Probst, T., Jiang, L., & Benson, W. (2018). Job insecurity and anticipated job loss: A primer and exploration of possible interventions. In U.-C. Klehe & E. A. J. van Hooft (Eds.), *Oxford handbook on job loss and job search* (pp. 31–53). Oxford University Press.

Probst, T., Chizh, A., Hu, S., Jiang, L., & Austin, C. (2020). Explaining the relationship between job insecurity and creativity. A test of cognitive and affective mediators. *Career Development International, 25*(3), 247–270. https://doi.org/10.1108/CDI-04-2018-0118

Quinlan, M., Mayhew, C., & Bohle, P. (2001). The global expansion of precarious employment, work disorganization and consequences for occupational health: Placing the debate in a comparative historical context. *International Journal of Health Services, 31*, 507–536. https://doi.org/10.2190/22BK-9XC0-AK7L-M6QH

Repenning, N. P. (2000). Drive out fear (unless you can drive it in): the role of agency and job security in process improvement. *Management Science, 46*(11), 1385–1396. https://doi.org/10.1287/mnsc.46.11.1385.12084

Robinson, S., & Rousseau, D. (1994). Violating the psychological contract: not the exception but the norm. *Journal of Organizational Behavior, 15*, 245–259.

Roll, L. C., Siu, O.-l., Li, S. Y. W., & De Witte, H. (2015). Job insecurity: Cross-cultural comparison between Germany and China. *Journal of Organizational Effectiveness: People and Performance, 2*(1), 36–54.

Roll, L., De Witte, H., & Wang, H.-J. (2023). Conceptualization and Validation of the Occupation Insecurity Scale (OCIS): Measuring employees' occupation insecurity due to automation. *International Journal of Environmental Research and Public Health, 20*, 2589. https://doi.org/10.3390/ijerph20032589

Roll, L. C., De Witte, H., & Rothmann, S. (2025). Introduction: The growing crisis of job insecurity in academia. In L. C. Roll, H. De Witte, & S. Rothmann (Eds.), *Global perspectives on job insecurity in higher education: Precarity in the Ivory Tower* (pp. 1–35). Springer.

Schaufeli, W. B., & Bakker, A. B. (2004). Job demands, job resources, and their relationships with burnout and engagement: A multi-sample study. *Journal of Organizational Behavior, 25*, 293–315.

Selenko, E., Mäkikangas, A., Mauno, S., & Kinnunen, U. (2013). How does job insecurity relate to self-reported job performance? Analysing curvilinear associations in a longitudinal sample. *Journal of Occupational and Organizational Psychology, 86*(4), 522–542. https://doi.org/10.1111/joop.12020

Selenko, E., Stiglbauer, B., & Batinic, B. (2020). More evidence on the latent benefits of work: Bolstered by volunteering while threatened by job insecurity. *European Journal of Work and Organizational Psychology, 29*(3), 364–376. https://doi.org/10.1080/1359432X.2019.1706487

Shoss, M. (2017). Job Insecurity: An integrative review and agenda for future research. *Journal of Management, 43*, 911–1939.

Shoss, M., Su, S., Schlotzhauer, A. E., & Carusone, N. (2022). Working hard or hardly working? An examination of job preservation responses to job insecurity. *Journal of Management*, 1–28. https://doi.org/10.1177/01492063221107877

Sparks, K., Faragher, B., & Cooper, C. (2001). Well-being and occupational health in the 21st century workplace. *Journal of Occupational and Organizational Psychology, 74*, 489–509.

Spector, P. E. (2003). *Industrial & organizational psychology. Research and practice* (3rd ed.). Wiley.

Spurk, D., Hofer, A., Hirschi, A., De Cuyper, H., & De Witte, H. (2022). Conceptualizing career insecurity: Toward a better understanding and measurement of a multidimensional construct. *Personnel Psychology, 75*, 253–294. https://doi.org/10.1111/peps.12493

Sverke, M., & Hellgren, J. (2002). The nature of job insecurity: Understanding employment uncertainty on the brink of a new millennium. *Applied Psychology: An International Review, 51*(1), 23–42.

Sverke, M., Hellgren, J., & Näswall, K. (2002). No security: A meta-analysis and review of job insecurity and its consequences. *Journal of Occupational Health Psychology, 7*(3), 242–264.

Sverke, M., Låstad, L., Hellgren, J., Richter, A., & Näswall, K. (2019). A meta-analysis of job insecurity and employee performance: Testing temporal aspects, rating source, welfare regime, and union density as moderators. *International Journal of Environmental Research and Public Health, 16*(14), 2536. https://doi.org/10.3390/ijerph16142536

Tomas, J., & Maslić Seršić, D. (2023). Job insecurity and job performance: Why do job-insecure employees not perform better? In N. De Cuyper, E. Selenko, M. Euwema, & W. Schaufeli (Eds.), *Job insecurity, Precarious employment and burnout. Facts and fables in work psychology research* (pp. 30–47). Edward Elgar Publishing Limited.

Van den Broeck, A., De Cuyper, N., De Witte, H., & Vansteenkiste, M. (2010). Not all job demands are equal: Differentiating job hindrances and job challenges in the Job Demands-Resources model. *European Journal of Work and Organizational Psychology, 19*(6), 735–759.

Van den Broeck, A., Van Ruysseveldt, J., Vanbelle, E., & De Witte, H. (2013). The job demands–resources model: Overview and suggestions for future research. In A. B. Bakker (Ed.), *Advances in positive organizational psychology* (Vol. 1, pp. 83–105). Emerald Group Publishing Limited.

Van Hootegem, A., Niesen, W., & De Witte, H. (2019). Does job insecurity hinder innovative work behaviour? A threat rigidity perspective. *Creativity and Innovation Management, 28*, 19–29. https://doi.org/10.1111/caim.12271

van Vuuren, T., de Jong, J., & Smulders, P. (2020). The association between subjective job insecurity and job performance across different employment groups. Evidence from a representative sample from the Netherlands. *Career Development International, 25*(3), 229–246. https://doi.org/10.1108/CDI-05-2018-0155

Vander Elst, T., & De Witte, H. (2024). An introduction to job insecurity. In C. Cooper & P. Brough (Eds.), *Elgar encyclopedia of occupational health psychology* (pp. 14–17). Edward Elgar Publishing Limited.

Vander Elst, T., Van den Broeck, A., De Witte, H., & De Cuyper, N. (2014). The role of quantitative and qualitative job insecurity in explaining counterproductive work behavior and innovation. *European Journal of Work and Organizational Psychology, 23*, 913–928.

Vander Elst, T., De Cuyper, N., Baillien, E., Niesen, W., & De Witte, H. (2016a). Perceived control and psychological contract breach as explanations of the relationships between job insecurity, job strain and coping reactions: Towards a theoretical integration. *Stress and Health, 36*(2), 100–116. https://doi.org/10.1002/smi.2584

Vander Elst, T., Näswall, K., Sverke, M., Bernhard Oettel, C., & De Witte, H. (2016b). The effect of job insecurity on employee health complaints: A within-person analysis of the explanatory role of threats to the manifest and latent benefits of work. *Journal of Occupational Health Psychology, 21*(1), 65–76. https://doi.org/10.1037/a0039140

Virtanen, M., Kivimäki, M., Joensuu, M., Virtanen, P., Elovainio, M., & Vahtera, J. (2005). Temporary employment and health: A review. *International Journal of Epidemiology, 34*, 610–622. https://doi.org/10.1093/ije/dyi024

West, M. A. (2002). Sparkling fountains or stagnant ponds: An integrative model of creativity and innovation implementation in work groups. *Applied Psychology: An International Review, 51*, 355–424.

West, M. A., & Farr, J. L. (1989). Innovation at work: Psychological perspectives. *Social Behaviour, 4*, 15–30.

Williams, L. J., & Anderson, S. E. (1991). Job satisfaction and organizational commitment as predictors of organizational citizenship and in-role behaviors. *Journal of Management, 17*, 601–617.

Hans De Witte (PhD in Psychology) was Full Professor in Work Psychology at the Faculty of Psychology and Educational Sciences of the KU Leuven, Belgium (Research Group Work, Organizational and Personnel Psychology). He is academically active since October 2023 as emeritus with assignment. He is also appointed as Extraordinary Professor at the North-West University of South Africa (Optentia Research Unit, Vanderbijlpark Campus). His research includes the study of the psychological consequences of job insecurity, unemployment, temporary employment and downsizing, as well as mobbing and burnout versus work engagement. He (co-) authored about 300 articles in English peer-reviewed journals, published 30 books (14 English and 16 in Dutch; most as co-editor) and is (co-)author of about 80 chapters in English academic books.

George Gunnesch-Luca is Associate Professor of Psychology at the University of Bucharest and a guest researcher at Friedrich-Alexander University Erlangen-Nürnberg, Germany. He is currently the President of the Large Scale Testing Laboratory, responsible for the implementation of international large-scale assessments in education. His research interests also include group behaviour, performance and dynamics, as well as personality in the workplace.

Dragos Iliescu is Professor of Psychology with the University of Bucharest. Dragos Iliescu has served in various capacities for a number of national and international professional associations; he is a Past-President (2016–2018) of the International Test Commission (ITC). He is the Editor-in-Chief for the European Journal of Psychological Assessment, and the author of over 200 scientific papers, book chapters and books, among them the co-Editor of the acclaimed ITC International Handbook of Testing and Assessment, published in 2016 by Oxford University Press, and the author of an important monography (Adapting tests in linguistic and cultural situations) published with Cambridge University Press.

Chapter 10
Qualitative Job Insecurity Is Associated with Lower Work Motivation, Work Adjustment, and Life Wellbeing Among Faculty Teaching Staff in China's Higher Education Institutions

Hao-Yun Zou and Hai-Jiang Wang

In recent years, China's higher education system has often made headlines in China, but not all of the news is positive. Alongside some extraordinary achievements, such as delivering education to 41 million college students, most countries in the world (Ministry of Education, China, 2021), higher education in China is facing its highest ever levels of stress among faculty teaching staff (Liu & Yan, 2020; Xu, 2019).[1] In October 2018, there were two cases of the sudden cardiac death of young faculty members in a week, which led many people to the realization that working in higher education is not as easy as they had believed (Mycos Research, 2018). The three main sources of pressure for faculty teaching staff are excessive teaching loads, demanding publication and grant requirements, and unnecessary administrative formalities ("red tape") (Persson, 2017; Su, 2021).

The pressures felt by faculty teaching staff are related to personnel system reforms in higher education. In 2003, Peking University's reform of its policies on teacher appointment and promotion drew widespread attention, and also prompted faculty appointment systems in China's colleges and universities to transition gradually from the "single-track" system of lifetime employment, known as the "iron rice bowl,[2]" to a "dual-track" of (non-) tenure system (Liu & Shen, 2017). Prior

[1] "Faculty teaching staff" refers here to tenure track (i.e., assistant professor, associate professor, and full professor) and non-tenure track (i.e., instructor, adjunct professor, clinical faculty, and research faculty) faculty members in colleges and universities in China.

[2] This Chinese term relates to the concept of lifetime employment and refers to an occupation that offers guaranteed job security (Friedman & Kuruvilla, 2015).

H.-Y. Zou · H.-J. Wang (✉)
Department of Human Resource and Organization Science, School of Management, Huazhong University of Science and Technology, Hongshan, Wuhan, Hubei Province, China
e-mail: zouhaoyun@hust.edu.cn; wanghaijiang@hust.edu.cn

L. C. Roll et al. (eds.), *Global Perspectives on Job Insecurity in Higher Education*, Aligning Perspectives on Health, Safety and Well-Being,
https://doi.org/10.1007/978-3-031-85772-0_10

to 2003, higher education institutions in China adopted a lifelong employment system for all faculty teaching staff, with promotion from lecturer to associate professor and then to professor on a single track. Since 2003, some universities have experimented with a tenure system to motivate faculty members by differentiating their status and corresponding salaries through two tracks: "tenure" and "non-tenure" (Gao, 2023). Under this system, institutions encourage newly hired and incumbent staff to work towards achieving the tenure criteria for permanent appointment to enjoy benefits in terms of resources, reputation, and authority (Zhu et al., 2017). Otherwise, newly hired staff who fail to pass the tenure assessment at the end of their pre-employment term will be dismissed (Shu et al., 2020), while existing staff who cannot meet the tenure standards will either remain in their current positions or choose to transfer to other non-teaching and research positions, offering lower salaries, less support, and fewer opportunities for career development (Zhang, 2014).

Considering the limited proportion of newly hired staff compared to the total faculty teaching staff (Liu & Shen, 2017), existing staff are more affected by the tenure system. They need to rejuvenate their work motivation in research, teaching, and service to qualify for tenure, otherwise they will not be able to access competitive salaries, support, and opportunities for career development (Gao, 2023; Zhang, 2021). As a consequence, qualitative job insecurity has become a salient stressor in China's higher education institutions. Job insecurity is defined as a *subjective* feeling of "*powerlessness to maintain desired continuity in a threatened job situation*" (Greenhalgh & Rosenblatt, 1984, p. 438). Different from quantitative job insecurity ("*concerns about the future existence of the present job*"), qualitative job insecurity refers to "*perceived threats of impaired quality in the employment relationship*" (Hellgren et al., 1999, p. 182). In addition to unstable employment, employees' perceptions and interpretations of their immediate work environment can also generate job insecurity (Lawrence et al., 2013; Lee et al., 2018). Literature shows that job insecurity has negative effects on work attitudes and behaviors (see Jiang & Lavaysse, 2018; Shoss, 2017 for a review) and that the negative impacts can even spill over from the work domain to the family domain (Hu et al., 2021; Lawrence et al., 2013; Nauman et al., 2020; Richter et al., 2010).

However, studies of job insecurity have exclusively focused on state-owned enterprises undergoing reform (Huang et al., 2012), private health institutions (Öztürk et al., 2017), or industrial organizations facing restructuring (Niesen et al., 2018). There is limited research on job insecurity—especially qualitative job insecurity—in higher education. It is important to fill this research gap for two main reasons. First, the experience of qualitative job insecurity among faculty teaching staff in colleges and universities might now be as strong as that among workers in other industries (Chen, 2019). Second, given that the major roles of faculty teaching staff are to educate students and generate research output, work stressors such as qualitative job insecurity might have negative consequences for the quality of education and research. For instance, qualitative job insecurity coupled with pressure to "publish or perish" might contribute to scientific misconduct (Goodstein, 2002).

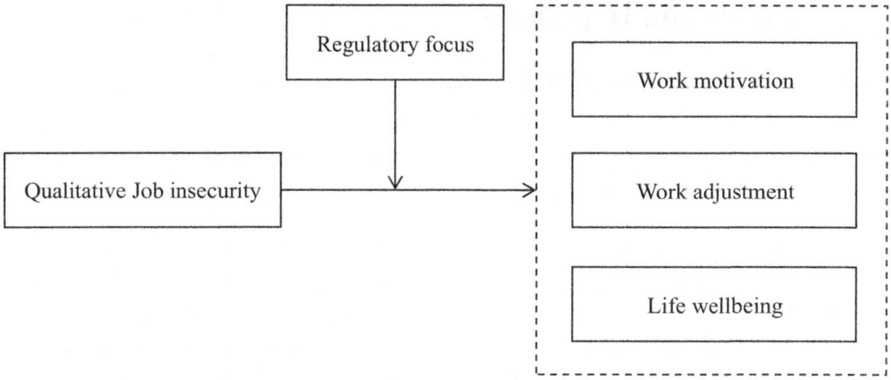

Fig. 10.1 Theoretical model

To address the above research gap, in this study, we investigated qualitative job insecurity and its consequences among faculty teaching staff at China's higher education institutions. Specifically, we examined the relationships between qualitative job insecurity and work motivation, work adjustment, and life wellbeing and further examined individual regulatory focus as a potential moderator of these relationships (see Fig. 10.1). Our findings make the following three main contributions to the literature and to higher education practice. First, our study is among the first to examine the qualitative job insecurity phenomenon in higher education in China. Therefore, the findings have theoretical and practical implications for researchers and policymakers with respect to the consequences of qualitative job insecurity among faculty teaching staff. Second, we theorize how qualitative job insecurity may negatively influence work engagement (work motivation), job crafting (work adjustment), and life meaning (life wellbeing) among faculty teaching staff through the lens of conservation of resources (COR) theory (Hobfoll, 1989; Hobfoll et al., 2018). Our findings therefore relate to a full range of qualitative job insecurity consequences across the work and life domains. Third, researchers have recently made increased efforts to test potential moderators of qualitative job insecurity from a range of theoretical perspectives (Jiang & Lavaysse, 2018; Lee et al., 2018; Shoss, 2017). We contribute to this line of research and advance the understanding of the different individual-level reactions to qualitative job insecurity by integrating COR with regulatory focus theory (Higgins, 1997; Scholer & Higgins, 2010).

10.1 Theory and Hypotheses

10.1.1 Higher Education in China

In 1977, China's college entrance examination system resumed after a 10-year hiatus. Higher education then entered a stage of rapid development in China. For instance, there were only 404 ordinary institutions of higher education in 1977, but by 2020, this number had increased to 2,738. In 1977, 625,000 students were enrolled, 273,000 were new students, and 194,000 were graduates; by 2020, these numbers had exploded to 32.85 million, 9.67 million, and 7.97 million, respectively. Over the past four decades, the gross enrollment ratio of higher education in China has increased from about 3% in 1977 to over 54% in 2020 (Ministry of Education, China, 2021), marking a successful transformation from an elite stage of higher education to a mass and universal stage (Trow, 1973).

Furthermore, as part of the reform and opening-up, China's Ministry of Education has put forward several key projects to advance higher education in China, including Project 211 (State Council, China, 1995), Project 985 (State Council, China, 1999), and First-class Universities and Disciplines of the World (Ministry of Education, China, 2015). According to the Times Higher Education (THE) World University Rankings for 2022, there were 97 universities in mainland China, trailing the U.S. (183), Japan (118), and the U.K. (101) as the country with the fourth largest number of universities; of these, 10 universities were ranked among the top 200, with Tsinghua University and Peking University sharing 16th place. THE's chief knowledge officer Phil Baty described China's investment in the higher education sector as successful and noted that Chinese universities were improving at a much faster rate than those in other countries and regions (Chen, 2021).

10.1.2 Qualitative Job Insecurity in Higher Education in China

With this rapid development of higher education in China, faculty teaching staff in colleges and universities are facing great challenges. For instance, the THE World University Rankings are based on five criteria: teaching (30%), research (30%), citation (30%), industry income (2.5%), and international outlook (7.5%). Universities strive for corresponding achievements in all of these criteria, and this objective is decomposed into output goals for faculty teaching staff. In an effort to increase output, China's Ministry of Education has been striving since the 1980s to break the iron rice bowls through reforms of the higher education system (e.g., *Guidance of the Ministry of Education on Deepening the Reform of the Assessment and Evaluation System for Teachers in Colleges and Universities*, Ministry of Education, China, 2016), and to strengthen competitive incentives by selecting outstanding faculty teaching staff in research, teaching, and service.

The implementation of a tenure system is the most pivotal of these reforms. This system is modeled after the tenure-track system used in American Higher education. At its core, the tenure system includes an "up-or-out" (similar to "publish or perish") pathway to lifetime appointment (Zhu et al., 2017). The tenure track offers faculty teaching staff the opportunity to secure tenure, receive promotions, and enjoy additional benefits. However, if they fail to meet the requirements, they may miss out on promotions, lose generous benefits, or even choose to leave their positions altogether (Shu et al., 2020; Zhang, 2021). For example, an experienced lecturer at Tsinghua University was transferred from a teaching position to an administrative position in 2014 because of the failure to meet the tenure requirements for publication (Shu et al., 2020). This and similar incidents have sparked public criticism of the system for prioritizing research over teaching, with some arguing that it contributes to a culture of impatience for academic success, where faculty teaching staff may focus on research output to avoid being eliminated and neglect teaching investment.

Colleges and universities in China have realized the drawbacks of the original system (Gao, 2023), namely that "up-or-out" is not applicable to all faculty teaching staff, and those who cannot meet the new tenure standards but still serve the colleges and universities well should also be respected (Zhang, 2014). Therefore, by establishing a competitive salary payment mechanism and career development security in the tenure system, Chinese higher education institutions encourage (rather than force) all faculty members to strive for tenure (Gao, 2023; Zhang, 2014). Newly hired staff are employed in a "pre-employment and long appointment" system, they are only given a long-term appointment if they pass the tenure assessment at the end of their pre-employment term, otherwise they will be dismissed. The pre-employment term lasts 3 to 6 years (Tian & Lu, 2017), which can protect the academic freedom of newly hired staff and greatly improve their work efficiency and academic output (Li & Jiang, 2021; Shu et al., 2020). Existing staffs who meet the tenure requirements can also apply to transfer into the tenure system, while those who do not can only continue to stay in their current position, choose to transfer to other non-teaching and research positions, or leave (Zhu et al., 2017). However, the tenure requirements have not changed. Whether they are newly hired or existing staff, they all face the fear of losing favorable salary and career opportunities if they do not qualify for tenure. Qualitative job insecurity has thus become an important issue in China's higher education institutions.

Indeed, the experience of job insecurity does not mean that an employee actually loses their job; rather, it means that the nature and continued existence of one's job are *perceived* to be at risk (Sverke & Hellgren, 2002, p. 27). Nonetheless, a central proposition of stress research is that the anticipation of a stressful event represents an equally important, or even greater, source of anxiety than the event itself (Lazarus & Folkman, 1984). In the job insecurity literature, researchers have made a conceptual distinction between quantitative and qualitative job insecurity (De Witte et al., 2010; Hellgren et al., 1999; Long et al., 2022; Tu et al., 2020). Employees can perceive not only threats of losing their job entirely (i.e., quantitative job insecurity; Hellgren et al., 1999) but also threats of losing valued features of their job (i.e., qualitative job insecurity; Hellgren et al., 1999), such as favorable work conditions, career opportunities, salary increases, and work responsibilities.

Success in tenure assessment is critical for faculty teaching staff to receive generous welfare benefits in China, with failure meaning that they will remain in their junior positions, transfer, or leave. This generates fears of losing valued features of their job (i.e., qualitative job insecurity; Hellgren et al., 1999). These characteristics of China's higher education system make it an appropriate context for studying qualitative job insecurity in higher education. In the following sections, we first draw on COR theory to elaborate on the relationships between qualitative job insecurity and work motivation, work adjustment, and life wellbeing. By integrating COR theory with regulatory focus theory, we then elaborate on the potential for an individual's prevention or promotion focus to moderate these hypothesized associations with qualitative job insecurity.

10.1.3 Qualitative Job Insecurity and COR Theory

COR theory is a theory of motivation that has been widely adopted in studies of stress (Hobfoll, 1989). Its basic tenet is that individuals strive to obtain, retain, foster, and protect the things they value most, namely, resources. Personal (e.g., professional skills), material (e.g., tools), emotional (e.g., positive affect), and situational (e.g., employment) resources are crucial to people's survival and goal attainment. COR theory maintains that employee stress results from (1) a loss of key resources, (2) the threat of such a loss, or (3) a lack of resource gain from a resource investment (Hobfoll et al., 2018). COR theory further posits that people have to invest their resources to deal with stressful conditions and prevent negative outcomes.

Qualitative job insecurity implies threats to people's psychological, social, and economic resources. As a signal of (potential) resource loss, qualitative job insecurity may lead individuals to focus on resource conservation instead of investing in additional resources (De Cuyper et al., 2012). However, such defense mechanisms also consume resources. As Halbesleben and Buckley (2004) noted, "the initial threat to resources is a stressor; however, the continued loss or threat to resources, particularly after a great deal of resource investment in work, is said to lead to burnout" (p. 862). In other words, when facing the threat of resource loss or an anticipation of resource loss (e.g., reduced career opportunities), individuals become vulnerable to the depletion of their remaining resources (Hobfoll, 2001). As a stressor that pertains to perceived threats to employment, qualitative job insecurity has been found to drain the personal resources of employees (Lee et al., 2018) and may therefore negatively affect their work motivation, work adjustment, and life wellbeing.

10.1.4 Qualitative Job Insecurity, Work Motivation, Work Adjustment, and Life Wellbeing

Qualitative job insecurity (i.e., uncertainty about retaining the desirable features of the present job) prevents employees from realizing their ideals and standards and decreases work meaningfulness, therefore distracting employees from fully engaging in their job performance (May et al., 2004; Wang et al., 2015). Conceptualizing work engagement as a motivational process, job demands–resources theory (Bakker & Demerouti, 2007) suggests that occupational and personal resources can have a positive effect on work engagement. Kahn (1990) defined role engagement at work as the harnessing of individuals' selves to their work roles. Engaged employees express and apply themselves physically, cognitively, and emotionally in performing their roles, find their work interesting and meaningful, and experience positive affect (Bakker & Demerouti, 2008). Høigaarda et al. (2011) found that work engagement was positively related to school teachers' job satisfaction and negatively related to their job burnout and intention to quit. Moreover, the engagement of faculty is critical for the development of higher education institutions (Raina & Khatri, 2015).

Qualitative job insecurity is often accompanied by psychological stress (Lee et al., 2018; Vander Elst et al., 2014a) and negative affect, such as anger and frustration (Kiefer, 2005), both of which are associated with a loss of personal resources. Qualitative job insecurity can also be viewed as a demand barrier, which has been shown to be negatively related to work motivation and performance (Van Laethem et al., 2019). The longitudinal study of Mauno et al. (2007) further demonstrated that qualitative job insecurity was negatively related to work engagement. We therefore expect that there is a negative association between qualitative job insecurity and work engagement (an indicator of work motivation) among faculty teaching staff. Accordingly, we propose the following hypothesis:

Hypothesis 1: *Qualitative job insecurity is negatively related to work engagement.*

The increased uncertainty of organizations and jobs highlights the importance of employee adjustment in the workplace. Employees' work adjustment behaviors benefit team effectiveness and organizational functioning (Parker & Bindl, 2016). Job crafting—the changes employees make in their jobs to optimize their functioning in terms of work-related wellbeing, attitudes, and behaviors (Vanbelle et al., 2023)—is a type of work adjustment behavior intended to improve person–environment fit (Parker et al., 2010). Employees can actively use elements of the job to craft their work: for example, they can change their task boundaries by altering the type or quantity of job tasks, change their cognitive boundaries by altering their view of work, or change their relational boundaries by altering the nature of their interactions at work (Wrzesniewski & Dutton, 2001). These changes can make people's work more engaging and meaningful and optimize their person–job fit (Tims & Bakker, 2010; Tims et al., 2016).

Faculty teaching staff can craft their jobs in many ways, such as refining the teaching methods and contents and altering the allocation of teaching and research time. However, qualitative job insecurity may reduce job crafting among faculty teaching staff. Crafting job demands and job resources can involve uncertain and risky behaviors that can be associated with potentially negative consequences (Tims et al., 2015). According to COR theory, individuals carefully consider the anticipated costs and benefits of their change-oriented actions and tend to adopt a defensive mode to preserve their resources when they are in a job-threatening situation (Hobfoll et al., 2018). In this case, perceived qualitative job insecurity makes people more conservative and less likely to engage in potentially risky behaviors, such as job crafting. People are more likely to engage in proactive behaviors when they feel psychologically safe (Edmondson, 2004). In other words, when people feel it is safe in their work environment to initiate change, they may be motivated to engage in job crafting (Plomp et al., 2019). Qualitative job insecurity, however, may turn people's attention to the potential risks of change, which might reduce job crafting behavior (an indicator of proactive work adjustment). Therefore, we propose the following hypothesis:

Hypothesis 2: *Qualitative job insecurity is negatively related to job crafting.*

Beyond its work-related consequences, qualitative job insecurity is also likely to influence employees' life wellbeing. Through the lens of COR theory (Hobfoll, 1989), qualitative job insecurity consumes personal resources, as employees seek to prevent the potential loss of valued job resources. Employees then have fewer resources available to invest in the life domain, which lowers their general wellbeing. Life meaning pertains to the significance of life or existence in general and is an important indicator of general wellbeing (Khaw & Kern, 2014). High life meaning is coupled with a sense of purpose, happiness, psychological fulfilment, and inner peace. Those who experience life in a more meaningful way have a sense of purpose and direction in life and present favorable evaluations of themselves and their values to others.

Qualitative job insecurity may reduce life meaning, as it creates negative experiences in both the work and family domains and leads to a more negative self-concept. As mentioned above, qualitative job insecurity triggers negative work attitudes, stress, and anxiety (De Witte et al., 2010; Lee et al., 2018; Vander Elst et al., 2014), which have cumulative effects on wellbeing (De Witte et al., 2016). Qualitative job insecurity and its associated negative affect also deplete employees' psychological resources, impair their work achievements and job performance, reduce their perceived value to the organization, and eventually weaken their self-identity and self-concept (Jiang & Lavaysse, 2018; Shoss, 2017). These considerations lead us to expect that qualitative job insecurity is associated with decreased life meaning.

Hypothesis 3: *Qualitative job insecurity is negatively related to life meaning.*

10.1.5 Qualitative Job Insecurity and Individual Regulatory Focus

Individual regulatory focus, which captures people's preferences in terms of goals and coping strategies, is likely to play an important role in guiding their reactions to stressful situations such as qualitative job insecurity. We draw on regulatory focus theory to explore how employees cope with qualitative job insecurity. Regulatory focus theory (Brockner & Higgins, 2001; Higgins, 1997; Molden et al., 2008) argues that prevention-focused people are driven by the need for security and safety; they are motivated to fulfil their duties and obligations and prefer using vigilant avoidance coping strategies in stressful situations. In contrast, promotion-focused people are driven by the need for nurturance and development; they are motivated to pursue growth and nurturance-related goals and prefer using eager approach coping strategies.

Sassenberg and Scholl (2013) showed that a prevention-focus orientation was positively related to a preference for job security. Prevention-focused employees tend to dwell on negative aspects of their work and are especially averse to resource loss (Gorman et al., 2012). Compared with their promotion-focused counterparts, prevention-focused employees may experience more stress in the face of qualitative job insecurity because they are more vulnerable to resource loss, especially when the vulnerable resources are related to satisfying their needs for security and safety. This will result in these employees feeling more psychologically depleted. Furthermore, their vigilant avoidance coping strategies, which are directed toward the conservation of resources, do not help them gain the extra resources they need to maintain their work motivation, work adjustment, and life wellbeing. Therefore, we propose the following hypothesis:

Hypothesis 4: *A prevention-focus regulatory orientation moderates the negative relationships between qualitative job insecurity and (4a) work engagement, (4b) job crafting, and (4C) life meaning (4c), such that these negative relationships are stronger when prevention focus is strong than when it is weak.*

A promotion focus is a motivational orientation that, unlike a prevention focus, is associated with aspirations and a preference for eager approach coping strategies (Higgins & Spiegel, 2004). Promotion-focused employees strive to achieve positive outcomes that fulfil their image of their ideal selves; they are likely to bring their preferred selves into their work roles, display high levels of work engagement and job crafting, and have higher life meaning (Lanaj et al., 2012). Furthermore, promotion-focused people are more attentive to resource gain than to resource loss. Because of their focus on self-development, promotion-focused employees may use approach coping strategies to pursue opportunities for personal growth even in situations that are threatening to the continuity of the valued aspects of their job. Compared with their prevention-focused counterparts, promotion-focused employees are therefore more willing to tolerate qualitative job insecurity, and their eager approach coping strategies may help them gain extra resources for use in maintaining positive work and life experiences, such as work motivation, work adjustment, and life wellbeing. Therefore, we propose the following hypothesis:

Hypothesis 5: *Promotion regulatory focus moderates the negative relationships between qualitative job insecurity and work engagement (5a), job crafting (5b), and life meaning (5c), such that these negative relationships are weaker when promotion focus is strong than when it is weak.*

10.2 Method

10.2.1 Sample and Procedures

We surveyed a sample of Chinese faculty teaching staff from two universities located in the central part of China. A research assistant distributed the questionnaires online to 350 potential participants. To ensure that these participants were faculty teaching staff in colleges and universities, we required them to indicate their employment status and excluded 62 participants who did not answer this question. We received 228 eligible questionnaires (for a response rate of 65%); 52.2% of the participants had a permanent contract (29.8% associate professors, 11.8% assistant professors, and 10.5% full professors), and 48.8% had a temporary contract (37.3% research and teaching faculty, 9.6% instructors, and 0.9% adjunct professors). Half of the sample ($n = 114$) were men, and half ($n = 114$) were women, with an average age of 38.59 years ($SD = 8.01$).

10.2.2 Measurements

The questionnaires were administered in Chinese. The original English scales were translated using back-translation procedures (Brislin, 1986).

Qualitative job insecurity. This construct was measured using the four-item Qualitative Job Insecurity Scale (QUAL-JIS) validated by Fischmann et al. (2022, see also Chap. 2). A sample item is "I think my job will change for the worse." The response scale ranged from 1 (*strongly disagree*) to 5 (*strongly agree*). Cronbach's alpha for this scale was .75 in the present study.

Work engagement. Work engagement was measured by the ultra-short three-item scale developed by Schaufeli et al. (2017). We asked the participants how they felt at work. A sample item is "At my work, I feel bursting with energy (vigor)." The response scale ranged from 1 (*never*) to 6 (*every day*). Cronbach's alpha for the work engagement scale was .90.

Job crafting. Job crafting was measured with four items developed by Vanbelle et al. (2023). The participants were asked to what extent they had shaped their jobs in recent months. A sample item is "I change my job so it better fits with who I am."

The response scale ranged from 1 (*never*) to 7 (*daily*). Cronbach's alpha for this scale was .91.

Life meaning. Life meaning was measured with three items developed by Khaw and Kern (2014). A sample item is "To what extent do you lead a purposeful and meaningful life?" The response scale ranged from 1 (*not at all*) to 5 (*completely*). Cronbach's alpha for this scale was .87.

Regulatory focus. Regulatory focus was measured with a scale developed by Neubert et al. (2008). The participants' prevention focus and promotion focus were measured with three items each. A sample item for prevention focus is "I focus my attention on avoiding failure at work"; a sample item for promotion focus is "I focus on accomplishing job tasks that will further my advancement." The response scale ranged from 1 (*strongly disagree*) to 5 (*strongly agree*). Cronbach's alphas for the two scales were .67 and .69, respectively, thus falling below the recommended cut-off of .70 (Mackenzie et al., 2011). We return to this issue in the Discussion section.

10.3 Results

10.3.1 Preliminary Analyses and Descriptive Statistics

We used an independent-sample *t* test for the association between the employment status of faculty teaching staff and their job insecurity. We created a dichotomous variable to represent contract type, where 0 = "temporary" ($n_{\text{temporary}} = 109$) and 1 = "permanent" ($n_{\text{permanent}} = 119$). The results showed that temporary staff had higher levels of job insecurity than those with permanent contracts ($M_{\text{temporary}} = 2.56$, $SD_{\text{temporary}} = .65$; $M_{\text{permanent}} = 2.32$, $SD_{\text{permanent}} = .74$; $t = 2.566$, $df = 226$, $p = .011$).

Before testing the hypotheses, we conducted a confirmatory factor analysis to examine the discriminant validity of our measures through maximum likelihood estimation with Mplus 7.4 (Muthén & Muthén, 1998–2015). The hypothesized model (with all items loading on the corresponding latent variable: qualitative job insecurity, work engagement, job crafting, and life meaning) had a better fit ($\chi^2 = 200.400$, $df = 71$, CFI = .93, TLI = .91, SRMR = 0.05, RMSEA = .09) than all alternative models (see Table 10.1). These results supported the discriminant validity of our focal variables.

Table 10.2 shows the means, standard deviations, correlations, and internal consistency reliability estimates for all of our study variables. As shown in Table 10.1, qualitative job insecurity was significantly and negatively related to work engagement ($r = -.24$, $p < .01$), job crafting ($r = -.15$, $p < .05$), and life meaning ($r = -.32$, $p < .05$). These results provided preliminary support for our hypotheses.

Table 10.1 Results of measurement models

Measurement Models	*df*	χ^2	CFI	TLI	SRMR	RMSEA
1. Hypothesis Model	71	200.400	0.933	0.914	0.053	0.089
2. Alternative Model 1 (combing qualitative job insecurity and work engagement)	74	411.280	0.826	0.786	0.108	0.141
3. Alternative Model 2 (combing qualitative job insecurity and job crafting)	74	426.866	0.818	0.776	0.119	0.145
4. Alternative Model 3 (combing qualitative job insecurity and life meaning)	74	386.568	0.839	0.802	0.095	0.136
5. Alternative Model 4 (combing work engagement, job crafting, and life meaning)	76	878.488	0.586	0.505	0.135	0.215

Table 10.2 Descriptive statistics, reliabilities, and inter-correlations

Variables	MEAN	*SD*	1	2	3	4	5	6	7
1. Employment contract	0.52	0.50	–						
2. Qualitative job insecurity	2.44	0.71	–.17*	(.75)					
3. Work engagement	4.27	1.31	.09	–.24**	(.90)				
4. Job crafting	3.61	1.31	.07	–.15*	.41**	(.91)			
5. Life meaning	3.26	0.81	.13	–.32*	.46**	.43**	(.87)		
6. Prevention focus	3.61	0.63	.05	−.08	.25**	.20**	.13	(.67)	
7. Promotion focus	3.65	0.60	.05	–.24**	.34**	.25**	.30**	.33**	(.69)

Note: $N = 228$. Alpha reliabilities are in parentheses on the diagonal. $^{*}p < .05$, $^{**}p < .01$

10.3.2 Hypothesis Testing

To test our hypotheses, we conducted multiple regression analyses in SPSS 25 to examine the proposed relationships, with employment contracts added in Model 1 as a control variable. As shown in Table 10.3 (Model 2), qualitative job insecurity was negatively related to work engagement ($\beta = -.29, p < .01$), work adjustment ($\beta = -.21$, $p < .05$), and life meaning ($\beta = -.24$, $p < .01$). These results supported Hypotheses 1–3. In Models 3 and 4, we added regulatory focus and its interactions with qualitative job insecurity. The results showed that promotion focus moderated the relationships between qualitative job insecurity and job crafting ($\beta = -.27$, $p < .01$) and between qualitative job insecurity and life meaning ($\beta = -.18, p < .01$) but did not moderate the relationship between qualitative job insecurity and work engagement ($\beta = -.04$, $p > .10$). As prevention focus did not moderate the

Table 10.3 Results of regression analyses: test the hypotheses of regulatory focus

	Work engagement				Job crafting				Life meaning			
Model 1												
Employment contract	.23	.14	.10	.11	.18	.11	.08	.12	$.21^{+}$	.13	.11	.14
Model 2												
Qualitative job insecurity		$-.29^{**}$	$-.24^{**}$	$-.24^{**}$		$-.21^{*}$	$-.17^{*}$	$-.17^{*}$		$-.24^{**}$	$-.21^{**}$	$-.21^{**}$
Model 3												
Prevention focus			$.21^{*}$	$.21^{*}$			$.19^{*}$	$.17^{*}$			.03	.02
Promotion focus			$.33^{**}$	$.33^{**}$			$.24^{**}$	$.23^{**}$			$.20^{**}$	$.20^{**}$
Model 4												
QJI × PREF				−.04				−.05				.01
QJI × PROF				−.06				$-.27^{**}$				$-.18^{**}$
R^2	.01	.06	.17	.18	.01	.03	.08	.14	.02	.10	.17	.22
ΔR^2		$.05^{**}$	$.11^{**}$	.01		$.02^{*}$	$.05^{**}$	$.06^{**}$		$.08^{**}$	$.07^{**}$	$.05^{**}$

Note: $N = 228$. Unstandardized coefficients are reported. *QJI* qualitative job insecurity; *PREF* prevention focus, *PROF* promotion focus. $+p < .10$, $^{*}p < .05$, $^{**}p < .01$

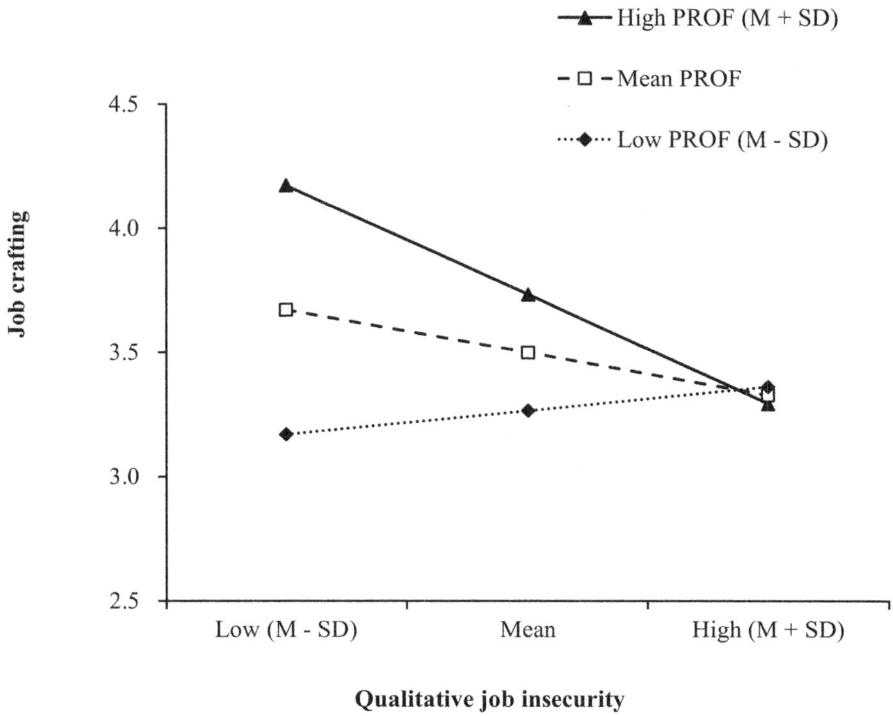

Fig. 10.2 The moderating role of promotion focus (PROF) in the relationship between qualitative job insecurity and job crafting

relationships between qualitative job insecurity and any of the focal outcomes, Hypothesis 4 was not supported.

To visualize the interaction effects (Table 10.4), we plotted the interactions at two conditional values of promotion focus (1 SD above and below the mean; see Figs. 10.2 and 10.3, respectively). As shown in Fig. 10.2, the negative relationship between qualitative job insecurity and job crafting was stronger when promotion focus was high (estimate = −.46, 95% confidence interval: [−.68, −.24]) than when it was low (estimate = .13, 95% confidence interval: [−.09, .34]). As shown in Fig. 10.3, the negative relationship between qualitative job insecurity and life meaning was stronger when promotion focus was high (estimate = −.38, 95% confidence interval: [−.51, −.25]) than when it was low (estimate = −.03, 95% confidence interval: [−.16, .09]). These results for the moderating effects of promotion focus were contrary to our Hypotheses 5b and 5c, which predict that the negative relationships will be weaker when promotion focus is high than when it is low; therefore, Hypothesis 5 was not supported.

Table 10.4 Simple Slope Test for promotion focus

IV: Qualitative job insecurity	Job crafting		Life meaning	
	Low	High	Low	High
Promotion focus	.13	$-.46^{**}$	−.03	$-.38^{**}$
CI (95%)	[−.09, .34]	[−.68, −.24]	[−.16, .09]	[−.51, −.25]

Note: $N = 228$. + $p < .10$, *$p < .05$, **$p < .01$

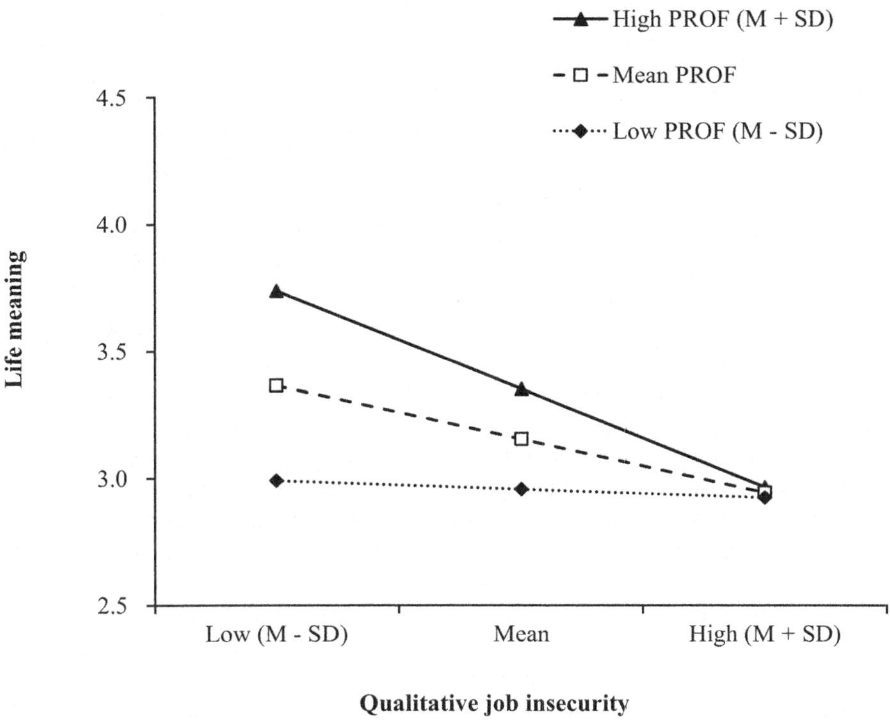

Fig. 10.3 The moderating role of promotion focus (PROF) in the relationship between qualitative job insecurity and life meaning

10.4 Discussion

Through the lens of COR and regulatory focus theories, our results showed that qualitative job insecurity was negatively related to individual work motivation (i.e., work engagement), work adjustment (i.e., job crafting), and overall wellbeing (i.e., life meaning) among faculty teaching staff at Chinese colleges and universities. Contrary to our expectations, we found that promotion-focused individuals suffered more from qualitative job insecurity than their counterparts and that prevention focus did not moderate the relationships between qualitative job insecurity and the tested outcome variables.

10.4.1 Theoretical and Practical Implications

Our preliminary analyses showed that the mean qualitative job insecurity scores for permanent staff and temporary staff were 2.32 ($SD = 0.74$) and 2.56 ($SD = 0.65$), respectively. These scores are comparable with those reported in previous studies using the same scale that has examined qualitative job insecurity among white-collar workers ($M = 2.53$, $SD = 0.82$; Urbanaviciute et al., 2018) and hospital staff ($M = 3.04$, $SD = 0.85$; Van Hootegem & De Witte, 2019). This suggests that faculty teaching staff in higher education experience qualitative job insecurity as strongly as workers in other organizations and industries. The challenges of meeting tenure requirements under China's reestablished tenure system include increased competition in publishing (Larkin, 1999; Tian et al., 2016), teaching difficulties for inexperienced staff, and service demands that consume limited personal resources. Permanent staff, those with long-term contracts but not necessarily with tenure qualifications, face an up-or-remain/transfer situation: if they do not produce enough high-quality research output (e.g., publications, foundation items) in a certain number of years, they may not be allowed to supervise postgraduates in research-oriented programs and might be transferred to teaching-oriented positions. If their teaching quality does not meet the stated requirements over an extended period and is considered unlikely to improve, permanent staff might be transferred to administrative positions, which would result in downgrades in their pay levels, promotion opportunities, and policy support. For temporary staff, those with short-term contracts who need to pass the tenure assessment, the consequences are even worse, as they are likely to quit their jobs (Tian et al., 2016; Zhang, 2014, 2021). They have higher levels of qualitative job insecurity than permanent staff because of the greater pressure they are under to retain the valued features of their job. Especially for newly hired staff, if they fail to pass the tenure assessment, the academic protection and policy support they received during pre-employment will be revoked. Therefore, the reforms to personnel and performance appraisal systems in higher education institutions in China have affected almost everyone, both permanent and temporary staff, working in Chinese colleges and universities.

Our results suggest that qualitative job insecurity is a contributing factor to decreased work motivation, work adjustment and life wellbeing among faculty teaching staff. These findings corroborate those of previous studies that have examined the consequences of qualitative job insecurity in other contexts (e.g., Van Hootegem & De Witte, 2019; Urbanaviciute et al., 2018). Qualitative job insecurity may have additional costs in higher education. The work and life experiences of faculty teaching staff may be directly related to how they educate students. A lecturer with low levels of work motivation, work adjustment, and life wellbeing is unlikely to deliver interesting and stimulating classes. In addition, our study provides further empirical evidence to that provided by the work of Tu et al. (2020) for the role of individual regulatory focus in reactions to job insecurity. However, contrary to our expectations, we found that promotion focus strengthened (instead of mitigated) the negative relationships between qualitative job insecurity and work adjustment (i.e., job crafting) and wellbeing (i.e., life meaning). A possible explanation for these unexpected findings is that qualitative job insecurity threatens advancement and growth because it calls career development opportunities into question. Qualitative job insecurity may therefore be particularly frustrating for employees with strong desires for personal growth at work, thus leading to more negative reactions. There was also a lack of support for the expected moderating role of prevention focus, which could be related to the inadequate reliability of the measures. Unreliable measures can prevent supposed significant relationships from emerging from the data. The reliability issue is further discussed in the study limitations below.

Until recently, scholars have not paid adequate attention to the issue of qualitative job insecurity in higher education. Having witnessed great change and reforms in colleges and universities, scholars have now come to realize the worldwide prevalence and influence of qualitative job insecurity. Based on our findings, we suggest that policymakers and other stakeholders need to be aware of the adverse effects of qualitative job insecurity in higher education. Qualitative job insecurity is not only directly and negatively related to faculty teaching staff's positive work motivation, work behaviors, and life wellbeing, as revealed in our findings but also probably has additional indirect costs for education, as shown by Su's (2021) findings of poor-quality teaching and the unsustainable development of education. Teaching staff assistance programs, such as teacher development centers, are commonly established in colleges and universities to help faculty teaching staff improve their research and teaching skills and better communicate with students (Li et al., 2014; Su, 2021). However, these programs are not specifically designed to help faculty teaching staff manage the stressful threat of job insecurity. To reduce stress among faculty teaching staff and avoid the regrettable events reported at the beginning of this chapter, we recommend that teaching staff assistance programs be tailored for greater effectiveness according to the different needs and situations of faculty teaching staff.

10.4.2 Limitations and Directions for Future Research

Several limitations of our study should be noted. First, as cross-sectional data were used in our study, the findings do not suggest causation. Studies have shown that the relationship between job insecurity and various outcomes may be reciprocal (De Witte et al., 2016; Hellgren & Sverke, 2003): for example, employees may feel greater job insecurity when they do not adjust well to their job. Future research could be conducted to replicate our findings with longitudinal data. Second, to measure regulatory focus, we used a short scale with only three items for each focus, which is considered suitable for East Asian cultures (Shin et al., 2017; Yang et al., 2018). Studies (He et al., 2019; Shin et al., 2017; Yang et al., 2018) using this scale have reported Cronbach's alpha values above .70—ranging from .73 to .84 for prevention focus and from .79 to .83 for promotion focus. In our study, however, Cronbach's alpha fell below the threshold for reliability for both regulatory focus subscales. McDonald's omega—an alternative to Cronbach's alpha (Dunn et al., 2014)—for the two scales was .69 and .71 for prevention focus and promotion focus, respectively, which is more acceptable. We also analysed the correlation between the scale used in this study and the 18-item regulatory focus scale developed by Neubert et al. (2008) using a different dataset ($N = 281$), and the results showed that there was a strong correlation for both prevention focus ($r = .85, p < .001$) and promotion focus ($r = .86, p < .001$). Nevertheless, we suggest that researchers examine the role of regulatory focus with more reliable scales in future studies.

10.5 Conclusion

Alongside quantitative job insecurity, qualitative job insecurity has become salient in higher education across the world due to reforms of personnel and performance appraisal systems in colleges and universities. Our study of faculty teaching staff in China showed that qualitative job insecurity was negatively associated with their work motivation, work adjustment, and life wellbeing. These negative relationships were even stronger for those who had a great desire for personal growth at work. Given that qualitative job insecurity may continue to increase as education reforms proceed, we recommend that policymakers and other key higher education stakeholders help faculty teaching staff manage the negative influences of qualitative job insecurity.

10.6 Take Home Message

In the context of the rapid development and reform of China's higher education system, especially the implementation of a tenure system, temporary faculty teaching staff reported higher levels of qualitative job insecurity than permanent faculty teaching staff. Qualitative job insecurity had a negative association with work motivation (i.e., work engagement), work adjustment (i.e., job crafting), and wellbeing (i.e., life meaning) among faculty teaching staff in Chinese colleges and universities. Surprisingly, a stronger promotion focus is more likely to reinforce the negative effects of qualitative job insecurity than it is to reduce them.

Acknowledgment We acknowledge the financial support from the National Natural Science Foundation of China (Project 72071086; 72132001).

References

Bakker, A. B., & Demerouti, E. (2007). The Job Demands-Resources model: State of the art. *Journal of Managerial Psychology, 22*(3), 309–328.

Bakker, A. B., & Demerouti, E. (2008). Towards a model of work engagement. *Career Development International, 13*(3), 209–223.

Brislin, R. W. (1986). The wording and translation of research instruments. In W. J. Lonner & J. W. Berry (Eds.), *Cross-cultural research and methodology series, vol. 8. Field methods in cross-cultural research* (pp. 137–164). Sage.

Brockner, J., & Higgins, E. T. (2001). Regulatory focus theory: Implications for the study of emotions at work. *Organizational Behavior and Human Decision Processes, 86*(1), 35–66.

Chen, M. (2019). Research on the relationship between college teachers' job insecurity, job burnout and organizational support. *Education Review, 1*, 122–127.

Chen, X. L. (2021, March 10). *Chinese universities lead in latest THE emerging economies university rankings*. Xinhua. Retrieved September 27, 2021, from https://www.shine.cn/news/nation/2103105723/

De Cuyper, N., Mäkikangas, A., Kinnunen, U., Mauno, S., & Witte, H. D. (2012). Cross-lagged associations between perceived external employability, job insecurity, and exhaustion: Testing gain and loss spirals according to the Conservation of Resources Theory. *Journal of Organizational Behavior, 33*(6), 770–788.

De Witte, H., De Cuyper, N., Handaja, Y., Sverke, M., Näswall, K., & Hellgren, J. (2010). Associations between quantitative and qualitative job insecurity and well-being: A test in Belgian banks. *International Studies of Management and Organization, 40*(1), 40–56.

De Witte, H., Pienaar, J., & De Cuyper, N. (2016). Review of 30 years of longitudinal studies on the association between job insecurity and health and well-being: Is there causal evidence? *Australian Psychologist, 51*(1), 18–31.

Dunn, T. J., Baguley, T., & Brunsden, V. (2014). From alpha to omega: A practical solution to the pervasive problem of internal consistency estimation. *British Journal of Psychology, 105*, 399–412.

Edmondson, A. C. (2004). Psychological safety, trust, and learning in organizations: A group-level lens. In R. M. Kramer & K. S. Cook (Eds.), *The Russell Sage Foundation series on trust. Trust and distrust in organizations: Dilemmas and approaches* (pp. 239–272). Russell Sage Foundation.

Fischmann, G., De Witte, H., Sulea, C., Vander Elst, T., De Cuyper, N., & Iliescu, D. (2022). Validation of a Short and Generic Qualitative Job Insecurity Scale (QUAL-JIS). *European Journal of Career Assessment, 38*(5), 397–411.

Friedman, E., & Kuruvilla, S. (2015). Experimentation and decentralization in China's labor relations. *Human Relations, 68*(2), 181–195.

Gao, C. Y. (2023). A study on the orientation of faculty appointment system reform in Chinese universities from the perspective of the logic of the tenure system. *China Higher Education Research, 01*, 85–92.

Goodstein, D. (2002). Scientific misconduct. *Academe, 88*(1), 28–31.

Gorman, C. A., Meriac, J. P., Overstreet, B. L., Apodaca, S., McIntyre, A. L., Park, P., & Godbey, J. N. (2012). A meta-analysis of the regulatory focus nomological network: Work-related antecedents and consequences. *Journal of Vocational Behavior, 80*(1), 160–172.

Greenhalgh, L., & Rosenblatt, Z. (1984). Job insecurity: Toward conceptual clarity. *Academy of Management Review, 9*(3), 438–448.

Halbesleben, J. R. B., & Buckley, M. R. (2004). Burnout in organizational life. *Journal of Management, 30*(6), 859–879.

He, Y., Li, Y., Xia, D., Zhang, T., Wang, Y., Hu, L., et al. (2019). Moderating effect of regulatory focus on public acceptance of nuclear energy. *Nuclear Engineering and Technology, 51*(8), 2034–2041.

Hellgren, J., & Sverke, M. (2003). Does job insecurity lead to impaired well-being or vice versa? Estimation of cross-lagged effects using latent variable modelling. *Journal of Organizational Behavior: The International Journal of Industrial, Occupational and Organizational Psychology and Behavior, 24*(2), 215–236.

Hellgren, J., Sverke, M., & Isaksson, K. (1999). A two-dimensional approach to job insecurity: Consequences for employee attitudes and well-being. *European Journal of Work and Organizational Psychology, 8*(2), 179–195.

Higgins, E. T. (1997). Beyond pleasure and pain. *American Psychologist, 52*(12), 1280–1300.

Higgins, E. T., & Spiegel, S. (2004). Promotion and prevention strategies for self-regulation: A motivated cognition perspective. In R. F. Baumeister & K. D. Vohs (Eds.), *Handbook of self-regulation: Research, theory, and applications* (pp. 171–187). The Guilford Press.

Hobfoll, S. E. (1989). Conservation of resources: A new attempt at conceptualizing stress. *American Psychologist, 44*(3), 513–524.

Hobfoll, S. E. (2001). The influence of culture, community, and the nested-self in the stress process: Advancing conservation of resources theory. *Applied Psychology, 50*(3), 337–421.

Hobfoll, S. E., Halbesleben, J., Neveu, J. P., & Westman, M. (2018). Conservation of resources in the organizational context: The reality of resources and their consequences. *Annual Review of Organizational Psychology and Organizational Behavior, 5*, 103–128.

Høigaarda, R., Giske, R., & Sundsli, K. (2011). Newly qualified teachers' work engagement and teacher efficacy influences on job satisfaction, burnout, and the intention to quit. *European Journal of Teacher Education, 35*(3), 1–11.

Hu, S., Jiang, L., Probst, T. M., & Liu, M. (2021). The relationship between qualitative job insecurity and subjective well-being in Chinese employees: The role of work-family conflict and work centrality. *Economic and Industrial Democracy, 42*(2), 203–225.

Huang, G. H., Niu, X., Lee, C., & Ashford, S. J. (2012). Differentiating cognitive and affective job insecurity: Antecedents and outcomes. *Journal of Organizational Behavior, 33*(6), 752–769.

Jiang, L., & Lavaysse, L. M. (2018). Cognitive and affective job insecurity: A meta-analysis and a primary study. *Journal of Management, 44*(6), 2307–2342.

Kahn, W. A. (1990). Psychological conditions of personal engagement and disengagement at work. *Academy of Management Journal, 33*(4), 692–724.

Khaw, D., & Kern, M. (2014). A cross-cultural comparison of the PERMA model of well-being. *Undergraduate Journal of Psychology at Berkeley, University of California, 8*(1), 10–23.

Van Hootegem, A., & De Witte, H. (2019). Qualitative job insecurity and informal learning: A longitudinal test of occupational self-efficacy and psychological contract breach as mediators. *International Journal of Environmental Research and Public Health, 16*(10), 1847.

Kiefer, T. (2005). Feeling bad: Antecedents and consequences of negative emotions in ongoing change. *Journal of Organizational Behavior, 26*(8), 875–897.

Lanaj, K., Chang, C.-H., & Johnson, R. E. (2012). Regulatory focus and work-related outcomes: A review and meta-analysis. *Psychological Bulletin, 138*(5), 998–1034.

Larkin, M. J. (1999). Pressure to publish stifles young talent. *Nature, 397*(6719), 467–467.

Lawrence, E. R., Halbesleben, J. R., & Paustian-Underdahl, S. C. (2013). The influence of workplace injuries on work-family conflict: Job and financial insecurity as mechanisms. *Journal of Occupational Health Psychology, 18*(4), 371–383.

Lazarus, R., & Folkman, S. (1984). *Stress, appraisal, and coping*. Springer.

Lee, C., Huang, G. H., & Ashford, S. J. (2018). Job insecurity and the changing workplace: Recent developments and the future trends in job insecurity research. *Annual Review of Organizational Psychology and Organizational Behavior, 5*, 335–359.

Li, L. M., & Jiang, L. (2021). The origin, dilemma and trend of "Tenure-Track"—"Tenured" system in colleges and universities in China. *Modern Education Management, 7*, 105–111.

Li, Q. Q., Gong, X. Y., & Chen, M. D. (2014). Job insecurity and intervention strategies of teachers in private colleges and universities. *Heilongjiang Education, 09*, 54–55.

Liu, Z. R., & Shen, H. (2017). Tenure system reform in American Research University: Dispute, reform and reference. *Research in Educational Development, 23*, 56–63.

Liu, M., & Yan, Y. (2020). Anxiety and stress in in-service Chinese University Teachers of Arts. *International Journal of Higher Education, 9*(1), 237–248.

Long, L. R., Tu, Y., Wang, H. J., & Jiang, L. (2022). The content of the threat matters: The differential effects of quantitative and qualitative job insecurity on different types of employee motivation. *Journal of Business and Psychology, 37*(2), 297–310.

MacKenzie, S. B., Podsakoff, P. M., & Podsakoff, N. P. (2011). Construct measurement and validation procedures in MIS and behavioral research: Integrating new and existing techniques. *MIS Quarterly, 35*(2), 293–334.

Mauno, S., Kinnunen, U., & Ruokolainen, M. (2007). Job demands and resources as antecedents of work engagement: A longitudinal study. *Journal of Vocational Behavior, 70*(1), 149–171.

May, D. R., Gilson, R. L., & Harter, L. M. (2004). The psychological conditions of meaningfulness, safety and availability and the engagement of the human spirit at work. *Journal of Occupational and Organizational Psychology, 77*(1), 11–37.

Molden, D. C., Lee, A. Y., & Higgins, E. T. (2008). Motivations for promotion and prevention. In J. Y. Shah & W. L. Gardner (Eds.), *Handbook of motivation science* (pp. 169–187). The Guilford Press.

Ministry of Education of the People's Republic of China. (2021). 2020 Statistical Bulletin on National Education Development, http://www.moe.gov.cn/jyb_sjzl/sjzl_fztjgb/202108/t20210827_555004.html.

Muthén, L. K., & Muthén, B. O. (1998–2015). *Mplus user's guide* (7th ed.). Muthén & Muthén.

Mycos Research. (2018, November 14). Heartbreaking! Two college teachers in their 30s died suddenly in a week! How many other teachers are over-drafted? *SOHO*. Retrieved September 17, 2021, from https://www.sohu.com/a/275075391_121294

Nauman, S., Zheng, C., & Naseer, S. (2020). Job insecurity and work–family conflict: A moderated mediation model of perceived organizational justice, emotional exhaustion and work withdrawal. *International Journal of Conflict Management, 31*(5), 729–751.

Neubert, M. J., Kacmar, K. M., Carlson, D. S., Chonko, L. B., & Roberts, J. A. (2008). Regulatory focus as a mediator of the influence of initiating structure and servant leadership on employee behavior. *Journal of Applied Psychology, 93*(6), 1220–1233.

Niesen, W., Van Hootegem, A., Vander Elst, T., Battistelli, A., & De Witte, H. (2018). Job insecurity and innovative work behaviour: A psychological contract perspective. *Psychologica Belgica, 57*(4), 174–189.

Öztürk, E. B., Karagonlar, G., & Emirza, S. (2017). Relationship between job insecurity and emotional exhaustion: Moderating effects of prevention focus and affective organizational commitment. *International Journal of Stress Management, 24*(3), 247–269.

Parker, S. K., & Bindl, U. K. (Eds.). (2016). *Proactivity at work: Making things happen in organizations*. Taylor & Francis.

Parker, S. K., Bindl, U. K., & Strauss, K. (2010). Making things happen: A model of proactive motivation. *Journal of Management, 36*(4), 827–856.

Persson, R. S. (2017). *The management and mismanagement of academic staff worldwide: A systemtised cross-national literature review of stress and work satisfaction in higher education and research*. ICIE.

Plomp, J., Tims, M., Khapova, S. N., Jansen, P., & Bakker, A. B. (2019). Psychological safety, job crafting, and employability: A comparison between permanent and temporary workers. *Frontiers in Psychology, 10*, 974.

Raina, K., & Khatri, P. (2015). Faculty engagement in higher education: Prospects and areas of research. *On the Horizon, 23*(4), 285–308.

Richter, A., Näswall, K., & Sverke, M. (2010). Job insecurity and its relation to work-family conflict: Mediation with a longitudinal data set. *Economic and Industrial Democracy, 31*(2), 265–280.

Sassenberg, K., & Scholl, A. (2013). If I can do it my way…The influence of regulatory focus on job-related values and job attraction. *Journal of Economic Psychology, 38*, 58–70.

Schaufeli, W. B., Shimazu, A., Hakanen, J., Salanova, M., & De Witte, H. (2017). An ultra-short measure for work engagement: The UWES-3 validation across five countries. *European Journal of Psychological Assessment, 35*(4), 577–591.

Scholer, A. A., & Higgins, E. T. (2010). Regulatory focus in a demanding world. In R. H. Hoyle (Ed.), *Handbook of personality and self-regulation* (pp. 291–314). Blackwell.

Shin, Y., Kim, M. S., Choi, J. N., Kim, M., & Oh, W. K. (2017). Does leader-follower regulatory fit matter? The role of regulatory fit in followers' organizational citizenship behavior. *Journal of Management, 43*(4), 1211–1233.

Shoss, M. K. (2017). Job insecurity: An Integrative Review and Agenda for Future Research. *Journal of Management, 43*(6), 1911–1939.

Shu, F., Quan, W., Chen, B., Qiu, J., Sugimoto, C. R., & Larivière, V. (2020). The role of Web of Science publications in China's tenure system. *Scientometrics, 122*(3), 1683–1695.

Su, Y. L. (2021). Analysis on career stress of young teachers in colleges and universities under the background of "Double-First Class" and coping strategies. *Survey of Education, 10*(25), 85–88.

Sverke, M., & Hellgren, J. (2002). The nature of job insecurity: Understanding employment uncertainty on the brink of a new millennium. *Applied Psychology: An International Review, 51*, 23–42.

The Times Higher Education World University Rankings 2022. (2021, September 2). Retrieved September 27, 2021, from https://www.timeshighereducation.com/world-university-rankings/2022/world-ranking#!/

Tian & Lu. (2017). What price the building of world-class universities? Academic pressure faced by young lecturers at a research-centered University in China. *Teaching in Higher Education, 22*(8), 957–974.

Tian, M., Su, Y., & Ru, X. (2016). Perish or publish in China: Pressures on young Chinese scholars to publish in internationally indexed journals. *Publications, 4*(2), 9.

Tims, M., & Bakker, A. B. (2010). Job crafting: Towards a new model of individual job redesign. *SA Journal of Industrial Psychology, 36*, 1–9.

Tims, M., Bakker, A. B., & Derks, D. (2015). Examining job crafting from an interpersonal perspective: Is employee job crafting related to the well-being of colleagues? *Applied Psychology: An International Review, 64*(4), 727–753.

Tims, M., Derks, D., & Bakker, A. B. (2016). Job crafting and its relationships with person-job fit and meaningfulness: A three-wave study. *Journal of Vocational Behavior, 92*, 44–53.

Trow, M. (1973). *Problems in the transition from elite to mass higher education*. Carnegie Commission on Higher Education.

Tu, Y., Long, L., Wang, H. J., & Jiang, L. (2020). To prevent or to promote: How regulatory focus moderates the differentiated effects of quantitative versus qualitative job insecurity on employee stress and motivation. *International Journal of Stress Management, 27*(2), 135–145.

Urbanaviciute, I., Lazauskaite-Zabielske, J., Vander Elst, T., & De Witte, H. (2018). Qualitative job insecurity and turnover intention: The mediating role of basic psychological needs in public and private sectors. *Career Development International, 23*(3), 274–290.

Van Laethem, M., Beckers, D. G. J., de Bloom, J., Sianoja, M., & Kinnunen, U. (2019). Challenge and hindrance demands in relation to self-reported job performance and the role of restoration, sleep quality, and affective rumination. *Journal of Occupational and Organizational Psychology, 92*(2), 225–254.

Vanbelle, E., Griep, Y., Van den Broeck, A., & De Witte, H. (2023). Development and validation of a short broad job crafting scale. *Group and Organization Management, 0*(0), 1–35.

Vander Elst, T., De Witte, H., & De Cuyper, N. (2014). The Job Insecurity Scale: A psychometric evaluation across five European countries. *European Journal of Work and Organizational Psychology, 23*(3), 364–380.

Vander Elst, T., Richter, A., Sverke, M., Näswall, K., De Cuyper, N., & De Witte, H. (2014a). Threat of losing valued job features: The role of perceived control in mediating the effect of qualitative job insecurity on job strain and psychological withdrawal. *Work & Stress, 28*(2), 143–164.

Wang, H. J., Lu, C. Q., Siu, O., & l. (2015). Job insecurity and job performance: The moderating role of organizational justice and the mediating role of work engagement. *Journal of Applied Psychology, 100*(4), 1249–1258.
Wrzesniewski, A., & Dutton, J. E. (2001). Crafting a job: Revisioning employees as active crafters of their work. *Academy of Management Review, 26*(2), 179–201.
Xu, L. (2019). Teacher–researcher role conflict and burnout among Chinese university teachers: A job demand-resources model perspective. *Studies in Higher Education, 44*(6), 903–919.
Yang, F., Qian, J., & Liu, J. (2018). Priming employees' promotion focus: How and when servant leadership enhances customer service behaviors. *Management Decision, 56*(11), 2308–2324.
Zhang. (2021). Current situation and problems of the reform of pre-employment long appointment system in "double first-class" universities: Analysis of teacher employment system in 42 "double first-class" universities. *Journal of Higher Education Research, 44*(04), 77–82+120.
Zhang, J. (2014). Developing excellence: Chinese university reform in three steps. *Nature, 514*(7522), 295–296.
Zhu, J. W., Ma, C. M., & Li, Y. C. (2017). From breaking "iron rice bowls" to reestablishing "lifetime appointments". *Journal of Higher Education, 38*(5), 21–25.

Hao-Yun Zou is a PhD student majoring in Business Administration at the School of Management, Huazhong University of Science and Technology, China. Her research interests include job stress, social network, and newcomer socialization. She has co-authored several peer-reviewed publications, including articles in *Human Resource Management Journal, Journal of Advanced Nursing* and *Journal of Career Development.*

Hai-Jiang Wang is a Professor of Industrial and Organizational Psychology at the School of Management, Huazhong University of Science and Technology, China. His research interests include work design, job crafting, and job stress. His research has been published in peer-reviewed journals such as *Journal of Applied Psychology, Journal of Management, Human Relations, Human Resource Management Journal, Journal of Business Ethics, Journal of Vocational Behaviors, European Journal of Work and Organizational Psychology,* and *Journal of Occupational and Organizational Psychology.* He currently serves as the associate editor of *Journal of Business Research* and the editorial board member of *Management and Organization Review.*

Chapter 11
How Workplace Social Capital Moderates the Effects of Job Insecurity: Greece as a Case Study

Andreas Tsounis, Despoina Xanthopoulou, Konstantinos Kafetsios, and Evangelia Demerouti

Rapid socio-economic changes during the past decades have resulted in a growing number of temporary employment contracts and flexible work arrangements that have increased job insecurity (JI; Gallie et al., 2017). At the same time, employees tend to worry more about their job stability (i.e., quantitative JI) as well as the quality of their job in the future (i.e., qualitative JI) during a crisis (e.g., financial downturn, pandemic; Chung & van Oorschot, 2010; Forbes & Krueger, 2019). The global economic recession that started in 2008 is such a crisis, whose aftermath is still evident in some countries, including Greece. Ever since 2009, Greece has been confronted with its most severe economic crisis post-war resulting in enormous unemployment levels and precarious working conditions (Mavridis, 2018). Considering the systematic empirical evidence that supports the unfavorable effects of JI on occupational well-being and work-related behaviors (i.e., reduced job satisfaction, work engagement, job performance and safety behaviors, and increased burnout and absenteeism; Jiang & Lavaysse, 2018; Sverke et al., 2019), research on the

A. Tsounis (✉) · D. Xanthopoulou
School of Psychology, Aristotle University of Thessaloniki, Thessaloniki, Greece
e-mail: atsounis@psy.auth.gr; dxanthopoulou@psy.auth.gr

K. Kafetsios
School of Psychology, Aristotle University of Thessaloniki, Thessaloniki, Greece

Department of Psychology, Palacký University, Olomouc, Czech Republic
e-mail: kkafetsios@psy.auth.gr

E. Demerouti
Department of Industrial Engineering and Innovation Sciences, Eindhoven University of Technology, Eindhoven, Netherlands

Department of Industrial Psychology and People Management, University of Johannesburg, Johannesburg, South Africa
e-mail: e.demerouti@tue.nl

L. C. Roll et al. (eds.), *Global Perspectives on Job Insecurity in Higher Education*, Aligning Perspectives on Health, Safety and Well-Being,
https://doi.org/10.1007/978-3-031-85772-0_11

conditions under which employees' negative responses to JI can be buffered is relevant for understanding and promoting successful employee coping in unstable contexts.

In the present study, we focus on the public higher education sector in Greece—an occupational setting that has been severely affected by the financial crisis—with the aim of investigating whether workplace social capital (WSC) may facilitate employee functioning in times of high quantitative and qualitative JI. WSC refers to those features of organizational life, such as trust, reciprocity and network, that promote employees' optimal functioning (Kouvonen et al., 2007; Ommen et al., 2009). Based on job demands-resources (JD-R; Bakker & Demerouti, 2017) and conservation of resources (COR; Hobfoll, 1989) theories, we argue that WSC is an organizational job resource that may mitigate the unfavorable effects of JI on work engagement and in-role performance. Specifically, we focus on individual (and not shared) employee perceptions of the WSC of their organization and adopt an individual-level approach to investigate whether, when facing job insecurity, employees who perceive higher levels of WSC are better off than those who perceive lower levels of WSC.

The current analysis adds to the JI and WSC literatures in the following ways. First, we contribute to the JI literature by exploring whether WSC helps us understand when JI is particularly unfavorable for employees. Although WSC, as a job resource, may facilitate employee adaptation in insecure conditions, its role is underrepresented in the JI literature (Inoue et al., 2016). Hence, we enrich this literature by exploring whether WSC may buffer the unfavorable effects of JI next to similar, unique job resources (i.e., social support from colleagues and supervisors; Cheng et al., 2014; Lim, 1997; Schreurs et al., 2012). This is because WSC, as a higher-order construct, incorporates specific resource aspects (e.g., trust, reciprocity and networking) that may complement each other in facilitating employees' satisfaction of the basic psychological needs of belongingness and competence that are frustrated in conditions of high insecurity (Van der Elst et al., 2012). In this way, we also shed light on additional boundary conditions that may explain employees' responses to JI that may be promoted in organizational interventions. Second, the current investigation contributes to the WSC literature and resource theories (i.e., JD-R theory, Bakker & Demerouti, 2017; COR theory, Hobfoll, 1989) by highlighting the role of WSC as a contextual resource that may help employees deal effectively with threatening aspects of the work environment. This is important because WSC integrates resourceful aspects, such as networking, that were largely neglected from the relevant literature. Lastly, by focusing on the Greek organizational context that was severely affected by the financial crisis, we contribute to better understanding the factors that may mitigate the unfavorable consequences of JI perceptions in crisis situations that enhance uncertainty (e.g., mass utilization of online labor platforms because of the COVID-19 pandemic).

11.1 Job Insecurity: The Greek Context

Most researchers agree that JI refers to the uncertainty that employees feel regarding their job continuity and the continuity of valued job features and that it has three main characteristics: (1) it is a subjective experience, (2) it implies uncertainty for the future and (3) it is involuntary (De Witte et al., 2015). Uncertainty about one's job continuity in the future is termed quantitative JI, while uncertainty about the quality of someone's job in the future is termed qualitative JI (De Witte et al., 2015; Hellgren et al., 1999). A large body of research has documented the unfavorable consequences of both quantitative and qualitative JI on employees' mental and physical health and work-related attitudes and behaviors (for meta-analyses, see Cheng & Chan, 2008; Jiang & Lavaysse, 2018; Sverke et al., 2019). For example, a recent review of 57 longitudinal studies showed that JI impairs physical health and psychological well-being over time and that it increases burnout and decreases job satisfaction and work engagement (De Witte et al., 2016).

Some of the most important factors contributing to JI that have been identified in the literature can be categorized into subjective characteristics (e.g., perceived employability, family responsibility, role ambiguity), factors related to objective situations (e.g., labor market characteristics, organizational uncertainty, employment contracts, organizational changes), as well as personal characteristics (e.g., age, tenure, locus of control and self-esteem; De Witte, 2005; Hartley et al., 1991; Keim et al., 2014; Kinnunen & Nätti, 1994). However, JI may also be sparked by broader societal factors, such as the global financial crisis (Erlinghagen, 2007; László et al., 2010). Indeed, cutback-related organizational changes that elicit perceptions of JI are more likely to be implemented during a financial recession (Petrou et al., 2017). Given that in Greece, the economic downturn after 2009 brought rapid changes in the macro environment (i.e., income reduction, high country unemployment, changes in legislation standards, increase of temporary employment, and deregulation of labor relationships) that promote JI, studies concerning JI in such a financially unstable context may add to the literature.

Traditionally, the Greek economy has been characterized by structural weaknesses like chronic fiscal and external deficits, large public debt and low competitiveness. However, in 2010, under the fear that Greece could be forced to default on its debt, the European Commission, the European Central Bank and the International Monetary Fund discussed the option of a possible bailout with the Greek government. As a result, Greece received financial assistance that was accompanied by a memorandum of fiscal policies that the country had to implement (Bank of Greece, 2011). Due to austerity and budgetary cuts in the period between 2008 and 2016, the gross domestic product of Greece shrank by 26.5% (Matsaganis, 2017). At this time, wages decreased on average by 20%, while the proportion of the population at risk of poverty increased from 16.4% to 49.5%, resulting in a humanitarian crisis (Filippidis et al., 2017). Meanwhile, unemployment rates rose from 9.4% in 2009 to 23.5% in 2016, reaching a peak of 28.7% in November 2013 (Matsaganis, 2017).

These unprecedented unemployment rates affected working conditions and labor relationships, since unemployment not only impairs the mental and physical health of those who are excluded from the labor market (Norström et al., 2014; Paul & Moser, 2009) but also touches those employed. Higher unemployment rates increase individuals' concerns about their own future employment prospects and the quality of their jobs in the future, while the anticipation of redundancies may be as distressing as the experience of job loss itself (Clark et al., 2010; De Witte, 1999). Hence, it is not surprising that Greek employees reported the highest JI levels among the OECD countries in 2018 (OECD, 2018). However, even before the current crisis, the uncertainty concerning the continuance of employment relationships was higher in Greece than in most European countries (Erlinghagen, 2007). Moreover, unemployment and JI are closely related phenomena, not only because unemployment leads to higher JI but also because they share similar outcomes (De Witte et al., 2019). A systematic review of studies investigating the health-related risks of both JI and unemployment revealed that JI might be as harmful as job loss, yet these constructs are distinct: although both phenomena were equally strongly related to poorer mental health, JI was more strongly associated with more somatic symptoms, while unemployment was associated with impaired general health and higher mortality (Kim and von dem Knesebeck 2015).

In addition to the uncertainty caused by the sharp rise in unemployment, several changes in the Greek labor market that resulted from the financial recession also affected JI perceptions. Given the demands for budgetary cuts and reforms in the public sector that was characterized by bureaucracy, high centralization, increased administrative costs and low performance, the Greek government implemented a series of changes. In 2012, a personnel mobility framework was implemented that envisaged—for the first time—the layoff of civil servants (Nella et al., 2015). Moreover, many reforms, including merging, job relocation and salary cuts, were imposed. These unfavorable changes and the continuous demand for additional reforms to reduce administrative costs led to an increased sense of insecurity among public sector employees. According to a study among 316 Greek primary teachers during that period, the unplanned organizational changes that were out of teachers' control (e.g., reduction of wages, assessment of personnel using the forced distribution method) were found to relate positively with perceived stress (Mouza & Souchamvali, 2016). Analogous were the findings of a study conducted among 811 Greek civil servants (Mouza, 2017).

The unfavorable effects of the financial crisis and the resulting reforms have also affected those employed in higher education. Results of an interview study with 36 university administrative employees awaiting repositioning (investigation group), 36 co-workers not at risk and 28 employees of a local hospital not at risk (control groups) revealed that employees at risk of losing their current position perceived higher levels of stress and negative emotion and lower levels of positive emotion compared to employees who were not at risk (Nella et al., 2015). All in all, this evidence suggests that JI among Greek higher education employees became a relevant issue, particularly considering the numerous structural weaknesses of this occupational sector that contribute to the unfavorable consequences of the financial recession.

11.2 Higher Education in Greece: Structure and the Role of the Financial Crisis

The educational system in Greece is tuition-free at all levels (except post-graduate studies in some cases). Public tertiary education is divided into (i) university education, provided by higher educational institutes, and (ii) higher technological education, provided by technological educational institutes (Giousmpasoglou et al., 2016). Private tertiary education also exists, but the provided degrees are usually not equivalent to those of public institutions. The academic personnel of Greek universities that consist of civil servants are selected by the institutions themselves, but they are under the authorization of the central government. The labor contracts of the other employees of Greek universities (e.g., administration or technical employees) vary considerably. Administrative staff mainly consists of civil servants, lab or technical staff consists of both permanent workers and employees with temporary work contracts, while the supportive staff (e.g., cleaners, security) is usually outsourced.

Various factors were considered problematic in higher education in Greece before the economic downturn, namely, bureaucracy, favoritism, political involvement, trade unionism, the formation of unnecessary departments in rural areas to satisfy local economies, and low competitiveness (Asderaki, 2009; Giousmpasoglou et al., 2016; Kokosalakis, 2001; Livanos & Pouliakas, 2011). However, the situation has been aggravated by the financial crisis. Austerity policies led to severe reductions in funding, while salary cuts (>30%) were imposed on the academic and administrative staff (Koulouris et al., 2014). Meanwhile, many faculty positions were abolished when staff was retired, while some academics modified their retirement plans and went earlier on pension due to the uncertain economic environment. At the same time, funding shortages and reduced possibilities for recruiting part-time staff created additional problems for many institutions that strongly relied on temporary teaching and research staff (Giousmpasoglou et al., 2016; Koulouris et al., 2014).

To face the shortage in funds, the Ministry of Education took a number of initiatives to reorganize the academic map of the country (Zmas, 2015). Many departments, particularly in the technological sector, were merged. Since 2012, the number of higher education institutions has decreased from 42 to 40, while the number of departments has decreased to 408 from 528 (Giousmpasoglou et al., 2016). Also, after 2017, many technological educational institutes reformed into higher educational institutions with a continuous process of merging. Thus, higher education institutions had to address growing demands with reduced resources when higher education employees were confronted with increased JI as a result of budgetary cuts and potential reforms.

Hence, it becomes evident that the context of higher educational institutions in Greece is particularly relevant for studying JI and potential factors, such as WSC, that may mitigate its unfavorable effects for employees. WSC constitutes a contextual resource that refers to norms (e.g., trust, reciprocity) and network connections within an organization (Meng et al., 2018; Ommen et al., 2009) that may enable employee functioning (Ooi et al., 2015). As such, it may operate as a buffer of the negative consequences of JI stemming from the economic downturn.

11.3 Workplace Social Capital (WSC)

Social capital (SC) is commonly viewed as an individual or ecological characteristic. In line with the individualistic approach, SC refers to benefits individuals may gain through their participation in social networks, through which they secure access to different forms of support (Bourdieu, 1985), while in line with the ecological approach (Putnam, 1995), SC is viewed as a feature that characterizes a social group or a community and is available to its members. Research evidence supports the beneficial effects of SC for both individuals and the community. For instance, a systematic review of 20 systematic reviews suggested that SC relates to better mental and physical health (Ehsan et al., 2019). These findings may be attributed to the unobstructed access to medical information and health services, the development of informal support and care, the restriction of social isolation and stigma, the empowerment of reciprocal relationships and the development of sustained supportive networks of those with high levels of SC (Rocco & Suhrcke, 2012; Salehi et al., 2018).

Given its relevance for health and well-being, SC has also been investigated in the workplace. Most organizational studies define and measure WSC as a contextual (i.e., organizational) and not as an individual resource (Eguchi et al., 2017; Kouvonen et al., 2007; Meng et al., 2018; Ommen et al., 2009; Pejtersen et al., 2010). This is because contextual resources are more likely to be promoted via organizational interventions aimed at enhancing employee well-being. In contrast, WSC as an individual resource strongly depends on individual actors' actions that often fall outside the scope and control of organizations (i.e., personal family networks). In line with this approach, in the current analysis, we focus on WSC as an organizational resource and investigate employees' individual (and not shared) perceptions of the WSC of their organization (for similar approaches, see Driller et al., 2011; Kowalski et al., 2010; Ommen et al., 2009; Tsuboya et al., 2015).

Empirical studies have documented the positive consequences of WSC as a contextual resource for both employees and organizations. Higher levels of WSC relate to higher job satisfaction (Framke et al., 2019; Ommen et al., 2009) and work engagement (Meng et al., 2018) and lower emotional exhaustion (Driller et al., 2011; Framke et al., 2019; Kowalski et al., 2010), long-term sickness absence (Hansen et al., 2018; Török et al., 2018) and psychological distress among employees (Firouzbakht et al., 2018; Tsuboya et al., 2015).

Since there is no consensus regarding the conceptualization of WSC as a contextual resource (Oksanen et al., 2013), Tsounis et al. (2023) conducted a literature review to identify the core elements of WSC. According to their analysis, the most prominent distinctions found in the extant literature are between bonding and bridging WSC (e.g., Ferlander, 2007; Harpham et al., 2002; Kreuter & Lezin, 2002) and between structural and cognitive WSC (e.g., Grootaert & Bastelaer, 2002; Krishna, 2001; Uphoff & Wijayaratna, 2000). The former distinction refers to the level of measurement of WSC and the latter to its components or dimensions. Namely, the bonding/bridging distinction allows identifying the different forms of WSC on the basis of the proximity of social linkages and the hierarchical levels at which these are developed (e.g., among employees or across subordinates and supervisors), while the cognitive/structural distinction determines the main components of WSC (e.g., trust, reciprocity, network).

More specifically, the bonding/bridging distinction concerns the linkages that exist between the different members of the organization, as well as the direction of action (Gittell & Vidal, 1998; Kreuter & Lezin, 2002). Bonding WSC refers to close ties between individuals within a homogeneous group (e.g., colleagues from the same hierarchical level), and it has an inwards direction (e.g., connections among employees), while bridging WSC refers to more distal connections among people of heterogeneous groups or from other hierarchical levels (e.g., employees and supervisors) and has outwards direction (e.g., connections across organizational levels and even beyond the organization; Harpham et al., 2002; Kreuter & Lezin, 2002; Putnam, 2001). The distinction between structural and cognitive WSC captures the specific components of WSC. Structural WSC mainly refers to the quality aspect of networking (e.g., quality of social relationships among colleagues, possibilities for expanding the professional network outside of the organization) that facilitates access to the resources of the organization and not to the amount of social connections (i.e., quantitative aspect of network) (Tsounis et al., 2023). Cognitive WSC mainly concerns perceptions of trust and reciprocity. Trust refers to expectations of honest behavior and the exchange of information that makes the various parties during a social interaction reliable (Fukuyama, 1997), and reciprocity refers to social support exchanges and mutual assistance between different actors (Harpham et al., 2002).

Based on their review, Tsounis et al. (2023) synthesized these core distinctions and defined WSC as a higher-order contextual resource that concerns employees' beliefs regarding trust, reciprocity (i.e., cognitive WSC), and network connections (i.e., structural WSC) that exist both between peers (i.e., bonding WSC) and among individuals across different hierarchical levels or organizations (i.e., bridging WSC). This conceptual definition of WSC is depicted in Fig. 11.1. Given that this definition encompasses all main aspects and components of WSC, it was adopted in the present study.

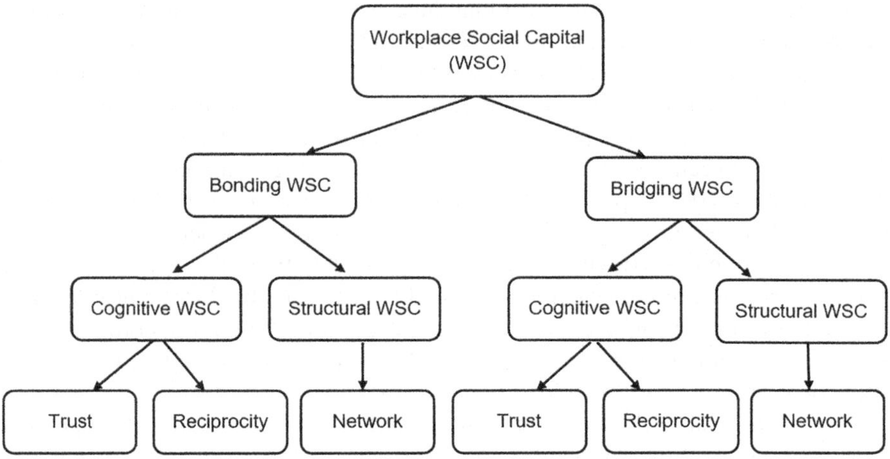

Fig. 11.1 Workplace social capital construct definition. Note: The bonding/bridging form of WSC refers to the level of measurement and to the direction of social interaction. The cognitive/structural form of WSC refers to its content (i.e., trust, reciprocity and network dimensions)

11.4 The Present Study

We drew on JD-R (Bakker & Demerouti, 2017) and COR (Hobfoll, 1989) theories to investigate WSC as a resource that may buffer the adverse effects of JI on employee functioning. Specifically, we focused on two indicators of employee functioning (work engagement and in-role performance) that were found to be particularly relevant for employees and organizations (Demerouti & Cropanzano, 2010; Salanova et al., 2005). Work engagement is "a positive, fulfilling work-related state of mind that is characterized by vigor, dedication and absorption" (Schaufeli et al., 2002, p. 74). Vigor refers to working with high levels of energy accompanied by eagerness to accomplish one's work tasks, dedication refers to a sense of significance with regard to one's work combined with feelings of enthusiasm and pride, and absorption refers to a situation where one is fully and happily immersed in their work. In-role performance refers to those behaviors directed towards formal duties, tasks and responsibilities that are included in one's job description and for which employees are held accountable (Williams & Anderson, 1991).

JD-R theory (Bakker & Demerouti, 2017) postulates that employee functioning depends on the characteristics of the work environment that can be distinguished into two broad categories: job demands and job resources. Job demands refer to "those physical, social or organizational aspects of the job that require sustained physical or mental effort and therefore, associate with certain physiological and psychological costs"(Demerouti et al., 2001; p. 501). In contrast, job resources refer to "those physical, psychological, social or organizational aspects of the job that may do any of the following: (a) be functional in achieving work goals, (b) reduce job demands and the associated physiological and psychological costs; (c) stimulate personal growth and development" (Demerouti et al., 2001; p. 501). In the context of JD-R theory (Bakker & Demerouti, 2017), we argue that both quantitative (i.e., uncertainty about keeping one's job; Hellgren et al., 1999) and qualitative (i.e., uncertainty about the quality of one's job in the future; De Witte et al., 2015) JI can be perceived as threatening aspects of the work environment. Although JI is not a characteristic of the job per se but a subjective perception of one's work condition, it shares certain facets with job demands. Namely, employees who experience high levels of JI need to invest overwhelming effort—with often uncertain outcomes—to deal with this threatening situation, which leads to energy depletion and reduced performance (Sverke et al., 2019).

Also, considering the definition of WSC proposed by Tsounis et al. (2023), it may be argued that WSC is an aspect of the organizational environment that may be perceived as a job resource (Bakker & Demerouti, 2017). This is because the components of WSC are similar to typical job resources such as supervisor support, colleague support and positive climate. For instance, the reciprocity sub-dimension of bonding WSC refers to the mutual exchange of instrumental and emotional support among employees in a workplace, the reciprocity sub-dimension of bridging WSC refers to social support provided across hierarchy levels that facilitates problem solving via the promotion of cooperation, and the network sub-dimension of bonding WSC reflects the quality of social relationships between colleagues, which is part of a positive organizational climate. Moreover, previous empirical evidence suggests that WSC functions as a job resource. Specifically, WSC was found to buffer the effect of high job demands on unhealthy behaviors such as smoking (Sapp et al., 2010) and to facilitate personal development in the workplace through work engagement (Meng et al., 2018) and job satisfaction (Ommen et al., 2009). Thus, we expect that WSC, as a resource, will mitigate the unfavorable consequences of JI on work engagement and performance (see Bakker et al., 2007).

COR theory (Hobfoll, 1989; Halbesleben et al. 2014) may help explain why WSC may buffer the unfavorable consequences of JI on work engagement and in-role performance. According to the main tenets of COR theory, individuals tend to retain, protect and build resources that they value because available resources may be invested to address threatening aspects of the environment and prevent well-being impairments. Resources under the prism of COR theory can be objects (e.g., a car), personal characteristics (e.g., self-efficacy), conditions (e.g., support) or energies (e.g., time; Hobfoll, 1989). WSC may be considered a condition since it reflects important aspects of the organizational context that create fertile ground for the conservation and gain of additional resources (Hobfoll et al., 2018).

COR theory (Hobfoll et al., 2018) postulates that employee well-being and performance are at stake when individuals face threatening and demanding situations (e.g., high JI) and do not possess the necessary resources to deal with these threats. In contrast, when employees possess adequate resources in the face of threatening situations, they may deal with these threats successfully and mitigate their unfavorable consequences. Employees who perceive high levels of WSC not only possess resources (e.g., trust, reciprocity and networking) but may also use these resources to gain further resources. Specifically, they may have better access to information and advice (i.e., trust dimension of WSC), they could receive support on the job (i.e., reciprocity dimension of WSC) and they may have qualitative connections with colleagues and opportunities to expand their professional and broader social network (i.e., network dimension of WSC). Thus, WSC may help employees cope better in insecure work conditions and protect themselves from future losses. Along these lines, Kahn and Byosiere (1992) claimed that facets of the work environment, including job resources (such as WSC), can buffer the effects of a demanding condition (i.e., JI) on employee functioning because employees who enjoy high levels of such resources are likely to appraise the demanding aspects of the work environment as manageable, thus limiting their unfavorable effects. In line with these theoretical assumptions, research has documented that job resources such as supervisor support, appreciation and positive organizational climate help teachers cope with their job demands, thus preventing decreases in their work engagement (Bakker et al., 2007).

In this context, we propose that in work environments characterized by high levels of trust and reciprocity among employees and across hierarchy levels, as well as opportunities for network expansion within and out of the organization, employees will be better equipped to cope with the demanding aspects of JI, thus preventing decrements in their engagement and in-role performance. For instance, employees may use the support provided in a context higher (vs. lower) in WSC to reappraise their perceptions of quantitative and qualitative JI, thus staying motivated and engaged. Also, a work environment that is characterized by higher levels of WSC may help employees successfully deal with insecure conditions and mitigate the negative effects of their perceived JI on their energy, dedication and absorption in their work task. These theoretical assumptions are supported by previous studies showing that job resources that resemble WSC not only promote employee functioning but may also buffer the negative impact of several job demands on work engagement (Bakker et al., 2007; Hakanen et al., 2005; Tadić et al., 2015). Of particular relevance for the present analysis, Cheng et al. (2014) found that social support from colleagues and supervisors buffered the negative effects of JI on vigor at work. Hence, we hypothesize the following:

Hypothesis 1: The negative relationship between quantitative and qualitative JI and work engagement will be stronger among those employees who perceive lower levels of WSC and weaker among those employees who perceive higher levels of WSC.

In regard to job performance, there is evidence for the buffering effect of support at work (i.e., a concept similar to the reciprocity sub-dimension of WSC) on the relationship between JI and lateness and absenteeism (Lim, 1997). Similarly, a weekly diary study concerning the moderating role of social support on the relationship between JI and in-role performance showed that on weeks employees received more (vs. less) support from their supervisors, their performance suffered less from JI (Schreurs et al., 2012). Based on these empirical findings, and in line with COR theory (Hobfoll, 1989), we expect that WSC will mitigate the relationship between JI and in-role performance. WSC may function as a protective factor for insecure employees, helping them cope with the fear of losing their job or changes for the worse regarding their job. When employees feel that they operate in an environment that is characterized by low levels of trust and mutual support and by a lack of opportunities for network expansion, perceptions of JI are more likely to affect their performance, making them unwilling to invest effort in their work tasks. In contrast, when employees feel that they work in a trustworthy, supportive and network-facilitating environment, the unfavorable impact of JI on performance will be weaker because they can invest these resources to counteract JI. Considering the above, we hypothesize the following:

Hypothesis 2: The negative relationship between quantitative and qualitative JI and in-role performance will be stronger among those employees who perceive lower levels of WSC and weaker among those employees who perceive higher levels of WSC.

11.5 Method

11.5.1 Participants and Procedure

Email invitations were sent to employees (academic faculty, administrative, other scientific and technical staff, post-doc researchers and other university support staff) of 14 Greek universities. In two universities, participants were informed through their university's intranet, while in all other cases, contact details (emails) were obtained from university websites. In total, 4245 individuals from 102 departments were invited to participate. Participants were informed about the purpose of the study, that participation was voluntary and anonymous and that their data would be treated confidentially. The study was reviewed and approved by the Research Ethics Committee of the School of Psychology, Aristotle University of Thessaloniki (# 020/03-01-2018).

The final sample included 376 employees (9% of those initially approached) (44.5% men, 50.9% women, 0.3% transgender), with a mean age of 47.91 ($SD = 8.24$) years. Fifty percent of participants were academic staff (i.e., professors, lecturers), 15.7% were administrative staff, 12.6% were expert scientific staff, 6.7% were technical/lab staff, 4.1% were scientific collaborators and tutors, 5.1% were post doc researchers and 2.1% were other staff (e.g., cleaner or other elementary occupation). The vast majority (90%) worked full-time.

11.5.2 Measures

Quantitative Job Insecurity was assessed with the 4-item scale validated by Vander Elst et al. (2014). An example item is "I feel insecure about the future of my job". Items were rated on a 5-point scale, ranging from (1) "totally disagree" to (5) "totally agree" and the scale was reliable (alpha = .84).

Qualitative Job Insecurity was measured with four items (Fischmann et al., 2022). An example item is "I think my job will change for the worse" (alpha = .86). Items were scored with the same 5-point scale used to assess quantitative JI. It is important to note that there is evidence supporting the factorial validity and equivalence of both JI sub-scales across different countries, including Greece (see Chaps. 2 and 3).

Workplace Social Capital was measured with the 24-item Workplace Social Capital Inventory (WoSCi; Tsounis et al., 2023), which evaluates structural (i.e., network) and cognitive (i.e., trust, reciprocity) WSC both at the bonding (11 items) and bridging (13 items) levels. Example items for bonding WSC are "In the organization where I work, colleagues trust each other" (trust), "Colleagues support each other even if they are not asked" (reciprocity), and "Employees develop and participate in common actions (e.g., organizing events, excursions) also outside of the workplace" (network). Example items for bridging WSC are "In the organization where I work, there is trust toward management" (trust), "Employees feel that the management will support (stand by) them if needed" (reciprocity) and "The organization where I work invests in collaborating with other organizations" (network). All items were scored on a 5-point scale, ranging from (1) "fully disagree" to (5) "fully agree". Cronbach's alpha was .95 for the total scale ($\alpha = .94$ and $\alpha = .93$ for bonding and bridging WSC, respectively).

WSC is conceptualized as an organizational job resource that may be operationalized within a multilevel framework, where employees (level 1) nested in organizations (level 2) evaluate the WSC of their organizations, and these scores are aggregated to level 2. For that, inter-rater (within-unit) agreement and inter-rater reliability (between and within units) must be supported (Le Breton & Senter, 2008). However, in the present study, only inter-rater agreement (i.e., $r_{wg} = .96$; and average deviation index = .67) but not inter-rater reliability (i.e., intra-class correlation coefficient-ICC) could be estimated; thus, we could not fully assess all necessary criteria for aggregation. The inability to calculate ICC values was attributed to the small number of units at level 2 and the sample distribution within each unit that varied substantially (i.e., from 1 or two to 71 employees across units). As a result, WSC was treated as an individual employee variable reflecting individual perceptions of WSC of one's organization (for similar approaches, see, Firouzbakht et al., 2018; Tsuboya et al., 2015).

Work Engagement was measured with the 3-item version of the Utrecht Work Engagement Scale (UWES-3; Schaufeli et al., 2017). The UWES-3 measures vigor ("At my work I feel bursting with energy"), dedication ("I am enthusiastic about my job") and absorption ("I am immersed in my work") with the use of a 7-point scale, ranging from (0) "never" to (6) "always". Cronbach's alpha was .77.

In-role Performance was measured with four items from Van Dyne and LePine' s (1998) scale. Example items were "I fulfill the responsibilities specified in my job description" and "I meet performance expectations". Items were scored on a 5-point scale, ranging from (1) "totally disagree" to (5) "totally agree", and the scale was reliable (alpha = .92).

11.5.3 *Strategy of Analysis*

Given the small number of organizations at level 2 ($N = 14$) and the inability to calculate the intra-correlation coefficient due to the sample distribution across the different organizations, we tested all hypothesized effects at the individual level of analysis without accounting for the multilevel structure of the data. To test the proposed main and moderating effects, we performed hierarchical multiple regression analyses with three steps and work engagement and in-role performance as dependent variables. In the first step, we entered quantitative and qualitative JI; in the second step, we added WSC; and in the final step, we added the respective interaction effects. The predictors (quantitative and qualitative JI) and the moderator (WSC) were standardized prior to calculating the cross-product interaction terms (Aiken et al., 1991). Significant interaction effects were probed with the simple effects approach and were plotted +/− 1 SD of the moderators (Preacher et al., 2006).

11.6 Results

11.6.1 *Descriptive Statistics*

Means, standard deviations and correlations between the variables are presented in Table 11.1.

11.6.2 *Moderating Effects*

The results of the regression analyses are presented in Table 11.2. Regarding main effects, results showed that quantitative JI was negatively related to both work engagement and in-role performance in all analyses, while qualitative JI was

Table 11.1 Means, standard deviations and correlations between the study variables (N = 376)

		Mean	*SD*	1	2	3	4	5	6
1	JI Quantitative	2.16	.87	–					
2	JI Qualitative	3.14	.88	.51**	–				
3	WSC	3.17	.64	−.17**	−.41**	–			
4	Bonding WSC	3.11	.71	−.07	−.28**	.87**	–		
5	Bridging WSC	3.22	.73	−.22**	−.43**	.91**	.60**	–	
6	Work Engagement	4.32	1.26	−.23**	−.27**	.30**	.21**	.32**	–
7	In-role Performance	4.44	.57	−.20**	−.05	−.02	−.06	.01	.28**

**$p < .01$, *$p < .05$

Table 11.2 Interactions of qualitative and quantitative job insecurity (JI) with workplace social capital (WSC) in explaining work engagement and in-role performance (N = 376)

		Work engagement			In-role performance		
	Variables	β (SE)	ΔR^2	F	β(SE)	ΔR^2	F
Step 1	Quantitative JI	−.13 (.07)*			−.23 (.03)***		
	Qualitative JI	−.20 (.07)***	.08	16.22***	.07 (.03)	.04	8.39
Step 2	Quantitative JI	−.14 (.07)*			−.23 (.03)***		
	Qualitative JI	−.10 (.08)			.05 (.04)		
	WSC	.24 (.07)***	.05	20.10***	−.04 (.03)	.001	.531
Step 3	Quantitative JI	−.13 (.07)*			−.24 (.03)***		
	Qualitative JI	−.10 (.08)			.05 (.04)		
	WSC	.25 (.07)***			−.02 (.03)		
	Quantitative JI = WSC	.03 (.07)			−.04 (.03)		
	Qualitative JI = WSC	−.11 (.06)*	.01	2.05*	−.12 (.03)*	.02	4.12*

*$p < .05$, **$p < .01$, ***$p < .001$

negatively related only to work engagement. Also, WSC was found to relate positively with work engagement, but it was unrelated to in-role performance.

According to Hypothesis 1, we expected that WSC would buffer the negative relationships between quantitative and qualitative JI and work engagement. Table 11.2 shows that only the interaction of qualitative JI and WSC was significant in explaining work engagement ($\beta = -.11$, $p = .04$). Results of simple slopes tests revealed that the relationship between qualitative JI and work engagement was negative and significant in conditions of higher WSC (+1SD: estimate = −.25, $t = -2.55$. $p = .01$), while it was not significant in conditions of lower WSC (−1SD: estimate = −.01, $t = -.06$, $p = .95$; see Fig. 11.2). Thus, Hypothesis 1 was rejected.

According to Hypothesis 2, we expected WSC to buffer the negative link between quantitative and qualitative JI and in-role performance. As shown in Table 11.2, results revealed that qualitative JI interacted with WSC ($\beta = -.12$, $p = .03$) in explaining in-role performance. Simple slopes tests showed that the relationship between qualitative JI and in-role performance was positive and significant in conditions of lower WSC (−1SD: estimate = .09, $t = 2.02$, $p = .04$), while it was not significant in conditions of higher WSC (+1SD: estimate = −.04, $t = -.74$, $p = .46$; Fig. 11.3). Thus, Hypothesis 2 was also rejected.

11.6.3 Post hoc Analyses

To shed more light on the moderating role of WSC on the outcomes of JI, we examined the interactions of quantitative and qualitative JI with bonding and bridging WSC separately. The results of these regression analyses (see Tables 11.3

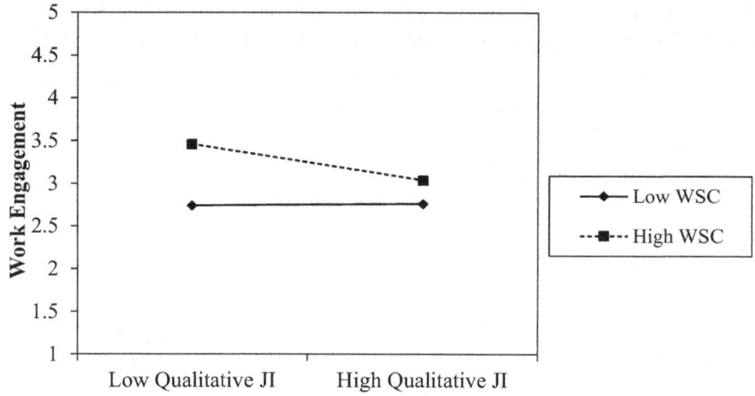

Fig. 11.2 Interaction effect of qualitative job insecurity (JI) and workplace social capital (WSC) in explaining work engagement

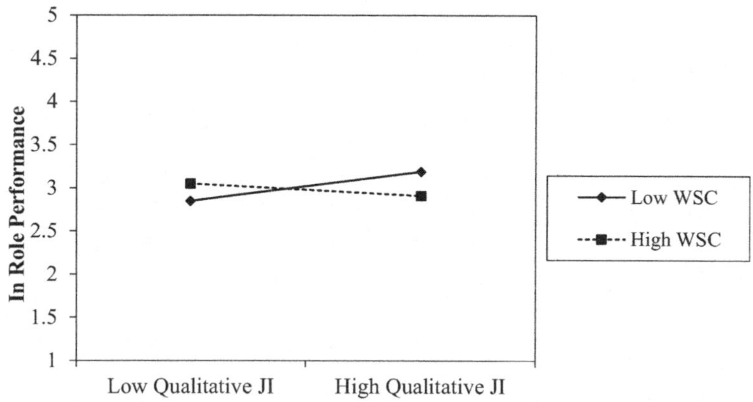

Fig. 11.3 Interaction effect of qualitative job insecurity (JI) and workplace social capital (WSC) in explaining in-role job performance

and 11.4) revealed that only bridging WSC interacted with qualitative JI in explaining both work engagement ($\beta = -.13$, $p = .02$) and in-role performance ($\beta = -.12$, $p = .03$).

Simple slope tests of the significant interaction effects also revealed that the relationship between qualitative JI and work engagement was negative and significant only for higher bridging WSC (+1SD: estimate = −.26, $t = -2.60$, $p = .01$)

Table 11.3 Interactions of qualitative and quantitative job insecurity (JI) with bonding workplace social capital (WSC) in explaining work engagement and in-role performance ($N = 376$)

		Work engagement			In-role performance		
	Variables	β (SE)	ΔR^2	F	β (SE)	ΔR^2	F
Step 1	Quantitative JI	−.13 (.07)*			−.23 (.03)***		
	Qualitative JI	−.20 (.07)***	.08	16.22***	.07 (.03)	.04	8.39
Step 2	Quantitative JI	−.13 (.07)*			−.23 (.03)***		
	Qualitative JI	−.15 (.08)*			.05 (.04)		
	Bonding WSC	.16 (.07)**	.02	9.26**	−.06 (.03)	.003	1.27
Step 3	Quantitative JI	−.14 (.07)*			−.23 (.03)***		
	Qualitative JI	−.15 (.08)*			.05 (.04)		
	Bonding WSC	.17 (.07)***			−.04 (.03)		
	Quantitative JI = Bonding WSC	−.00 (.07)			−.07 (.03)		
	Qualitative JI = Bonding WSC	−.09 (.07)	.01	1.53	−.10 (.03)	.02	3.72

$*p < .05$, $**p < .01$, $***p < .001$

Table 11.4 Interactions of qualitative and quantitative job insecurity (JI) with bridging workplace social capital (WSC) in explaining work engagement and in-role performance ($N = 376$)

		Work engagement			In-role performance		
	Variables	β(SE)	ΔR^2	F	β(SE)	ΔR^2	F
Step 1	Quantitative JI	−.13 (.07)*			−.23 (.03)***		
	Qualitative JI	−.20 (.07)***	.08	16.22***	.07 (.03)	.04	8.39
Step 2	Quantitative JI	−.13 (.07)*			−.23 (.03)***		
	Qualitative JI	−.09 (.08)			.05 (.04)		
	Bridging WSC	.25 (.07)***	.05	22.31***	−.04 (.03)	.00	5.31
Step 3	Quantitative JI	−.13 (.07)*			−.24 (.03)***		
	Qualitative JI	−.09 (.08)			.05 (.04)		
	Bridging WSC	.27 (.07)***			−.02 (.03)		
	Quantitative JI = Bridging WSC	.05 (.07)			−.04 (.03)		
	Qualitative JI = Bridging WSC	−.13 (.06)*	.01	2.65*	−.12 (.03)*	.02	4.12*

$*p < .05$, $**p < .01$, $***p < .001$

and non-significant for lower bridging WSC (−1SD: estimate = .03, $t = .32$, $p = .75$). Also, the relationship between qualitative JI and in-role performance was positive and significant for lower bridging WSC (−1SD: estimate = .10, $t = 2.20$,

$p = .028$) and non-significant for higher bridging WSC (+1SD: estimate $= -.03$, $t = -.62$, $p = .54$).[1,2]

11.7 Discussion

The objective of the study presented in this chapter was to investigate the mitigating role of WSC on the negative relationship between (quantitative and qualitative) JI on the one hand and work engagement and in-role job performance on the other hand among higher education employees in Greece. We considered Greece to be a relevant setting for testing the study aim because the financial recession of the past decade has formed a demanding and precarious work context. In such a context, the study of recourses that may potentially buffer the adverse effects of JI may add to theory development and to developing targeted organizational interventions.

Based on JD-R (Bakker & Demerouti, 2017) and COR (Hobfoll, 1989) theories, we argued that WSC (as a contextual job resource) will mitigate the unfavorable impact of JI on work engagement and in-role performance. In line with expectations and previous studies (Clausen et al., 2019; Fujita et al., 2016; Lehner et al., 2013; Meng et al., 2018; Van Bogaert et al., 2014), WSC was found to relate positively with work engagement (but not in-role performance). Also, WSC was found to moderate the relationship between qualitative JI and both work engagement and in-role performance. However, the direction of these interaction effects was not in line with our expectations. Namely, results showed that qualitative JI was negatively related to work engagement in conditions of higher WSC, while the relationship was non-significant in conditions of lower WSC. Also, qualitative JI related positively to in-role performance in conditions of lower WSC and non-significantly in conditions of higher WSC. Post-hoc analyses showed that mainly the network sub-dimension of bridging WSC was responsible for these findings. The theoretical and practical implications of these findings are discussed in the following sections.

[1]We also performed additional analyses to examine the interactions of quantitative and qualitative JI with each sub-dimension of WSC (i.e., trust, reciprocity and network of both bonding and bridging WSC). These results showed that mainly the network dimension of bridging WSC interacted with qualitative JI in predicting both work engagement and in-role job performance, in the same direction as with the main analyses.

[2]In line with the motivational process and the boosting hypothesis of JD-R theory (Bakker & Demerouti, 2017), we considered JI as a moderator on the relationship between WSC and work engagement and in-role performance. Simple slope tests revealed that the relationship between WSC and work engagement was positive and significant in conditions of both lower and higher qualitative JI. However, the relationship was stronger in conditions of lower (vs. higher) JI. These results did not support the boosting effect of JI on the motivational process.

11.7.1 Theoretical Implications

In line with JD-R theory (Bakker & Demerouti, 2017), we found that WSC functions as a job resource that relates positively to work engagement. However, the buffering role of WSC on the unfavorable consequences of JI was not supported. Contrary to the assumptions of COR theory (Hobfoll, 1989), our results showed that in conditions of high qualitative JI, lower and not higher levels of WSC were more favorable for work engagement and performance. Work engagement was lowest in conditions of higher JI and higher WSC, while in-role performance was highest in conditions of higher JI and lower WSC.

The unexpected findings regarding work engagement resemble those of Rothmann and Jordaan (2006). Their study among academics from higher education institutions in South Africa showed that the negative relationship between overload (amount of work, quantitative and emotional load) and dedication was weaker under conditions of lower than higher organizational support. Similarly, the study of Probst et al. (2020) among working adults in the U.S. showed that the positive relationship between quantitative JI and moral disengagement was stronger under conditions of higher (vs. lower) perceived organizational support. These findings suggest that job resources, and interestingly those interpersonal in nature, do not always buffer the unfavorable effects of job demands and JI.

Portes (1998) mentioned that SC is conceptualized as something "by definition"positive, although it may cause diverse effects (Kawachi et al., 2008). Loizos (2002), who studied the life of immigrants, observed the trend of social relationships to be strongly confined within an ethnic group. Although this helped people face difficulties encountered in a foreign country, it led to the normalization of social isolation. Also, research evidence suggests that different forms of SC may have differential effects. Some studies have indicated that higher bonding SC may provide instrumental support, but at the same time, it may contribute to the perpetuation of social isolation, preventing the development of social ties with the broader community (Caughy et al., 2003; Mitchell & La Gory, 2002; Takahashi & Magalong, 2008). Other studies have also shown that the cognitive form of SC is more beneficial than the structural form (De Silva et al., 2005; Eriksson et al., 2010, 2011). This is in line with our findings suggesting that in conditions of higher structural WSC (i.e., network), JI was negatively related to work engagement. This implies that in some cases, close ties between colleagues in a workplace and opportunities for expanding professional and social network may deteriorate employees' capability to confront JI consequences on work engagement.

A possible explanation may be attributed to one's position in the organizational network. The study of Sparrowe et al. (2001) showed that individual job performance related positively to centrality in advice networks (i.e., networks comprised of relationships through which actors share information, guidance and assistance) and negatively to centrality in hindrance networks (i.e., networks characterized by negative exchange relations such as interference, sabotage, rejection and threats). In our study, we did not differentiate between advice or hindrance networks and did not investigate employees' positioning in social networks. Rather, we focused on the existence of positive close relationships between colleagues and opportunities for network expansion. However, it is likely that not all individuals within an organization have access to its high network WSC and the resources that can be derived from such an asset. Lack of access to resources may lead to a sense of isolation that may explain why social network does not function as a resource in threatening conditions. Specifically, high WSC may be interpreted as something useful only if someone may take advantage of it when facing threatening conditions. On the contrary, the presence of a resource that is not accessible, when needed, may lead to reduced motivation and engagement since it could be interpreted as a lost opportunity.

An alternative explanation for the unexpected moderating effect on work engagement could be that employees who are strongly connected with others and have expanded networks through their organization (i.e., higher WSC) are likely to be affected more strongly by job insecurity and become disengaged. This is in line with organizational identification theory (Riketta, 2005), according to which employees who have a strong bond with their organization and feel that they are an important part of it are more likely to react negatively in conditions that indicate a threat to their organizational identity (i.e., high JI; see also Ellemers, 2003).

Results were also unexpected with regard to in-role performance. First, the analyses did not support the main effect of WSC on in-role performance. Also, the significant interaction effect suggested that the relationship between qualitative JI and in-role performance was positive in conditions of lower WSC and non-significant in conditions of higher WSC. This is an unexpected finding because it suggests that in insecure conditions, employees are more likely to perform better when they do not have access to WSC. Although our hypothesis was not supported, our results suggest that the absence of positive networking interactions may enhance the pressure for productivity in insecure conditions. Research evidence suggests that employees who face JI may concentrate on productivity aspects that are typically rewarded by organizations (Probst et al., 2007). Thus, our results may imply that when WSC is low and employees cannot rely on their organization, they may choose to rely on their own strengths and invest additional effort to protect from future losses through better performance (Gilboa et al., 2008).

Another possible explanation for the unexpected moderating effects of WSC (and particularly its structural component) may relate to the impact of the financial crisis on individuals' understanding of the self, which, in turn, may affect collective reactions. A study of 15 independent samples collected between 2004 and 2016 (Kafetsios, 2017, 2022) found that compared to the pre-crisis years, during crisis-stricken years, young persons in Greece did not report higher interdependent self-construal as expected in a society high in collectivism. Interdependent self-construal refers to individuals' thoughts, feelings and actions as a result of positioning and understanding the self as connected with others and especially those from an in-group (Markus & Kitayama, 1991). Uncertainty resulting from the economic crisis would have led to increased proximity to others and higher interdependent self-construal, as observed in the US (Greenfield, 2009; Park et al., 2014). However, this was not observed in Greece, a collectivistic culture, suggesting that the related aspects of WSC may be differentially affected by the crisis. In a period of uncertainty, people may adopt individual strategies for confronting JI, while networking may reflect "alliances" with a negative connotation or may be interpreted under this prism. The results, moreover, highlight the precarious effects of bridging WSC in insecure job conditions, a facet of WSC that may be typical for collectivistic societies (Yamagishi & Hashimoto, 2016).

Also, the study was conducted in a period of ongoing changes that may influence employees' subjective perceptions that their job may be in danger (quantitative JI) or that they will confront negative changes as far as the quality of their current job (qualitative JI) (De Witte, 2005). The study of Smet et al. (2016) revealed that rumours, which mainly refer to informal communication between employees (i.e., unverified information about something important to a group of people or an organization; DiFonzo & Bordia, 2002), mediate the relationship between organizational change communication and JI and vice versa. Thus, we could also expect that in a period of ongoing changes in higher education in Greece where negative rumours may have risen, some employees who do not perceive themselves as a "part of a team" within an organization with high WSC may be negatively affected and feel less engaged with their current job.

Results could also be explained by the higher education context in Greece, where the study took place. Specifically, obstacles related to bureaucratic processes and a lack of a culture that brings about the social meaning of networking may increase competitiveness and negative alliances, thus highlighting the "dark side''of networking. This may explain why WSC have unfavorable consequences in insecure conditions.

11.7.2 Practical Implications

By taking into account the findings of our research and relevant studies that confirm the positive relationship between WSC and work-related attitudes such as work engagement (Fujita et al., 2016; Lehner et al., 2013; Meng et al., 2018; Van Bogaert et al., 2014) and job satisfaction (Framke et al., 2019; Ommen et al., 2009), it may be proposed that strengthening the WSC of an organization may contribute to optimal employee functioning. However, our results also suggested that high WSC may have adverse outcomes when combined with high JI. This may be because not all employees have access to the potential benefits derived from WSC. Thus, organizations should try to take the necessary steps in order to mitigate employees' perceptions of JI and, at the same time, to ensure that all employees have access to and benefit from WSC. Additionally, efforts to enhance network connections within an organization (e.g., encourage employees to develop positive social relationships as a group) could be accompanied by measures that reassure that no employee is excluded from these networks.

Our study was conducted at the end of a severe period of economic crisis. This prolonged financial downturn presents similarities with the current crisis caused by the COVID-19 pandemic that also resulted in several unfavorable changes (e.g., pay cuts, unemployment, job intensification, greater financial concerns, Xiao et al., 2021). Under these circumstances, employees' perceptions of both quantitative and qualitative JI are elevated, and the findings of our study may also be relevant.

11.8 Limitations and Future Research

The research presented in this chapter has some limitations. First, due to the cross-sectional nature of the study, causal inferences cannot be made. Second, the response rate, although it cannot be estimated accurately, was rather low. Although more than 4000 people were contacted about the study via email, we cannot estimate (i) how many accounts were active, (ii) how many employees were on leave, while (iii) 2/3 of those alerted did not open the sent email. Although such low response rates (between 5 and 15%) are common on web-surveys and do not necessarily imply differences between respondents and non-respondents (Sappleton & Lourenço, 2016), they may indicate some kind of auto-selection effects (e.g., more engaged employees participated), which may limit the validity and reliability of the study findings.

A major study limitation was that due to the sample distribution and missing data, we could not aggregate WSC scores at the organizational level of analysis or perform multilevel analyses. Future studies should examine whether individual employee scores of WSC may be aggregated at the organizational level of analysis and should adopt multilevel designs in order to capture the interdependence that exists when employees are nested within organizations. Furthermore, future studies should employ longitudinal designs in order to capture causal changes. Additionally, the moderation effects of WSC on the relationship between JI and other important organizational outcomes (e.g., exhaustion, turnover intentions) could be studied since JI has a number of unfavorable consequences on a variety of work-related states, while WSC was found to be relevant for many of these states. Finally, the network sub-dimension of WSC, which was proven to be mainly responsible for the unfavorable interaction effects, could be captured in more detail by exploring the perceptions of employees regarding the main pros and cons of networks and networking policy in the workplace, by measuring the position of employees in the network of their organization or by examining the participation of employees in their organization's network. This would help us understand which aspects of networking are particularly unfavorable for employees facing insecure working conditions.

11.9 Conclusion

JI is particularly threatening for employees in crisis conditions. Thus, the study of contextual resources that may mitigate its unfavorable effects on employee functioning (i.e., work engagement and in-role performance) is of great importance. In this chapter, we investigated whether WSC, as a contextual job resource, may buffer the adverse effects of JI. Contrary to expectations, our results revealed that JI related to lower engagement in conditions of higher (instead of lower) WSC and that it related to higher in-role performance in conditions of lower (instead of higher) WSC. To better understand these unfavorable effects of WSC, future studies should focus on the positioning of employees in the network of their organization and the way that they interpret the possibilities of network expansion through their organization.

11.10 Take Home Message

As a take-home message, our findings suggest that although WSC facilitates work motivation and goal attainment, an employee's positioning in and access to the organizational network is relevant under insecure conditions. This is because an existing but non-accessible resource may be perceived as a threat or as a lost opportunity, rather than as a framework for advancement.

References

Aiken, L. S., West, S. G., & Reno, R. R. (1991). *Multiple regression: Testing and interpreting interactions*. Sage.

Asderaki, F. (2009). The impact of the Bologna Process on the development of the Greek quality assurance system. *Quality in Higher Education, 15*(2), 105–122. https://doi.org/10.1080/13538320902995758

Bakker, A. B., & Demerouti, E. (2017). Job demands–resources theory: Taking stock and looking forward. *Journal of Occupational Health Psychology, 22*(3), 273–285. https://doi.org/10.1037/ocp0000056

Bakker, A. B., Hakanen, J. J., Demerouti, E., & Xanthopoulou, D. (2007). Job resources boost work engagement, particularly when job demands are high. *Journal of Educational Psychology, 99*(2), 274–284. https://doi.org/10.1037/0022-0663.99.2.274

Bank of Greece. (2011). *Governor's report for the year 2010*. Bank of Greece.

Bourdieu, P. (1985). The forms of capital. In J. G. Richardson (Ed.), *Handbook of theory and research for the sociology of education* (pp. 241–258). Greenwood.

Caughy, M. O., O'Campo, P. J., & Muntaner, C. (2003). When being alone might be better: Neighborhood poverty, social capital, and child mental health. *Social Science and Medicine, 57*(2), 227–237. https://doi.org/10.1016/S0277-9536(02)00342-8

Cheng, G. H. L., & Chan, D. K. S. (2008). Who suffers more from job insecurity? A meta-analytic review. *Applied Psychology, 57*(2), 272–303. https://doi.org/10.1111/j.1464-0597.2007.00312.x

Cheng, T., Mauno, S., & Lee, C. (2014). Do job control, support, and optimism help job insecure employees? A three-wave study of buffering effects on job satisfaction, vigor and work-family enrichment. *Social Indicators Research, 118*, 1269–1291. https://doi.org/10.1007/s11205-013-0467-8

Chung, H., & van Oorschot, W. (2010). *Employment insecurity of European individuals during the financial crisis: A multi-level approach.* Reconciliation of Work and Welfare in Europe Working Paper No. 14/2010. Available at SSRN: https://doi.org/10.2139/ssrn.1769770.

Clark, A., Knabe, A., & Rätzel, S. (2010). Boon or bane? Others' unemployment, well-being and job insecurity. *Labour Economics, 17*(1), 52–61. https://doi.org/10.1016/j.labeco.2009.05.007

Clausen, T., Meng, A., & Borg, V. (2019). Does social capital in the workplace predict job performance, work engagement, and psychological well-being? A prospective analysis. *Journal of Occupational and Environmental Medicine, 61*(10), 800–805. https://doi.org/10.1097/JOM.0000000000001672

De Silva, M. J., McKenzie, K., Harpham, T., & Huttly, S. R. (2005). Social capital and mental illness: A systematic review. *Journal of Epidemiology and Community Health, 59*, 619–627. https://doi.org/10.1136/jech.2004.029678

De Witte, H. (1999). Job insecurity and psychological well-being: Review of the literature and exploration of some unresolved issues. *European Journal of Work and Organizational Psychology, 8*(2), 155–177. https://doi.org/10.1080/135943299398302

De Witte, H. (2005). Job insecurity: Review of the international literature on definitions, prevalence, antecedents and consequences. *SA Journal of Industrial Psychology, 31*(4), 1–6. https://hdl.handle.net/10520/EJC89073

De Witte, H., Vander Elst, T., & De Cuyper, N. (2015). Job insecurity, health and well-being. In J. Vuori, R. Blonk, & R. H. Price (Eds.), *Sustainable working lives* (pp. 109–128). Springer. https://doi.org/10.1007/978-94-017-9798-6_7

De Witte, H., Pienaar, J., & De Cuyper, N. (2016). Review of 30 years of longitudinal studies on the association between job insecurity and health and well-being: Is there causal evidence? *Australian Psychologist, 51*(1), 18–31. https://doi.org/10.1111/ap.12176

De Witte, H., Selenko, E., & De Cuyper, N. (2019). Unemployment and job insecurity: Surprisingly identical twins. In T. Taris, M. Peeters, & H. De Witte (Eds.), *The fun and frustration of modern working life. Contributions from an occupational health psychology perspective. Festschrift for Prof. dr. Wilmar Schaufeli* (pp. 45–57). Pelckmans Pro.

Demerouti, E., & Cropanzano, R. (2010). From thought to action: Employee work engagement and job performance. In A. Bakker & M. Leiter (Eds.), *Work engagement: A handbook of essential theory and research* (pp. 147–163). Psychology Press.

Demerouti, E., Bakker, A. B., Nachreiner, F., & Schaufeli, W. B. (2001). The job demands-resources model of burnout. *Journal of Applied Psychology, 86*(3), 499–512. https://doi.org/10.1037/0021-9010.86.3.499

DiFonzo, N., & Bordia, P. (2002). Corporate rumor activity, belief and accuracy. *Public Relations Review, 28*(1), 1–19. https://doi.org/10.1016/S0363-8111(02)00107-8

Driller, E., Ommen, O., Kowalski, C., Ernstmann, N., & Pfaff, H. (2011). The relationship between social capital in hospitals and emotional exhaustion in clinicians: A study in four German hospitals. *International Journal of Social Psychiatry, 57*(6), 604–609. https://doi.org/10.1177/0020764010376609

Eguchi, H., Tsutsumi, A., Inoue, A., & Odagiri, Y. (2017). Psychometric assessment of a scale to measure bonding workplace social capital. *PLoS One, 12*(6), e0179461. https://doi.org/10.1371/journal.pone.0179461

Ehsan, A., Klaas, H. S., Bastianen, A., & Spini, D. (2019). Social capital and health: A systematic review of systematic reviews. *SSM - Population Health, 8*, 100425. https://doi.org/10.1016/j.ssmph.2019.100425

Ellemers, N. (2003). Identity, culture, and change in organizations: A social identity analysis and three illustrative cases. In S. A. Haslam, D. Van Knippenberg, M. Platow, & N. Ellemers (Eds.),

Social identity at work: Developing theory for organizational practice (pp. 191–204). Psychology Press. https://doi.org/10.4324/9781315784137

Eriksson, M., Dahlgren, L., Janlert, U., Weinehall, L., & Emmelin, M. (2010). Social capital, gender and educational level impact on self-rated health. *The Open Public Health Journal, 3*, 1–12. https://doi.org/10.2174/1874944501003010001

Eriksson, M., Ng, N., Weinehall, L., & Emmelin, M. (2011). The importance of gender and conceptualization for understanding the association between collective social capital and health: A multilevel analysis from northern Sweden. *Social Science and Medicine, 73*(2), 264–273. https://doi.org/10.1016/j.socscimed.2011.05.013

Erlinghagen, M. (2007). Self-perceived job insecurity and social context: A multi-level analysis of 17 European countries. *European Sociological Review, 24*(2), 183–197. https://doi.org/10.1093/esr/jcm042

Ferlander, S. (2007). The importance of different forms of social capital for health. *Acta Sociologica, 50*(2), 115–118. https://doi.org/10.1177/0001699307077654

Filippidis, F. T., Gerovasili, V., Millett, C., & Tountas, Y. (2017). Medium-term impact of the economic crisis on mortality, health-related behaviours and access to healthcare in Greece. *Scientific Reports, 7*, 46423. https://doi.org/10.1038/srep46423

Firouzbakht, M., Tirgar, A., Oksanen, T., Kawachi, I., Hajian-Tilaki, K., Nikpour, M., Muodi, S., & Sadeghian, R. (2018). Workplace social capital and mental health: A cross-sectional study among Iranian workers. *BMC Public Health, 18*, 794. https://doi.org/10.1186/s12889-018-5659-3

Fischmann, G., De Witte, H., Sulea, C., Vander Elst, T., De Cuyper, N., & Iliescu, D. (2022). Validation of a short and generic qualitative job insecurity scale (QUAL-JIS). *European Journal of Career Assessment, 38*(5), 397–411. https://doi.org/10.1027/1015-5759/a000674

Forbes, M. K., & Krueger, R. F. (2019). The great recession and mental health in the United States. *Clinical Psychological Science, 7*(5), 900–913. https://doi.org/10.1177/2167702619859337

Framke, E., Sørensen, O. H., Pedersen, J., Clausen, T., Borg, V., & Rugulies, R. (2019). The association of vertical and horizontal workplace social capital with employees' job satisfaction, exhaustion and sleep disturbances: A prospective study. *International Archives of Occupational and Environmental Health, 92*, 883–890. https://doi.org/10.1007/s00420-019-01432-5

Fujita, S., Kawakami, N., Ando, E., Inoue, A., Tsuno, K., Kurioka, S., & Kawachi, I. (2016). The association of workplace social capital with work engagement of employees in health care settings: A multilevel cross-sectional analysis. *Journal of Occupational and Environmental Medicine, 58*(3), 265–271. https://doi.org/10.1097/JOM.0000000000000605

Fukuyama, F. (1997). *Social capital, Tanner lecture on human values*. Oxford University.

Gallie, D., Felstead, A., Green, F., & Inanc, H. (2017). The hidden face of job insecurity. *Work, Employment and Society, 31*(1), 36–53. https://doi.org/10.1177/0950017015624399

Gilboa, S., Shirom, A., Fried, Y., & Cooper, C. (2008). A meta-analysis of work demand stressors and job performance: Examining main and moderating effects. *Personnel Psychology, 61*(2), 227–271. https://doi.org/10.1111/j.1744-6570.2008.00113.x

Giousmpasoglou, C., Marinakou, E., & Paliktzoglou, V. (2016). Economic crisis and higher education in Greece. In P. O. de Pablos & R. D. Tennyson (Eds.), *Impact of economic crisis on education and the next-generation workforce* (pp. 120–148). IGI Global). https://doi.org/10.4018/978-1-4666-9455-2.ch006

Gittell, R., & Vidal, A. (1998). *Community organizing: Building social capital as a development strategy*. Sage.

Greenfield, P. M. (2009). Linking social change and developmental change: Shifting pathways of human development. *Developmental Psychology, 45*(2), 401–418. https://doi.org/10.1037/a0014726

Grootaert, C., & Bastelaer, T. (2002). *Understanding and measuring social capital: A multidisciplinary tool for practitioners, directions in development*. World Bank.

Hakanen, J. J., Bakker, A. B., & Demerouti, E. (2005). How dentists cope with their job demands and stay engaged: The moderating role of job resources. *European Journal of Oral Sciences, 113*(6), 479–487. https://doi.org/10.1111/j.1600-0722.2005.00250.x

Halbesleben, J. R., Neveu, J. P., Paustian-Underdahl, S. C., & Westman, M. (2014). Getting to the "COR": Understanding the role of resources in conservation of resources theory. *Journal of Management, 40*(5), 1334–1364. https://doi.org/10.1177/0149206314527130

Hansen, A. S. K., Madsen, I. E., Thorsen, S. V., Melkevik, O., Bjørner, J. B., Andersen, I., & Rugulies, R. (2018). Does workplace social capital protect against long-term sickness absence? Linking workplace aggregated social capital to sickness absence registry data. *Scandinavian Journal of Public Health, 46*(3), 290–296. https://doi.org/10.1177/1403494817721672

Harpham, T., Grant, E., & Thomas, E. (2002). Measuring social capital within health surveys: Key issues. *Health Policy and Planning, 17*(1), 106–111. https://doi.org/10.1093/heapol/17.1.106

Hartley, J., Jacobson, D., Klandermans, B., & Van Vuuren, T. (1991). *Job insecurity: Coping with jobs at risk.* Sage Publications.

Hellgren, J., Sverke, M., & Isaksson, K. (1999). A two-dimensional approach to job insecurity: Consequences for employee attitudes and well-being. *European Journal of Work and Organizational Psychology, 8*(2), 179–195. https://doi.org/10.1080/135943299398311

Hobfoll, S. E. (1989). Conservation of resources: a new attempt at conceptualizing stress. *American Psychologist, 44*(3), 513–524. https://doi.org/10.1037/0003-066X.44.3.513

Hobfoll, S. E., Halbesleben, J., Neveu, J. P., & Westman, M. (2018). Conservation of resources in the organizational context: The reality of resources and their consequences. *Annual Review of Organizational Psychology and Organizational Behavior, 5*(1), 103–128. https://doi.org/10.1146/annurev-orgpsych-032117-104640

Inoue, A., Kawakami, N., Eguchi, H., & Tsutsumi, A. (2016). Buffering effect of workplace social capital on the association of job insecurity with psychological distress in Japanese employees: A cross-sectional study. *Journal of Occupational Health, 58*(5), 460–469. https://doi.org/10.1539/joh.16-0129-OA

Jiang, L., & Lavaysse, L. M. (2018). Cognitive and affective job insecurity: A meta-analysis and a primary study. *Journal of Management, 44*(6), 2307–2342. https://doi.org/10.1177/0149206318773853

Kafetsios, K. (2017). Temporal variation and co-variation in insecure attachment and self-construal over the last twelve years in Greece. *Oral presentation at the18th General Meeting of the European Association of Social Psychology*, Granada, Spain, 5–8 July.

Kafetsios, K. (2022). Self-construal and insecure attachment variation and co-variation during a period of economic crisis. *Journal of Cross-Cultural Psychology, 53*(2), 239–259. https://doi.org/10.1177/00220221211060458

Kahn, R. L., & Byosiere, P. (1992). Stress in organizations. In M. D. Dunnette & L. M. Hogh (Eds.), *Handbook of industrial and organizational psychology* (Vol. 3, pp. 571–650). Consulting Psychologists Press.

Kawachi, I., Subramanian, S. V., & Kim, D. (2008). Social capital and Health: A decade of progress and beyond. In I. Kawachi, S. V. Subramanian, & D. Kim (Eds.), *Social capital and health* (pp. 1–26). Springer. https://doi.org/10.1007/978-0-387-71311-3_1

Keim, A. C., Landis, R. S., Pierce, C. A., & Earnest, D. R. (2014). Why do employees worry about their jobs? A meta-analytic review of predictors of job insecurity. *Journal of Occupational Health Psychology, 19*(3), 269–290. https://doi.org/10.1037/a0036743

Kim, T. J., & von dem Knesebeck, O. (2015). Is an insecure job better for health than having no job at all? A systematic review of studies investigating the health-related risks of both job insecurity and unemployment. *BMC Public Health, 15*, 985. https://doi.org/10.1186/s12889-015-2313-1

Kinnunen, U., & Nätti, J. (1994). Job insecurity in Finland: Antecedents and consequences. *European Journal of Work and Organizational Psychology, 4*(3), 297–321. https://doi.org/10.1080/13594329408410490

Kokosalakis, N. (2001). Lifelong learning in Greek universities: Policies, practices and prospects. *European Journal of Education, 36*(3), 329–339. https://doi.org/10.1111/1467-3435.00071

Koulouris, A., Moniarou-Papaconstantinou, V., & Kyriaki-Manessi, D. (2014). Austerity measures in Greece and their impact on higher education. *Procedia - Social and Behavioral Sciences, 147*, 518–526. https://doi.org/10.1016/j.sbspro.2014.07.147

Kouvonen, A., Kivimäki, M., Vahtera, J., Oksanen, T., Elovainio, M., Cox, T., Pentti, J., Cox, S., & Wilkinson, R. G. (2007). Psychometric evaluation of a short measure of social capital at work. *BMC Public Health, 7*, 90. https://doi.org/10.1186/1471-2458-6-251

Kowalski, C., Ommen, O., Driller, E., Ernstmann, N., Wirtz, M. A., Köhler, T., & Pfaff, H. (2010). Burnout in nurses–the relationship between social capital in hospitals and emotional exhaustion. *Journal of Clinical Nursing, 19*(11-12), 1654–1663. https://doi.org/10.1111/j.1365-2702.2009.02989.x

Kreuter, M. W., & Lezin, N. (2002). Social capital theory. In R. J. DiClemente, R. A. Crosby, & M. C. Kegler (Eds.), *Emerging theories in health promotion practice and research: Strategies for improving public health* (pp. 228–284). Wiley.

Krishna, A. (2001). Moving from the stock of social capital to the flow of benefits: The role of agency. *World Development, 29*(6), 925–943. https://doi.org/10.1016/S0305-750X(01)00020-1

László, K. D., Pikhart, H., Kopp, M. S., Bobak, M., Pajak, A., Malyutina, S., Salavecz, G., & Marmot, M. (2010). Job insecurity and health: A study of 16 European countries. *Social Science and Medicine, 70*(6), 867–874. https://doi.org/10.1016/j.socscimed.2009.11.022

Le Breton, J. M., & Senter, J. L. (2008). Answers to 20 questions about inter-rater reliability and interrater agreement. *Organizational Research Methods, 11*(4), 815–852. https://doi.org/10.1177/1094428106296642

Lehner, B. L., Kowalski, C., Wirtz, M., Ansmann, L., Driller, E., Ommen, O., Oksanen, T., & Pfaff, H. (2013). Work engagement of hospital physicians: Do social capital and personal traits matter? *Psychotherapie, Psychosomatik, Medizinische Psychologie, 63*(3-4), 122–128. https://doi.org/10.1055/s-0032-1333289

Lim, V. K. (1997). Moderating effects of work-based support on the relationship between job insecurity and its consequences. *Work & Stress, 11*(3), 251–266. https://doi.org/10.1080/02678379708256839

Livanos, I., & Pouliakas, K. (2011). Wage returns to university disciplines in Greece: Are Greek higher education degrees trojan horses? *Education Economics, 19*(4), 411–445. https://doi.org/10.1080/09645290903546363

Loizos, P. (2002). Are refugees social capitalists? In F. John, T. Schuller, & S. Baron (Eds.), *Social capital: Critical perspectives* (pp. 269–296). Oxford University Press.

Markus, H. R., & Kitayama, S. (1991). Culture and the self: Implications for cognition, emotion, and motivation. *Psychological Review, 98*(2), 224–253. https://doi.org/10.1037/0033-295X.98.2.224

Matsaganis, M. (2017). The impact of the great recession on child poverty in Greece. In B. Cantillon, Y. Chzhen, S. Handa, & B. Nolan (Eds.), *Children of austerity. Impact of the great recession on child poverty in rich countries* (pp. 94–117). United Nations Children's Fund & Oxford University.

Mavridis, S. (2018). Greece's economic and social transformation 2008–2017. *Social Sciences, 7*(1), 9. https://doi.org/10.3390/socsci7010009

Meng, A., Clausen, T., & Borg, V. (2018). The association between team-level social capital and individual-level work engagement: Differences between subtypes of social capital and the impact of intra-team agreement. *Scandinavian Journal of Psychology, 59*(2), 198–205. https://doi.org/10.1111/sjop.12435

Mitchell, C. U., & La Gory, M. (2002). Social capital and mental distress in an impoverished community. *City and Community, 1*(2), 195–215. https://doi.org/10.1111/1540-6040.00017

Mouza, A. M. (2017). Continuous unplanned changes and stress in Greek public sector due to economic crisis. *International Journal of Humanities and Social Science, 7*(9), 70–78.

Mouza, A. M., & Souchamvali, D. (2016). Effect of Greece's new reforms and unplanned organizational changes on the stress levels of primary school teachers. *Social Indicators Research, 128*, 981–994. https://doi.org/10.1007/s11205-015-1065-8

Nella, D., Panagopoulou, E., Galanis, N., Montgomery, A., & Benos, A. (2015). Consequences of job insecurity on the psychological and physical health of Greek civil servants. *BioMed Research International, 2015,* Article ID 673623. https://doi.org/10.1155/2015/673623.

Norström, F., Virtanen, P., Hammarström, A., Gustafsson, P. E., & Janlert, U. (2014). How does unemployment affect self-assessed health? A systematic review focusing on subgroup effects. *BMC Public Health, 14,* 1310. https://doi.org/10.1186/1471-2458-14-1310

OECD. (2018). *OECD jobs strategy. How does Greece compare.* https://www.oecd.org/greece/jobs-strategy-GREECE-EN.pdf

Oksanen, T., Suzuki, E., Takao, S., Vahtera, J., & Kivimäki, M. (2013). Workplace social capital and health. In I. Kawachi, S. Takao, & S. Subramanian (Eds.), *Global perspectives on social capital and health* (pp. 23–63). Springer. https://doi.org/10.1007/978-1-4614-7464-7_2

Ommen, O., Driller, E., Köhler, T., Kowalski, C., Ernstmann, N., Neumann, M., & Pfaff, H. (2009). The relationship between social capital in hospitals and physician job satisfaction. *BMC Health Services Research, 9,* 81. https://doi.org/10.1186/1472-6963-9-81

Ooi, N., Laing, J., & Mair, J. (2015). Social capital as a heuristic device to explore sociocultural sustainability: A case study of mountain resort tourism in the community of Steamboat Springs, Colorado, USA. *Journal of Sustainable Tourism, 23*(3), 417–436. https://doi.org/10.1080/09669582.2014.957211

Park, H., Twenge, J. M., & Greenfield, P. M. (2014). The Great Recession: Implications for adolescent values and behavior. *Social Psychological and Personality Science, 5*(3), 310–318. https://doi.org/10.1177/1948550613495419

Paul, K. I., & Moser, K. (2009). Unemployment impairs mental health: Meta-analyses. *Journal of Vocational Behavior, 74*(3), 264–282. https://doi.org/10.1016/j.jvb.2009.01.001

Pejtersen, J. H., Kristensen, T. S., Borg, V., & Bjorner, J. B. (2010). The second version of the Copenhagen Psychosocial Questionnaire. *Scandinavian Journal of Public Health, 38*(3), 8–24. https://doi.org/10.1177/1403494809349858

Petrou, P., Demerouti, E., & Xanthopoulou, D. (2017). Regular versus cutback-related change: The role of employee job crafting in organizational change contexts of different nature. *International Journal of Stress Management, 24*(1), 62–85. https://doi.org/10.1037/str0000033

Portes, A. (1998). Social capital: Its origins and applications in modern sociology. *Annual Review of Sociology, 24,* 1–24. https://doi.org/10.1146/annurev.soc.24.1.1

Preacher, K. J., Curran, P. J., & Bauer, D. J. (2006). Computational tools for probing interactions in multiple linear regression, multilevel modeling, and latent curve analysis. *Journal of Educational and Behavioral Statistics, 31*(4), 437–448. https://doi.org/10.3102/10769986031004437

Probst, T. M., Stewart, S. M., Gruys, M. L., & Tierney, B. W. (2007). Productivity, counterproductivity and creativity: The ups and downs of job insecurity. *Journal of Occupational and Organizational Psychology, 80*(3), 479–497. https://doi.org/10.1348/096317906X159103

Probst, T. M., Petitta, L., Barbaranelli, C., & Austin, C. (2020). Safety-related moral disengagement in response to job insecurity: Counterintuitive effects of perceived organizational and supervisor support. *Journal of Business Ethics, 162,* 343–358. https://doi.org/10.1007/s10551-018-4002-3

Putnam, R. D. (1995). Bowling alone: America's declining social capital. *Journal of Democracy, 6,* 65–78.

Putnam, R. D. (2001). *Bowling alone: The collapse and revival of American community.* Simon and Schuster. https://doi.org/10.1145/358916.361990

Riketta, M. (2005). Organizational identification: A meta-analysis. *Journal of Vocational Behavior, 66*(2), 358–384. https://doi.org/10.1016/j.jvb.2004.05.005

Rocco, L., & Suhrcke, M. (2012). *Is social capital good for health? A European perspective.* WHO Regional Office for Europe.

Rothmann, S., & Jordaan, G. M. E. (2006). Job demands, job resources and work engagement of academic staff in South African higher education institutions. *SA Journal of Industrial Psychology, 32*(4), 87–96. https://hdl.handle.net/10520/EJC89106

Salanova, M., Agut, S., & Peiró, J. M. (2005). Linking organizational resources and work engagement to employee performance and customer loyalty: The mediation of service climate. *Journal of Applied Psychology, 90*(6), 1217–1227. https://doi.org/10.1037/0021-9010.90.6.1217

Salehi, A., Ehrlich, C., Kendall, E., & Sav, A. (2018). Bonding and bridging social capital in the recovery of severe mental illness: A synthesis of qualitative research. *Journal of Mental Health, 28*(3), 331–339. https://doi.org/10.1080/09638237.2018.1466033

Sapp, A. L., Kawachi, I., Sorensen, G., LaMontagne, A. D., & Subramanian, S. V. (2010). Does workplace social capital buffer the effects of job stress? A cross-sectional, multilevel analysis of cigarette smoking among US manufacturing workers. *Journal of Occupational and Environmental Medicine, 52*(7), 740–750. https://doi.org/10.1097/JOM.0b013e3181e80842

Sappleton, N., & Lourenço, F. (2016). Email subject lines and response rates to invitations to participate in a web survey and a face-to-face interview: The sound of silence. *International Journal of Social Research Methodology, 19*(5), 611–622. https://doi.org/10.1080/13645579.2015.1078596

Schaufeli, W. B., Salanova, M., González-Romá, V., & Bakker, A. B. (2002). The measurement of engagement and burnout: A two sample confirmatory factor analytic approach. *Journal of Happiness Studies, 3*, 71–92. https://doi.org/10.1023/A:1015630930326

Schaufeli, W. B., Shimazu, A., Hakanen, J., Salanova, M., & De Witte, H. (2017). An ultra-short measure for work engagement: The UWES-3 validation across five countries. *European Journal of Psychological Assessment, 35*(4), 577–591. https://doi.org/10.1027/1015-5759/a000430

Schreurs, B. H., Hetty van Emmerik, I. J., Günter, H., & Germeys, F. (2012). A weekly diary study on the buffering role of social support in the relationship between job insecurity and employee performance. *Human Resource Management, 51*(2), 259–279. https://doi.org/10.1002/hrm.21465

Smet, K., Vander Elst, T., Griep, Y., & De Witte, H. (2016). The explanatory role of rumours in the reciprocal relationship between organizational change communication and job insecurity: a within-person approach. *European Journal of Work and Organizational Psychology, 25*(5), 631–644. https://doi.org/10.1080/1359432X.2016.1143815

Sparrowe, R. T., Liden, R. C., Wayne, S. J., & Kraimer, M. L. (2001). Social networks and the performance of individuals and groups. *Academy of Management Journal, 44*(2), 316–325. https://doi.org/10.5465/3069458

Sverke, M., Låstad, L., Hellgren, J., Richter, A., & Näswall, K. (2019). A meta-analysis of job insecurity and employee performance: Testing temporal aspects, rating source, welfare regime, and union density as moderators. *International Journal of Environmental Research and Public Health, 16*(14), 2536. https://doi.org/10.3390/ijerph16142536

Tadić, M., Bakker, A. B., & Oerlemans, W. G. (2015). Challenge versus hindrance job demands and well-being: A diary study on the moderating role of job resources. *Journal of Occupational and Organizational Psychology, 88*(4), 702–725. https://doi.org/10.1111/joop.12094

Takahashi, L. M., & Magalong, M. G. (2008). Disruptive social capital: (Un)Healthy socio-spatial interactions among Filipino men living with HIV/AIDS. *Health and Place, 14*(2), 182–197. https://doi.org/10.1016/j.healthplace.2007.06.002

Török, E., Clark, A. J., Jensen, J. H., Lange, T., Bonde, J. P., Bjorner, J. B., Rugulies, R., Hvidtfeldt, U. A., Hansen, Å. M., Ersbøll, A. K., & Rod, N. H. (2018). Work-unit social capital and long-term sickness absence: a prospective cohort study of 32 053 hospital employees. *Occupational and Environmental Medicine, 75*(9), 623–629. https://doi.org/10.1136/oemed-2017-104954

Tsounis, A., Xanthopoulou, D., Demerouti, E., Kafetsios, K., & Tsaousis, I. (2023). Workplace social capital: Redefining and measuring the construct. *Social Indicators Research, 165*(2), 555–583. https://doi.org/10.1007/s11205-022-03028-y

Tsuboya, T., Tsutsumi, A., & Kawachi, I. (2015). Change in psychological distress following change in workplace social capital: Results from the panel surveys of the J-HOPE study. *Occupational and Environmental Medicine, 72*(3), 188–194. https://doi.org/10.1136/oemed-2014-102427

Uphoff, N., & Wijayaratna, C. M. (2000). Demonstrated benefits from social capital: The productivity of farmer organizations in Gal Oya, Sri Lanka. *World Development, 28*(11), 1875–1890. https://doi.org/10.1016/S0305-750X(00)00063-2
Van Bogaert, P., van Heusden, D., Timmermans, O., & Franck, E. (2014). Nurse work engagement impacts job outcome and nurse-assessed quality of care: Model testing with nurse practice environment and nurse work characteristics as predictors. *Frontiers in Psychology, 5*, 1261. https://doi.org/10.3389/fpsyg.2014.01261
Van Dyne, L., & LePine, J. A. (1998). Helping and voice extra-role behaviors: Evidence of construct and predictive validity. *Academy of Management Journal, 41*(1), 108–109. https://doi.org/10.5465/256902
Vander Elst, T., Van den Broeck, A., De Witte, H., & De Cuyper, N. (2012). The mediating role of frustration of psychological needs in the relationship between job insecurity and work-related well-being. *Work & Stress, 26*(3), 252–271. https://doi.org/10.1080/02678373.2012.703900
Vander Elst, T., De Witte, H., & De Cuyper, M. (2014). The Job Insecurity Scale: A psychometric evaluation across five European countries. *European Journal of Work and Organizational Psychology, 23*(3), 364–380. https://doi.org/10.1080/1359432X.2012.745989
Williams, L. J., & Anderson, S. E. (1991). Job satisfaction and organizational commitment as predictors of organizational citizenship and in-role behaviors. *Journal of Management, 17*(3), 601–617. https://doi.org/10.1177/014920639101700305
Xiao, Y., Becerik-Gerber, B., Lucas, G., & Roll, S. C. (2021). Impacts of working from home during COVID-19 pandemic on physical and mental well-being of office workstation users. *Journal of Occupational and Environmental Medicine, 63*(3), 181–190. https://doi.org/10.1097/JOM.0000000000002097
Yamagishi, T., & Hashimoto, H. (2016). Social niche construction. *Current Opinion in Psychology, 8*, 119–124. https://doi.org/10.1016/j.copsyc.2015.10.003
Zmas, A. (2015). Financial crisis and higher education policies in Greece: Between intra-and supranational pressures. *Higher Education, 69*, 495–508.

Andreas Tsounis is employed as a psychologist at the Centers for the Prevention of Addictions and Promoting Psychosocial Health of Municipality of Thessaloniki, Greece, since 2007. He has also been employed as an Adjunct Lecturer at the Department of Psychology of University of Western Macedonia, Greece, and at the Department of Educational and Social Policy of University of Macedonia, Greece. He obtained his PhD in Organizational Psychology from School of Psychology, Aristotle University of Thessaloniki, Greece. He is an author of numerous articles in the field of Health and Organizational Psychology, and his research has been published in peer-reviewed journals such as Social Indicators Research, BMC Psychology, Health Psychology Research and Substance Abuse Treatment, Prevention and Policy.

Despoina Xanthopoulou is Full Professor in Organizational Psychology at the School of Psychology, Aristotle University of Thessaloniki, Greece. Her research interests include job (re)design and job crafting, (job and personal) resources, employee well-being and job performance, and recovery for job demands. Also, she specializes in advanced research methodologies (i.e., quantitative diary studies) and statistical analyses. Her research has been published in peer-reviewed journals such as Journal of Applied Psychology, Human Relations, and Journal of Organizational Behavior. She is Associate Editor of European Journal of Work & Organizational Psychology and she serves at the editorial boards of Journal of Occupational Health Psychology, Journal of Personnel Psychology, Occupational Health Science and Stress & Health. Since 2022, she serves as Education Forum Chair of the Executive Committee of the European Academy of Occupational Health Psychology.

Konstantinos Kafetsios is an Associate Professor in Social Psychology at the School of Psychology, Aristotle University of Thessaloniki. Also a Visiting Professor at the Psychology Department, Palacký University, Czech Republic. He has previously held research and teaching positions at the University of Crete, Anglia Ruskin University and University of Cambridge. His research interests revolve around examining emotion in interpersonal and social interaction, in hierarchical relationships at work, and in social relationships across cultures. This research has been published in peer-refereed articles such as Social Psychological and Personality Science, Emotion, Personality and Social Psychology Bulletin, The Leadership Quarterly and Journal of Nonverbal Behavior. He serves as an Associate Editor for Journal of Experimental Social Psychology and European Journal of Social Psychology and a consulting editor for Journal of Personality and Social Psychology and Hellenic Journal of Psychology.

Evangelia Demerouti is a Full Professor in Work and Organizational Psychology at Eindhoven University of Technology. Since 2015, she has been a Distinguished Visiting Professor at the University of Johannesburg, South Africa, and since 2017, she has been Chief Diversity Officer at Eindhoven University of Technology. Her research focuses on the processes enabling performance, including the effects of work characteristics, individual job strategies (including job crafting and decision-making), occupational well-being, and work-life balance. She has developed the Job Demands-Resources model, and her recent work concerns the development and implementation of bottom-up job redesign interventions (i.e., job crafting) to improve employee well-being and functioning. She has published over 250 national and international papers and book chapters on these topics. Her work has been published in high impact journals such as Journal of Applied Psychology, Journal of Management, Journal of Organizational Behavior and Journal of Occupational Health Psychology. She is often invited as keynote speaker in European and international congresses, and the European Academy of Occupational Health Psychology awarded her a lifetime fellowship. Currently she is associate editor of Journal of Occupational Health Psychology and the president of the European Association of Work and Organizational Psychology.

Chapter 12
Epilogue

Hans De Witte, Lara Christina Roll, Wilma Coetzee, and Sebastiaan Rothmann

12.1 Introduction

The idea for this edited volume emerged in 2017 during a visit to the Optentia Research Unit at North-West University, South Africa. At the time, Lara Roll was a postdoctoral fellow at Optentia, working under the guidance of Ian Rothmann, while Hans De Witte was visiting to explore potential collaborations. During this meeting, the idea to study a timely and increasingly relevant topic—job insecurity in academia—was conceived. Initially, the plan was to gather data from our own countries, but this quickly expanded into a larger project, inviting colleagues from other countries to join our research consortium. This collaboration eventually brought together scholars from 10 countries, who have since met at various conferences to further refine their ideas and present papers. A comprehensive questionnaire was developed, translated into multiple languages, and data collection took place in 2018 (see Chap. 1).

H. De Witte (✉) · L. C. Roll
Research Group Work, Organizational and Personnel Psychology (O2L-WOPP), FPPW, KU Leuven, Leuven, Belgium

Optentia Research Unit, North-West University, Vanderbijlpark, South Africa
e-mail: hans.dewitte@kuleuven.be

W. Coetzee
Optentia Research Unit, North-West University, Vanderbijlpark, South Africa

Unit for Data Science and Computing, North-West University, Vanderbijlpark, South Africa
e-mail: Wilma.Coetzee@nwu.ac.za

S. Rothmann
Optentia Research Unit, North-West University, Vanderbijlpark, South Africa
e-mail: ian@ianrothmann.com

L. C. Roll et al. (eds.), *Global Perspectives on Job Insecurity in Higher Education*, Aligning Perspectives on Health, Safety and Well-Being,
https://doi.org/10.1007/978-3-031-85772-0_12

This book contains the results of the activities of this research consortium. It contains 11 chapters, written by 26 authors from 10 countries—spanning four of the six continents of the globe. All separate country-specific datasets were combined into a global dataset, and every scholar was invited to develop a chapter based on that joint dataset and their research interest. Thereby, our homogeneous starting point (a joint dataset) lead to a diversity of views and analyses, in which each author team focussed on a specific topic and research question. In this epilogue, we aim to integrate and discuss some of the key findings from the various chapters, with a focus on the overarching results across countries. Country-specific results and differences will only be mentioned occasionally, as the convenience samples collected in each country do not support a thorough or reliable comparison. Throughout the chapters, the country-specific data were primarily used to assess the robustness and generalisability of our findings. Therefore, this epilogue will concentrate on the overall patterns or common threads observed in most countries.

The content of this book can be divided into four parts. The first part (three chapters) 'sets the scene' for the remaining chapters. The first chapter gives an overview of the context of academia in the various countries, and presents the research consortium, the analytic framework of the study, and details the questionnaire, data collection and samples. The next two chapters present the results of thorough analyses of the measurement invariance of the job insecurity measures (Chap. 2) and nine scales to measure the predictors, moderators, mediators and outcomes of this research (Chap. 3). Such a methodological test of construct equivalence is crucial in cross-national studies, even though this issue is often ignored. As such, these chapters lay the much-needed foundation for the various comparisons that follow in the next chapters of this book. The second part of the book contains six chapters (Chaps. 4 until 9) in which the total dataset of all (or most) countries is used to examine a specific research question. The topics analysed are tailored to the academic sector. The findings, however, can probably also be generalised outside academia, as most of the chapters focus on a rather universal research question (like mediation or moderation of relationships) in the job insecurity domain. The third part contains only two chapters (Chaps. 10 and 11) with country-specific results. These are case studies in which a specific topic is explored, sometimes with variables specifically added to the questionnaire in this country only (like in Chap. 11). The last part of the book refers to this epilogue, in which the findings are integrated and discussed.

This epilogue is structured as follows. First, we focus on the *independent variables* of this book: what can we conclude regarding the measurement and conceptualisation of insecurity, country differences and associations with outcomes. Second, we focus on the *outcomes*: well-being versus performance. What are the consequences of insecurity in the academic sector for health, well-being and work-related behaviours? The latter includes a discussion of whether insecurity motivates academics to work harder and better or whether insecurity hinders them from performing well. The third section integrates the findings regarding the *explanations* of the job insecurity-outcomes relationship in academia, whereas the fourth section focusses on the various tests of *moderators* of that relationship. These sections allow testing new forms of mediation and moderation. This increases our scientific knowledge in this field and helps determining boundary conditions for the consequences of job insecurity, in and probably also outside academia. Both are important for policy and practice in this field, as it helps develop evidence-based interventions to tackle the issue of insecurity. One of the specificities of research in academia is that there are (at least) three large professional categories: professors (academic staff), PhD students and post-doctoral fellows, and administrative (support) staff. The latter is probably more similar to white-collar workers in other sectors, whereas professors and PhD students are rather specific for the academic sector. Therefore, we summarise the eventual differences in results between these three broad *professional categories* in the fifth section. In discussing the research findings in this epilogue, we will systematically compare the framework reported in Chap. 1 with the topics analysed in all chapters. This discussion will include an integration of limitations and suggestions for future research in each section. One interesting topic not highlighted in this book thus far will be discussed in the sixth section: the *causal attributions* of job insecurity by our respondents. We will present descriptives on the main causes for job insecurity in academia as perceived by our respondents, and will present some country differences and differences in causal attributions according to their professional category. The seventh section will discuss the impact of *technology* and *artificial intelligence*. It seemed relevant to include a reflection of these topics in this epilogue, as they did not receive a lot of research attention in this book thus far. The reason partly relates to the pre-covid years in which the dataset was gathered. Since 2020, ICT applications have been booming and have been affecting the academic sector to an even larger extent than before. Some additional reflection on these topics thus seemed appropriate. We conclude the epilogue by integrating *policy and practice suggestions* developed in the various chapters. As such, we also hope to contribute to reducing and mitigating job insecurity and its consequences in academia.

We will refer to the various chapters by their number only rather than their authors. This way, we hope to simplify the discussion and reduce repetition. Obviously, this is not meant to be disrespectful or to lack appreciation for the work of the various authors. The editorial team is highly indebted to their hard work and dedication—without their efforts (and patience …), this book would never have been possible.

12.2 Insecurity Comes in Many Forms: Temporary Employment and Quantitative Versus Qualitative Job Insecurity

In the introductory Chap. 1 and in many of the other chapters in this book, a picture has been painted of large-scale changes in academia. Due to various phenomena such as restructuring, educational reforms, and reductions in budgets, insecurity has become part of academic existence. As a consequence, insecurity in its various forms became the core variable on which all chapters in this book focussed their analyses.

The first topic to discuss then, is the content of the insecurity concept. Two views are prevailing in science: the objective operationalisation versus the subjective one. Sociologists often favour the *objective* operationalisation of insecurity: a temporary (or fixed-term) employment contract. Psychologists more often highlight the *subjective* experience of insecurity, as exemplified in the perception of job insecurity. The objective employment contract was only analysed once (Chap. 9), and was used as control variable in some other chapters.

Two dimensions have been advanced in this book when focussing on the subjective operationalisation of insecurity. *Quantitative* job insecurity is related to the uncertainty that one can keep the actual job or will be dismissed, whereas qualitative job insecurity refers to uncertainty about retaining valued job features (Hellgren et al., 1999). Quantitative job insecurity involves an 'all or nothing' evaluation; qualitative job insecurity is not related to keeping (or losing) the actual job, but to the continuation of its quality in the future. The addition of both operationalisations to our research design offers several interesting scientific opportunities. One can first of all explore the *dimensionality* of the job insecurity construct in more depth. Some authors have advanced the view that especially the distinction between cognitive versus affective job insecurity is important (Borg, 1992; Jiang & Lavaysse, 2018; Probst, 2003). The cognitive dimension refers to the perceived probability that the job might be lost, whereas the affective dimension relates to the worries related to that perception. Others have been advancing the distinction between quantitative versus qualitative job insecurity, as used in this book (Chirumbolo et al., 2017; Greenhalgh & Rosenblatt, 1984; Hellgren et al., 1999). In this study, the authors measured quantitative versus qualitative job insecurity with several items and made sure that cognitive as well as affective items were used for both operationalisations. Additionally, specific care was given to the order of the items when answering the questionnaire: first, the cognitive items were presented together (regardless of whether they referred to quantitative or qualitative job insecurity), followed by the affective items of both dimensions. In other words, they were presented is such a way that the cognitive versus affective dimensionality became more eye-catching than the quantitative versus qualitative dimensionality. The results in Chap. 2 nevertheless show that only the quantitative versus qualitative dimensionality was found in the dataset (and in the separate countries). These findings thus show the distinction between quantitative versus quantitative job insecurity to be more prominent in the perception of the respondents than the distinction between cognitive versus affective insecurity. These results align with findings in other studies, like those of Chirumbolo et al. (2020), and are seemingly not confined to the academic sector. The authors of Chap. 2 additionally conclude that both measures of job insecurity can be successfully used by researchers in a wide range of countries, and state that the results of their studies can also (to some extent) be compared. To spur future research, they also report a nuanced overview of items to be used in cross-country comparisons in the future.

Chapter 2 thus added to the scientific debate about the dimensionality of the job insecurity construct. The thorough analysis in that chapter also enabled the cross-national use of both job insecurity measures in the remaining chapters of this book.

An interesting descriptive illustration was the figure in Chap. 2, in which all countries were plotted on both dimensions of job insecurity. Strikingly, Greece appeared as the country in which high scores on qualitative job insecurity were combined with low scores on the quantitative dimension. While further research is needed to fully understand the reasons behind this, several possible explanations can be drawn from the earlier discussion in Chap. 1. For example, Greece's prolonged economic crisis led to austerity measures and significant budget cuts across the public sector, including universities (Kottaridi & Tsakloglou, 2020; Ladi, 2014). This reduction in funding for higher education institutions may have negatively impacted qualitative job security for academic staff. Additionally, Greece's efforts to align its higher education system with European standards—part of the broader process of Europeanization—have often resulted in increased workloads for the remaining staff, further contributing to qualitative job insecurity (Featherstone, 2016; Papadimitriou, 2015). At the same time, those already in their positions appear less concerned about losing their jobs, reflecting lower levels of quantitative job insecurity.

South Africa and Switzerland showed the opposite pattern, with lower scores on qualitative job insecurity and higher scores on its quantitative variant. While this research does not provide a definitive interpretation, Chap. 1 suggests that the underlying reasons may vary significantly between the two countries. In South Africa, for instance, the recent memory at the time of data collection of the "Fees Must Fall" movement may have led individuals to question the future of higher education and, consequently, their job security (Svongoro, 2023). In Switzerland, by contrast, economic shifts, technological advancements, and evolving business models may have increasingly challenged the traditional psychological contract, potentially leading to higher levels of perceived quantitative job insecurity (Chan et al., 2020; OECD, 2023).

The UK demonstrated high scores on both qualitative and quantitative job insecurity, which may reflect the ongoing strikes in the higher education sector at the time (University and College Union, 2022). In contrast, Romania scored the lowest on both dimensions, possibly due to the relative job stability once an individual is appointed. However, caution is necessary, as the research design does not permit strict comparisons. The sampling procedures across countries are not identical, and none of the samples are representative of the respective countries. Therefore, comparisons should be approached with care.

The various chapters in this book also offer interesting information regarding the *nomological network* of both kinds of job insecurity. In seven chapters, both dimensions of job insecurity were analysed together. This allows us to determine their relative importance for specific outcomes ('consequences' of job insecurity). Note that 'antecedents' of both job insecurity dimensions have not been analysed in the various chapters, a gap to be filled in future research. When comparing the results in the seven chapters that analysed both dimensions, a striking picture emerges. When looking at indicators of *well-being*, *qualitative* job insecurity appeared more important as predictor than quantitative job insecurity. The results in Chap. 8, for instance, show that qualitative job insecurity correlates stronger with job satisfaction, burnout and work engagement than its quantitative counterpart. Also, the profiles of the combinations of burnout and work engagement in Chap. 4 correlated more strongly with the qualitative dimension. Interestingly, this pattern was even reflected in associations with the mediators as introduced in the overall research model in Chap. 1. Qualitative job insecurity (in contrast to quantitative job insecurity) correlated more strongly with variables such as identification with the job and with the working population (Chap. 6), overall justice (Chap. 7) and workplace social capital (Chap. 11). However, when looking at *performance*, the opposite picture emerged. Here, *quantitative* job insecurity showed to be the most important predictor compared to qualitative job insecurity, as shown in Chap. 5 (in-role behaviour and counterproductive behaviour) and Chap. 9 (all indicators of performance, including innovative work behaviour).

This differentiated finding is rather surprising. In their seminal article, Greenhalgh and Rosenblatt (1984) originally expected quantitative job insecurity to have stronger consequences for workers than its qualitative counterpart, as quantitative insecurity is more encompassing than qualitative insecurity, and includes the latter: losing the whole job also means losing valued job characteristics. This resulted in the hypothesis that quantitative job insecurity would be more strongly associated with all kinds of outcomes. Empirical studies, however, often failed to find clear differences in outcomes (e.g. De Witte et al., 2010) or found that qualitative job insecurity was more strongly associated with well-being and organisational attitudes than quantitative job insecurity (Chirumbolo et al., 2020). The longitudinal study of Nawrocka et al. (2021) extended this to a larger set of outcomes and found qualitative job insecurity to be the only predictor of well-being and performance indicators over time. The finding of differentiated outcomes, with quantitative insecurity more important for performance and qualitative insecurity for well-being, thus seems to diverge from the current state of knowledge. Is this typical for the academic sector? Are the high-performance demands in academia the cause of the prominence of quantitative job insecurity over its qualitative variant when dealing with performance[1]? Future research in which several sectors are systematically compared will need to answer this research question.

We can conclude that including both quantitative *and* qualitative job insecurity in future research is important, as both cover a different facet of the broader job insecurity concept, and seem to have partly different outcomes. Only by adding both dimensions to the research design can one analyse the global experience of insecurity (in academia and elsewhere). Adding the employment contract to (subjective) job insecurity is preferable too, as this objective operationalisation of insecurity was only analysed once in this book. The lack of interest in the employment contract is probably due to the disciplinary background of most authors (psychology). It is, however, also one-sided. Psychologists can learn a lot by adding objective variables like the employment contract to their research designs, as shown

[1]Note that the association of quantitative job insecurity with performance is a *negative* one, as will be discussed later on in this epilogue.

by the results of the international Psycones study (Guest et al., 2010). Additionally, the increase in temporary contracts in academia highlights its importance when analysing insecurity in this sector. Combining objective and subjective operationalisations in a research design also enables analysing their combination and interaction. Klandermans and van Vuuren (1999) suggested that it is especially the subjective 'translation' of objective insecurity that matters for outcomes (see also Klandermans et al., 2010). Stated otherwise: a temporary contract only resulted in negative consequences when the respondents *perceived* their job to be insecure. This view is to some extent reverberated in the results of Chap. 9, showing that the employment contract was less important in the prediction of various performance outcomes once indicators of subjective job insecurity are controlled for. The addition of the employment contract to job insecurity in analysing associations with outcomes in the other chapters of this book could have helped checking whether this finding can be generalised. Note that insecurity in its various forms is just one of the possible indicators of precarity (in academia and elsewhere). As noted in Chap. 6 and in Fig. 1.1 of Chap. 1, these indicators could be complemented by others like financial strain or underemployment to cover the full experience of precarity in academia in future research.

To conclude this section on insecurity, it is interesting to notice that two chapters only focussed on qualitative job insecurity, whereas not a single chapter solely analysed quantitative job insecurity. This reflects the wish of our authors to focus on novel aspects rather than on aspects that received most research attention in the past. While substantial research exists on quantitative job insecurity, our understanding of qualitative job insecurity has only recently begun to grow. The case for a focus on qualitative job insecurity was well motivated in Chap. 10. These authors analyse data from China, and justify their choice for qualitative job insecurity by referring to the rapid development and intense educational reforms in the academic sector in China. They hence clearly link this insecurity dimension to structural changes in academia in their country, motivating its importance specifically for academics. One can, however, wonder whether limiting the analysis to just one insecurity dimension is the best choice to make. The various reforms in China, for instance, also have implications for quantitative job insecurity, and the inclusion of both in the analysis would allow to perform a competitive test of their relative importance in determining outcomes. This could also be relevant for the analysis in Chap. 7, where the association of qualitative job insecurity with burnout and performance indicators was analysed. Given the interesting results in that chapter, one wonders what the results would have been if both job insecurity dimensions had been included in the analysis. As discussed above, the quantitative insecurity dimension appears more relevant for performance than its qualitative variant. So, testing the theoretical framework of Chap. 7 by adding the quantitative dimension seems recommendable in future research.

12.3 On the Outcomes: Well-Being Versus Performance

The chapters in this edited volume examine various aspects of well-being and performance. Given the interest of the individual authors, not all variables highlighted in our conceptual model (see Fig. 1.1 in Chap. 1) have been covered to the same extent. Most of the chapters concentrate on *well-being* in academia, with a particular emphasis on burnout (discussed three times) and work engagement (addressed four times). Additionally, job satisfaction is explored twice, while psychological well-being and general physical health are each covered once. The general conclusion regarding the impact of job insecurity was rather similar, regardless the operationalisation of well-being: job insecurity is associated with lower levels of work engagement, job satisfaction, psychological well-being and general health, and with higher levels of burnout complaints. In other words, the results of the various chapters firmly confirm that job insecurity is bad for health and well-being, *also* in academia. These findings align with the findings from literature reviews and meta-analyses in this domain (e.g. Cheng & Chan, 2008; De Witte et al., 2015, 2016; Jiang & Lavaysse, 2018; Klug et al., 2024; Probst et al., 2018; Sverke & Hellgren, 2002; Sverke et al., 2002; Vander Elst & De Witte, 2024), suggesting that workers in academia 'are just ordinary workers', who comply with what is found outside academia. The associations with unwell-being were rather robust, as differences between countries were rather limited. This also complies with findings from international comparative studies (see e.g. Klug et al., 2024). Above, we already indicated that qualitative job insecurity shows somewhat stronger associations with well-being than quantitative job insecurity. This also aligns with the recent literature in the field (e.g. Chirumbolo et al., 2020; Nawrocka et al., 2021). Note, however, that quantitative job insecurity was also associated with unwell-being, after controlling for qualitative job insecurity. In other words, *both* are associated with reduced health and well-being in academia, suggesting that both merit policy attention from academic management and governments.

In discussing well-being in academia, media and scientists have the tendency to highlight the negative side. Studies typically show that academics experience lower levels of well-being than other professional categories, and that their jobs are often characterized by high demands and inadequate resources (Kinman, 2001; Kinman et al., 2006; Tytherleigh et al., 2005; Winefield et al., 2003). The picture arising from such studies is, however, one-sided. This is well illustrated by the results of Chap. 4, in which burnout and work engagement were combined in profiles. It was striking to observe that the positive side strongly outnumbered the negative side. About 70% of the respondents in the total dataset could be classified as 'engaged', with high scores on work engagement and low scores on burnout. Less than 8% of the respondents belonged to the opposite profile (the 'exhausted'), with high scores for burnout and low scores for work engagement. This clearly indicates that workers in academia are far more engaged than burned out, a finding that is once again also typical for the entire working population (see Chap. 4).

In addition to well-being, several chapters also address *performance*. Specifically, in-role performance is discussed five times, while innovative work behaviour appears only twice, and extra-role behaviour or organizational citizenship behaviour is examined only once. Counterproductive work behaviour is covered twice. Most chapters focus on only one or two aspects of performance; however, Chap. 9 is unique in that it analyses all four operationalisations. While in-role behaviours represent the most exemplary productive behaviours at work, limiting the analysis to these behaviours constrains our understanding of the insecurity-performance relationship. Future research in academia should complement this focus by exploring a broader range of performance aspects.

The association of job insecurity with well-being does not evoke much controversy in the research literature. The finding of a negative association is a robust one (see also Klug et al., 2024). Its association with performance indicators created somewhat more discussion. A minority stream in the job insecurity literature maintains that job insecurity could motivate workers to perform (Shoss, 2017). In contrast, most studies point towards a negative association between job insecurity and productive behaviours, as underpinned by several reviews and meta-analyses (e.g. Cheng & Chan, 2008; De Cuyper & De Witte, 2021; De Witte, 2024; De Witte & Van Hootegem, 2021; Jiang & Lavaysse, 2018; Klug et al., 2024; Probst et al., 2018; Sverke et al., 2019; Vander Elst & De Witte, 2024). Academia is an interesting context to examine these contrasting views due to the high-performance demands and the requirements to 'publish or perish'. The dominant finding emerging from the various tests in this book clearly points towards a *hindrance* effect of insecurity among academics: job insecurity is associated with less productive work behaviour and with more counterproductive work behaviour (see for instance Chap. 9). This association was quite robust when looking at the association of *quantitative* job insecurity with *in-role behaviour*. The findings were less convincing regarding other operationalisations of performance (like innovative work behaviour or counterproductive work behaviour), as also non-significant associations were reported. No associations of (subjective) job insecurity and extra-role behaviour were observed, probably due to the limited operationalisation of this concept as person-related rather than organisation-related organisational citizenship behaviour. The conclusion that those in academia who fear losing their job perform worse is an important one, and its relevance cannot be underestimated. It means that quantitative job insecurity is not conductive to the development of scientific knowledge, but rather jeopardises its creation and dissemination. The fear to lose one's job is a threat to science.

As stated before, qualitative job insecurity was much less important in determining performance than quantitative job insecurity. This dimension was mostly analysed in relationship to in-role behaviour (five chapters: Chaps. 5, 7, 8, 9 and 11). In four of the five chapters, a non-significant association with in-role work behaviour was reported. This finding aligns with the non-significant original (zero-order) correlation between both variables in the total dataset. Only in Chap. 5, a small positive association between qualitative job insecurity and in-role performance was reported. However, this relationship was not robust, as it was only replicated in two out of ten countries and in one out of three occupational categories. The relationship was not replicated in the other chapters neither. These chapters sometimes added additional control variables to the analysis, like the employment contract (Chap. 9). The finding in Chap. 5 thus seems to point to a spurious association, probably due to statistical suppression. Given the lack of robustness of the association between qualitative job insecurity and in-role behaviour and methodological reasons for the small positive relationship as a statistical artefact, it seems premature to conclude that support was found for the job preservation motivation view of Shoss (2017) when analysing qualitative job insecurity. The associations of quantitative job insecurity with performance found in the various chapters of this book also dominantly refute this view.

12.4 How to Link Insecurity to Outcomes: Explaining the Association

Taking stock of possible associations between insecurity and outcomes is a first and necessary step in scientific research. Psychologists, however, generally want to go one step further, by also explaining these associations. This leads to testing mediational models, preferably in longitudinal designs. The data of this book, however, were only cross-sectional. This obviously limits a thorough (and convincing) examination of explanatory relationships. Four chapters nevertheless explored some explanatory relationships in an attempt to advance our understanding of the outcomes of job insecurity in academia. The framework depicted in Chap. 1 lists no less than seven mediators to explain the job insecurity-outcomes relationship. However, the authors in this book focused on testing innovative explanations rather than explanatory frameworks that already received confirmation in the past. Mediators such as perceptions of control and psychological contract breach have already been tested widely in previous studies (e.g. De Cuyper & De Witte, 2006; Vander Elst et al., 2016) and were consequently not tested in any of the chapters.

Chapter 8 summarised the literature on the role of organisational justice as antecedent and mediator and suggests that justice perceptions can indeed explain part of the job insecurity-outcomes relationship. As this relationship was already tested before, the authors decided not to test mediation in their chapter. As an overview of the existing literature, this part of their chapter is very informative and can be used to inspire future research.

The three remaining chapters did perform an empirical test of mediation, focussing on self-undermining (Chap. 5), identity threat (Chap. 6) and burnout (Chap. 7), the latter as indicator of the health impairment process in the well-known Job Demand-Resources model (Demerouti et al., 2001; Bakker et al., 2023; Schaufeli & Bakker, 2004). The self-undermining viewpoint suggests that job demands (like job insecurity) create obstacles that undermine one's performance. Employees behave in a self-undermining manner to cope with the stressor. This behaviour, however, risks to result in a loss cycle, as it increases the negative impact of job insecurity. Consequently, job insecurity leads to a negative spiral in which coping with job stressors becomes increasingly problematic. Chapter 6 tests an explanation that already received some confirmation in the literature, based on social identity theory (see e.g. Selenko et al., 2017). The author applies this theory to academia, and presents a detailed analysis of how academic work impacts on the social self-identification of academics. She expects (and finds) that academics identify more strongly with their job. Job insecurity is supposed to threaten that identity, resulting in un-wellbeing (operationalised as burnout complaints). Chapter 7 continues this logic to some extent, by analysing the importance of burnout in explaining the association of qualitative job insecurity with two aspects of performance (in-role and innovative work behaviour) in academia. The core idea here is that job insecurity, as hindrance stressor, exhausts the physical and psychological resources of the employee, making them unable and unwilling to perform. The results of these three chapters are promising, even though not all hypotheses are corroborated. The authors of Chap. 5, for instance, find that all their tests of mediation are statistically significant. However, the associations of quantitative job insecurity with self-undermining are twice negative instead of positive, as hypothesised. Quantitative job insecurity reduced (rather than increased) self-undermining acts, contradicting the hypothesis. Also, the social identification hypotheses in Chap. 6 were not all corroborated. The author expected the identification with (a) the job and (b) the working population to mediate the association between both kinds of insecurity and burnout complaints. Of the four tested mediations, only one was significant: qualitative job insecurity was associated with less identification with the working population, which in turn was associated with more burnout complaints. The identification with the job was not shown to mediate, whereas especially this kind of identification was found to be typical for professors. The results in Chap. 7, finally, also corroborated only half of the hypotheses. Burnout was found to mediate the association between qualitative job insecurity and in-role behaviour in most countries, but not the relationship with innovative work behaviour. This suggest that the explanatory framework was perhaps more outcome-specific that expected.

Taken together, one can conclude that the new mediational pathways advanced by the authors are relevant but may also need refinement. The frameworks were also insecurity-specific. When both aspects of job insecurity were analysed (Chaps. 5 and 6), the hypothesised explanations were more relevant to explain the associations with qualitative job insecurity than those with quantitative job insecurity. Is this due to the specific sector in which they were tested (academia)? Or is their relevance restricted to this dimension of job insecurity? Future research could try to answer this question. Future research would also benefit from performing competitive tests, in which several explanatory frameworks are tested against each other (see e.g. De Witte, 2016). Such tests should also include explaining variables that have proven to be relevant in the past, such as perceptions of control and psychological contract breach. By testing the new explanatory frameworks against explanations that have already shown to be valid, one can examine whether the new explanations have additional value. Such a competitive test will increase the value of the proposed explanation when it is shown to significantly add to the already know explanations of the consequences of job insecurity. Such a competitive test could even show that part of the explanatory power of the traditional frameworks is due to newer frameworks that have not been tested before.

12.5 In Search of Boundary Conditions: Moderators

At the start of the millennium, an appeal was made to analyse moderators of the job insecurity-outcome relationship (e.g. Sverke & Hellgren, 2002). The search for moderators reveals whether there are boundary conditions for the consequences of job insecurity: can specific variables buffer (or strengthen) the association of insecurity with outcomes? Such boundary conditions are important for policy and practice, as they might help develop interventions to reduce the negative consequences of insecurity in academia. The proposed research model in Chap. 1 lists no less than 10 such possible moderators, classified as organisational, interpersonal, and individual. Moderation was examined in four chapters of this book (Chaps. 8, 9, 10 and 11), but only one analysed a moderator covered in the research model (regulatory focus; Chap. 10). In Chap. 11, a new moderator was added to the picture (workplace social capital), which was only measured in that specific country (Greece). In the other two chapters, variables were analysed as moderator that were expected to be a mediator (justice; Chap. 8) or an economic stressor (the employment contract, Chap. 9). This shows that the classification of a variable as a moderator or mediator also depends on the research question, and on the theoretical underpinning thereof.

The results of the moderation analyses in this book were not always successful, suggesting that 'good moderators are often hard to find'. The results were mostly opposite to expectations and required some interpretation afterwards. Chapter 8 advanced overall justice as a moderator that was neglected in the job insecurity literature thus far. The authors found overall justice perceptions to buffer the negative association between (both dimensions of) job insecurity and job satisfaction, as expected. Workers in academia who perceived being treated fairly experienced job insecurity in a slightly less negative way. All other significant moderation effects were opposite to expectations, as high levels of overall justice strengthened (instead of buffered) the negative impact of job insecurity on in-role performance, work engagement and burnout. The authors interpreted their surprising results by inferring "that in high justice conditions, the occurrence of job insecurity is experienced as particularly stressful because it contradicts the idea of a fair organisation". This may drain the energetic resources of the employees when they try to cope with job insecurity.

In Chap. 10, the authors advanced a promotion versus prevention focus as moderators among faculty members (professors) in China. This time, none of the hypotheses were corroborated. Contrary to expectations, the authors did not find a prevention focus to moderate the association of (qualitative) job insecurity with three different outcomes (work engagement, job crafting and life meaning). Instead, no significant moderation effects were found. Two out of three tests of a promotion focus as moderator were significant, but in the opposite direction: the negative relationship between (qualitative) job insecurity and job crafting or life meaning was stronger (instead of weaker) when the promotion focus was high. The authors explained their findings by stating that "insecurity threatens advancement and growth because it calls career development opportunities into question. Insecurity may therefore be particularly frustrating for employees with strong desires for personal growth at work". A high promotion focus is related to such stronger desires.

The authors in Chap. 11 advanced yet another possible moderator: workplace social capital (WSC further on), encompassing trust, reciprocity and networking. This new organisational resource complements already existing variables like social and organisational support. They expected WSC to play a buffering role. Here again, only half (two out of four) of the tested interactions were significant. And the significant ones were again opposite to expectations. The association of insecurity with work engagement, for instance, was only significantly negative in the condition of higher WSC (instead of lower WSC—as hypothesised). Here again, the interpretation stated that "employees who are strongly connected with others and have expanded networks through their organisations (i.e. high WSC) are likely to be affected more strongly by job insecurity and become disengaged". The opposite moderation trends observed in all three chapters were consistently explained by reversing the logic. It was stated that individuals who score high on the expected moderator are more likely to experience problems rather than fewer. Future research will need to demonstrate whether this ad hoc interpretation can be replicated and generalised.

In Chap. 9, contrasting hypotheses were developed and tested regarding the moderating role of the 'objective' indicator of insecurity: the employment contract. The authors hypothesised that a temporary contract could intensify ('intensification hypothesis') or buffer ('violation hypothesis') the association of (subjective) job insecurity with performance. About 25% of all tested interactions were significant, and all but one corroborated the violation hypothesis. Job insecurity appeared to be specifically problematic for those working on a permanent contract, presumably because insecurity was perceived as a breach of the psychological contract by this category of employees. Employees with a temporary contract did probably not expect security to the same extent, and consequently perceived less psychological contract breach. These findings are consistent with previous studies in the field (De Cuyper & De Witte, 2006; Mauno et al., 2005; van Vuuren et al., 2020). It was interesting to notice that most interactions related to quantitative job insecurity and in-role behaviours. This again suggests that specifically the threat to losing the current job has relevance for task-related productive behaviour in academia.

12.6 Identical Results for All Professional Categories in Academia?

Academia is an 'interesting' context for the study of job insecurity and its consequences for a variety of reasons. This sector has been the subject of important educational reforms and governmental cutbacks, as highlighted in Chap. 1 and several chapters in this book. The 'publish or perish' logic puts high-performance demands on its employees in conditions of increasing insecurity. Additionally, its composition in terms of professional categories is rather special. At least three important categories can be distinguished: professors (or academic staff), PhD students and post-doctoral fellows, and administrative (or support) staff. These categories differ regarding position, job characteristics, demographical features and future perspectives. The professors and PhD students (plus post-doctoral fellows) are typical 'academic personnel', even though their age, level of job autonomy and authority, and future perspectives are often quite different. The administrative staff members are possibly more similar to white-collar workers in other sectors, even though their job content and future perspective are obviously also impacted by the conditions of the sector in which they work. In other words, academia is a heterogeneous context. This permits another test of the universality of the analyses reported in this book, and also enables exploring each professional category's specificity when facing insecurity.

This issue was explored in five chapters. The general conclusion is that there appears to be *universality* in findings across professional categories, rather than huge differences, even though some smaller differences could be noticed. Chapter 2 offers the foundation for comparisons, as the authors show that the job insecurity measures are invariant across professional position. In other words: the job insecurity construct was interpreted in a conceptually equivalent manner by all professional categories. Looking at well-being indicators also suggests robustness of the reported associations across professional categories. In Chap. 4, three profiles of combinations of burnout and work engagement are presented. The size of these profiles is almost identical for professors, PhD students and administrative staff, highlighting that all categories experience much more work engagement than burnout. Only among the PhD students somewhat more 'exhausted' respondents could be found, compared to the other categories (9.5% versus about 6%). This difference is however rather limited. When analysing performance, also large similarities across professional categories are observed, rather than differences. The test of a specific explanatory mediational model in Chap. 5 shows that the indirect association of qualitative job insecurity with in-role and counterproductive work behaviours through self-undermining behaviour is the same for all professional categories. In other words, qualitative job insecurity impacts performance because it increases self-undermining acts among professors, PhD students and administrative staff alike. The results of Chap. 9 complement this, by showing that especially quantitative job insecurity is a hindrance stressor for in-role behaviours for every professional category. Additionally, quantitative job insecurity also interacted with the employment contract in associating with in-role behaviours for all professional categories under scrutiny. The main conclusions regarding the negative association of job insecurity with in-role behaviours in Chap. 9 are thus confirmed for all categories of employees in academia.

Note, however, that one can also observe occasional *deviations*, suggesting that some of the findings might be category specific. These deviations are limited, however, and require verification and replication in future research. The small difference regarding exhaustion observed in Chap. 4 has already been mentioned, with *PhD students* scoring somewhat higher on burnout complaints. Next, it is noticeable that especially *professors* (academic staff) sometimes seem to deviate for the general trends highlighted above. The results in Chap. 6, for instance, show that academic staff members identified more strongly with their job than employees in administration or PhD students. This stronger identification might have resulted in different results for this professional category. In Chap. 5, the authors also note that the mediational path between quantitative job insecurity and performance through self-undermining is somewhat different for the academic staff. For this category, the fear of losing the actual job was associated with a reduction (rather than the expected increase) in self-undermining behaviour. This effect was rather limited, however. The results in Chap. 9 demonstrate the specific position of professors regarding innovative work behaviour. Only among this specific professional category, quantitative job insecurity was associated with a reduction of the generation and implementation of new ideas. Additionally, only professors showed a deviating interaction between the employment contract and quantitative job insecurity regarding innovative work behaviour. For professors on a permanent contract, quantitative job insecurity was *not* associated with innovative work behaviour. Only those on a temporary contract showed an association, in line with the challenge view: quantitative job insecurity was associated with an increase in innovative work behaviour among professors on a temporary employment contract. Looking at the figure of the interaction effect however clarified that the temporary workers were not outperforming their colleagues with a permanent contract. Rather they seemed to 'catch up their backlog', in that their score equalled the score of their counterparts when both experience insecurity. In other words, the difference in innovative work behaviour could have been avoided by offering the professors a permanent contract from the start.

Finally, it is interesting to notice that qualitative job insecurity only related to aspects of performance among *administrative staff* (see Chaps. 5 and 9). The results of Chap. 9, for instance, suggest that specifically this professional category showed less in-role and more counterproductive work behaviour when they felt insecure about the continuation of valued job characteristics. It is unclear why qualitative job insecurity is less important for performance among professors and PhD students, once quantitative job insecurity (and the employment contract) have been controlled for. Future research needs to explore this issue more thoroughly and needs to check whether these differences can be replicated. These findings seem to suggest that administrative workers are indeed more alike to white-collar workers, as they react to quantitative and qualitative job insecurity in a more or less similar way (see e.g. De Witte et al., 2010).

12.7 Not All Pieces of the Puzzle Have Already Been Placed Thus Far: Perceived Causes of Job Insecurity in Higher Education

One key question that arises in discussions of job insecurity in higher education is: what do employees in higher education perceive as the primary causes of this insecurity? This question has not yet been addressed in this book, even though we gathered data on this issue. It seemed like an interesting opportunity to add some descriptive findings to this epilogue. In our research, we aimed to explore this by directly asking participants about the factors they believe contribute to job insecurity within their institutions. Specifically, we measured causal attributions using a 7-item scale, based on the one developed by Van Vuuren (1990), which was slightly modified for this study to include an additional factor—technological advancement. The scale used a 5-point Likert format and mainly focused on external causal attributions, with an emphasis on evaluating general trends rather than personal experiences.

Participants were asked to indicate the extent to which they believed that the following seven factors contributed to job insecurity in their respective countries: poor employee performance, poor managerial decision-making, technological advancements, declining organizational performance, union policies, governmental policies, and the broader economic situation of the country. In addition to comparing causal attributions across 10 countries, we also examined how these perceptions differed between the various professional categories in academia.

Our analysis aligns with the broader literature that underscores the psychological impact of attributing job insecurity to external causes. Van Vuuren was one of the first authors to emphasise the importance of causal attributions in the job insecurity literature (van Vuuren, 1990; see also Hartley et al., 1991). Jiang and Lavaysse (2018) demonstrated through their meta-analysis that job insecurity attributed to external factors—such as economic downturns and technological changes—has significant adverse effects on employees' mental health and overall well-being. These external attributions, perceived as uncontrollable, tend to exacerbate stress and feelings of helplessness. Similarly, Keim et al. (2014) found that external factors like organisational changes and economic conditions play a major role in shaping employees' perceptions of job insecurity. In particular, organisational changes were strongly linked to heightened insecurity, further emphasising the negative impact when employees feel powerless over these broader forces. Finally, in a recent longitudinal study, Vander Elst et al. (2024) explored whether specific kinds of causal attributions of insecurity moderated the relationship between insecurity and psychological contract breach. They hypothesised that a causal attribution to the

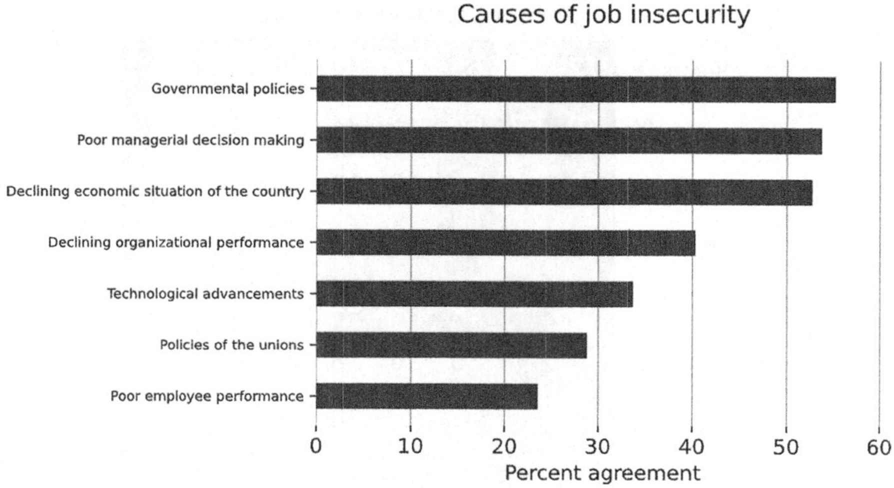

Fig. 12.1 Percentages of perceived causes of job insecurity as rated across 10 countries

organisation would amplify this relationship, and an attribution to the economic situation would buffer the relationship.

Figure 12.1 shows the percentages by which respondents across 10 countries ranked the causes of job insecurity. Governmental policies, poor managerial decision-making, and the declining economic situation of the country emerged as the top three contributors, with very similar rankings. In contrast, union policies and poor employee performance were seen as the least impactful causes. Interestingly, technological advancements were ranked in the middle. With the increasing prominence of AI, including tools like ChatGPT, and ongoing debates about automation, this attribution may rise in significance, as discussed further below.

The heat map in Figure 12.2 illustrates significant differences in how employees in academia across the 10 countries perceive the causes of job insecurity. As stated earlier on, the various samples in this book were gathered in different ways, and were all convenience samples. This makes an international comparison risky. Given the importance of this topic, we nevertheless report this comparison, as it might indicate some relevant differences, which will need to be confirmed in future research. Romania and the UK emerge as the countries where governmental policies and declining economic conditions are perceived as the most significant contributors to job insecurity. In Greece, governmental policies and the nation's economic decline are rated the highest, which is unsurprising given the financial challenges the country has faced since the 2008 economic crisis (see Chap. 1 for further details). Similarly, in South Africa, the declining economic situation is seen as the primary cause, which aligns with the country's ongoing economic difficulties.

In the USA, poor managerial decision-making is perceived as the most prominent factor, and technological advancements are rated higher than in any other country. Lithuania and Croatia did not identify any specific cause as the most or least

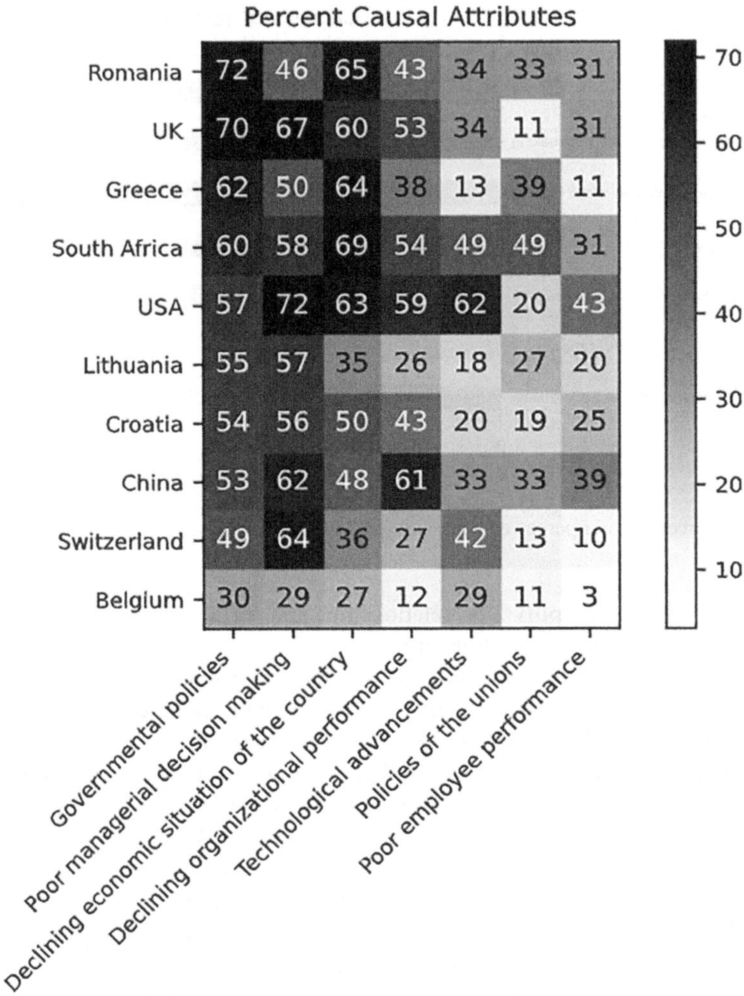

Fig. 12.2 Heat map of perceived causes of job insecurity by country

significant compared to other countries, though both generally followed the trend of highlighting governmental policies and poor managerial decisions as key contributors.

In China, poor managerial decision-making and declining organizational performance ranked highest, with none of the other factors being rated particularly low. This suggests a broad distribution of responsibility across different causes, with none seen as insignificant.

In Switzerland, poor managerial decision-making was rated the top concern, while union policies and employee performance were rated lower overall. In Belgium, all categories received relatively low ratings, with declining organizational

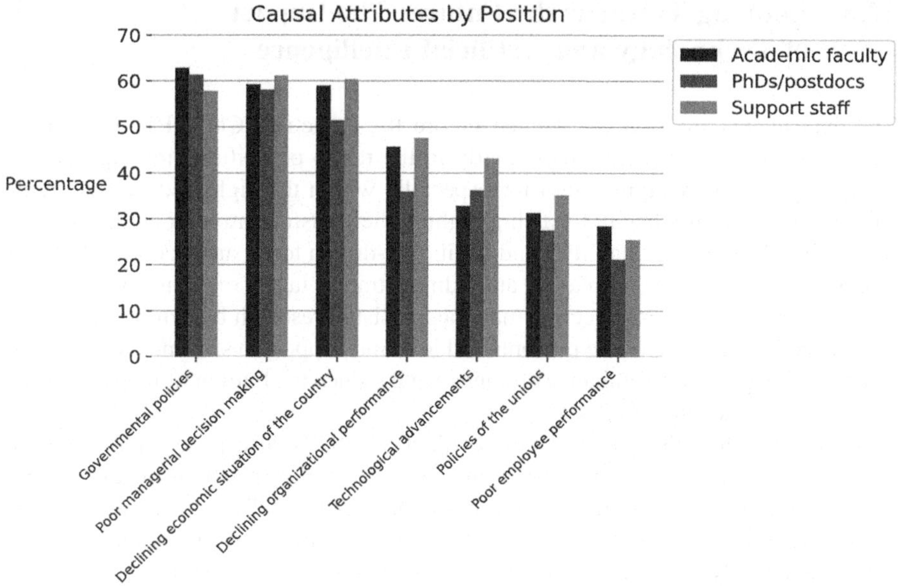

Fig. 12.3 Perceived causes of job insecurity in higher education by position across all countries

performance, union policies, and poor employee performance emerging as the least significant causes.

Interestingly, poor employee performance was rated lowest in all countries, indicating a general perception among academia that job insecurity is not due to the employees themselves.

Figure 12.3 illustrates how the various professional categories or positions ranked the causes of job insecurity. The overall pattern is consistent across all positions, with governmental policies, poor managerial decision-making, and the declining economic situation being rated the highest, while poor employee performance is consistently rated the lowest. Generally, all three groups—PhDs and postdocs, academic faculty (professors), and administrative support staff—rated the potential causes similarly, though PhDs and postdocs tended to report lower percentages compared to academic faculty and support staff. One notable exception is technological advancements, which received the lowest ratings from academic faculty staff. Additionally, declining organizational performance was rated lower by PhDs and postdocs compared to the other groups.

12.8 Looking Towards the Future: The Impact of Technology and Artificial Intelligence

The data in this study was collected before the launch of ChatGPT. Since then, technological advancements, particularly in the realm of artificial intelligence, are likely to play a more significant role, especially within the higher education sector. The introduction of ChatGPT has highlighted the transformative potential of automation in this domain. ChatGPT, and similar AI-driven tools, are increasingly being integrated into teaching, research, and administrative tasks, offering the ability to automate grading, generate lecture materials, assist in research by synthesising large amounts of data, and provide personalised learning support to students. This has the potential to significantly enhance efficiency and reduce the burden of repetitive tasks for educators and support staff.

However, while these benefits are evident, ChatGPT also poses challenges. Its capacity to generate academic content and answer complex questions raises concerns about academic integrity and the future role of educators. There is growing apprehension that the widespread use of AI could diminish the need for certain academic roles, particularly those related to administrative tasks, content creation, and student support. As such, the presence of ChatGPT in higher education introduces not only the prospect of increased efficiency but also the potential for significant disruption and reshaping of roles within the sector.

In response to these technological disruptions, a new phenomenon has emerged: the fear that entire occupations may disappear or undergo significant changes due to automation. This phenomenon has been termed 'occupation insecurity' (Roll et al., 2023). It can be further divided into two distinct types: 'global occupation insecurity', which refers to the fear that automation may render entire jobs obsolete, and 'content occupation insecurity', which relates to concerns that the nature of one's role will change significantly as a result of automated technologies.

As technological innovations like ChatGPT continue to evolve, these concerns may become even more pronounced across various sectors, including higher education. Addressing them is crucial to ensure that the integration of AI into academic environments supports rather than undermines the sector's core values and roles. Without thoughtful planning and adaptation, there is a risk that technology could exacerbate job insecurity, lead to a loss of valuable human interaction in education and undermine the critical thinking and originality that universities aim to cultivate.

The rapid rise of AI tools demands proactive measures, including updating curricula to equip staff and students with the skills to work alongside AI technologies and revising job roles to harness AI to enhance rather than replace human contributions. Ensuring transparency, fostering collaboration between technology developers and educators, and promoting the ethical use of AI are essential steps in addressing these challenges.

Additionally, higher education institutions need to implement policies that balance automation's efficiency with preserving the human elements essential to education. This includes addressing concerns about academic integrity, ensuring fair employment practices, and providing retraining opportunities for staff whose roles may evolve as AI takes on more administrative and instructional tasks. By taking such steps, higher education can remain resilient in the face of technological change while continuing to uphold its mission of fostering learning, critical thinking, and innovation.

12.9 And Now for Policy and Practice: What to Do?

One of the main conclusions—if not *the* main conclusion—of the various studies in this book is that job insecurity is present in academia, and that it has adverse effects on everyone working in this sector. Job insecurity was found to impact a large variety of health and well-being indicators and decrease work engagement and increase burnout complaints. It additionally reduced productive work behaviours and increased counterproductive work behaviours. Job insecurity is thus problematic for professors, PhD students and post-doctoral fellows, and the administrative staff in academia. It hinders their functioning and, as a consequence, also negatively impacts the academic education of students and the development and accumulation of science. Consequently, many of this book's chapters discussed the practical implications of their findings (see especially Chaps. 5, 7, 8, 10 and 11). Encompassing summaries of possible interventions have already been presented in several overview chapters of the job insecurity literature (see e.g. De Witte et al., 2015; De Witte, 2024; Probst et al., 2018). In this final section of this epilogue, some of these recommendations will be summarised so that policymakers and practitioners can decide how to intervene in practice in academia.

The first issue to highlight is the need to reduce job insecurity through *structural* interventions. Governmental policies in many countries increased insecurity by restructuring academia, increasing educational demands, and generalising the use of temporary contracts when hiring academics. China is a good example of these trends, as documented in Chap. 11. These evolutions, however, are not limited to this country, as discussed in many other chapters of this book (and in Chap. 1). Questioning these trends seems a good starting point. These changes have probably been initiated to strengthen the academic performance and output in the countries involved. They, however, risk to result in the opposite, as they have adverse effects on well-being and performance. Additionally, investing in permanent contracts, research funding and in labour market policies that support academics is probably the first important structural action to undertake.

Subjective concerns regarding job security also need to be dealt with. Developing interventions requires a solid theoretical foundation and needs to be evidence-based. An overall theoretical framework in which all explanations of job insecurity are integrated is, however, lacking at the moment. Therefore, some authors have been advancing ideas based on just one theoretical foundation. One such view relates to the idea that insecurity mainly works through a lack of (perceived) control (see, e.g. De Witte et al., 2015). In this view, interventions need to be developed that focus on (a) directly reducing job insecurity (perceptions) and (b) mitigating the negative consequences of job insecurity. The first route focuses on the *antecedents* of job insecurity, whereas the second route tries to strengthen specific *moderators* that could *buffer* its negative consequences. Four such interventions have been advanced in the past, and many authors in this book have been referring to these interventions: communication, participation, organisational justice and employability. All four have the capacity to strengthen control perceptions and, as such, are able to reduce job insecurity and/or buffer its consequences.

Communication relates to transparency regarding eventual transformations and the transition process involved. Here, it seems crucial to openly and clearly communicate about organisational changes and their eventual impact. Involving employees in *decision-making* reduces feelings of powerlessness and strengthens their perceptions of control over the process. This also increases the perception that one has been treated respectfully during the organisational transition. The latter is an aspect of organisational *justice*. Employees who perceive to be treated fairly know what to expect and what the outcomes will be of actions taken by their organisation. *Employability* relates to the perception that one can easily find a suitable job elsewhere, in case one gets dismissed. Career development and skill enhancement programs developed by universities will improve the employability of those working on academia, especially for PhD students and post-doctoral fellows. Providing career counselling services will also help these categories to explore alternative career paths and will prepare them for potential job transitions.

Several chapters in this book also highlighted the need to develop specific *support programs* for academics. Teaching staff assistance programs, for instance, could be better tailored to the specific needs of faculty teaching staff, as suggested in Chap. 11. Enhancing workplace social capital, in which trust, reciprocity and network connections are promoted, could optimise employee functioning (Chap. 10). Investing in strengthening social support at various levels in academia will additionally help buffering adverse phenomena, like job insecurity. And for those who feel negatively affected by insecurity and changes, stress management and well-being programs offered by their university might be helpful in dealing with their problems.

12.10 Take Home Message

Job insecurity is part of the academic experience nowadays, as shown in the surveys conducted in 10 countries across the globe. The results show that quantitative versus qualitative job insecurity are the core dimensions of the insecurity construct. Qualitative job insecurity in academia was more strongly associated with lower levels of health and well-being. Quantitative job insecurity was more strongly related to reduced productive and increased counterproductive work behaviours. Both kinds of job insecurity thus appeared as hindrance stressors with negative consequences, contradicting the view that job insecurity can motivate or energise employees. These findings were roughly similar for the three main professional categories in academia: academic staff (professors), Ph.D. students and post-doctoral fellows, and administrative (support) staff. Interventions to reduce job insecurity and buffer its negative consequences are thus important in order to safeguard the future of academia.

References

Bakker, A., Demerouti, E., & Sanz-Vergel, A. (2023). Job demands–resources theory: Ten years later. *Annual Review of Organizational Psychology and Organizational Behavior, 10*(1), 13–29. https://doi.org/10.1146/annurev-orgpsych-120920-053933

Borg, I. (1992). Ueberlegungen und untersuchungen zur messung der subjektiven unsicherheit der arbeitsstelle. *Zeitschrift fur Arbeits- und Organisationspsychologie, 36*(3), 107–116. https://nbn-resolving.org/urn:nbn:de:0168-ssoar-69691

Chan, W. Y., Ho, G. W. K., Chernyshenko, O. S., Ho, R., & Sam, Y. L. (2020). Stress adaptation and resilience of academics in higher education. *Asia Pacific Education Review, 21*(1), 23–33.

Cheng, G. H. L., & Chan, D. K. S. (2008). Who suffers more from job insecurity? A meta-analytic review. *Applied Psychology-an International Review, 57*(2), 272–303. https://doi.org/10.1111/j.1464-0597.2007.00312.x

Chirumbolo, A., Urbini, F., Callea, A., Lo Presti, A., & Talamo, A. (2017). Occupations at risk and organizational well-being: An empirical test of a job insecurity integrated model. *Frontiers in Psychology, 8*, 1–13. https://doi.org/10.3389/fpsyg.2017.02084

Chirumbolo, A., Urbini, F., & Callea, A. (2020). Dimensionality, reliability and validity of a Multidimensional Job Insecurity Questionnaire. *Preliminary Findings in the Italian Context. Rassegna di Psicologia, 37*, 35–46. https://doi.org/10.13133/1974-4854/16722

De Cuyper, N., & De Witte, H. (2006). The impact of job insecurity and contract type on attitudes, well-being and behavioural reports: A psychological contract perspective. *Journal of Occupational and Organizational Psychology, 79*, 395–409. https://doi.org/10.1348/096317905X53660

De Cuyper, N., & De Witte, H. (2021). *Job insecurity*. Oxford University Press. https://doi.org/10.1093/acrefore/9780190236557.013.17

De Witte, H. (2016). On the scarring effects of job insecurity (and how they can be explained). *Scandinavian Journal of Work and Environmental Health, 42*(2), 99–102. https://doi.org/10.5271/sjweh.3545

De Witte, H. (2024). Job Insecurity. In M. Bal (Ed.), *Encyclopedia of Organizational Psychology*. Edward Elgar Publishing Limited. https://doi.org/10.4337/9781803921761

De Witte, H., & Van Hootegem, A. (2021). Job insecurity: Challenge or hindrance stressor? Review of the Evidence and empirical test on entrepreneurs. In C. Korunka (Ed.), *Flexible working practices and approaches: Psychological and social implications of a multifaceted phenomenon* (pp. 213–229). Springer. https://doi.org/10.1007/978-3-030-74128-0_11

De Witte, H., De Cuyper, N., Handaja, Y., Sverke, M., Näswall, K., & Hellgren, J. (2010). Associations Between Quantitative and Qualitative Job Insecurity and Well-Being. A Test in Belgian Banks. *International Studies of Management & Organization.*. Special Issue on Job Insecurity, *40*(1), 40–56. https://doi.org/10.2753/IMO0020-8825400103

De Witte, H., Vander Elst, T., & De Cuyper, N. (2015). Job insecurity, health and well-being. In J. Vuori, R. Blonk, & R. H. Price (Eds.), *Sustainable working lives: Managing work transitions and health throughout the life course* (pp. 109–128). Springer.

De Witte, H., Pienaar, J., & De Cuyper, N. (2016). Review of 30 years of longitudinal studies on the association between job insecurity and health and well-being. Is there causal evidence? *Australian Psychologist, 51*(1), 18–31. https://doi.org/10.1111/ap.12176

Demerouti, E., Bakker, A. B., Nachreiner, F., & Schaufeli, W. B. (2001). The job demands-resources model of burnout. *Journal of Applied Psychology, 86*, 499–512. https://doi.org/10.1037/0021-9010.86.3.499

Featherstone, K. (2016). The Greek crisis and the challenge to reform higher education. *Journal of Modern Greek Studies, 34*, 323–345.

Greenhalgh, L., & Rosenblatt, Z. (1984). Job insecurity: Toward conceptual clarity. *Academy of Management Review, 9*(3), 438–448. https://doi.org/10.2307/258284

Guest, D., Isaksson, K., & De Witte, H. (2010). *Employment contracts, psychological contracts, and employee well-being. An international study*. Oxford University Press.

Hartley, J., Jacobson, D., Klandermans, B., & Van Vuuren, T. (1991). *Job insecurity. Coping with jobs at risk*. Sage Publications.

Hellgren, J., Sverke, M., & Isaksson, K. (1999). A two-dimensional approach to job insecurity: consequences for employee attitudes and well-being. *European Journal of Work and Organizational Psychology, 8*, 179–195. https://doi.org/10.1080/135943299398311

Jiang, L., & Lavaysse, L. M. (2018). Cognitive and affective job insecurity: A meta-analysis and a primary study. *Journal of Management, 44*(6), 2307–2342. https://doi.org/10.1177/0149206318773853

Keim, A. C., Landis, R. S., Pierce, C. A., & Earnest, D. R. (2014). Why do employees worry about their jobs? A meta-analytic review of predictors of job insecurity. *Journal of Occupational Health Psychology, 19*(3), 269–290. https://doi.org/10.1037/a0036743

Kinman, G. (2001). Pressure Points: A review of research on stressors and strains in UK academics. *Educational Psychology, 21*(4), 473–492. https://doi.org/10.1080/01443410120090849

Kinman, G., Jones, F., & Kinamn, R. (2006). The well-being of the UK Academy, 1998-2004. *Quality in Higher Education, 12*(1), 15–27. https://doi.org/10.1080/13538320600685081

Klandermans, B., & van Vuuren, T. (1999). Job insecurity: Introduction. *European Journal of Work and Organizational Psychology, 8*(2), 145–153. https://doi.org/10.1080/135943299398294

Klandermans, B., Klein Hesselink, J., & van Vuuren, T. (2010). Employment status and job insecurity: On the subjective appraisal of an objective status. *Economic and Industrial Democracy, 31*(4), 557–577. https://doi.org/10.1177/0143831X09358362

Klug, K., Selenko, E., Van Hootegem, A., Sverke, M., & De Witte, H. (2024). A lead article to go deeper and broader in job insecurity research: Understanding an individual perception in its social and political context. *Applied Psychology: International Review, , 73*(4), 1960-1993. https://doi.org/10.1111/apps.12535

Kottaridi, C., & Tsakloglou, P. (2020). The impact of the economic crisis on higher education in Greece. *Higher Education Policy, 33*, 5–24.

Ladi, S. (2014). Austerity politics and administrative reform: The Eurozone crisis and its impact upon Greek public administration. *Comparative European Politics, 12*, 184–208.

Mauno, S., Kinnunen, U., Mäkikangas, A., & Nätti, J. (2005). Psychological consequences of fixed-term employment and perceived job insecurity among health care staff. *European Journal of Work and Organizational Psychology, 14*(3), 209–237. https://doi.org/10.1080/13594320500146649

Nawrocka, S., De Witte, H., Brondino, M., & Pasini, M. (2021). On the Reciprocal Relationship between Quantitative and Qualitative Job Insecurity and Outcomes. Testing a Cross-Lagged Longitudinal Mediation Model. *International Journal of Environmental Research and Public Health, 18*, 6392. https://doi.org/10.3390/ijerph18126392

OECD. (2023). *Education at a glance 2023: OECD indicators*. OECD Publishing. https://doi.org/10.1787/69096873-en

Papadimitriou, A. (2015). Higher education reforms in Greece: An international comparative perspective. *European Journal of Higher Education, 5*, 49–65.

Probst, T. M. (2003). Development and validation of the Job Security Index and the Job Security Satisfaction scale: A classical test theory and IRT approach. *Journal of Occupational and Organizational Psychology, 76*, 451–467. https://doi.org/10.1348/096317903322591587

Probst, T., Jiang, L., & Benson, W. (2018). Job Insecurity and Anticipated Job Loss: A Primer and Exploration of Possible Interventions. In K. Ute-Christine Klehe & E. A. J. van Hooft (Eds.), *Oxford handbook on job loss and job search* (pp. 31–53). Oxford University Press.

Roll, L., De Witte, H., & Wang, H.-J. (2023). Conceptualization and validation of the Occupation Insecurity Scale (OCIS): Measuring employees' occupation insecurity due to automation. *International Journal of Environmental Research and Public Health, 20*, 2589. https://doi.org/10.3390/ijerph20032589

Schaufeli, W. B., & Bakker, A. B. (2004). Job demands, job resources, and their relationships with burnout and engagement: a multi-sample study. *Journal of Organizational Behavior, 25*, 293–315. https://doi.org/10.1002/job.248

Selenko, E., Mäkikangas, A., & Stride, C. B. (2017). Does job insecurity threaten who you are? Introducing a social identity perspective to explain well-being and performance consequences of job insecurity. *Journal of Organizational Behavior, 38*(6), 856–875. https://doi.org/10.1002/job.2172

Shoss, M. (2017). Job Insecurity: An integrative review and agenda for future research. *Journal of Management, 43*, 911–1939. https://doi.org/10.1177/0149206317691574

Sverke, M., & Hellgren, J. (2002). The nature of job insecurity: Understanding employment uncertainty on the brink of a new millennium. *Applied Psychology: An International Review, 51*(1), 23–42. https://doi.org/10.1111/1464-0597.0077z

Sverke, M., Hellgren, J., & Näswall, K. (2002). No security: A meta-analysis and review of job insecurity and its consequences. *Journal of Occupational Health Psychology, 7*(3), 242–264. https://doi.org/10.1037/1076-8998.7.3.242

Sverke, M., Låstad, L., Hellgren, J., Richter, A., & Näswall, K. (2019). A meta-analysis of job insecurity and employee performance: testing temporal aspects, rating source, welfare regime, and union density as moderators. *International Journal of Environmental Research and Public Health, 16*(14), 2536. https://doi.org/10.3390/ijerph16142536

Svongoro, P. (2023). Understanding higher education: Alternative perspectives (2022) by C. Boughey, and S. McKenna. - African Minds, Cape Town. *Journal of Education (University of KwaZulu-Natal), 93*, 212–218.

Tytherleigh, M., Webb, C., Cooper, C., & Ricketts, C. (2005). Occupational stress in UK higher education institutions: a comparative study of all staff categories. *Higher Education Research & Development, 24*(1), 41–61. https://doi.org/10.1080/0729436052000318569

University and College Union. (2022). *Biggest ever university strike begins in fight over pay, pensions and conditions.* Retrieved from https://www.ucu.org.uk

van Vuuren, T. (1990). *Met ontslag bedreigd. Werknemers in onzekerheid over hun arbeidsplaats bij veranderingen in de organisatie. (Threatened with dismissal. Insecure workers about their job during organizational changes).* PhD dissertation,. VU Uitgeverij.

van Vuuren, T., de Jong, J., & Smulders, P. (2020). The association between subjective job insecurity and job performance across different employment groups. Evidence from a representative sample from the Netherlands. *Career Development International, 25*(3), 229–246. https://doi.org/10.1108/CDI-05-2018-0155

Vander Elst, T., & De Witte, H. (2024). An introduction to job insecurity. In C. Cooper & P. Brough (Eds.), *Elgar encyclopedia of occupational health psychology* (pp. 14–17). Edward Elgar Publishing Limited. https://doi.org/10.4337/9781035313389

Vander Elst, T., De Cuyper, N., Baillien, E., Niesen, W., & De Witte, H. (2016). Perceived Control and Psychological Contract Breach as Explanations of the Relationships Between Job Insecurity, Job Strain and Coping Reactions: Towards a Theoretical Integration. *Stress & Health, 36*(2), 100–116. https://doi.org/10.1002/smi.2584

Vander Elst, T., Griep, Y., Sverke, M., & De Witte, H. (2024). The relationship between job insecurity and psychological contract breach as conditional upon causal attributions: A within-person approach *Scandinavian Journal of Work and Organizational Psychology, 9*(1), 7, 1–18. https://doi.org/10.16993/sjwop.277

Winefield, A. H., Gillespie, N., Stough, C., Dua, J., Hapuarachchi, J., & Boyd, C. (2003). Occupational stress in Australian university staff: Results from a national survey. *International Journal of Stress Management, 10*(1), 51–63. https://doi.org/10.1037/1072-5245.10.1.51

Hans De Witte (PhD in Psychology) was Full Professor in Work Psychology at the Faculty of Psychology and Educational Sciences of the KU Leuven, Belgium (Research Group Work, Organizational and Personnel Psychology). He is academically active since October 2023 as emeritus with assignment. He is also appointed as Extraordinary Professor at the North-West University of South Africa (Optentia Research Unit, Vanderbijlpark Campus). His research includes the study of the psychological consequences of job insecurity, unemployment, temporary employment and downsizing, as well as mobbing and burnout versus work engagement. He (co-) authored about 300 articles in English peer-reviewed journals, published 30 books (14 English and 16 in Dutch; most as co-editor) and is (co-)author of about 80 chapters in English academic books.

Lara Christina Roll (PhD in Work and Organizational Psychology) is a Senior Associate at PwC Belgium, an External Researcher at KU Leuven (Belgium) and an Extraordinary Professor with the Optentia Research Unit at North-West University (South Africa). Her primary research focuses on workplace insecurity, particularly on how employees perceive the impact of technological advancements on their occupations. From 2022 until 2024 she has served as vice-chair of Algorigth e.V., a think tank comprised of young scholars to support research exchange and good digitalisation in Germany (https://algoright.de/). Furthermore, from 2023 to 2024, she served as an expert panel member for the Flemish Minister for Economy, Innovation, Work, Social Economy, and Agriculture, contributing to the development of future scenarios on the role of technology in creating an inclusive job market.

Wilma Coetzee is a Statistics Lecturer in the Department of Mathematical and Statistical Sciences and a Researcher at the Unit for Data Science and Computing at the North-West University, South Africa. She has worked as a statistical consultant in the industry for several years before joining academia. Her research interests include statistics education, employability, and educational analytics.

Sebastiaan Rothmann Sr. Ph.D. is Professor in industrial/organizational psychology at the North-West University (Vanderbijlpark Campus) and Director of the Optentia Research Unit in South Africa. His research journey started with the topics of stress, burnout, and work engagement and has evolved toward prospering and flourishing of people in work and organizational contexts. People who prosper in work and organizational contexts are satisfied with their jobs; experience positive emotions; are energetic, learning, and dedicated; experience satisfaction.

The manufacturer's authorised representative in the EU is Springer Nature Customer Service Centre GmbH, Europaplatz 3, 69115 Heidelberg, Germany. If you have any concerns regarding our products, please contact ProductSafety@springernature.com

Printed and bound by CPI Group (UK) Ltd, Croydon, CR0 4YY
30/09/2026
02225570-0011